W9-AGL-026

Santa Fe & Taos

Paige R Penland

Contents

TAOS
p142

SANTA FE
p70

ALBUQUERQUE
p54

Lonely Planet books provide independent advice. Lonely Planet does not accept advertising in guidebooks, nor do we accept payment in exchange for listing or endorsing any place or business. Lonely Planet writers do not accept discounts or payments in exchange for positive coverage of any sort.

Los libros de Lonely Planet ofrecen información independiente. Lonely Planet ni acepta publicidad en sus guías ni cobra por incluir o recomendar cualquier lugar o establecimiento. Los escritores de Lonely Planet no aceptan descuentos o pagos a cambio de cualquier tipo de trato de favor.

Destination: Santa Fe & Taos

Those who sniff that this is a young country have never seen this place. Sculpted from the earth itself, lustrous in the high-desert light, are ancient capitals that have stood watch over these treasures for millennia: slumbering volcanoes that betray still liquid hearts with hot and healing springs; minarets worn by piercing winds from a sunset-painted desert; and sheer cliffs that rise, inexorably, toward the fierce and empty sky.

And rending such beauty asunder in a dark canyon gash is a great river, winding and fertile, which alone allowed those who would brave such unforgiving elements to build their cities here. There were no riches, not those the Spanish Crown sought, yet her people have remained. And the Rio Grande they christened has since slaked the thirsts of those consumed with passions for art, God and science.

Santa Fe, steeped in all this myth and magic, now guards these ancient lands, inviting those intrigued by such tales to thread her maze of adobe and imagination, partake of her famed and fiery cuisine, and rest a while before exploring all that she protects. There is no end to her charms, from the most delicate silver bracelet crafted by the woman who sits beneath the plaza portal to soaring arias performed beneath the stars.

And follow the river north to Taos, past villages of miracles and apricots, to even wilder places where creativity remains the single highest virtue. Nothing here is entirely tame, and if you give yourself up to the spirit of this place, it may well reveal the shackles of your own domestication. Don't cling to them. Watch the sun rise instead.

ANDREW MARSHALL & LEANNE WALKER

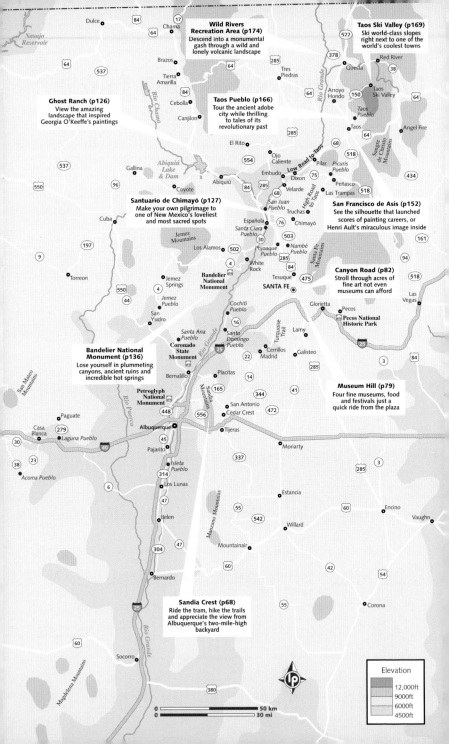

Clear high-desert sunlight spilling across Northern New Mexico's surreal splendor stirs the finest photographers: Adam Clark Vroman recorded **Taos Pueblo** (p166) in 1900, while Ansel Adams' striking desertscapes caused critics to comment that 'Santa Fe and Taos were his Rome and Paris.' Later, Paul Strand, Edward Weston and Laura Gilpin, famed for portraits of Georgia O'Keeffe at **Ghost Ranch** (p126), were joined by those inspired by wonders like **Wild Rivers Recreation Area** (p174) and ancient **Bandelier** (p136). But keep your own aperture open for those quirky roadside displays, yard art taken to its (il)logical extreme.

KARL LEHMAN

Scoop up some sacred earth at **Santuario de Chimayó** (p127), known for its healing powers

Boasting Taos' most famous buttresses, **San Francisco de Asis** (p152) is a vision in adobe

MARK NEWMAN

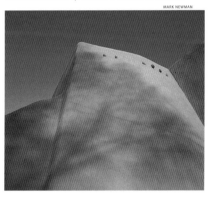

Even the mailboxes on **Canyon Road** (p82) illustrate the artsy influence of Santa Fe's most famous collection of galleries

JOHN HAY

KARL LEHMANN

The Miraculous Staircase at Santa Fe's
Loretto Chapel (p85) uses no nails nor
obvious structural support

The **Santuario de Guadalupe's** (p85)
colorful *retablo* came from Mexico
City to Santa Fe in 1783

RICHARD CUMMINS

The **Earthship 'Suncatcher'** (p152) shows off its passive solar design: half-buried walls cool,
and angled windows heat, the futuristic Taos home

KARL LEHMAN

KARL LEHMANN

Sandia Crest (p68) glows watermelon pink as the sun sets over Albuquerque

RICHARD CUMMINS

A Diné (Navajo) dancer brings prayer and performance together at Santa Fe's **Museum Hill** (p79)

Watch that first step at **Taos Ski Valley** (p169): it's a doozy!

KARL LEHMANN

KARL LEHMANN

The **Rio Grande** (p152) flows between two massive tectonic plates pulling the continent apart

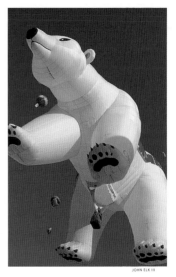

JOHN ELK III

Folks who can't bear to be earthbound love the **Albuquerque International Balloon Fiesta** (p60)

After surviving the Class IV **Taos Box,** (p153) happy rafters get ready to splash through the Racecourse

KARL LEHM

Getting Started

To quote former New Mexico Governor Lew Wallace, 'All calculations based on our experiences elsewhere fail in New Mexico.'

If you're used to following a strict itinerary, keep in mind that here, more than many places, plans tend to go absurdly awry. Taos Pueblo will inexplicably close. The party that friendly locals invited you to – a 2-mile hike from anything – lasts all weekend. Something, anything, will simply spontaneously arise on the Tuesday scheduled for Museum Hill.

If you're visiting New Mexico for a specific event, particularly during the jam-packed late summer months of Santa Fe's Indian Market and Opera Season, planning ahead is most definitely necessary – reserve your rental car and hotel room as far in advance as possible.

But if you're coming just to explore, do reserve the rental car in advance, and perhaps a hotel room for the first couple of nights. Create a loose itinerary of things you'd like to see and do, but don't be determined to stick to it. Temptations arise, mañana time happens and someone will point you toward the experience that changes your life.

WHEN TO GO

Northern New Mexico is a year-round destination, with four distinct seasons and 300 days of sunshine annually. Spring is unpredictable, and visitors from April through early June should bring both winter coats and shorts to wear while meandering among lilacs and blooming fruit trees.

See Climate Charts (p184) for more information.

Though the Albuquerque summer can be unbearable, easily topping 100°F, the higher elevations of Santa Fe and Taos mellow the burn. Folks intent on exploring the desert should take the extreme temperatures into consideration, but this is the perfect time for getting outside in the mountains.

Cooling afternoon storms that begin in late July make things much more pleasant, just in time for Santa Fe's peak tourist season: either come to experience the Opera and Indian Market, or do yourself a favor and steer clear until September. Fall – with crisp mornings and the smell of roasting green chile in the air – is the most pleasant time to visit, though camping gets nippy. Oddly enough, this is when also when New Mexico gets the least traffic.

From November to March, it's ski season. Early December and mid-January are the lulls, with good deals on lift tickets, and the Christmas holidays are peak periods, when room rates skyrocket and rental cars are difficult to find.

There's no bad time to visit this region; just figure out what your priorities are and plan accordingly. The sun will always be shining, no matter when you cruise through.

COSTS

Unless you plan to stick to the cities, travel by car is the least expensive and most convenient way to get around. Greyhound is affordable, but the private shuttles and tours you'll need to get off the beaten path cost money and time.

Off-season car rental rates run as low as $100 a week for subcompacts, $150 or more during peak season, plus $10 a day for insurance. 4WD vehicles can be as high as $90 a day; keep in mind that only two roads mentioned in this book – to abandoned gold mines – require them.

You can camp for free on Bureau of Land Management (BLM) land, pay $6 to $15 for developed wilderness sites, or $20 to $30 at full-service campgrounds with pools, full hookups and convenient in-town locations. Youth hostels charge around $15 for a dorm bed, and sleazier motels (not really available in Santa Fe or Taos) can be had for $25 a double.

Motels charging $35 to $50 for a double tend to be extremely well kept, if basic. Hotels close to the plaza start at around $80 and go way, way up, while B&B prices start at $70 or so for small rooms serving continental breakfasts and $90 to $150 for the real, antique-packed deal. A luxury suite – and Santa Fe has some truly fine accommodations – usually runs $350 to $450, though you can certainly spend more.

Good Southwestern fast food (healthy if you're careful) can be as cheap as $3 to $6 for a substantial meal. Full-service restaurants will still fill you up for $10 or less, while fine cuisine is often available as prix-fixe menus (more common in the off-season) for as low as $20 or as much as three times that (not including wine).

PRE-DEPARTURE READING

If you've already discounted pleas to conserve water as just hand-wringing by those Lonely Planet lefties, read *Cadillac Desert: The American West and Its Disappearing Water,* by Marc Reisner, a thorough and entertaining account of this land's dripping-to-dry history. *Touring New Mexico Hot Springs,* by Matt Bischoff, with maps and reviews of the state's finest soaks, will cheer you up afterward.

New Mexico's Sanctuaries, Retreats and Sacred Places, by Christina Nealson, is a predictably New Agey but fabulous rundown of spiritual spots, with maps and lore galore. Jack Kutz' *Mysteries and Miracles of New Mexico* may not have maps, but the strange (and sometimes scary) tales he tells will have you doing your own research, perhaps to find certain lost mines.

Pueblos of the Rio Grande is Daniel Gibson's indispensable guide (though the 2001 edition was a tad outdated) for anyone interested in Native New Mexico. Others offering insight into Pueblo culture include Leslie Marmon Silko's *Almanac of the Dead* and N Scott Momaday's *House Made of Dawn.*

The laugh-out-loud *Turn Left at the Sleeping Dog: Scripting the Santa Fe Legend 1920–1955,* by John Pen La Farge, is oral history at its finest, with interviews of local characters who discuss Dennis Chávez, Georgia O'Keeffe and the whole 'Old Santa Fe Trail' thing with absolutely no respect for the tourist bureau's rosy tricultural rap.

For more grassroots New Mexico culture, peruse the excellent *Low 'N Slow: Lowriding in New Mexico,* by Carmella Padilla, Jack Parsons and Juan Estevan Arellano, a lavishly illustrated look at the finest art on wheels.

INTERNET RESOURCES

New Mexico Department of Tourism (www.newmexico.org) Information and links to accommodations, attractions and other useful sites.

Santa Fe New Mexican (www.santafenewmexican.com) Online visitor information and top local stories from Santa Fe's newspaper.

State of New Mexico (www.state.nm.us) Facts, stats and state government sites, plus links to public transportation, USGS and street maps, and other official business.

New Mexico CultureNet (www.nmcn.org) Articles about the artists, writers and history of New Mexico, with events listings of the most enriching sort.

Lonely Planet (www.lonelyplanet.com) An online guide with up-to-date visa regulations, events that could affect your visit and the Thorn Tree forum, where you can ask other travelers what they think.

HOW MUCH?

Breakfast burrito: $3-6

Nongourmet tamale: $1

Latte with two shots: $3

Lift tickets: $19-55

Margarita: $4-8

USFS campsite: $6-10

Day-use fee at trailheads: $1-5

Hourly parking in downtown Santa Fe: $2-6

Hourly Internet access at café: $6-12

Half-hour tarot-card reading: $30

TOP TENS

TOP TEN FESTIVALS & EVENTS

New Mexico doesn't settle for the average celebration. This is a creative culture – three of them, actually – and there's always something spectacular going on. For more listings, check the Santa Fe , Taos and Albuquerque chapters, as well as sections on smaller towns and pueblos.

- Taos Talking Pictures
  (Taos), April (p156)

- Gathering of Nations Powwow
  (Albuquerque), April (p60)

- San Felipe Feast Day & Green Corn Dances
  (San Felipe Pueblo), May (p65)

- Solar Music Festival
  (Taos), June (p157)

- Spanish Market
  (Santa Fe), July (p92)

- Indian Market
  (Santa Fe), August (p92)

- Santa Fe Fiestas
  (Santa Fe), September (p92)

- International Balloon Fiesta
  (Albuquerque), October (p60)

- Cambalache
  (Questa), October (p173)

- Las Posadas
  (Taos), December (p157)

TOP TEN TINY MUSEUMS

This is the land of roadside attractions, where eclectic and eccentric collections raise one eyebrow with their clutter but mesmerize everyone else, revealing more in their cheerful anarchy than more-revered museums ever could.

- Tinkertown Museum (p67)
  Cedar Crest

- Awakening Museum (p81)
  Santa Fe

- Turquoise Museum (p57)
  Albuquerque

- Classical Gas Museum (p131)
  Embudo

- Rattlesnake Museum (p57)
  Albuquerque

- Elizabethtown Museum (p177)
  Elizabethtown

- Museum of Archaeology (p67)
  Cedar Crest

- Cerrillos Turquoise Mining Museum (p68)
  Cerrillos

- Huichol Indian Museum (p84)
  Santa Fe

- Legends of New Mexico Museum (p65)
  Off I-25

TOP TEN SPOTS TO TRANSCEND

Whether you're a dedicated spiritual seeker or just casually interested in keeping your karma clean, there are plenty of places for miracles and meditation in this state.

- El Santuario de Chimayó (p127)
  Chimayó

- Zozobra (p93)
  Santa Fe

- Ojo Caliente Hot Springs Resort (p124)
  Ojo Caliente

- Kasha-Katuwe Tent Rocks (p67)
  Cochiti Pueblo

- The Blue Lakes Wilderness (p167)
  Taos Pueblo

- Ghost Ranch (p126)
  Abiquiú

- Shrine of the Stone Lions (p136)
  Bandelier

- Loretto Chapel (p85)
  Santa Fe

- New Buffalo Inn (p172)
  Arroyo Hondo

- Vietnam Veterans Memorial (p178)
  Angel Fire

Itineraries

CLASSIC ROUTES

NORTHERN NEW MEXICO: THE VACATION CIRCUIT   1 week

Escape the **Albuquerque Sunport** (p62) and stop at **The Frontier** (p62) to recuperate, remembering to order your green chile on the side. Then it's up the **Turquoise Trail** (p67) with a quick detour to **Tinkertown Museum** (p67), perhaps making your way up the mountain for the quick hike to **Sandia Man Cave** (p68) and fabulous views of Albuquerque from the top.

Continue north, poke around picturesque **Madrid** (p67) for an hour, stop at the **Cerrillos Turquoise Mining Museum & Petting Zoo** (p68), and then cruise into Santa Fe.

Stretch your legs at the plaza, then watch the sun set from **La Fonda** (p97). Spend **three days** (p73) exploring the area, then jump on the Low Road as you begin the **two-day tour** (p145) of Taos; if you get a late start, have lunch at the state's first microbrewery, **Embudo Station** (p131). If you've seen enough museums in Santa Fe, consider arranging a **white-water rafting** (p88) trip.

After returning to Santa Fe, relax – you deserve it! Perhaps it's a good night to soak in an outdoor hot tub at **10,000 Waves** (p99).

Wake up early and head down I-25 to **Kasha-Katuwe Tent Rocks** (p67) for a hike. Need more souvenirs? Stop at **Bien Mur Marketplace** (p65) and finish your shopping. Go upscale for dinner at **High Finance** (p68) or savor your last green chile at **Los Cuates** (p62).

This roundtrip will put about 300 miles on your car. The three-day tour of Santa Fe includes one full day of exploration; consider taking more time. The two-day tour of Taos spends considerable time on the quicker High Road, but the Low Road is almost as scenic.

NORTHERN NEW MEXICO: THE GRAND TOUR   2 weeks

After escaping the **Sunport**, it's off to **Acoma Pueblo** (p59), then either a hike at **Petroglyph National Monument** (p59) or a few museums in **Old Town** (p57). Check the *Alibi* over dinner to see what's going on.

Wake up to the **Jemez Scenic Byway** (p66), bedding down in **Jemez Springs** (p66) after a soak. Get to **Bandelier National Monument** (p136) early to beat the crowds, then hit the free museums in **Los Alamos** (p132).

After a quick stop at **San Ildefonso Pueblo** (p118), you're finally headed to Santa Fe. Do the **four-day tour** (p73), but after leaving Abiquiú, get a hotel in **Española** (p121) and explore the pueblos as well as the galleries by day and casinos by night.

The next day, hit the **High Road to Taos** (p127), stopping at **El Santuario de Chimayó** (p127) (to either sightsee or collect allegedly miraculous earth) and **Rancho de Chimayó** (p128) for brunch before heading to Taos. At the end of the **five-day tour** (p145), make a left at Angel Fire and take the **Back Road** (p180) to Las Vegas.

Grab a room in **Las Vegas** (p138) and dinner at Estella's Café, then perhaps another soak at **Montezuma Hot Springs** (p141). Break up the two-hour drive back to Albuquerque with brunch at **Sad Café** (p138), then head back down the Turquoise Trail.

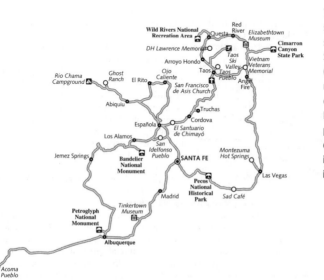

Though it's stunning, skipping Jemez Scenic Byway (140 winding miles) saves a full day. The 84-mile Enchanted Circle, part of the five-day Taos Tour, is best done in two days.

TAILORED TRIPS

THE GREAT OUTDOORS

Even Albuquerque has incredible hiking just minutes away, through **petroglyphs** (p59) or up and around **Sandia Crest** (p68). Head north to Santa Fe's **Public Lands Information Center** (p78) and peruse all the recommended activities, hikes and campgrounds.

Bandelier (p136), in the heart of an old volcano, is threaded with ancient trails – how about that three-day hike to **Stone Lion Shrine** (p136)? And for

camping at its loveliest, Abiquiú's **Rio Chama Campground** (p126) offers hikes aplenty, after which you can soak your cares away in **Ojo Caliente Mineral Springs** (p124).

Take the shortcut (NM 567) to **Pilar** (p131), with **white-water rafting** and more at **Orilla Verde National Recreation Area** (p132).

Taos is the gateway to even more outdoor options, odd outfitters, and the world-renowned **Ski Valley** (p169). The Enchanted Circle is lined with campsites, fishing holes and hikes that could last a week, plus lonely **Wild Rivers Recreation Area** (p174) and lovely **Cimarron Canyon State Park** (p177). The **Back Road to Las Vegas** (p180) accesses two fine state parks.

The **Gallinas Canyon Complex** (p139) is a green and gorgeous spot, or carve your own adventure from the peaks of **Pecos Wilderness** (p137).

NATIVE NEW MEXICO

The Rio Grande Valley is one of very few places where Native Americans have continuously held their ancestral lands. Start at Albuquerque's **Indian Pueblo Cultural Center** (p57) for Pueblo Art and History 101, then hike **Petroglyph National Monument** (p59) or **Coronado State Monument** (p65) to

experience both up close.

End the day at posh **Prairie Star Restaurant** (p65) or with a show at **Sandia Casino** (p65) before heading out to explore the many pueblos, bookended by dramatic **Acoma** (p59) and stunning **Taos** (p166). The six Tewa-speaking **pueblos** (p115) are clustered around Española, making it the perfect base for exploration.

Make a detour to **Bandelier** (p136), the ruins of a massive city, or continue into the volcanic wilderness to **Jemez State Monument** (p66), once home to the Jemez Pueblo, which now operates the **Museum of Pueblo Culture** (p66).

On the **High Road** (p127), don't skip **Picuris Pueblo** (p130), which gets remarkably few tourists, and explore Taos' many fine **Native galleries** (p165). Santa Fe has a few, too, but more impressive are the **Museum of Indian Arts and Culture** (p79) and **Institute of American Indian Arts Museum** (p80). Take the Turquoise Trail back to Albuquerque and stop at **Sandia Man Cave** (p68), the first known human encampment on the continent, where perhaps it all began.

The Author

PAIGE R PENLAND

Paige is a native of Oak Ridge, Tennessee, sister city to Los Alamos and home to many unhappily relocated nuclear scientists. When she was a teenager, one such expat pointed up into a particularly sapphire afternoon and said, 'That's what the sky in New Mexico looks like.' Intrigued, Paige enrolled at UNM on the (ahem) six-year program, which allowed plenty of time to invest her misspent youth exploring the region. It was only later, however, as a writer for *Lowrider* magazine, that she came to appreciate the area's outstanding automotive artistry. She's since written several Lonely Planet guides covering the nation's most beautiful places, but not one could compare to New Mexico.

My Santa Fe & Taos

As a one-time resident of more down-to-earth (well, relatively) Albuquerque, both Santa Fe and Taos have always seemed a bit mystical to me. My first visit to the capital was for Zozobra (p93), which was mind-blowing to begin with, and later trips reinforced my first impressions – that Northern New Mexico was basically a David Lynch film played out on sets painted by Georgia O'Keeffe.

Wandering through the sculptures at Shidoni (p110), catching a show at the sweeping Paolo Soleri Amphitheatre (p107), or having your fortune told in the lobby of La Fonda (p97) are all such rare experiences. Taos and the other villages are gems of tradition and character, but it is their setting – the high desert in all its variety – that I love best.

CONTRIBUTING AUTHOR:

David Goldberg MD wrote the Health chapter (p196). Dr Goldberg completed his training in internal medicine and infectious diseases at Columbia-Presbyterian Medical Center in New York City, where he has also served as voluntary faculty. At present, he is an infectious diseases specialist in Scarsdale, New York, and the editor-in-chief of the website MDTravelHealth.com.

Snapshot

New Mexicans love a good political discussion, and in the northern part of the state, it's generally the Democrats versus folks much farther left (pity the neo-cons around here). Newspapers feature regularly outraged op-eds decrying everything from the fate of the two-inch-long silvery minnow, which may be sacrificed as a species so folks can keep their lawns green, to bigger fish like US Secretary of Defense Donald Rumsfeld, whose vacation home in Taos enjoyed a porch packed with protesters during the recent wars and their sketchy aftermaths.

One topic inspires a steady stream of commentary: water. It's most certainly not everywhere, and if you want a drop to drink at any restaurant, you'll have to ask for it – by law. What really gets folks in a lather is that the posh Las Campañas Golf Community, where President George W Bush takes a swing when he's in town, has been awarded water rights more suitable for Seattle while the rest of the capital suffers Stage III Water Restrictions, which forbid planting new grass or watering existing (brown) yards more than twice a week. There's even a hotline number to report offenders.

In some ways, however, New Mexico is the greenest state in the union, thanks to David Bacon's 2002 run for governor on the Green Party ticket, which earned 5% of the vote and successfully reestablished the Greens' major-party status, earning future candidates the right to participate in debates and use public funds earmarked for campaigning. Not that they were short on cash in the 2002 elections: Republican Party State Chairman John Dendahl donated a 'six-figure' sum to the party, just to keep the Greens in competition. Ahem.

They didn't play spoiler (this time), however, and New Mexicans elected former UN ambassador and Secretary of Energy Bill Richardson to the governor's mansion. The seasoned diplomat has had his name kicked around for years as a potential Democratic vice presidential candidate – which would make him the first Hispanic to hold the job. He's been making plenty of headlines at home, however, and not just because he's had his mug plastered on tourism ads from Times Square to Los Angeles; he recently signed a living wage bill as well as the landmark hate crimes bill that protects not only gays and lesbians but also transsexuals (unique in the nation).

Although Santa Fe's cost of living is well above the national average, most jobs are in the low-paying service industry sector. Since March 2003, however, larger companies have had to pay at least $8.50 an hour; they'll have to pay $10.50 an hour by 2008. Socialism? Hardly. Look at area rentals and do the math. There's still a lot of ramen being served around here.

Ramen with organic local produce, that is. Recent interest in rescuing heirloom varieties and traditional farming methods from agribusiness' genetically modified clutches has resulted in truly marvelous selection at area farmers markets. Frugal gourmets can even trade farm work for vegetables through Community Supported Agriculture, which connects consumers to the fields, profiting everyone. Now that's the way to use the water.

FAST FACTS

New Mexico population: 1.8 million

New Mexico area: 121,356 sq miles

Santa Fe's altitude: 7200ft (the highest US state capital)

Maximum roadrunner speed: 20mph

Per capita income: $17,200

Homeless population working full- or part-time: 35%

Annual reported UFO sightings: 400 to 650 (most in USA)

History

About the same time that the Brits were building Stonehenge and Indians (in India) were beginning to weave cotton, New Mexicans were learning to farm and organizing into permanent settlements. By the time Charlemagne was crowned emperor in Europe and Nara was named the first capital of Japan, Chaco Canyon, Bandelier and other major regional cities were thriving metropolises regularly trading with Central America and the US Midwest. Heck, the first cities in Mesopotamia may not be much older than some of the irrigation ditches around here.

And as the Pilgrims settled down to that first Thanksgiving, bustling Santa Fe was celebrating its second decade as the Spanish capital of New Mexico, complete with political tensions involving the surrounding, and far older, cities. The USA may be a young country in some respects, but New Mexico is ancient and enamored of its rich cultural inheritance, so well preserved in the dry desert air.

HUNTER-GATHERER PERIOD

Though you know that humans first came to the Americas atop a land bridge, formed along Alaska's Aleutian chain during the last ice age, consider the potential for a grain of truth in the Native American version: folks around here emerged from the Sipapu, a cavern somewhere in the mountains of Northern New Mexico.

Because, oddly enough, the oldest evidence of human habitation on the continent wasn't discovered in Alaska. Spearheads, dating back at least 12,000 years, found near Clovis, New Mexico, are widely accepted as the oldest human remains on the continent.

More controversial is Sandia Man Cave, just a few minutes from Albuquerque. The encampment was dated at 20,000 years old in the 1940s, shocking folks who thought humans had been here only 3000 years. Contemporary archaeologists recently dated remains at 8000 years old (others call Sandia Man a hoax), but the resulting fuss reveals only how little we do know.

Here's the official version: Nomadic Paleo-Indians first settled Northern New Mexico in about 10,000 BC (a suspiciously round number that experts from various fields argue over constantly). About 2000 years later, the ancestors of the linguistically distinct Zuñi tribe came from the Midwest to join them.

The shift from hunter-gatherer lifestyle to a more settled agricultural economy took place between 6000 and 3000 BC, when techniques and crops introduced from Mexico became widespread. By this time, trade routes with civilizations in Central America, California and the Midwest were well established. One of the first cultivated crops was tobacco, and by 1500 BC, thriving farms along the Rio Grande were producing corn, beans and squash – a reliable diet diversified with hunting and gathering.

RISE OF THE CITY-STATES

The growing agricultural economy gave people more time to pursue arts and sciences, including manufacturing goods for trade. One of the most valuable items available in Northern New Mexico was turquoise, taken from surface deposits that were eventually depleted.

In about AD 100, engineers dug North America's first mine, near Cerrillos; you can see stone taken from these mines at the Cerrillos

Turquoise Mining Museum & Petting Zoo, which also has tools that were used there. Jewelry made with Cerrillos turquoise has been unearthed all over North America.

Basketry, ceramics and other arts also improved rapidly during this period, and by AD 600, locally produced redware pottery was being shipped as far as California and Mexico.

Cities were springing up throughout the region, as advances in materials and design allowed complexes to reach five stories tall. Chaco Canyon – founded in the late 800s east of modern-day Cuba – was the capital of a city-state, immediately housing some 1200 people, while the surrounding communities may have had a population of 5000 more.

By AD 1000, Chaco was the region's most important financial and administrative center, facilitating communications and trade via some 400 miles of roads that connected it with other cities throughout the region, including Puyé and Bandelier. In turn, these cities probably acted as local centers of government for surrounding communities.

Religious iconography of the period bears a strong resemblance to that of the Aztec empire, built in the 1200s by people who called their ancestral home, which is usually traced to this region, Aztlán (Nahuatl for 'Land of the Blue Herons'), indicating a much moister environment.

Like all empires, Chaco fell. Modern research suggests that long-term warming trends and increasingly depleted resources, including lumber and fertile soil, may have led to a period of civil unrest. The abandonment of Chaco and other major cities between 1150 and 1270 remains somewhat mysterious, however.

Many of the 19 modern pueblos were founded in the wake of this exodus, including San Juan Pueblo. There, a central government for a loose confederation of regional city-states was established as early as the 1200s. It is still the seat of both the Eight Northern Indian Pueblos Council and Bureau of Indian Affairs Northern Pueblo Agency.

THE SPANISH INCURSION

Although the new, smaller cities maintained communication and trade with one another, the loss of an effective central government took its toll. Some arts, including mural painting and the development of polychrome pottery, continued to evolve, but the period of rapid technological advance was over.

In about 1400, groups of Diné (Navajo) and Apache emigrated from Colorado to the region. Though many of these nomadic peoples pursued a peaceful and profitable relationship with the Pueblo Indians, this was, overall, a violent period. Skirmishes inspired advances in defensive architecture that would prove useful when the next new neighbors moved in.

The Spanish government sent two preliminary teams into the area, one in 1536 and another in 1539, when missionary Fray Marcos de Niza

PETROGLYPHS *By Jennifer Rasin Denniston*

Throughout the Southwest, rocks, boulders and cliffs may be darkened with a blue-black layer called desert varnish. The dark color is caused by iron and manganese oxides that leach out of the rock over many centuries, leaving a thin and slightly shiny polish that sometimes streaks cliffs from top to bottom. Ancient Indians chipped away the varnish to expose the lighter rock beneath, thus creating the rock art known as petroglyphs.

erected a cross at Zuñi Pueblo and claimed the territory for Spain. It was the 1540 expedition led by Francisco Vasquez de Coronado, however, that fundamentally transformed the region.

Coronado was searching for the Seven Cities of Gold but found only heavily fortified cities of gold-toned adobe. He stopped first at Acoma Pueblo's mesa-top fortress, calling it among the strongest cities he'd ever seen. He then moved on to easier pickings, wintering at less-fortified Kuau'a, today Coronado State Monument.

Coronado and his men began appropriating food and clothing from area residents. Though most grudgingly acceded, one group, probably from Sandia Pueblo, drove off several of their horses. Enraged, Coronado ordered an attack on the pueblo, burning it to the ground.

The following spring, Coronado and other Spaniards made contact with several other cities, relying on negotiation – and intimidation – rather than violence. The goal was gold, but there simply wasn't any to be had.

Several other explorers followed, and in 1598 Don Juan de Oñate set out to colonize the region. When his contingent of some 400 priests and soldiers wintered near Acoma Pueblo, several men attempted to scale the fortress's cliffs and raid their winter stores; 13 were killed, including Oñate's nephew.

According to Acoma historians, retribution was severe: Oñate chopped one foot off every man over 25. Others call this exaggeration, as Oñate needed slave labor, and this would have cost him manpower. Whatever the truth, when a statue in Oñate's honor was erected in Española in 1998, clever vandals made off with one of its feet.

It was close to modern-day Española that Oñate founded the first permanent Spanish settlement of San Gabriel, declaring it the capital of the Kingdom of New Mexico, with himself as governor. About 800 Spaniards and lots of Mexican Indian laborers were joined by 18 Franciscan friars, who got to work converting the locals by any means necessary.

These friars had been born into and trained during the most brutal wave of the Spanish Inquisition. After successfully driving the Moors from Spain, an entrenched theocracy continued to torture and kill accused heretics in the name of God. This was something these men had lived their entire lives considering normal. Oñate likely encouraged them to do their worst. Beautiful missions were built using forced labor, children were sold as slaves in Mexico, and that was not the worst of it.

Eventually Oñate was removed from office, both for his failure to find gold and for his mistreatment of the locals. His replacement, Don Pedro de Peralta, chose to move the capital entirely, founding La Villa de Santa Fe (City of Holy Faith) in 1609. There he and those first families built the Casas Reales (Royal Houses), today called the Palace of the Governors; La Fonda; and eventually a thriving agricultural sector, built around present-day Canyon Road and Barrio de Analco.

In the pueblos, however, echoes of Inquisition only intensified.

PUEBLO REVOLT OF 1680

According to Native traditions, the only place a pan-Pueblo war could be declared was San Juan Pueblo, and only by one who lived there. In the 1670s, friars punished, publicly and horribly, perhaps 50 Native religious leaders who continued practicing the old religion, including a San Juan priest named Popé. Popé organized a meeting of pueblo representatives and told them they could beat the Spanish. They agreed to try.

San Juan was too close to Santa Fe, so Popé moved his base of operations to Taos Pueblo. He worked closely with other military leaders throughout

New Mexico Historical Maps (www.rootsweb.com/ ~nmguadal/ histmaps.html) has an online collection of maps covering Spanish land grants, mineral deposits and Indian lands through history.

New Mexico Genealogical Society (www.nmgs.org) provides an excellent and accurate rundown of the state's history.

the state, most notably Domingo Naranjo from Santa Clara and Catiti from Santo Domingo, who marshaled the Keres-speaking tribes.

They used the tools of the conquistadors against them: the Spanish language facilitated communication between the linguistically different tribes, and runners distributed yucca cords with knots untied each morning in a universal countdown.

The Spanish suspected subterfuge, and shortly before the uprising was due to begin, two Tesuque messengers were intercepted. When Fray Juan Pío arrived at Tesuque the next morning to give Mass, he was assassinated. It was too soon, and too late. Runners fanned out across the state.

The following day, Indians began laying siege to Santa Fe. San Miguel Mission, now touted as 'the Oldest US Church,' was the first to fall. Santa Feans barricaded themselves inside the Palace of the Governors as Indians torched homes and businesses.

Though the better-armed Spanish killed scores of Indian troops, reinforcements from the surrounding pueblos poured into the capital. For nine days the battle raged, until Indians diverted the palace's water supply.

Thirsty and exhausted, the Spanish surrendered. Pueblo leadership defined the terms of the truce: immediate removal of the Spanish from tribal lands. A rag-tag column of refugees made their way south to El Paso, more than 300 backbreaking miles.

The Indians occupied Santa Fe for twelve years, though old political rivalries quickly resurfaced, weakening the tenuous system of alliances formed during the occupation. Many returned to their homes.

The Spanish settlers were plotting their own return, and with the arrival of Don Diego DeVargas, a seasoned soldier and negotiator, set their plans into motion. DeVargas visited all the pueblos with a heavily armed contingent, basically aiming cannons at the city walls while asking for peace.

Popular history calls the Reconquista 'almost bloodless,' yet many tribes abandoned their pueblos entirely for several years, retreating to live with Apache and Plains Indian allies rather than face retribution. At least 80 people died resisting DeVargas, and that's according to historical accounts written by the Spanish.

But Pueblos were negotiating from a position, and since the revolt, the Indians have worshipped however they chose without interference (well, not as much). Many chose Catholicism or some combination of the two belief systems.

In October 1693, 70 families, 100 soldiers and 18 friars returned to Santa Fe.

EUROPEAN EXPANSION

After securing Santa Fe, Spanish settlers began populating the Rio Grande Valley in earnest. By the 1700s, Spanish control of the continent was being threatened by growing British and French colonies to the east, and the government encouraged settlers with land grants. Truchas, Taos, Albuquerque and many other cities were incorporated.

The region remained isolated from Spain, and agricultural communities were basically self-sufficient, developing distinctive crafts, in particular the colorful *reredos* and *retablos* – sacred art – that were markedly different from the European traditions.

Though the Pueblos had been largely subdued, retribution for the Pueblo Revolt was exacted in the form of high taxes and annexed land, and the Comanche, Apache and Navajo tribes began increasingly

What Caused the Pueblo Revolt of 1680? (Historians at Work), edited by David J Weber: Academic, but this collection of historical essays offers several different viewpoints on the continent's only successful Native uprising and, thus, is the definitive read.

coordinated attacks on these homesteads. Plazas and large haciendas, such as Chimayó's original plaza and La Hacienda de los Martinez in Taos, were designed to protect entire communities from these raids.

New Mexicans were becoming increasingly independent from Spain, and despite laws against trade with the newly independent United States of America, illegal trade along the Santa Fe Trail became increasingly common. When peace treaties were signed with the Comanche in 1804, only one barrier remained to free trade.

MEXICAN INDEPENDENCE

Though most New Mexicans were comfortable with – or, at least, could ignore – Spanish rule, revolution had been fomenting in central Mexico for decades. In September 1821, Mexican separatists declared victory. Santa Fe celebrated, and the end of the Santa Fe Trail became a popular spot for traders led by William Becknell, who brought in wares like nails, metal tools and new technologies that the isolated region had long done without.

Businesspeople like Doña Tules began opening saloons and gambling halls where these traders could come and lose their profits, building a formidable economy. By the 1840s Rio Grande weavers were exporting some 21,000 pieces annually; trade increased twentyfold in every sector.

Even as cultural and economic ties with the Americans strengthened, the local population was growing disenchanted with Mexican rule. Governor Manuel Armijo attached increasingly higher taxes on every transaction, and his corruption and cruelty won him few friends.

When the US declared war on Mexico in 1846, ostensibly because of skirmishes on the Texas border (but in reality because of a strategy to extend US control to Pacific ports), they met bitter resistance in much of the country. But in New Mexico, Armijo's troops put up no fight, and many people welcomed General Stephen Kearny with open arms.

The Wind Leaves No Shadow, by Ruth Laughlin: Breasts heave and empires fall in this immensely entertaining (if embellished) historical novel about Doña Tules, Governor Manuel Armijo and Santa Fe's transition through the Spanish, Mexican and US eras.

US RULE

Pockets of resistance remained after the state was annexed as a US territory. The first US governor, Charles Bent, was attacked and scalped at his home in Taos by a contingent of Spanish and Indians loyal to Armijo.

The event touched off a bloody reprisal on Taos Pueblo, where 150 women, children and elders were burned alive as they huddled inside the pueblo's mission. Today only the bell tower remains.

Relations between the US government and Native peoples continued to deteriorate, and in 1851 Governor James C Calhoun issued a proclamation authorizing volunteer forces to kill any Native American who looked threatening. The Diné and Apache 'Long Walk,' in which 10,000 POWs and civilian detainees were marched by Kit Carson, starving, for 400 miles to a concentration camp near Fort Sumner, was probably the worst episode.

Most of the state thrived under US rule, however, despite tensions between the largely Spanish-speaking population and their new government. A new wave of settlers began pouring in: young Jewish men, escaping persecution in Central Europe set up shop here. Solomon Jacob Spiegelberg arrived with Union forces in 1946 and operated a mercantile in Santa Fe until the 1870s. Solomon Bibo, who arrived in the region in the 1870s, married a Laguna Pueblo woman and was later elected governor of the tribe.

You can still have drinks in the home of prominent Santa Fean Abraham Staab, who helped finance Archbishop Jean-Baptiste Lamy in the construction of St Francis Cathedral. According to legend,

DID YOU KNOW?

Smokey Bear was rescued as a cub during a 1950 New Mexico forest fire and is buried at Smokey Bear Historical Park in Capitan.

Staab forgave the massive debts its construction incurred, inspiring the addition of the tetragrammaton (JHVH) above the entrance.

Lamy, a newly arrived French archbishop less than enchanted by the territory's independent Catholic leadership, suspended Albuquerque Padre José Manuel Gallegos, who went on to represent New Mexico in the US Congress. Lamy later excommunicated the beloved Padre Antonio José Martinez of Taos, who ignored him and continued to preach.

The archbishop also ordered many of the traditional *retablos* and *reredos* removed from New Mexico churches; they were squirreled away in private homes and returned to their altars after his death in 1888.

By this time, the railroad linked Santa Fe and Albuquerque to the rest of the country; it was only a matter of time before the territory gained full statehood.

Death Comes for the Archbishop, by Willla Cather: The story of Father Jean Latour (based on Archbishop Lamy) and his European pals' efforts to reform New Mexican Catholicism (and build one very nice cathedral) in the decades following US annexation has been criticized as Anglo-centric, but is nevertheless a classic and well-written tale.

STATEHOOD

After New Mexico finally achieved statehood in 1912, writers and artists began coming to the arid state to recuperate from tuberculosis and ended up falling in love with the place, then inviting their friends out to visit. Folks like Mabel Dodge Luhan, the Taos Society of Artists and Los Cincos Pintores in Santa Fe began adding their own surreal twists to local culture.

The growing Anglo community made several popular contributions to the increasingly pluralistic society, including Zozobra at the annual Santa Fe Fiestas. Though some saw this as the erosion of New Mexico's essentially Hispanic character by its latest nation, in 1936 the state returned the favor, sending the USA's first Hispanic senator, Dennis Chávez, to Washington.

Democrats didn't usually do too well in New Mexico; Chávez was originally appointed because prominent state Republicans supported him, perhaps doubting he would hold the office for long. He won subsequent elections, however, largely because of the Great Depression.

DENNIS CHÁVEZ: TEACHING THE SENATE SPANISH

It was New Mexico's most tumultuous election: Entrenched Republican Senator Bronson Cutting was known as 'patron' to many for his generous favors. Democrat Dennis Chávez was a junior-high-school dropout who had educated himself while working in a grocery store, going on to attend Georgetown University and serve in the US House of Representatives. It was 1934, the Great Depression, and one of the state's first elections by secret ballot.

When the votes were tallied, Cutting had won by less than 1%. Stormy accusations of fraud had still not been settled by 1936, when Cutting died in an airplane accident. Chávez was appointed to take his place, becoming the USA's first Hispanic senator.

As the only Spanish speaker in Congress, Chávez was quickly drafted to help build diplomatic relationships with Latin America and the territory of Puerto Rico, and he helped negotiate the Pan American Freeway. He used his growing influence to introduce legislation that protected Native American sovereignty and built Cochiti Lake. After WWII he criticized veterans programs that failed to provide treatment to Hispanic war heroes, famously noting, 'We are Americans when we go to war, and when we return, we are Mexicans.'

National policy began to change under Chávez's watch, prompting him to introduce the bill that he would fight for until his death: the Fair Employment Practices Commission, which would guarantee equal employment rights for all people.

Chávez died in 1962, two years before he would have seen his long battle won: the landmark Civil Rights legislation of 1964 included, finally, equal employment under federal law. The inscription beneath his image in the National Statuary reads (in Spanish, Diné and English), 'We have lost our voice.' But few have echoed so profoundly.

New Mexico was a primarily agricultural economy, so most folks didn't feel much of a pinch – it's tough to get fired from the family farm. But when the Works Progress Administration (WPA) began, New Mexicans began getting training and opportunities they'd never had before, new roads and buildings were built, and most people did better than ever – and changed their votes. Prior to 1936 New Mexico was a Republican state; ever since, it's voted Democrat in two out of three elections.

World War II transformed the state even more fundamentally. In 1943 the federal government took over an isolated mesa east of Santa Fe and built a secret city to construct a nuclear device, code-named the Manhattan Project. In 1945 Los Alamos unleashed its secret on Hiroshima and then Nagasaki, bringing WWII to an end. The blasts killed 120,000 people immediately, and perhaps three times as many in the years that followed.

Santa Fe and Taos, in the meantime, were experiencing a cultural bloom. Since the 1920s Taos patron Mabel Dodge Luhan and Santa Fe's Alice Corbin had been bringing writers and artists to the state. In the 1960s they were joined by a new breed of counterculture archetypes: hippies. New Buffalo Commune, made famous in the movie *Easy Rider*, was but one groovy Taos outpost where folks farmed naked, drove rattling VW buses around and in general irritated the traditionally conservative, Catholic residents.

There were incidents of violence and vandalism in Taos throughout the late 1960s and early 1970s as the two very different groups learned to get along. Particularly after the newcomers began donning clothing, things settled down. The precedent was set, and both Santa Fe and Taos were firmly entrenched on the hippie trail.

But it wasn't just the hippies: New Mexico, like the rest of the Southwest, was experiencing a huge general population boom, coinciding with the widespread availability of swamp coolers and air conditioning. The state's population has tripled since 1950.

In the 1980s New Agers, convinced that Santa Fe was at the crossroads of invisible lines of power, brought holistic healing, organic grocers and feng shui to the state capital. Microchip manufacturer Intel, convinced that Albuquerque's underground aquifer would never be depleted, built the world's largest chip manufacturing plant in the suburb of Rio Rancho in the 1990s.

The jury's still out on the New Agers, but Intel was wrong, and Albuquerque's primary source of water is being rapidly depleted. Water has become the most discussed and least addressed problem in the state.

DID YOU KNOW?

The nuclear weapon used on Nagasaki was named 'Fat Man' in honor of UK Prime Minister Winston Churchill, who possessed a similar silhouette.

Surely You're Joking, Mr Feynman!, by Richard P Feynman: The Nobel Prize winner's hysterical escapades picking locks, harassing generals and building bombs in WWII Los Alamos makes the Manhattan Project look fun.

Salt of the Earth (dir. Herbert J Biberman, 1954): Blacklisted actors and crews joined striking Silver City miners to film this important, hilarious and once-banned McCarthy-era film of dangerous picket lines, festive feminism and Operation Wetback.

The Culture

New Mexico pitches itself as proudly tricultural, a place where Native Americans, Hispanics and Anglos get along, if not in perfect harmony, at least better than most places. In general this is true, with a few simmering caveats. But most folks make a genuine effort to understand and respect one another, interracial relationships (heck, interracial relationships between heavily tattooed transsexuals walking their pet ferrets) don't warrant a second look, and new arrivals quickly pick up a few key Spanish phrases.

New arrivals don't always fit into those three categories, either. Large populations of African Americans, Asians and other folks are finding niches, particularly in Albuquerque but throughout the region. Most people who have been here a while think of themselves as New Mexicans, often distinct from Americans, and in a different category altogether from the rest of the Southwest, which tends to be more conservative politically and socially.

It's a consciously open-minded place, where a variety of traditional cultures are preserved in an atmosphere of mutual respect and where creative careers, fostered from an early age in the public schools, are encouraged and venerated. The result is a region of unusual diversity and impressive eclecticism.

REGIONAL IDENTITY

Though describing the three major New Mexican cultures is a good introduction to the state, just keep in mind that many people hail from more than one of them, and most of the rest feel little need to judge their

---

WHAT'S IN A NAME?

Though the stereotypes that too often accompany racial labels are largely ignored in New Mexico, it's still a challenge for publishers to figure out the most accurate (and politically correct) term for various ethnic groups. Here's the rundown on our terminology for New Mexico's big three:

Native American: After introducing themselves to one very confused Christopher Columbus, the original Americans were labeled 'Indians.' The name stuck, and 500 years later folks from Mumbai are still trying to explain that, no, they don't speak a word of Tewa. 'Native American' is recommended by every major news organization, but in New Mexico, most tribal members remain comfortable with the term 'Indian.' Both terms are used in this book.

Anglo: Though 'Caucasian' is the preferred moniker (even if their ancestors hailed from nowhere near the Caucuses) and 'White' is the broadest and most useful word for European-Americans, in New Mexico, the label for non-Iberian Europeans is 'Anglo' ('of England'). Even English speakers of Norwegian-Polish ancestry are Anglo around here, so get used to it.

Hispanic: This is the one that has editors pulling their hair out. AP prefers hyphens: 'Mexican-American,' 'Venezuelan-American,' etc. Obviously, it's easier, if less precise, to use 'Latino' to describe people hailing from the Spanish-speaking Americas (yes, this includes the USA – or are Spanish-speaking US citizens more properly 'American-Americans'?). Add to that list 'Chicano,' 'Raza,' and 'Hispano,' a de-anglicized term currently gaining popularity, and everyone's confused. But, because New Mexico was part of Spain for 225 years and Mexico only 25, and many folks can trace an unbroken ancestry back to Spain, 'Hispanic' ('of Spain') is the term used throughout this state and book, sprinkled with 'Spanish' and all the rest.

neighbors by the color of their skin. With so many characters around, that's the barometer folks have been relying on for centuries.

Native Americans

There are about 153,000 Native Americans officially enrolled in tribes in New Mexico, making up around 11% of the population: 107,000 Diné, 40,000 Pueblo Indians and 6000 Jicarilla and Mescalero Apaches.

The pueblos and reservations have only recently achieved any level of economic independence. Until gaming became widespread, the vast majority of Indians lived beneath the poverty level, many subsisting on bare-bones federal stipends that are, as one person put it, 'the government's way of proving that socialism doesn't work.'

When the casinos started going up in the mid-1980s, critics argued that gambling would destroy lives and communities, not to mention the traditional Native way of life. This has perhaps proven true, at least in part: one painting displayed in Santa Fe depicted an Indian in ceremonial garb, his eyes replaced with quarters.

But the tradeoff is clear to anyone visiting a gaming versus a nongaming pueblo: luxurious homes, rising from the earth where doublewide trailers once parked, stand in stark contrast to the almost ramshackle buildings that house residents of more isolated – or more stubborn – pueblos.

All the pueblos are diversifying their economies, adding everything from business parks for environmentally friendly corporations to luxurious resorts and golf courses, and gaming profits have been efficiently invested in schools, roads, clinics and other long-needed infrastructure. Many tribes have undertaken buffalo reintroduction programs, while others have used their growing power to lobby for environmental protection and cleanup.

Most tribes remain very protective of their culture, inviting visitors to watch their dances but declining to share the details. But when the evergreen boughs come off and Native locals get back to business, whether on or off the pueblo, they are increasingly well represented in government and business. It sometimes seems as though the injustices inherited unhappily through too many generations are finally being transcended – sometimes. When Pojoaque Governor Jacob Villareal stood in the middle of NM 84/285 and threatened to shut down the vital corridor connecting Santa Fe to Los Alamos if state legislators did not concede to the right of his people to develop (what was left of) their land as they chose, it revealed a great deal.

Hispanics

About 42% of New Mexico's population is Hispanic, the highest proportion of any state in the USA. Moreover, New Mexico's Hispanics command more wealth, own more businesses and are better represented in politics at every level than anyplace else in the country. The state's constitution designates New Mexico as officially bilingual, and about 30% of New Mexicans speak Spanish at home.

This massive influence exerts itself not only in New Mexico but also throughout the country. The country's first Hispanic senator, Dennis Chávez, was a fierce proponent of civil rights; and Dolores Huerta, cofounder of the United Farm Workers, was the first person to ever negotiate a contract between immigrant farm workers and the wealthy landowners who had historically taken advantage of them.

New Mexico's power players serve as a beacon in a nation where Hispanics are often marginalized. The effects of this commitment to

The Pueblo of Santa Ana Calendar of Native American Events and Dances (www.santaana.org/calendar.htm) offers comprehensive listings of dances and feast days at all New Mexico pueblos.

DID YOU KNOW?

More than 200 of 562 Indian tribes participate in gaming, employing 300,000 people (about 25% of whom are Native Americans) and generating $12.7 billion annually.

Milagro Beanfield War, by John Nichols: This one's required reading (or watching – the movie is almost as good) about the tiny village of Milagro, wealthy Anglo developers and one very important hill of beans.

diversity are as seemingly insignificant as a reluctance to ban lowrider cruising, resulting in this small state's consistent national supremacy in the sport, to the election of Governor Bill Richardson, which keeps the USA's most prominent Hispanic politician very much on the national and international stages.

The Hispanic community does not always reach out to more recent immigrants from Mexico and Central America, however. Still, it must be a relief to this growing community of immigrants that they can speak to their boss or state representative with those nuances that fluency imparts, something unusual elsewhere in the USA.

New Mexico Department of Cultural Affairs (www.nmoca.com) offers a rundown on museums, national monuments and historical parks and other highbrow attractions.

Anglos

Anglos make up about 44% of the state's population, a number that has grown disproportionately over the past fifty years. In Northern New Mexico most live in the major population centers and, particularly in Santa Fe, many are young and somewhat transient, moving to New Mexico for a few years and then drifting away.

Los Alamos has the most unusual Anglo-majority population, an insular clutch of nuclear scientists here for one reason: to keep Los Alamos National Laboratory (LANL) running. Many other new arrivals retire here because of the climate. But the most visible White populations, and the ones that have helped define the culture of Northern New Mexico the most, are the artists, hippies and spiritual types who feel drawn to this place.

Racial roles are in some ways reversed in New Mexico, compared to the rest of the United States: many Anglos feel that they are the outsiders, working to fit into a New Mexican culture that has largely retained its Hispanic character. Some newcomers move to New Mexico and immediately attempt to integrate themselves with the community, efforts that often inspire letters to the editor that begin, 'Why do people move here and then try to change everything?,' followed by a diatribe about the latest lefty venture in their neighborhood.

But Anglo contributions to the arts, sciences and progressive politics of Northern New Mexico (the Southern half of the state is quite different, with a strong, and much more conservative ranching culture dominated by Anglo businesspeople) are seen as aspects of the now-entrenched Northern New Mexican culture that few would want to erase.

The People: Indians of the American Southwest, by Stephen Trimble: Trimble traveled, interviewed and photographed Native peoples for almost a decade before publishing this excellent book, much of it in the words of the Indians themselves.

LIFESTYLE

The lifestyle in Northern New Mexico can best be described as laid-back. Although many folks have a taste for the finer things – the number of excellent gourmet restaurants is your first clue – you can wear jeans absolutely anywhere. Locals are casual and community-oriented, people know their neighbors and you'll get smiles anywhere you go. It's outdoorsy, and one reason the nightlife is a tad anemic is because many people's idea of a good time is to load everyone in the van and head for the hills rather than attempt to look chic at Swig.

The commitment to creativity is probably the most captivating part of the culture. Richard Florida's book *The Rise of the Creative Class* ranked Albuquerque first in midsize US cities on his 'creativity index,' determined by the community's involvement with the arts, the economic opportunities for creative types and overall diversity, particularly with respect to minorities, recent immigrants, gays and lesbians.

The 'creative class' attracted to the region, however, tends to be young and transient, and this is the sort of place where people wear a badge of pride in how long their family has lived here; those whose families came with Oñate can lord it over those who didn't get here until after DeVargas. There is a certain level of resentment – or at least eye rolling – among those born here toward the recent arrivals. Hey, there's only so much water to go around.

Santa Fe in particular has a love-hate relationship with tourists. Yes, they provide jobs and money. But behind the server's smile as you send back the too-hot chile, there may be some muttering about 'tourons.' On the other hand, community seating at area restaurants and a culture of friendliness and acceptance make it easy to mix with locals, who are in much better moods after getting off work in the city's inflated and underpaid service sector.

And, like many tourist economies, the region has a serious drug problem. The old Camino Real brings more drugs up from Mexico than inexpensive manufactured goods. The porous border, perhaps less heavily guarded here than in California and Texas, has made the region something of a distribution center for heroin and cocaine.

The attendant crime is high. New Mexico ranks number one in violent crimes, burglary and aggravated assault, and is near the top in most other crimes, not to mention car accidents, drunk driving and other indicators. All this prompted Morgan Quitno Press to rate New Mexico 'the most dangerous state' in 2000. The situation has improved in recent years, but it's something to keep in mind during your visit.

It's still the Wild West, but bravado here comes fabulously accessorized. Individuality (even eccentricity) is highly regarded, and 'keeping up with the Joneses' often translates into having the neighborhood's best yard art, welded or raku-fired by hand in the studio out back. There's a sense of freedom beneath the enormous sky, and a big part of the unspoken social contract is to live and let live.

POPULATION

Like most Southwestern states, New Mexico has a young population, with the median age of 34 somewhat skewed by the number of retirees who choose to live here. Because water availability is a constant concern, most people are concentrated in urban areas; almost half the population of the state lives in Albuquerque and the endless suburbs of tract housing that surround it.

About 20% of New Mexicans work directly for the state or federal government, and the state receives more government funding (though much of this is for weapons labs and military bases) than any other. It is still among the poorest states; as New Mexicans say, 'Thank goodness for West Virginia.'

There is a cycle to this: with less money spent on education, not to mention health care and other infrastructure, locals often graduate high school unprepared to live up to their potential. And when the transient creative population moves in, locals find themselves out-competed for prime jobs.

This doesn't paint a pretty picture, but keep in mind that in many ways New Mexico has forged a solid link between US, Mexican and Native American cultures, and displays many of the political and economic indicators of all. People are less concerned with conspicuous consumption, preferring to sacrifice suit-and-tie success to build strong families and communities and maintain their particular culture's traditions.

Many New Mexicans are also committed to voluntarily living a 'sustainable lifestyle,' using as few resources as possible to be comfortable and generally making less money. And because art – rarely the road to riches – is considered such an important part of these communities,

> **DID YOU KNOW?**
> Albuquerque-based Rollerz Only is the only car club ever to have been named 'Lowrider Club of the Year' twice.

> *Skinwalkers,* by Tony Hillerman: Just one of the best in a series of novels by the award-winning mystery author about Navajo police officers Jim Chee and Joe Leaphorn.

even nonprofessionals invest significant amounts of time and money in creative pursuits rather than committing wholeheartedly to the rat race. It's a different mindset, and if a life well lived means foregoing the creature comforts prized elsewhere in the USA, so be it.

RELIGION

Perhaps because of its enforced isolation and (since 1680, anyway) tradition of tolerance, Northern New Mexico is considered a spiritual center to a variety of faiths, which exist here in unusual harmony, particularly considering how things are elsewhere in the world. The cultural geography that this has engendered is inspiring.

Native American Religions

The specifics of Pueblo Indian religious practices are not generally revealed to outsiders, and each tribe has its own traditions. But spiritual life centers on the kiva, a circular sacred space buried partially underground, as a reminder of humanity's essential connection to the earth. All Native practices are characterized by a respect for nature that is often de-emphasized in modern interpretations of Western religions.

New Mexico's Cultural Treasures (www.nmculture.org) features endless opportunities for enrichment, including museum exhibits, pueblo dances and more.

Dances held on saints' feast days nominally praise each mission's Catholic patron but also honor more ancient deities; other dances don't bother with the saint. Visitors are welcome to observe some dances as long as proper respect is maintained.

Festivities center on the plaza, where long lines of dancers, sometimes painted in earth and wearing pine boughs, fur pelts and fetching dresses – the costuming is different for each tribe and celebration – move to drums and chanting provided primarily by men. The gatherings are prayers, but are festive – expect food stands and plenty of roaming about after the prayer is complete.

Catholicism

The dominant religion in New Mexico is Roman Catholicism, and about 30% of the population is baptized Catholic, though not all practice regularly. Traditions remain stronger here than most places in the USA.

In the Holy Week leading up to Easter, some 75,000 pilgrims from as far away as Albuquerque make the pilgrimage the Santuario de Chimayó. Christmas traditions, called Las Posadas, go way beyond Santa Claus: farolitos and luminarias line streets and cemeteries, and many families celebrate not on December 25 (though most businesses are closed that day) but on King's Day, January 6, as in Spain. Some businesses, particularly in rural areas, are closed during the weeks between.

Judaism

Some of the original Spanish settlers were probably Crypto-Jews, Jews who converted to Catholicism to avoid persecution under the Inquisition. Families still haunted by rumors of heresy back in Spain could start fresh here. Research into this aspect of New Mexican history is ongoing but understandably complicated given the long-standing need for secrecy.

Beginning in the 1850s, a wave of openly Jewish young men, fleeing persecution in Central Europe, established businesses and homes here, particularly in Santa Fe, and remain an important part of the community. According to legend, the Tetragrammaton (JHVH) above the entrance of St Francis Cathedral was to give thanks for the Staab family's financial contribution to its construction, but it may also honor those for whom Catholicism and Judaism have been intertwined for 400 years.

Other Religions

In the 1970s and 1980s, Santa Fe in particular became a mecca for New Age types. This migration has led to a proliferation of pagan and other traditions: 'What's your sign?' isn't just a pickup line around here; be prepared to know your ascendant and moon signs as well.

Large communities of Muslims, Sikhs, Quakers, and most other major Protestant sects have been joined by the recent diaspora from Tibet, refugees who note the prophesy of Padmasambhava, founder of Tibetan Buddhism: 'When the iron bird flies and horses run on wheels…the Dharma will come to the land of the Red Man.'

And when a contingent of maroon-clad monks approached area tribes to tell that strange tale, they learned of a parallel Hopi prophesy: A 'tribe of red hat and red cloaked people' would arrive from the east 'by air.' This, unfortunately, is a precursor to the cleansing of Earth by fire; see the Los Alamos section for more.

GOVERNMENT

Though not everyone realizes it, New Mexico is part of the USA. The state maintains close ties with old Mexico, particularly the neighboring states of Chihuahua and Sonora, as well as strong cultural ties with Spain, all facilitated by the fact that many in state government speak Spanish with some degree of fluency.

All recognized Native American tribes are technically sovereign nations, but in reality are subject to most US laws and lots of red tape spewed forth with every attempt at economic development. Tribal members are also full US citizens and hold several important offices and positions in New Mexico government. Pueblo governments covered in this book vary, but are all led by a governor, usually appointed by a council of elders rather than voted into office in general elections.

This complex political landscape has historically hobbled Native influence in the state and nation, and local organizations – including the 22 Native American Tribes of New Mexico, the All Indian Pueblo Council (AIPC), the Eight Northern Indian Pueblo Council (ENIPC) and the federally administrated Bureau of Indian Affairs – seem to just add to the bureaucratic maze. But since gaming began infusing the tribes with money, the pueblos' political power has grown exponentially, and structures are most certainly in place to flex that muscle.

The New Mexico state legislature (www.legis.state.nm.us), which goes into session the third Tuesday of January and lasts two months during odd years, one during even years, provides entertainment at its finest, which you're welcome to watch at the Roundhouse. Any citizen with a beef is allowed to talk for as long as they want about anything, then ask audience members what they think. The possibilities, clearly, are endless.

Though New Mexico tends to vote Democrat in most elections, the politics of personality remain more important than party affiliations. Republican US Senator Pete Dominici has served five six-year terms in office; many folks tick his name off right along with Democrats Senator Jeff Bingaman and Representative Tom Udall.

The Green Party always gets a large turnout, and in part because of their efforts New Mexico underwent a voting recount similar to Florida in the 2000 presidential election, with Al Gore carrying the state by 368 votes. Of course, since New Mexico gets only five representatives in the Electoral College, it wouldn't have made much difference either way. The Green Party did draw away enough votes from the Democrats to

The Devil's Butcher Shop: The New Mexico Prison Uprising, by Roger Morris: A brutal portrayal of the 1980 prison uprising, the worst in US history, and the greed, corruption and abuse that led up to it.

Alburquerque, by Rudolfo Anaya: A magical history tour through the city and its 'fictional' inhabitants, including the powerbrokers, politicians and outcasts who make it so strange, by the seminal Chicano novelist and UNM professor emeritus.

help elect former Republican Governor Gary Johnson to office in 1994, causing much rejoicing among Republicans – until he began his maverick crusade to decriminalize marijuana.

Current Governor Bill Richardson, longtime prominent state politician and former UN ambassador and secretary of energy, is also a force to be reckoned with. The governments of Cuba, Iraq and North Korea have requested the seasoned diplomat to help negotiate with both the Clinton and Bush administrations, making him a major player on the international stage. Most New Mexicans think that's pretty cool, even when he has to rush off to some last minute-negotiations to avert international crises and whatnot rather than posing for tourism billboards back home.

GOVERNOR GARY 'BIG J' JOHNSON: LIFE OF THE REPUBLICAN PARTY

After President Clinton's pronouncement that he 'didn't inhale,' reporters nationwide began asking their own politicians if they had ever used marijuana. New Mexico's 1994 Republican gubernatorial candidate, Gary Johnson, answered 'yes.' He had quit years earlier, however, noting that being stoned made it more difficult to read.

Supporters worried that such honesty equaled political suicide, but with the inadvertent help of the Green Party, Johnson smoked the competition. The former owner of Big J Construction quickly earned a reputation as the nation's most fiscally conservative governor and in 1998 became New Mexico's first Republican governor to serve a second, and final, term.

Term limits give leaders the freedom to have their say, and in June 1999 Governor Johnson said, 'I'm not advocating breaking the law, but personally I don't think you should go to jail for smoking marijuana.' He also called the War on Drugs 'a miserable failure.'

The firestorm was immediate and severe. Drug Czar Barry McCaffrey nicknamed him 'Puff Daddy Johnson,' and the Republican Party called on him to step down – or at least shut up. Johnson refused, complaining that drug arrests had increased 2000% since 1980 and that more than half of his law enforcement budget went to fighting nonviolent drug users.

Politically Incorrect host Bill Maher called Johnson his hero. The Libertarian Cato Institute called to ask if he'd be their keynote speaker. And fans of New Mexico's number-two cash crop (after hay) called on Johnson to legalize it. In 2001 Johnson introduced eight such bills to the legislature, from medical use to decriminalization. Not one passed.

State marijuana laws remain harsh: for one big J, you could spend 15 days in jail; even paraphernalia ('tobacco accessories') carry a large fine. But on leaving office, Johnson, an Ironman triathlete who advocates quitting both alcohol and coffee (in addition to all currently illegal drugs) vowed to continue working for a sane national drug policy – right after his vacation.

Quite fittingly, Johnson began private life by getting higher than anyone else on Earth: in May 2003 he successfully scaled Mount Everest. Gary, this bud's for you.

Arts

Santa Fe is no ordinary art colony: it's the third-largest art market in the USA, after New York City and running neck-in-neck with Los Angeles. Around 10,000 of Santa Fe's 70,000 residents are directly employed in the creative scene. It's not just about expressing yourself: this is big business, to the tune of $200 million a year.

Art is an integral part in the daily lives of almost everyone in the Santa Fe and Taos corridor. Gallery openings aren't just for the upper crust – they're community events. Local artists, many of whom have collectors all over the world, hang their pieces in every bar and coffee shop in town. No venue is too humble to become a showcase for the next Agnes Martin.

Portrait of an Artist, by Laura Lisle: Thorough and deeply personal, this is considered the quintessential book on Georgia O'Keeffe, her work and her role in the American art scene.

While most Americans consider the pursuit of art an interesting hobby, at best, in New Mexico it's a respected vocation. Art is heavily promoted in both public and private schools, and kids are encouraged to develop their skills through a variety of programs and special events.

The region's museums and galleries are a feast for the eyes that can send your brain happily into meltdown. If you're thinking of investing, do some research before you head out. Grab a couple of the fat freebie publications that are available just about anywhere: The **Collector's Guide** (www .collectorsguide.com) has gallery, accommodations and events listings for Taos, Santa Fe and Albuquerque, and a great searchable website; **the essential guide** (www.essentialguide.com) covers galleries and restaurants in Taos and Santa Fe; and **Inside Santa Fe** (www.insidesf.com) has more of the same, but just for Santa Fe.

VISUAL ARTS

If you're just here to browse, you're bound to have a ball – it seems like every square foot of wall space is covered with fine art. If there are particular types of art you're interested in seeing, however, do your research.

Southwestern Association for Indian Arts (www.swaia.org), the home of Indian Market, features an online gallery, artist profiles and links to specific sites.

Native American Arts

Each of New Mexico's tribes has a specialty, although artisans at each pueblo pursue different – sometimes radically so – directions. The Indian Pueblo Cultural Center in Albuquerque is a great introduction to the finest art of each tribe, broken down pueblo by pueblo, while the Institute of American Indian Arts Museum in Santa Fe shows the community's cutting-edge pieces. Indian Market, Santa Fe's annual juried show, attracts the very best Native artists from all over the continent.

Several other museums throughout the state feature great Native work, but the galleries are better endowed: Santa Fe's Canyon Road has more Maria Martinez pottery than her namesake museum at San Ildefonso Pueblo.

Art New Mexico (artnewmexico.com) covers arts all over the state, with museums, galleries, artists, openings and more.

The best places to buy are, of course, the pueblos and reservations, where beautiful pottery and other work often are sold from the artists' homes. Fine jewelry is sold beneath the famed Palace of the Governors portal in Santa Fe, but shops carrying pawn at good prices are best found in Albuquerque. If you just want to look, however, the Millicent Rogers Museum in Taos has an outstanding collection.

New Mexico Masters

Between roughly 1910 and 1940, Northern New Mexico attracted and inspired some of the finest painters in the world. Georgia O'Keeffe is probably the most famous, and the largest collection of her work anywhere is on display in Santa Fe.

Santa Fe's first serious collective, Los Cincos Pintores (Freemont Ellis, Willard Nash, Jozef Bakos, Walter Mruk and Will Shuster) and members of the Taos Society of Artists also command large followings – and high prices. Several museums have excellent collections of their paintings, particularly the Blumenschein and Harwood in Taos and the Museum of Fine Arts in Santa Fe. The Gerald Peters and Nedra Matteucci Galleries in Santa Fe also display their work.

Fourteen Families in Pueblo Pottery, by Rick Dillingham and JJ Brody: Pottery techniques are family affairs, and this illustrated guide introduces you to the artists and their work, and even includes contact information.

Western realists, including cowboy sculptor Frederic Remington and landscape artists Maynard Dixon and Charlie Russell, are also best found on Canyon Road; try the Altermann Galleries.

Spanish Arts

New Mexico's traditional Spanish arts are not as well known outside the state, except to serious art historians and collectors, which is an oversight. Sacred art – the tradition of painted altar pieces, called *retablos* and *reredos*, and carved saints, or *santos*, are well worth seeing, particularly those by artists selected by the Works Progress Administration (WPA) during the 1930s, including Santiago Matta, José Dolores López and most famously Patrociño Barela, whose sensual *bultos* won accolades over O'Keeffe's work when displayed in the 1930s.

New Mexico Santos (www.nmsantos.com) is the best online guide to Hispanic sacred art, including book recommendations, photos and events listings.

You can find collections of their work at the Harwood and Millicent Rogers Museums in Taos and at the Museum of Spanish Colonial Art in Santa Fe. The best places to see the original pieces are in the Catholic churches scattered throughout Northern New Mexico. Spanish Market, a juried show held in late July in Santa Fe, showcases modern masters of the santero traditions.

Cordova is renowned for its distinct wooden carvings, while Chimayó has been producing some of the world's finest wool weavings for 400 years.

Contemporary Art

Just try to avoid it: in every hotel, coffee shop, bar and restaurant, fine art by local artisans is on display and often on sale. Collectors make Santa Fe a regular destination, and many internationally known artists, both local and otherwise, show in galleries in Santa Fe, specifically close to the plaza or Canyon Road, and downtown Taos. Lesser-known local artists often show a bit off the beaten path, where rents are lower.

Baca St in Santa Fe and less-touristed spots in both the capital and Taos are great places to find cutting-edge artists. Several small communities scattered throughout the region have become something of art colonies: Truchas, Dixon, Abiquiú, Madrid and Arroyo Seco.

DID YOU KNOW?

More than 30% of the global population lives in adobe buildings, making it the world's most popular building material.

ARCHITECTURE

Though New Mexicans have probably been building with adobe for 6000 years or more, the well-preserved examples at Chaco Canyon and Bandelier date back to only about AD 800. The loveliest and best-preserved example of original adobe architecture is Taos Pueblo, built around 1100.

When the Spanish came they introduced improvements to adobe building, mixing the mud with straw and forming it into more easily transportable brick rather than just cutting it from riverbanks. Spanish colonial architecture was simple: usually single-story homes without dirt floors (iron tools weren't available to early settlers) and walls plastered with a mixture of oxblood and clay or tierra blanca, wheat paste mixed with white micaceous clay, to keep the dust under control.

After US annexation in 1846, the less curvaceous Territorial Style was introduced. Also adobe, these featured wooden porches and columns, including the famed Palace portico and framework.

In 1912 Santa Fe enacted its famous adobe-only law, requiring new buildings to return to that pristine pueblo look. The Museum of Fine Arts was one of the first, inspiring architect John Gaw Meem to create what's now known as pueblo revival, or Santa Fe style.

Today, pueblo revival style is being combined with alternative technologies; buildings are laid out to take advantage of passive solar energy, and many are made using inexpensive straw-bale construction. Like modern-day barn raisings, groups of people arrange bales of hay, then spray them down with special stucco mixtures for an incredibly well-insulated and soundproofed home – and it can be done in a weekend.

LITERATURE

Immediately after the United States annexed New Mexico, the state began to attract an unusual assortment of literati. Governor Lew Wallace wrote part of his popular passion play *Ben Hur: A Tale of Christ* during his term, while his wife, Susan Wallace, recorded her own impressions of the territory, collected as *The Land of the Pueblos*.

It was Alice Corbin, however, who established what's now termed 'The Writer's Era' in Northern New Mexico. Like many artists, she came to

---

ALMA LOPEZ & THE BIKINI OF ROSES

When Los Angeles artist Alma Lopez read Sandra Cisneros' essay 'Guadalupe the Sex Goddess' (*Goddess of the Americas*, Ana Castillo, ed), she was inspired by the author's desire to 'lift Guadalupe's robes' to see if the Virgin was real, like herself. What would such an act reveal? Lopez was sure it would be roses.

Lopez, an award-winning digital artist and cofounder of Homegirl Productions, got to work. Fellow artist Raquel Salinas posed, arms akimbo and chin defiant, as the Virgin, while activist Raquel Gutierrez revealed her breasts as the butterfly-winged angel holding the mother of Christ aloft. Lopez adorned both women with roses, much, she thought, like those Juan Diego filled his cloak with after the Virgen de Guadalupe revealed herself to him in 1531. She called the piece *Our Lady*.

In February 2001 the work was included in the International Folk Art Museum's CyberArte exhibit, but not everyone appreciated it. 'You may find yourself in some serious trouble with our Raza in Northern New Mexico,' community activist Jose Villegas wrote Lopez in mid-March, adding that he would 'find her supporters' and publicly 'hold their actions accountable.' Lopez was shocked, particularly after a 200-person vigil was held outside the museum, demanding that the piece be removed.

'I see this woman's legs and belly,' she told the *LA Times*, 'and I don't see anything wrong.' Others did, however, calling the garlanded depiction of the Patroness of the Americas insensitive and sacrilegious.

Archbishop Michael J Sheehan called the piece 'particularly offensive...in a state-funded institution.' The First Amendment notwithstanding, museum officials held a public meeting to address the controversy. Because of a legal technicality, a later judge ruled that the painting could stay. Museum officials chose to close the entire exhibition four months early anyway, 'in a spirit of reconciliation.'

'Half a slice of pie is better than none at all,' Sheehan commented. In October 2001 the roses came down.

Lopez has not wilted, however. 'If we grow up with the image of the Virgen de Guadalupe,' she explained, 'then we have and should be able to express our relationship with her.' Her work may never again be displayed in Santa Fe, but this is cyber art; you can see for yourself at www.almalopez.net. Or you can choose not to.

convalesce from tuberculosis in 1916, bringing her husband, William Penhallow Henderson, illustrator of *Brothers of Light: The Penitentes of the Southwest.*

Corbin's 1928 anthology of poetry, *The Turquoise Trail,* included pieces by many of the writers she hosted in the city: Carl Sandburg, Ezra Pound, Paul Horgan and Witter Bynner, the poet who would go on to found his own collective of kooky characters.

Together Corbin and Henderson founded Santa Fe's first publisher, Rydal Press, in 1932. The growing literary culture racked up some unusual accomplishments: in addition to Willa Cather's *Death Comes for the Archbishop,* one of Lynn Riggs' plays was adapted into the musical *Oklahoma!* Boy Scout cofounder Ernest Thomas Seton's short stories became the basis of the Disney classic *Bambi.*

DID YOU KNOW?

Los Cincos Pintores, the original Santa Fe arts collective, were also known as 'the five little nuts in adobe huts.'

Mabel Dodge Luhan was something of Corbin's rival – the heiress was known for her bitter insults to the Santa Fe crowd. Her own collective included such notables as DH Lawrence, Robinson Jeffers and Jean Toomer.

In the late 1960s John Muir, a former California aerospace engineer (and distant cousin of the famed conservationist of the same name), joined the hippie migration to New Mexico, writing the seminal *How to Keep Your Volkswagen Alive,* which he was forced to distribute through the Whole Earth Catalog; it ended up selling more than two million copies.

He used his unexpected profits to found John Muir Publications, which touched off something of a renaissance in the Santa Fe writing scene. Though it's since moved, magazines including *Mothering* and *Outside,* numerous book publishers, and some 700 full-time professional writers keep Santa Fe alive with the sound of tapping keyboards.

FILM

Ever since Tom Mix arrived in 1915 to commit cowboy mythology to the silver screen, New Mexico – the first state to ever form a film commission – has had its endless vistas and picturesque ghost towns captured on camera.

The region has wooed many a movie star to remain after filming, including Academy Award–winning actress Greer Garson, who made

---

TURQUOISE – OR NOT?

Though New Mexico is famed for its high-quality Native American jewelry, you should know that those authentic Zuñi and Navajo pieces aren't always what they seem. Several Southeast Asian countries have created quite a cottage industry imitating the fine work, and manufacturers use synthetic turquoise in pieces that appear almost identical to the originals to the untrained eye. Though required by law to display an import sticker, many unscrupulous dealers continue to market the jewelry as genuine.

Even if the piece is made in New Mexico by Native artisans, you still might not be getting the turquoise you think you are. There are five 'grades' of turquoise: expensive natural turquoise, which is hard enough to simply cut and set; stabilized turquoise, softer stone treated with an epoxy resin, and which makes up the bulk of fine jewelry; treated turquoise, which has been dyed; reconstituted turquoise, ground stone that has been colored and formed into cakes; and imitation turquoise, an entirely different stone, usually howlite, dyed to look like the real thing.

How do you tell the difference? Educate yourself at Albuquerque's Turquoise Museum before spending any serious money, and buy from either reputable shops or direct from the artisan. Genuine pieces are generally stamped and signed (though counterfeiters are clued into this as well), and tend to cost a bundle. If a deal seems too good to be true, it probably is.

her home in the Pecos Wilderness, and Dennis Hopper, who purchased the Mabel Dodge Luhan House in Taos, attracting all manner of scruffy counterculture celebrities to the region.

The movie-making industry has transformed New Mexico in many ways. *Easy Rider,* which popularized the hip 1960s scene in Taos, inspired a youthful immigration that painted the town tie-dye. *The Milagro Beanfield War,* the excellent adaptation of John Nichols book, forced star and director Robert Redford to build an authentic looking plaza in Truchas, after the town of Chimayó declined to allow movie crews to overrun their own. Even the road to Acoma Pueblo, previously accessible only via a steep footpath, was built for a John Wayne flick.

More than 300 major films and countless smaller ones have been made in New Mexico, and many of them are screened at film festivals throughout the year. August in Santa Fe features the Native Cinema Showcase Film Festival, which coincides with Indian Market, but the biggest bash is mid-April's Taos Talking Pictures, where independent films – including lots of Hispanic, Native American and teen offerings – are viewed by fans from all over the country.

100 Years of Filmmaking in New Mexico, edited by Mikelle Cosandaey: Covering everything from *Young Guns* to *Salt of the Earth,* this is the ultimate guide to tinsel-topped scenes set in the Land of Enchantment.

PERFORMING ARTS

All New Mexico is a stage: from the elaborate ceremonial dances of the Pueblo Indians and pageantry of the Santa Fe Fiestas, ritual as performance art has long been an integral part of life.

High culture, however, came to Santa Fe with John Crosby. A New York City native who attended the Los Alamos Boy's School, Crosby became a classical composer and opera aficionado after WWII. Disillusioned with the scene on Broadway, he came to Santa Fe with a dream: to build a stage where young performers could hone their skills in the creative atmosphere fostered by the region's artistic tradition.

In 1957 he established the Santa Fe Opera. With an open-air theater seating 450, and local as well as international talent – Igor Stravinsky was drafted to oversee production of the first shows – his dream was realized. A fire in 1967 allowed the company, which had grown in size and reputation, to expand the theater; today's stage is among the finest anywhere.

The Opera became the hub of a world-class performance art scene with followers worldwide. The Santa Fe Chamber Music Festival began in 1972, with performances by top musicians and composers that roughly coincide with the Opera's late summer season. Together they attract hundreds of thousands of culture junkies to the region annually.

One of Santa Fe's most renowned dance troupes is Maria Benitez Teatro Flamenco, perhaps the finest performers of the quintessential Spanish dance in the nation. Santa Fe is something of a flamenco center, where you can catch performances by the National Institute of Flamenco, located here, as well as the renowned Ottmar Leibert and co-conspirator James Bobchak, making this the committed flamenco capital of North America.

Try to see a performance while you're in town, particularly by artists like Ramón Bermudez Jr, who calls his unique sound 'flamenco fusion' (check out his award-winning *Fuego en Alma*); Wayne Wesley Johnson, who specializes in 'jazzmenco'; or the band Manzanares, whose rock-flamenco sound is showcased on *Nuevo Latino* at venues all over New Mexico.

Environment

Folks from less arid climes often think the term 'desert' refers to vast wastelands, uninspiring tracts of hostile and boring sand where cacti provide the only shade. Anyone who crosses the state on I-40 is likely to feel these beliefs justified.

But deserts are richly varied, and in New Mexico they rise to scenic heights that include most of the world's most important life zones, almost none of which fit the description above. The Rocky Mountains end here and are richly forested with all manner of flora and fauna adapted to the aridity.

This is where the tectonic plates that make up North America meet, on either shore of the Rio Grande, and their interaction has inspired all manner of geological wonders. Only South Africa boasts volcanic features that can compare to the Jemez Mountains, and the highlands of the Enchanted Circle are alive with creatures that would feel more at home in the Alps than anything portrayed in those Roadrunner cartoons.

Leave your misconceptions in Albuquerque as you make your way toward the 'deserts' of Northern New Mexico, where ski slopes, streams and shady trails invite the traveler to redefine what that word actually means.

THE LAND

There are portions of New Mexico that are endless, barren, Lawrence-of-Arabia-style sand dunes – that's White Sands National Monument, outside the range of this book, and even that's a geographic anomaly.

Northern New Mexico, on the other hand, is at the tail end of the Rocky Mountains, with forests of ponderosa pine and aspen skirting several peaks that reach well over 12,000ft. The high-desert plateau from

---

RESPONSIBLE TRAVEL

All the usual rules of responsible travel apply in New Mexico: don't litter, tip well, respect the locals and make an attempt to appreciate as well as enjoy this land. Indian Pueblos in particular ask more sensitivity of visitors.

Common sense also applies when camping and hiking. The desert may seem tough, but is extremely sensitive to overuse; stay on trails and practice low-impact camping in the backcountry. Take special care with campfires (and cigarettes), as wildfires are a huge concern.

Several recreational opportunities offered disturb the environment, though their proponents argue otherwise. ATV use in the National Forests is causing serious damage, and 'varmint hunts,' which target coyotes, bobcats and other inedible animals, remove necessary predators from the New Mexico ecosystem.

But the most important contributions you can make revolve around New Mexico's most precious resource, water. Keep conservation in mind at all times: this is not the place to indulge in long showers, let the faucet run while you brush your teeth, or ask hotel staff to wash towels used only once.

Consider carefully before patronizing golf courses: sure, many are on Native American land, use gray water systems and so on, but there are probably better uses for all that water. Golf courses belong in Scotland, where it rains.

Northern New Mexico has been experiencing a renaissance of sorts in the area of sustainable agriculture, based on small farms often growing heirloom and other rare crops. These are available at roadside stands and **farmers markets** (☎ 983-4098; www.farmersmarketsnm.org), and a dollar spent there is a vote for New Mexico's future.

which these mountains rise loses elevation as the state slants to the south; Albuquerque is at the lowest elevation covered, and at more than 5000ft is only slightly lower than Denver, Colorado.

To Albuquerque's east are the rose-tinted granite cliffs of Sandia Crest, rising another mile from the Earth's crust like a trap door opening at the crumpled-granite hinge of Cedar Crest. The uplift that began about 10 million years ago continues to grow another couple of centimeters each year. At the top, hardened, layered limestone formed by the ocean that covered the region during the Paleozoic Era (544 million to 245 million years ago) is studded with the fossils of sea creatures.

The uplift and granite are volcanic in origin, and the region is defined by tectonic activity along the Rio Grande Rift, marked by the great river coursing through the gorge, most dramatically displayed on the Low Road to Taos. This is where tectonic plates floating atop a sea of magma chafe against one another, pulling apart to create the Rio Grande Valley and sometimes inspiring enormous violent eruptions.

The Jemez Mountains are one of the largest volcanic fields in the world, where volcanoes began rising 13 million years ago, forming the pyroclastic tuffs of Bandelier National Monument and the unusual formations of Kasha-Katuwe Tent Rocks. Valles Caldera is at the heart of a huge volcano that once reached perhaps 30,000ft; you could see it from Texas, where pieces of it are still found. These volcanoes are dormant, not dead.

East of the Continental Divide are the high plains of the Llano Estacado, watered by the Pecos River pouring from the Sangre de Cristo Mountains, one of the world's longest chains, which rose from the Earth about 27 million years ago to 13,101ft Truchas and 12,280ft Baldy Peaks.

The granddaddy of New Mexico mountains is 13,161ft-tall Wheeler Peak, surrounded by alpine plains populated with wildlife suited to Canada and topped with year-round ice that some folks argue is a tiny glacier.

Roadside Geology of New Mexico, by Halka Chronic: This excellent guide for the curious nongeologist describes the volcanoes, rifts and other views you can see right from the road.

DID YOU KNOW?

More than 40% of the USA's uranium deposits are found at Mt Taylor, 70 miles west of Albuquerque.

WILDLIFE

Northern New Mexico's flora and fauna are fascinating but difficult to observe. Adapted to the aridity and extremes in temperature, many creatures are nocturnal. And hunted almost to extinction by humans, most larger beasts are timid.

Plant life is not limited to cacti, which actually are rather rare in the northern highlands. But all plants must survive without water, particularly in the recent drought, and have some tricks that will fascinate the amateur botanist. The average tourist, however, will be much more taken with the dramatic geology than the wily and weird biology of the high deserts.

Animals

The New Mexico state bird, the roadrunner, bears little resemblance to its cartoon mascot. For one, *Geococcyx californianus* isn't purple; the 2ft-long critters are dusty brown and cruise low to the ground. While fairly common, you're likely to miss the well-camouflaged birds as they race around looking for tasty lizards.

The mountains are home to black bears that seem more familiar with garbage pickup schedules than many humans and come into the cities specifically for the event. Bobcats are more elusive.

Those exploring the regions north of Santa Fe and Taos may see squirrel, turkey, quail, elk, mule deer, javelina (small boars) and, if you're

New Mexico Wildlife Viewing Guide, by Jane S MacCarter: Learn about scores of spots to see wildlife, including information on access and the probability of seeing the most important species at specific sites.

lucky, those adorable marmots of the Enchanted Circle, fat little rodents that are sometimes attracted to the heat of recently parked cars.

Big-horned sheep became extinct in New Mexico in the early 1900s, the victims of overhunting and diseases introduced by domesticated sheep. They were reintroduced into the Pecos Wilderness and Wheeler Peak region in the 1990s and by all accounts are thriving.

Trout still ply the waters in abundance, as New Mexico stocks rivers and lakes with the tasty salmonoids. Rare wetlands have several unusual birds, but it's the rare Rosy Finch, which winters in the Sandias, that brings in the birders.

Those who stay in Santa Fe will likely have to settle for groundhogs, which locals pay $20 a pop to have removed. Insect and reptile lovers have a ball in the lower elevation deserts surrounding Albuquerque, where creepy crawlies like tarantulas, scorpions, rattlesnakes and lizards make their home. Perhaps the most successful insect at press time was the piñon bark beetle, which is currently transforming the state most fundamentally.

Plants

Vegetation of the high desert must survive serious extremes in temperature and lack of water. Though cacti are less common in the region north of Albuquerque, most plants you see have similar survival strategies: they collect sunlight during the day and process it at night, when evaporation is less of an issue. Other plants, like the omnipresent sage bushes, have volatile oils that effectively protect their stores of water from marauding deer, who don't like the taste.

At the higher elevations encompassing Santa Fe and Taos, the most notable vegetation is large stands of ponderosa pine, which is extensively logged. Other plants found here are cedar, Gambel's oak and various shrubs.

PIÑON BARK BEETLES

Squat, green piñon trees that stud the blushing sandstone hills, silhouetted against a turquoise sky – this is the enduring image of New Mexico captured by O'Keeffe and others, forever etched in the memory of visitors. The scent of burning piñon wood, the rich flavor of its nut – this tree, the state tree, is deeply rooted in the heart of New Mexico.

And in 2002 another 160,000 acres, twice as many as the year before, fell prey to tiny Ips pini, no larger than a grain of rice; together with its cousins in the Ips and Dendrodoctonus genii, it has become the scourge of North American evergreen forests. The piñon bark beetle, as it's known in New Mexico, burrows under the bark of the tree, laying eggs that will hatch into larva, devour the tender wood (leaving it a tinder-dry husk of deadwood) and take to the air to start the cycle once again.

Long a part of every healthy pine ecosystem, the beetles have always targeted trees so weakened by age and drought that they were no longer able to cast the larva out in a flood of pitch, their bodies felled to nourish another generation. But about 20 years ago, from Alaska to Mexico, the beetles began reproducing more rapidly, even as evergreens wilted in the globally increasing heat. The piñon, as well as all those that rely on its fruit, is suffering with the beetles. Los Alamos, the Enchanted Circle and other regions are hard hit. More menacingly, the beetle has jumped species in the Jemez, now attacking the Ponderosa pine.

The economic impact, from shrinking piñon crops and growing wildfire risk, is as yet incalculable. The Forest Service says this is just part of the natural cycle of things. 'There are just too many trees,' explained one ranger. Years of fire suppression have led to more piñon than this place was ever supposed to cradle. This plague, though hard to watch, will restore an ancient balance. Besides, only rain or a hard winter could possibly reverse it, and Mother Nature has not been forthcoming.

From about 8000ft to 9500ft the predominant trees are Douglas firs and aspens, which turn a dramatic gold in the fall, as well as white fir and juniper; the shading of these thick forests precludes the growth of many other plants.

From 9500ft to 11,500ft other conifers tend to predominate, including Engelmann spruce, subalpine fir and bristlecone pine, though these last plants are generally rare in the steppes of the Enchanted Circle. Above the tree line (11,500ft) is the Alpine zone, characterized by small tundra-like plants.

The state tree is the piñon. Long the dominant feature of the high deserts between the moister regions of Northern New Mexico, these trees are the most visible victims of the current drought.

GreenMoney Journal (www.greenmoney journal.com) is a great guide to environmentally friendly businesses in New Mexico.

NATIONAL, STATE & REGIONAL PARKS

The best place to start your exploration of New Mexico's wilderness is the **Public Lands Information Center** (☎ 438-7542, 877-276-9404; www.publiclands.org; 1474 Rodeo Rd, Santa Fe; ☻ 9am-4:30pm), with information about all federal, state and locally administered public lands. No national parks are covered in this book.

About only 1.6 million acres of public land in New Mexico – about 2.2% of the state's area, a much smaller percentage than in other western states – are protected as wilderness. Indian lands are protected, but in general access is either highly restricted, available only through a guided tour or administrated in conjunction with the Bureau of Land Management and noted here as such.

State Parks

The **New Mexico State Parks** office in Santa Fe has information on the state's 31 state parks, 28 of which offer camping that can be reserved by phone or online up to 90 days in advance. Campgrounds are usually open May through September, depending on elevation. Not all have running water but do have access to water that can be treated.

Cimarron Canyon features gold mines, the Cimarron Palisades and developed campsites. Fish, hike or rock climb here from May to November.

Coyote Creek boasts a lake with some of the state's best fishing. It's small and uncrowded and good for camping, especially May to September.

Hyde Memorial, close to Santa Fe, is New Mexico's highest state park (9400ft), with aspen forests perfect for hiking, mountain biking, Nordic skiing and llama trekking year-round.

Morphy Lake is isolated and hard to reach, but its well-stocked lakes and primitive campsites make a good retreat for anglers seeking solitude. It's best from May to November.

Storrie Lake, convenient to Las Vegas, is a year-round destination for fishing, camping or just wandering the short trails through the pine forest in search of bears and deer.

Villanueva offers a dramatic desert landscape, complete with red rock canyons and the Pecos River. Come here to take short hikes or fish from April to November.

If Mountains Die: A New Mexico Memoir, by John Nichols: The state's most famous author watches while his adopted Taos Valley fights development; photos really make an impression.

National Forests

National forests are multiuse areas, which includes logging, ATV and snowmobile trails, hunting and private ski areas. Developed campsites are administrated independently; you can pick up a backcountry pass and camp for free, usually within 30ft of an established trail. Many national forests include wilderness areas, which are off-limits to most development.

Carson offers opportunities to do it all, year-round: ski, boat, hike, snowmobile, go horseback riding or wildlife-watching (look for elk, deer, marmots and big-horned sheep). Near Wheeler Peak and the Red River, the forest includes four ski areas and 30 developed campgrounds.

Cibola, close to Albuquerque, gives you access to Sandia Crest, Sandia Ski Park and Sania Man Cave. There's hiking, skiing, wildlife-watching, and even fine dining, year-round.

Santa Fe boasts hot springs, ancient ruins, Rio Chama, Truchas and Baldy Peaks, plus 23 campgrounds and 1000 miles of trails. After you hike, ski, scale a few rocks, or ride the rapids, you can soak away your aches year-round.

Wilderness Areas

Generally wilderness areas are those portions of a national forest set aside to be kept pristine. Some commercial activity, including grazing animals and approved mining, is allowed, but ATVs, hunting, ski areas and logging are banned. Campsites don't often have running water or campfire grills, and usually their costs range from free to $6.

Chama Canyon features incredible desert scenery, with access to Pedernal, El Vado Lake, Rio Chama and Abiquiú. Go for great camping, white-water rafting and fishing May to September.

Dome, adjacent to Bandelier National Monument, offers a chance to see St Peters Dome and abandoned pueblos. Expect prime hiking, mountain biking and rock climbing May to October.

Pecos boasts the best hiking in the state, plus fishing and backcountry camping amid almost lush forests and mountain lakes in the Sangre de Christo Mountains. Visit from May to September.

Sandia Mountain is easy to reach from Albuquerque. Hike through pine forests populated by eagles and bears to archaeological sites. You can hike, backcountry camp, mountain bike or just enjoy the great view year-round.

Wheeler Peak offers hiking, rock climbing, fishing in alpine lakes and wildlife-watching; watch out for marmots, elk, and big-horned sheep. Wheeler's at its best June to September.

ENVIRONMENTAL ISSUES

New Mexico is currently undergoing a massive ecosystems overhaul. The drought, combined with a long-standing policy of fire suppression that has allowed more vegetation to accumulate than is theoretically natural, has led to outbreaks of massive forest fires.

Rangers and wildlife experts explain that this is normal and healthy, and a program of controlled burns has been implemented – with some setbacks. The Cerro Grande Fire of 2000 resulted from a controlled burn near Los Alamos and raged through 43,000 acres surrounded LANL. The federal government refused to tell residents what is – or was – stored out there, but folks familiar with nuclear weapons have made educated guesses.

Plutonium and uranium, both incredibly toxic, as well as radioactive isotopes of beryllium and cesium, were dumped in the area throughout the Cold War, and there is neither accountability nor information from any quarter. What was in that smoke, and what continues to flow with water following heavy rains down the mountain to Española, Santa Fe and the surrounding pueblos, are the subject of much uniformed debate. It can't be good.

High and Dry: The Texas-New Mexico Struggle for the Pecos River, by G Emlen Hall: Whose water is it anyway? Find out in this funny, fact-filled rundown of the 20-year showdown between the states.

Santa Fe Water Crisis (www.santafewater crisis.com) features articles, op-eds and photos of what's not coming down in Santa Fe – rain.

DID YOU KNOW?

During summer the average 18-hole golf course in Northern New Mexico uses more than one million gallons of water a day.

Water is, of course, the other hot-button issue. Massive aquifers – porous sediment that accumulates at the foothills of large granite peaks like the Sandia Mountains – are New Mexico's primary source of water. Politicians, who compared Albuquerque's aquifer to the Great Lakes in an effort to lure businesses to the area, have long been cheerfully overestimating reserves. Water tables throughout the region are dropping, and there is no effective policy to deal with it. However, that hasn't stopped developers from building more golf courses.

WATER: NEW MEXICO'S MOST VALUABLE RESOURCE *By Annette Rodriguez*

Northern New Mexico's varied topography and abundance of adapted plant and wildlife make it easy to forget that New Mexico is indeed a desert, with meager precipitation and low relative humidity. And like other Southwestern states, it has experienced enormous metropolitan growth. Water availability has not been able to keep pace with population expansion.

Statewide, the average annual precipitation varies between 7 inches in the high desert of the northwest to about 20 inches in the central mountain region. Most falls during what New Mexicans call the 'monsoon season,' characterized by afternoon thunderstorms in July and August. While the dry climate makes for vast blue skies and a horizon line that seems just feet off the ground, regular periods of meager rainfall or snowmelt also result in widespread water shortages. Recent dry conditions have resulted in states of emergency throughout New Mexico and are expected to persist.

Population growth coupled with the hot, dry climate has produced conditions resulting in widespread wildfires, state park closings and water-use restrictions in both urban and rural areas. Numerous skirmishes regarding water use include bitter interstate water rights disputes, political finger pointing, and the years-long battle regarding the much-maligned Rio Grande silvery minnow.

Awareness of water issues has increased since the early 1990s, when the Unites States Geological Survey concluded that New Mexico's water levels were dropping significantly and highlighted the need for water conservation. They noted that about 90% of communities rely on ground water – the state's principal source for agricultural, industrial and public uses – yet this water has been extracted far more quickly than nature has been able to replenish it.

What does this mean for you? In many areas, most notably Santa Fe, Los Alamos and Albuquerque, water use restrictions are put into place during dry spells. Municipalities have their ways of letting you know, usually with friendly signs posting reminders, full-page ads in area newspapers and banners hanging in hotels that announce how often they'll be able to legally wash your linens (during a Stage III alert, that's every four days).

If you are a returning visitor, you'll notice that there are fewer ornamental fountains, and most outdoor pools are covered or drained. Many communities have begun replacing lush, grassy lawns with xeriscaping, a recent local specialty that promotes the use of native or adapted plants for the Southwest climate. These include buffalo and maidenhair grasses, ornamental cacti, and blooming sages and flax.

There are public xeriscape demonstration gardens throughout the state, the largest of which is at El Rancho de las Golondrinas. Don't expect acres of cacti, but a peek at these xerophytes is worthwhile; their diversity and beauty are quite remarkable.

Outdoors

Outdoorsy types will love this statistic: of the 50 states, New Mexico ranks 45th in population density. This means that there's plenty of unspoiled nature to get out into. The opportunities are just about endless; many are described in the Albuquerque, Taos and Santa Fe Activities sections.

Some of the more stunning options not listed here include the hikes and climbs surrounding Los Alamos; the day hikes at Ghost Ranch, through the landscape made famous by Georgia O'Keeffe; and the outstanding trails to the hot springs of the Jemez Mountains.

The **Public Lands Information Center** (Map p75; ☎ 438-7542, 877-276-9404; www.publiclands.org; 1474 Rodeo Rd, Santa Fe) and **Carson National Forest Supervisor's Office** (☎ 758-6200; www.fs.fed.us/r3/carson; 208 Cruz Alta Rd, Taos) are the best places to start, but ranger stations and visitors centers always have information on the finest trails and most original outfitters around.

Order maps ($7) from the **Forest Service** (☎ 842-3292; 517 Gold Ave SW, Albuquerque 87102) or download them for free (sar.lanl.gov/maps_by_name.html).

In Taos, the gateway to the wild northeast, **Taos Outdoor Recreation** (www .taosoutdoorrecreation.com) provides an online rundown of all your options, and **Native Sons Adventures** (Map p147; ☎ 758-9342, 800-753-7559; www.nativesonsadventures .com; 1033 Paseo del Pueblo Sur) offers advice and every sort of guided tour.

Faust Transportation (☎ 758-3410, 888-830-3410; www.newmexiconet.com/trans/faust/ faust.html) will get you to the trailhead for less money than most outfits.

A Word of Caution

Even the healthiest folks from lower, moister climes should keep in mind that there are reasons why such a beautiful land hasn't sprouted the usual varicose veins of interstates and tract housing: altitude, aridity and extremes in temperature.

Take time to acclimate to the altitude before embarking on any serious climbs, and carry at least a gallon of water per person, per day, while hiking. Try not to rely on 'reliable' water sources, particularly in summer months; they have a dangerous tendency to dry up right when you need them.

Temperatures can vary up to 50°F from day to night, and hikers have gotten hypothermia on top of their sunburns. And there's a lot less atmosphere protecting you from the sun – wear a hat, sunscreen and shades at all times. For more information, see the Health chapter.

HIKING

The cheapest and easiest way to get out into the New Mexico wilderness is on foot; with a pair of sturdy shoes, a gallon of water per day, a hat and lots of sunscreen, you're ready to take on dozens of day trips. With a little more preparation, you could stay out for several sunsets.

Day Hikes

New Mexicans love to get outside, and every visitors center and ranger station has maps to local trails of every length and difficulty. Ask for recommendations.

Kasha-Katuwe Tent Rocks National Monument (Cochiti Pueblo) With two short (under 2 miles) and incredible day hikes, you could do both.

La Luz Trail (Albuquerque) Albuquerque's pride and joy, this 8-mile hike from the desert to the woods includes a 3800ft altitude gain. Bonus: you can take the tram back down.

Clear Creek Canyon Trail (Eagle Nest) Perhaps the prettiest day hike on the Enchanted Circle, this trail is a golden tunnel of aspen in fall.

North and South Dale Ball Trails (Santa Fe) More than 20 miles of trails, from 3-mile loops to all-day adventures, are just minutes from the plaza.

Atalaya Trail (Santa Fe) This 7-mile loop, not far from downtown, tops 9121ft Atalaya Mountain. It's perfect at sunset.

Hikes with Kids

Even though these hikes are easy enough for even small children, always take extra precautions: sunscreen, shades and plenty of liquids.

Rio Grande Nature Center (Albuquerque) Follow the Rio Grande through the bosque on short interpretive nature trails.

Randall Davey Audubon Center (Santa Fe) Just 3 miles north of the plaza, this 135-acre preserve along the acequias of Santa Fe Canyon offers two fine trails.

Nambé Falls (Nambé Pueblo) Two great 20-minute hikes offer ample excuses to stretch your legs on the High Road to Taos.

Hikes Through History

These hikes make an impression that lasts long after the soreness is gone.

Bandelier National Monument (Los Alamos) Trails through this once-mighty city make this a trip highlight; climb the ladders to sky-scraping Ceremonial Cave.

Petroglyph National Monument (Albuquerque) Intriguing hikes past thousands of ancient petroglyphs are only a half hour from downtown.

Sandia Man Cave (Albuquerque) Perfect for even little kids, this is where Boy Scouts discovered the oldest human encampment in North America. Bring a flashlight.

Pioneer Canyon Trail & Placer Creek Trail (Red River) Two rough roads pass dozens of dilapidated gold mines, with rusting equipment, old machinery and abandoned shafts.

Serious Hikes

You'll need all the equipment – real boots, water filtration systems, USGS maps and more information than this book provides – for these hikes.

Stone Lion Shrine (☎ 672-3861; www.nps.gov/band; Los Alamos; car $10 for 7 days; ⏰ 7am-7:30pm) This 28-mile, three-day walkabout through the Jemez Mountains takes you to two ancient and sacred stone carvings.

Hermit Mountain (☎ 425-3534; 1926 N 7th St, Las Vegas; ⏰ 8am-5pm Mon-Fri) Hike 14 miles through Gallinas Canyon Complex to the scenic spot where the eccentric Giovanni Maria Angoste performed his miracles.

Truchas Peak (☎ 757-6121; Hwy 63; ⏰ 8am-4:30pm Mon-Fri, also Sat in summer) There are at least three ways to the top of 13,101ft Truchas Peak: from Cowles, near Pecos; from Truchas; and from Santa Barbara Campground, near Peñasco.

Wheeler Peak The two main trails to the highest point in New Mexico – 13,161ft Wheeler Peak – begin at Taos Ski Area and near Red River, perhaps the prettier ascent.

BIKING

You may need to acclimate to the altitude for a few days, but with back roads and scenic byways seemingly made for the sport and mountain-bike trails with fans all over the country, who needs four wheels?

You can rent bikes in Albuquerque, Santa Fe and Taos; rates drop for longer rentals. Santa Fe rates are about double those elsewhere.

Road Biking

In general road biking is not allowed on the interstates, but the scenic byways are all yours. Top tours include the Enchanted Circle, 84 miles of alpine intensity, and the Turquoise Trail, with opportunities to park next to the Harleys in Madrid and prove that you don't need internal combustion to look cool.

Albuquerque has an elaborate system of bike trails that run throughout the city, many of which are off-limits to automobiles. Santa Fe Rail Trail offers a fun 18-mile trail, almost entirely paved, that follows the rail line to Lamy.

There are several guided tours available that take you two-wheeling all over the state, including **Native Sons** (Taos); **Known World** (☎ 800-983-7756; www.knownworldguides.com) and **The World Outdoors** (☎ 303-413-0926, 800-488-8483; www.theworldoutdoors.com).

Mountain Biking

Many mountain-biking trails, including Santa Fe's Dale Ball Trails and Atalaya Trail, are multiuse. Forest roads are also maintained with mountain bikers in mind and tend to be rated beginner or moderate – except after it rains, when they can quickly become intermediate or difficult.

Other options really run the gamut of abilities. These are listed from easiest to most challenging, and represent only a taste of what's out there.

Both **Sandia Peak Ski Park** (Albuquerque) and **Red River Ski Area** (Red River) allow mountain bikers to take the lifts up and slopes down in summer.

West Rim Trail (Pilar) This moderate 9-mile trek offers stunning views of the Rio Grande Gorge.

Windsor Trail (Santa Fe) Take this 10-mile intermediate trail through the aspens and views of Santa Fe Ski Area; the path forms the spine of several other trails, and some folks say they're best when snow is on the ground.

Carson National Forest (Taos) The USFS maintains a huge system of mountain-bike and multiuse trails between Taos, Angel Fire and Picuris Peak.

South Boundary Trail (Taos) Considered one of the best mountain-bike trails in the nation, this 28-mile adventure is for experienced bikers with maps and more information.

WHITE-WATER RAFTING

Folks in the desert know how to appreciate their waterways like no one else, and if you're ready, they're willing to take you on some serious white-water rapids. The screamer is the **Class IV Taos Box** ($100), which is for rafters 12 years and older, while the **Class III Racecourse** ($50) and even mellower **Class III Lower Gorge** ($50) are suitable for anyone over the age of six.

These last two trips put in at Pilar, but a variety of outfitters in Santa Fe and Taos take busloads of budding river rats there daily from April through October. May and June, when all that snowmelt really gets things rolling, are tops. You *will* get wet.

Even more relaxed options include a leisurely float to **Embudo Station** (Embudo) and an all-ages trip offered by **Los Rios River Runners** (Taos).

The **Class III Rio Chama** ($350-750), near Abiquiú, is usually taken as a three-day all-inclusive excursion, with meals and tents included in your fee. **Far Flung Adventures** (Pilar) offers custom trips that could also include horseback riding.

FISHING

If you plan to spend much time camping on your trip, bring your fishing pole. New Mexico stocks its lakes and streams with rainbow,

German brown and cutthroat trout (the state fish!), and some lakes even have salmon. There are fishing holes with full wheelchair access, and others you'll hike all day to find, but no matter what, you'll need a license.

New Mexico Game and Fish (☎ 800-862-9310; www.gmfsh.state.nm.us) issues several licenses for nonresidents: one-year (adult/child $45/25), five-day ($22) and one-day ($14), including the $5 WHI (Wildlife Habitat Improvement) stamp that's required to fish on USFS and BLM lands. New Mexicans pay about half that.

Your bag limit is five fish for trout and salmon, with a maximum of two cutthroat trout per day. Sporting goods stores, tackle shops and RV parks (and some gas stations near popular fishing areas) sell licenses, and you can often rent a rod and tackle for $10 to $20.

The Enchanted Circle has the best access and is lined with campsites known for fishing. Red River and the Rio Grande are tops September through April, while Cimarron Canyon State Park, parks on the Back Road to Las Vegas and the area lakes are best between May and September. **Ed Adams** (www.edadamsflyfishing.com; Questa) leads guided fly-fishing trips and maintains an online river schedule and fishing reports.

Closer to Santa Fe, Abiquiú, Nambé Lakes and Rio Chama can also hook you up with dinner. Jemez Springs, the Las Vegas Gallinas Canyon Complex and Pecos Wilderness are great places to reel one in, and many pueblos maintain stocked fishing ponds where you can catch a fish or five for $7 to $10 a day.

If you're looking to learn the fine art of fly fishing, or just want access to less-crowded private lands, there are several outfitters who'll lead the way. Prices, which are just a bit higher for an extra person, vary widely ($75-250), so shop around.

In Santa Fe **High Desert Angler** (☎ 988-7688, 888-988-7688; www.highdesert angler.com) is the leader, while Taos has **Los Rios Anglers** (☎ 758-2798, 800-748-1707; www.losrios.com) and **Taos High Mountain Angler** (☎ 770-1419; www.highmountain angler.com). Independent guides are generally much less expensive and leave flyers at ranger stations and visitors centers.

HOT AIR BALLOONING

If you've ever wanted to get up, up and away, here's the place to do it. The silence is perhaps the most surprising part, as you float in a wicker basket high above the desert landscape.

Though commercial flights generally last an hour, allow four for the entire experience. They'll pick you up early (around 6am) and take you to some remote spot where a rainbow sheath, your only anchor to the heavens, is being inflated with roaring flames. You'll step into the basket through a waist-high gate – folks used to flying in planes may be taken aback.

Champagne is the traditional, and appropriate, way to toast your homecoming and is included with each flight. You may even get a certificate or some such souvenir, as if you could ever forget the experience.

Make reservations two days in advance to take to the skies with Albuquerque outfits, such as **Discover Balloons**. Taos and Angel Fire also have several, including **Pueblo Balloon**.

If the price seems extravagant, and if the timing is right, simply head to a balloon festival. New Mexico's largest are the **Albuquerque International Balloon Fiesta** (early Oct) and **Wings over Angel Fire** (late July), but there are several throughout the year.

Loitering about the colorful grounds is encouraged, and plenty of balloonists will have a basket with room for one more. Bring cash – $75 should do the trick – and offer to slip it to the pilot when folks paying full price aren't looking.

NEW MEXICO IN THE SNOW

North-central New Mexico, almost entirely enfolded into the Rocky Mountains, boasts all sorts of opportunities for appreciating its winter wonderland. Take snowmobile tours to abandoned mining towns from Red River; ice skate the lakes near Questa; or, for something a bit different, try snowskating (on skateboards without wheels!) or snowbiking (on bikes with skis!), available at Angel Fire and other resorts. There's even an **Adaptive Ski Program**, offering lessons and special equipment for folks with all sorts of disabilities.

And you thought this was the desert. Actually, aridity is a factor in maintaining the fine powder that brings in top skiers from all over the world.

Ski season generally runs from November through March, depending on altitude and the weather, and resort schools will show you the slopes if you don't know how. The dozen or so free ski guides, available at any visitors center, include *Ski New Mexico* (www.skinewmexico.com), which, in addition to providing ski reports and links to resorts, offers a discount card that might work for you.

Of all the cross-country ski trails, **Enchanted Forest** (www.enchantedforestxc.com; Red River), is the most beloved, with some 25 miles of groomed trails lit up with luminarias for Christmas. Less-developed options include the Nordski Trail near Santa Fe, and dozens of trails in the Carson National Forest, described in the free guide, *Where to Go in the Snow*.

The main attraction, however, is the cool collection of ski resorts scattered across New Mexico's sunny peaks. Here's a rundown of what each has to offer, but check town sections for more information:

- **Angel Fire Resort** (www.angelfireresort.com; Angel Fire) With 210 inches of snowfall enhanced with many machines, this sprawling, all-inclusive resort boasts a 2077 vertical foot drop, the state's only snowboarding half-pipe, and special areas for kids, plus all sorts of activities and amenities geared toward families.

- **Pajarito Ski Area** (www.skipajarito.com; Los Alamos) Short lines, long lifts and all-natural snow make this cozy spot a good place to just get in touch with the mountain.

- **Red River Ski Area** (www.redriverskiarea.com; Red River) Though it doesn't have the most challenging slopes in the state, this adorable resort community capitalizes on its easy-to-tackle runs with family packages and activities for kids – plus, it's close to Enchanted Forest and lots of opportunities for snowmobiling.

- **Sandia Peak Ski Park** (www.sandiapeak.com) Close proximity to Albuquerque and a tram to get you there make this a sweet treat when it snows – but mild winters have left it a bit barren the past few years.

- **Santa Fe Ski Basin** (www.skisantafe.com) Just 16 miles from the capital, lifts take you to the top of the highest skiable slope in the state – 12,003ft. The views of the Sangre de Cristos are legendary, the 1600ft of vertical drop are challenging and 44 trails are rated for every level, so it's no wonder it's popular; plan for crowds.

- **Sipapu** (www.sipapunm.com; Peñasco) Family-owned and out of the way, this small resort with a 1055ft vertical drop has lots of little-used acreage and some of the least expensive rates in the state.

- **Taos Ski Valley** (www.taosskivalley.com) Among the nation's top ski areas, with 312 inches of natural snow, 2612ft vertical drop (that's 3274ft, if you're willing to hike), award-winning instructors and all the amenities (well, except snowboards – sorry, dudes and dudettes), this is the big one.

Food & Drink

The Official State Question (seriously; it was enacted in 1999) is 'Red or green?,' which is your first clue that you'll be eating well on this trip. More than the balloon fiestas, pueblo revival architecture or even art galleries, chile is the pride of New Mexico. Not Mexican – and most definitely not Texican – these fiery flavors have won adherents the world over.

Don't expect your first heavenly meal to arrive at the table as a distinct entree and a couple of neatly arranged side dishes – it's all piled together, usually richly seasoned rice or potatoes, beans that are the pride of any serious cook, flanking something like a chile-and-cheese covered burrito just bursting with gooey goodness. You are expected to mix all this together and enjoy it as a symphony rather than a series of solos.

Pain is a flavor in New Mexico, and visitors unfamiliar with the concept should order their chile on the side – at first. Soon your body will realize that the fierce bite of capsaicin, the chemical that gives good chile its sting, is just the prelude to a chemical cascade involving endorphins (yep, the same hormone released during orgasm) that you will come to crave.

The cure for the burn is right beside you. Water does little or nothing to stop the tears, but any restaurant worth its deep fryer provides soft *sopapillas* (pillows of fried bread) and a plastic squirt bottle of honey, with which to douse the flames, on every table.

The Food of Santa Fe, by Dave Dewitt and Nancy Gerlach: The chile experts get down to business with some seriously spicy, easy-to-follow and easy-to-love recipes.

STAPLES & SPECIALTIES

Isolated geographically from Mexico and Spain, and culturally from the USA, New Mexico's cooking traditions are the result of a long line of unknown artists who have conjured from the simplest ingredients a cuisine unique in the world. The original crops were corn (introduced from Mexico), beans and squash, and still remain the basis of the state's fine food.

Corn is ground and patted into tortillas, served a multitude of delicious ways, or made into *masa*, which is elaborately folded into corn husks with some sweet or savory filling to create tamales, steamed to perfection. Or it is soaked in lye until tender and used in a rich stew called *posole*. These are just the most common recipes.

Beans have long been the staple protein of New Mexicans from every culture, and come in many colors, shapes and preparations. They are usually stewed with onions, chiles and spices (many say the micaceous pottery of the Picuris and other tribes is the best possible vessel for such preparations) and served either somewhat intact or refried to a creamy consistency just perfect for scooping with a corn chip.

Squash is no longer a real staple, as imported produce from more accommodating climes has largely replaced this desert standard, but if you see *calabasas* on the menu, give it a try.

New Mexico Farmers Markets (www.farmers marketsnm.org) offers your guide to the freshest food around, plus events listings and a harvest calendar.

The Spanish brought with them a whole new world of ingredients, hauling across the sands the first grapevines, ostensibly for sacramental wine; sheep, pigs and cattle; fruit trees; grains like rye and wheat; spices introduced by the Moors from North Africa, including the omnipresent cumin; and most important, chile.

Chile

From the sweet red bell pepper to brutish jalapeño, smoky chipotle to potent serrano, chiles are carefully cultivated across the globe. Hardy sources of vitamin C, flourishing where lesser plants fail, they are revered as much for their health benefits as their bite.

None can match the Hatch green chile, New Mexicans will tell you, and though the Chimayó red chile is perhaps not as revered, discriminating critics often prefer its more elegant flavor. Both are from the same plant but are harvested at different times. While the Chimayó is a close cousin to the mild Anaheim chile, the fruit's flavor is as much a reflection of environment and technique as mere genealogy.

Chiles are picked green in September and October, an event that fills every town in the state with the scent of the roast, done outdoors in special barrel-shaped contraptions designed for the task. Forty-pound burlap bags are hoisted onto the shoulders of slavering locals, who roast them at home to horde all winter long.

Those left on the plant are allowed to mature to a deep ruby red, then strung on ristras to dry, and laboriously ground into a paste that becomes the basis of rich red sauces, or a piquant spice for sprinkling atop almost anything.

Waitstaff immediately offer you the choice: 'Red or green?' If you don't yet have a favorite, simply reply: 'Which is better?' or, alternately, 'Which is hotter today?' Each batch varies according to harvest and preparation. If you can't decide, say 'Christmas,' and you'll get it half-and-half.

As a side note, *chili* is a word that refers not to New Mexico's most important harvest, but to a bean-and-meat stew classified as Texan around here.

Breakfast

Breakfast is serious business in New Mexico. This is a culture only recently divorced – well, amicably separated, anyway – from a subsistence farming economy. Even omelets and other egg breakfasts usually come with beans and some kind of potatoes on the side, plus a couple of flour tortillas and, of course, chile. Breakfast meats include all the usual suspects, plus *chorizo*, a soft and spicy sausage often scrambled right into the eggs.

Huevos rancheros are the quintessential New Mexican breakfast: eggs prepared to order are served on top of two fried corn tortillas, loaded with beans and potatoes, sprinkled with cheese, and served swimming in chile. Slightly less massive are breakfast burritos, a flour tortilla filled with eggs, bacon or chorizo, cheese, chile and sometimes beans, and usually served à la carte.

Main Dishes

You'll start just about every meal with a big bowl of corn chips and salsa. Almost everything comes with beans, rice and your choice of warm flour or corn tortillas, topped with chile, cheese and sometimes sour cream. Blue corn tortillas are one colorful New Mexican contribution to the art of cooking – they're just like regular tortillas but, shockingly, made with blue corn.

Enchiladas are made with your choice of blue or regular corn tortillas (blue usually costs a bit extra) and served either rolled Mexican-style around the filling (usually cheese or chicken) or flat, a New Mexican preference, layered like a lasagna with the filling and then baked.

Burritos are the staple: flour tortillas rolled around just about everything – beans, lamb, chicken, vegetables, cheese, whatever. Try the *carne adovada*: tender, slow-cooked pork baked in savory red chile. A chimichanga is a deep-fried burrito, just in case you're trying to gain weight for your next movie role. Stuffed sopapillas are similar to burritos,

DID YOU KNOW?

One chile – red or green, they're both the same fruit – has the same amount of vitamin C as an orange.

Cocinas de New Mexico (www.vivanewmexico.com/nm/food.recipes.cocinas.html) is an online cookbook with recipes for all things New Mexican.

Coyote Café, by Mark Miller: Santa Fe's most celebrated celebrity chef does fresh, gourmet twists on New Mexico classics, best attempted by cooks with some time on their hands.

but all that good stuff comes inside a sopapilla, which makes them that much better.

Chile rellenos really are the food of the gods. Usually green or serrano chiles are stuffed with cheese and sometimes other ingredients, thickly breaded and fried, then topped with more chile. Northern New Mexico's version is more delicate and eggy, while Albuquerque and points south tend to use a thicker, firmer cornmeal breading.

Green chile stew is, perhaps, the ultimate expression of chile cuisine, and most certainly the pride of every New Mexican cook. Chiles are joined by potatoes, corn and other vegetables, and usually ground beef, though the recipes vary. It is the only proven cure for the common cold and is probably a treat best saved for when you are more acclimated to the cuisine.

The Santa Fe School of Cooking Cookbook, by Susan Curtis: The recipes have been tested by both world-class chefs and confused students, so even you will soon be simmering great green chile stew.

Sopapillas & Desserts

Served alongside every meal, these delicate puffed breads are deep-fried and served hot – they're hollow, so don't wait to bite into one and breathe in its scent. Sopapillas serve two primary purposes: first, as an alternative to tortillas for scooping up dinner, and second, as a receptacle for honey, available at every table in handy squeezable plastic bottles. Together with the honey, the sopapillas cool off your palate after a fiery meal.

Other than sopapillas, dessert is something of a side note in New Mexican cooking, probably because meals are so huge. *Biscochitos* – the New Mexico State Cookie – are simple sugar cookies with anise flavoring, while flan, a rich custard with a caramelized sugar topping, is a traditional Spanish desert that's on a lot of menus. Empanadas, pastries folded around fruit, spices and other fillings (sometimes savory), are almost a meal in themselves.

Foods of the Southwest Indian Nations, by Lois Ellen Frank: Fabulous recipes use Native ingredients, transforming pumpkin, quail and prickly pears into spectacular dining.

Native Cuisine

Modern Indian cuisine bears little resemblance to the food eaten prior to the Spanish conquest, but it is distinctive from New Mexican cuisine nonetheless. Navajo and Indian tacos – fry bread usually topped with beans, meat, tomatoes, chile and lettuce – are the most readily available. Chewy *horno* bread is baked in the beehive-shaped outdoor adobe ovens (*hornos*) using remnant heat from a fire built inside, then cleared out before cooking.

Most other Native cooking is game-based and usually involves fry bread, beans, squash and locally harvested ingredients like berries and piñon nuts. Overall it's difficult to find; your best bets are stands at festivals and markets, casino restaurants or people's homes at the different pueblos.

The Tewa Kitchen, at Taos Pueblo, and Pueblo Harvest Cafe, at the Indian Pueblo Cultural Center in Albuquerque, are scrumptious exceptions, while Santa Fe's Anasazi Restaurant takes it upscale. You could also attend a feast day at one of the different pueblos, where you'll either be invited to someone's table for some serious home cooking or (more likely) grab some good grub at one of the stands that are set up for every dance.

The Cooking Post (www.cookingpost.com) offers free recipes for Native American cuisine, plus all the ingredients you'll want once you get hungry.

DRINKS

In case you hadn't noticed, New Mexico's in the middle of a drought. You can help save Santa Fe's golf courses, however, by drinking more fine New Mexican wine, a margarita or one of the excellent beers made right here.

Microbreweries to try include the state's first, Embudo Station, or Eske's in Taos, both of which do great green chile beers, or relaxed Kelly's Brewery in Albuquerque. Santa Fe's Blue Corn Café and Second Street Brewery make up for their ambiance with a fine selection of quality brews. Keep a lookout for Roswell Alien Amber, with the best label ever.

CELEBRATIONS

Christmas is when the really good food comes rolling out. Families get together for big tamale-making parties, biscochitos are baked by the hundreds and specially spiced hot chocolate is served at places all around town. Many restaurants put Christmas specials – usually the cook's family recipes – on the menu.

But it's the pueblos that really know how to throw a ceremony. Feast days, replete with dances, pole climbs, races and whatnot, are topped off with lots of great food. The biggest events are noted throughout the book, but refer to any of the free visitors guides or the Indian Pueblo Cultural Center website (www.indianpueblo.org) for more complete listings. Be sure to familiarize yourself with the etiquette and to have fun.

On Saturday evenings all summer, Albuquerque runs Summerfest, with food and entertainment. Santa Fe offers upscale food-related events, including late February's ARTfeast Edible Art Tour, with art, jazz and wine and gourmet cuisine, and the Santa Fe Wine & Chile Fiesta featuring wine tastings and dinner events in late September.

WHERE TO EAT & DRINK

First and foremost – and this is less true in Santa Fe than elsewhere, but still generally applies – get the heck away from the plaza. The food won't be bad, but you'll often pay extra for something less than spectacular.

Phenomenal four-star cuisine is available everywhere, although you'll pay through the nose for it. But if you're looking for quality New Mexican grub, ask the locals where they're having lunch. Places that gussy

---

ON THE VINE

There are three things a good wine grape needs: lousy soil, lots of sunshine and dedicated caretakers, all of which New Mexico has in spades. So why are folks so surprised at the state's growing wine industry?

According to the **New Mexico Wine Growers Association** (☎ 866-491-6366; www.nmwine.net), the state's 33 wineries produce some 350,000 gallons of various vintages annually – and a lot of it, according to both *Wine Spectator* and local wine snobs, is top-notch. Best of all, unlike wineries in California (where those upstarts didn't even start growing grapes until the 1770s, 150 years after Franciscan friars near Socorro planted their first cuttings), most still offer flights free of charge.

The star of the show is Gruet, in Albuquerque, with an outstanding Brut sparkling wine and several award-winning whites. La Chiripada, in Dixon, is well known for its Riesling and cabernet sauvignon, while Casa Rodeña, another Albuquerque entry, has a Cabernet Franc that's earned plenty of kudos.

But that's just the beginning. Stop into any fine winery and taste for yourself. Better yet, build your vacation around one of these festivals:

- **Albuquerque Wine Festival** (Balloon Fiesta Park; $13; late May) Gourmet grub on the grass
- **Santa Fe Wine Festival** (Rancho de los Golondrinas; $10; early July) Mariachis, art and more
- **New Mexico Wine Festival** (Bernalillo Fairgrounds; $10; late August) Biggest and best
- **!Traditions! Wine Festival** (!Traditions! Marketplace; free; early October) Celebrate the harvest, and shop, too

themselves up – this is not done for locals – are unlikely to be your best bets for authentic cuisine. Look for holes-in-the-wall with chipped Formica tables, Naugahyde booths and lines out the door.

VEGETARIANS & VEGANS

Thanks to the area's long-standing appeal to hippie-types, vegetarians and vegans will have no problem finding something delicious on most menus, even at fast food drive-thrus and tiny dives. Potential pitfall: traditional New Mexican cuisine uses lard in beans, tamales, sopapillas and flour (but not corn) tortillas, among other things. Be sure to ask about options – often, even the most authentic places are simmering a pot of vegetarian pintos just for you.

Almost every large town has a natural foods grocer, and Animal Protection of New Mexico (www.apnm.org/animalstation/VeggieGuides/santafe.html) keeps a list of restaurants with exceptional vegetarian menus. You'll eat better here than almost anywhere in the Southwest, so go nuts.

WHINING & DINING

All but the most upscale restaurants are marvelously kid-friendly and generally have children's menus, high chairs and large booths for big families, and often crayons or other toys to amuse the tots. Most folks will know to automatically omit the chile for younger kids, but tweens and teens should specifically ask for it on the side, if necessary.

If the kids are feeling surly, it's easiest to avoid the crowds by eating between 2pm and 5pm, just to give yourself a little more room.

COOKING COURSES

Considering the cost of cuisine around Santa Fe, it's no wonder that frugal foodies have inspired a cottage industry in cooking courses. It's a great way to immerse yourself in the tasty local culture, plus you may even learn to replicate that perfect burrito burned into your imagination.

Santa Fe School of Cooking (Map pp76-7; ☎ 983-4511, 800-982-4688; www.santafeschoolofcooking.com; 116 W San Francisco St; $55-95) The capital's most acclaimed cooking

> **DID YOU KNOW?**
>
> When the state legislature moved in 1989 to make the biscochito an official symbol, New Mexico became the first to have a state cookie.

AT THE GROCERY STORE

When you leave New Mexico, you might miss the sunshine or the laid-back attitude. But unless you've got an allergy, it's going to be the food that keeps you dreaming about coming back. Luckily modern technology now facilitates green chile addiction worldwide.

Bueno (☎ 800-952-4453; www.buenofoods.com) 'Did you bring the Bueno?' is the other state question; frozen green chile with red and green salsas and powders helps you answer affirmatively.

McGinn's Pistachio Tree Ranch (☎ 437-0602; www.pistachiotreeranch.com) Pistachios of every flavor come with a huge selection of spicy condiments, including Cannon's Sweethots (green chile for ice cream!).

Santa Fe School of Cooking (☎ 800-982-4688; www.santafeschoolofcooking.com) Small batches of gourmet New Mexican treats include everything from red chile peanut brittle and blue corn cookies to an endless variety of salsas.

Tamale Molly (www.tamalemolly.com) Proceeds go to feed the homeless, and you're fed all-veggie, all-natural, hand-tied tamales, from goat cheese with mint to honey pecan.

Tamaya Blue (☎ 888-867-5198; www.cookingpost.com) This company delivers Santa Ana Pueblo's own blue corn muffin mix, deer jerky and other Native treats to your door, and online recipes show you how to cook them.

A TASTE OF NEW MEXICO *By Beth Penland*

Already hungry but your flight doesn't leave for five more months? Begin preparing your taste buds today for the flavors of Santa Fe with these recipes. Note: there is no official state recipe for the state cookie (or what's likely to be the state stew the next time legislators get bored, for that matter), but these should do the trick.

BISCOCHITO

1lb pure lard (Yes, lard. Not butter, not shortening, vegetable oil
or any other fat substitute. Lard is the magic
behind the cookies' light, flaky texture.)
1 cup sugar
2 eggs
6 cups flour
¼ cup red wine, sherry or brandy
2 tsp slightly crushed anise seed
1 cup sugar mixed with 2-3 tsp cinnamon

Preheat oven to 350°F.
With an electric mixer, cream lard in a large bowl until fluffy.
Slowly add sugar, mixing well.
Continue mixing as you add one egg at a time.
Add anise seed, then the flour one handful at a time.
After flour is mixed in well, add enough wine to make dough soft.
Let stand about 10 minutes.
Roll out dough ¼-inch thick on lightly floured board and cut into shapes.
Bake for 15 minutes on ungreased cookie sheets.
Remove from sheets while hot and dip top side in sugar/cinnamon mixture.

GREEN CHILE STEW

½lb ground beef, pork or turkey
½lb boneless sirloin, cubed
4 cups chicken broth
½ cup beer
2lb fresh green chiles, roasted, peeled and chopped
1 tomato, chopped
1 medium onion, chopped
1 clove garlic, minced
½ cup fresh cilantro, chopped
1½ tsp oregano
2½ tsp cumin
1/8 cup parsley, chopped
1 tsp salt
1 tsp pepper

In a large pot, sauté ground meat and sirloin until done. Remove from pot.
Add onions, garlic and cilantro to pot and cook for three to five minutes
or until onions are softened.
Add chicken broth, beer, green chiles and tomato.
Bring to a boil and reduce to a simmer.
Add meat, oregano, cumin, parsley, salt and pepper.
Simmer for two hours, stirring occasionally.

FLAT (OR STACKED) ENCHILADAS

1 dozen corn tortillas
2 cups shredded cheddar cheese
2 cups red chile sauce (see recipe below) or 2 cans of prepared enchilada sauce
1 cup chopped onion
Olive oil

Heat 1 inch of oil in small skillet. Fry tortillas a few seconds until limp.
Place on paper towels to drain.
Dip tortilla in sauce one at a time and place on casserole dish,
covering the bottom without overlapping too much.
Sprinkle on some grated cheese and onion.
Repeat for two more layers.
Pour on any remaining sauce and sprinkle on remaining cheese and onions.
Put in broiler or oven for a few minutes, until cheese has melted, and serve.

RED CHILE SAUCE

20 dried chile pods
Water as needed (about ¼ cup)
6 garlic cloves
Salt
Mexican oregano

Remove the stems and seeds of the chile pods.
Simmer the pods for about 10 minutes.
Place chile and garlic in a blender with water; puree until smooth.
Add more water as needed to get desired consistency.
In a saucepan, add pureed chile with oregano and salt to taste.
Bring to a slow boil, and then simmer for 20 minutes.

school offers 2½-hour classes on everything from New Mexican favorites and Native American cuisine to a recommended class that begins with a trip to the farmers market. And yes, you get to eat what you make. There are also free demonstrations some Saturday afternoons.

Las Cosas Kitchen Shoppe & Cooking School (Map pp76-7; ☎ 988-3394, 877-229-7184; www.lascosascooking.com; 564 N Guadalupe St, DeVargas Center; $45-85) Area chefs teach you to cook at high altitudes, with green chile, or *au deux* at the Chocolate Lovers Workshop. There's also a four-day kid's camp ($250).

Chocolate Smith (Map p75; ☎ 473-2111; www.chocolatesmith.com; 1807 2nd St; $65-85) Hone your chocolate-dipping, truffle-making, chocolate pâté–creating skills at these three-hour evening workshops.

Comida de Campos (☎ 852-0017; www.comidadecampos.com; Hwy 75; $25-45) Spend a day on this working organic farm, picking veggies and then whipping them up with area chefs into a Native feast, berrylicious dessert or vegetarian cuisine. There's a **guesthouse** ($85/day including breakfast, of course) onsite and you'll leave with a bag full of fresh-picked produce.

Taos School of Cooking (Map p149; ☎ 751-4419; www.taoscooking.com; 123 Manzanares, Taos; $60) Area chefs who are over the whole green chile thing offer classes covering truffles, foie gras and caviar or French baking techniques, as well as a kid's camp ($150).

Albuquerque Area

Ah, Albuquerque, never considered a great beauty. Her sprawl is legendary, strip malls legion and contingent of Taco Bells® numbering no fewer than 18. This is the central nervous system of all New Mexico, the crossroads of freeways and manufacturer of computer chips, and no veneer of adobe could disguise the efficiencies that keep the traffic flowing.

As the regional transport hub, Albuquerque welcomes the vast majority of visitors to the state, even those who pause only long enough to rent a car or catch a bus. But there is such beauty in this city, though not offered up on any terra cotta platter: Albuquerque saves her best for those willing to uncover her less obvious charms, those who will hike La Luz, decipher her tangled streets and drink with her constituents in darkened downtown bars.

Will you make the effort? If not, there are other, perhaps prettier, places, far more easily explored. But those who linger in the shadow of the Sandias will find their time most brilliantly rewarded.

HIGHLIGHTS

■ **Sandia Crest** Trams, trails and North America's oldest encampment (p68)

■ **Albuquerque International Balloon Fiesta** Hundreds of hot-air balloons hung like lanterns from the heavens (p60)

■ **Tinkertown Museum** What one man did while you were watching TV (p67)

■ **Kasha-Katuwe Tent Rocks** More scenery per calorie than any other hike around (p67)

■ **Acoma Pueblo** Epic history, fine pottery and dramatic views from the continent's oldest city (p59)

■ **Indian Pueblo Center Cultural Center** Art, history and a great café (p57)

■ **Jemez Springs** Hot springs, wild and tame, for soaking away your cares (p66)

■ **Albuquerque Isotopes** Baseball's most coveted T-shirts (p63)

■ **Petroglyph National Monument** Artists who really rock (p59)

■ **The Frontier** Fiery green chile stew beneath John Wayne's inscrutable gaze (p62)

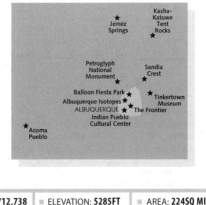

■ TELEPHONE CODE: **505**   ■ POPULATION: **712,738**   ■ ELEVATION: **5285FT**   ■ AREA: **224SQ MI**

ORIENTATION

Albuquerque is vast, locals give directions using compass points (north, south, etc) rather than saying 'right' or 'left,' and drivers venturing much off the beaten path will finally understand why Bugs Bunny was always making that wrong left turn here. Just remember that Sandia Crest is to the east and most of the city is built on a grid, and you'll be fine.

The Rio Grande runs north-south through the city, just west of Old Town. Across the river, the volcanoes visible from almost anywhere in the city are now protected as a part of Petroglyph National Monument (p59).

Central Ave (old Route 66, now NM 333) bisects the city running roughly east to west and connects most areas of interest: Nob Hill, downtown and Old Town. Addresses are designated by their relationship to the point where Central Ave crosses the railroad tracks, just east of First St downtown: NW, SW, NE and SE.

Two major interstates cross just north of downtown. I-40 (east-west) connects the city to Tucumcari and Acoma Pueblo, while I-25 (north-south) runs between Santa Fe and El Paso, Texas.

The International Sunport (it's an airport, but sunny – get it?) is in the SE quadrant, off I-40; it can also be reached by Yale Blvd, which intersects Central Ave near UNM (the University of New Mexico). The Turquoise Trail (NM 14) begins as you leave town on I-40 East, at the Tijeras exit.

Maps

The maps in this book cover Albuquerque's major sights and will get you to Santa Fe, but explorers should pick up a *Rand McNally* or *UniversalMap* folding map to the city. The *Rand McNally Albuquerque, Santa Fe & Taos Streetfinder* ($18) may be useful if you plan to stay a while. Check the Santa Fe maps section (p72) for more recommendations.

Holman's (☎ 449-3810; 6201 Jefferson St NE) may have the best selection of maps in the state. Other good spots to find maps include **Page One** (see Bookstores, below) and the **UNM Bookstore** (see Bookstores, below), which also gives out a free, no-frills map of the city.

INFORMATION

Bookstores

Page One (☎ 294-2026; 11018 Montgomery Blvd NE) Huge and comprehensive.

Page One Too (☎ 294-5623; 11200 Montgomery Blvd NE) Used bookstore across the street from Page One.

UNM Bookstore (Map p60; ☎ 277-5451; cnr Central Ave & Cornell St) Good selection of guides, maps and Southwestern literature.

Bookworks NM (☎ 344-8139; 4022 Rio Grande Blvd NW) Similar fare as the UNM Bookstore.

Newsland Bookstore (Map p60; ☎ 242-0694; 2112 Central Ave SE) Publications from all over the world.

Emergency

Fire, Police, Ambulance Immediate Dispatch (☎ 911)

Police (☎ 242-2677; 400 Marquette NW)

UNM Hospital Emergency (☎ 272-2411)

NM Poison Control Center (☎ 800-432-6866)

Internet Access

Main Library (Map p58; ☎ 768-5140; 501 Copper Ave NW) Free Internet access after you purchase a $3 library card.

Kinko's (Map p60; ☎ 255-9673; 2706 Central Ave SE; $12/hr) Pricey but open 24 hours, and with several locations.

Internet Resources

City of Albuquerque (www.cabq.gov) The city's excellent site, with information on public transport, area attractions and more.

Albuquerque Online (www.abqonline.com) Exhaustive listings and links for Albuquerque businesses.

Albuquerque.com (www.albuquerque.com) Attraction, hotel and restaurant information, with links.

Media

There are scores of radio and television stations; see the Santa Fe chapter (p74) for complete listings.

Albuquerque Journal (www.abqjournal.com) New Mexico's largest daily; publishes the evening *Tribune* and Friday *Venue*, an arts and entertainment pullout.

Alibi (www.alibi.com) This fun, free weekly features entertainment listings and more.

Crosswinds Weekly Another free publication that lists events listings, with lefty political commentary.

Local Flavor and *ABQ Arts* (www.abqarts.com) These free monthlies cover the restaurant and arts scenes.

Medical Services

University Hospital (Map p60; ☎ 272-2411, emergency 272-2411; 2211 Lomas Blvd NE) Head here if you forgot to buy insurance.

Presbyterian Hospital (☎ 841-1234, emergency 841-1111; 1100 Central Ave SE) This facility has shorter lines in the emergency room.

Walgreens (☎ 265-1548, 800-925-4733; 6201 Central Ave NE; ⊙ 24hrs) The 800 number locates other all-night-pharmacy locations.

Tourist Offices

Albuquerque Convention & Visitors Bureau (Map p58; ☎ 842-9918, 800-284-2282; www.itsatrip.org; 401 2nd St NW; ⊙ 9am-5pm Mon-Fri) Has information for all New Mexico.

Old Town Visitors Center (Map p58; ☎ 243-3215; www.itsatrip.org; 303 Romero St NW; ⊙ 9:30am-4:30pm daily) Covers Albuquerque; there's another branch at the **Sunport** (⊙ 9:30am-8pm daily).

Cibola National Forest Office (Map p58; ☎ 842-3292; www.fs.fed.us/r3/cibola; 517 Gold Ave SW, 5th floor; ⊙ 8am-4:30pm Mon-Fri) Features information on the surrounding wilderness, as does the BLM.

Bureau of Land Management (BLM; ☎ 761-8700; www.nm.blm.gov; 435 Montaño Rd NW; ⊙ 7:45am-4:30pm Mon-Fri)

SIGHTS

Most of Albuquerque's top tourist sites are concentrated in downtown and Old Town, convenient enough to walk from many hotels and a straight shot down Central Ave from the inexpensive hotel strip east of Nob Hill. Some of the best attractions, however – including the Indian Pueblo Cultural Center, Petroglyph National Monument and Sandia Tramway – are most easily accessible by car.

Downtown & Old Town

Old Town's most famous photo op is the 1793 **San Felipe de Neri Church** (Map p58; ☎ 243-4628; San Felipe Plaza; admission free; ⊙ 7am-7pm daily). But don't skip the **Turquoise Museum** (Map p58; ☎ 247-8650; 2107 Central Ave NW; $4; ⊙ 10am-4pm Mon-Sat), an enlightening crash course in determining which stones are high quality, or even real; or the **Rattlesnake Museum** (Map p58; ☎ 242-6569; www.rattlesnakes.com; 202 San Felipe St NW; adult/child $3/2; ⊙ 10am-5pm daily), with 45 different rattlers – survivors get a Certificate of Bravery.

The **Albuquerque Museum** (Map p58; ☎ 242-4600; www.albuquerquemuseum.com; 2000 Mountain Rd NW; admission free; ⊙ 8am-5pm Tue-Sun) explores the city's history and features a great gallery of New Mexican artists. The museum also offers **Old Town walking tours** (⊙ 11am Tue-Sun).

Across the street, the **Museum of Natural History & Science** (Map p58; ☎ 841-2800; 1801 Mountain Rd NW; adult/child $5/2; ⊙ 9am-5pm daily) is geared toward academically minded teens, and **!Explora! Science Center** (Map p58; ☎ 842-1537; www.explora.mus.nm.us; Mountain Rd; adult/child $4/2; ⊙ 10am-6pm Mon-Sat, noon-6pm Sun), next door, has hands-on scientific fun for smaller kids.

Nerds of all ages will love the **National Atomic Museum** (Map p58; ☎ 284-3243; www.atomicmuseum.com; 1905 Mountain Rd NW; adult/child $4/3; ⊙ 9am-5pm daily), with an outstanding collection of nuclear weapons. The **New Mexico Holocaust & Intolerance Museum** (Map p58; ☎ 247-0606; www.nmholocaustmuseum.org; 415 Central Ave NW; admission free; ⊙ 11am-4pm Tue-Sat) houses powerful exhibits on genocides worldwide, from Armenia to Acoma.

Operated by the All Indian Pueblo Council, the **Indian Pueblo Cultural Center** (☎ 843-7270; www.indianpueblo.org; 2401 12th St NW; adult/child $4/1; ⊙ 9am-5pm daily) is a must: the

---

WHAT HAPPENED TO THE 'R' IN ALBURQUERQUE?

Sly Don Francisco Cuervo y Valdez wanted to build a city on the Rio Grande, but in 1706 he still didn't have the required 30 families to do it. He knew, however, that the paperwork would be processed by one Viceroy Fernandez – the Duke of Alburquerque. In a shameless ploy to curry his favor, the new settlement – if approved – would be named to the Duke's eternal glory. And so Alburquerque was born.

After US annexation, English speakers poured into the Duke City, but found that first 'r' a bit difficult to pronounce. Besides, the sign at the new train station (this is a legend, perhaps) just wasn't long enough for that jumbled mouthful of letters. Somewhere along the way, that 'r' was lost forever.

Or perhaps not. Rudolfo Anaya, UNM professor emeritus and author of the seminal Chicano novel, *Bless Me, Ultima*, in 1992 published the not-quite-as-revered (but better) *Alburquerque*, resurrecting the city's proper name. And oddly enough, through a mist of magical realism, he was able to invoke the essence of this strange city, along with that long forgotten 'r.'

ALBUQUERQUE AREA

ALBUQUERQUE

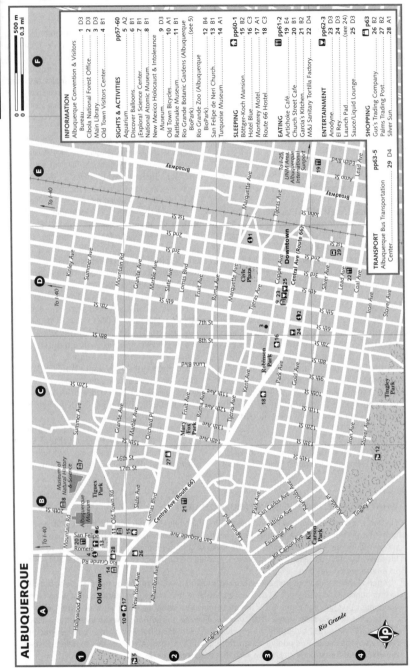

INFORMATION	
Albuquerque Convention & Visitors	
Bureau	1 D3
Cibola National Forest Office	2 D3
Main Library	3 D3
Old Town Visitors Center	4 B1

SIGHTS & ACTIVITIES	pp57-60
Aquarium	5 A2
Discover Balloons	6 B1
¡Explora! Science Center	7 B1
National Atomic Museum	8 B1
New Mexico Holocaust & Intolerance	
Museum	9 D3
Old Town Bicycles	10 A1
Rattlesnake Museum	11 B1
Rio Grande Botanic Gardens (Albuquerque	
BioPark)	(see 5)
Rio Grande Zoo (Albuquerque	
BioPark)	12 B4
San Felipe de Neri Church	13 B1
Turquoise Museum	14 A1

SLEEPING	🛏 pp60-1
Böttger-Koch Mansion	15 B2
Hotel Blue	16 C3
Monterey Motel	17 A1
Route 66 Hostel	18 C3

EATING	🍴 pp61-2
Artichoke Café	19 E4
Church Street Café	20 B1
Garcia's Kitchen	21 B2
M&J Sanitary Tortilla Factory	22 D4

ENTERTAINMENT	🎭 pp62-3
Anodyne	23 D3
El Rey	24 D3
Launch Pad	(see 24)
Sauce/Liquid Lounge	25 D3

SHOPPING	🛍 p63
Gus's Trading Company	26 B2
Palms Trading Post	27 B2
Silver Sun	28 A1

TRANSPORT	pp63-5
Albuquerque Bus Transportation	
Center	29 D4

0 _____ 500 m
0 _____ 0.3 mi

history exhibits are fascinating, while the arts wing shows the finest examples of each pueblo's work – come here before considering any major purchases. The onsite **Pueblo Harvest Cafe** (mains $4-7; ☾ 8am-3pm daily) serves Native cuisine, and there are art demonstrations, bread baking and dances on weekends.

University of New Mexico

With 30,000 students on its pueblo revival campus, **UNM** (Map p60; ☎ 277-5813; www.unm.edu; Central Ave NE) is an adobe wonderland with seven free museums and lots of public art. The **Visitors Center** (Map p60; ☎ 277-1989; Las Lomas Rd; ☾ 8am-5pm Mon-Fri) has information and maps.

Campus standouts include the **Maxwell Museum of Anthropology** (Map p60; ☎ 277-4404; Redondo Dr; ☾ 9am-4pm Mon-Sat), with artifacts galore and a fabricated dig; **University Art Museum** (Map p60; ☎ 277-4001; cnr Redondo & Cornell Drs), boasting a permanent collection of 24,000 pieces; and **Jonson Gallery** (Map p60; ☎ 277-4967; 1909 Las Lomas Rd; ☾ 9am-4pm Tue-Fri), specializing in challenging contemporary art.

Metropolitan Albuquerque

Albuquerque's most famous attraction is probably **Sandia Tram** (p68), and the newest is the **National Hispanic Cultural Center** (☎ 246-2261; www.nhccnm.org; 1701 4th St SW; adult/child $3/free; ☾ 10am-5pm Tue-Sat), with three galleries of art and the nation's premier Hispanic **genealogy library**.

The **Albuquerque BioPark** (Map p58; ☎ 764-6200; www.cabq.gov/biopark; adult/child $10/5 for all three parks, $7/3 for one park; ☾ 9am-5pm Mon-Sun) is basically a combo ticket to three kid-friendly attractions, good for one day. The **Rio Grande Zoo** (Map p58; 903 10th St SW), on 60 shady acres along the river, is home to more than 1300 animals. The **Albuquerque Aquarium** and **Rio Grande Botanic Gardens** (☎ 903 10th St NW), just west of Old Town, feature a 285,000-gallon shark tank and several conservatories housing desert plants. Both locations stage mellow **music events** (adult/child $7/4; ☾ 7pm Fri Jun-Aug).

The state's two best wineries, **Gruet Winery** (Map p64; ☎ 821-0055; 8400 Pan American Fwy NE; ☾ noon-5pm Mon-Sat) and **Casa Rondeña** (☎ 344-5911; 733 Chavez Rd NW; ☾ 1-5pm Thu-Sun), are in town and open for free tastings.

ACTIVITIES

Sandia Crest (p68) is Albuquerque's rural playground, and many trails begin in the foothills at **Elena Gallegos Picnic Area** (☎ 857-8334; $2; ☾ 7am-7pm). The **Rio Grande Nature Center** (☎ 344-7240; 2901 Candelaria Rd NE; $1; ☾ 8am-5pm daily), in the tree-lined bosque, has interpretive nature trails that are perfect for kids.

The **Petroglyph National Monument** (Map p64; ☎ 899-0205; www.nps.gov/petr; Unser Blvd; $2;

DETOUR: ACOMA PUEBLO

It's worth spending an hour on I-40 – or more, if you stop at **Laguna Pueblo** (Map p64; ☎ 552-6654; I-40 exit 114), a 1699 pueblo boasting **San Jose Mission** – to see this.

Sky City (Map p64; ☎ 470-4966; adult/child $10/7, photo permit $10; ☾ 8am-5pm daily), a cluster of ancient adobes atop a dramatic 367ft mesa, was described by Coronado as 'one of the strongest [cities] ever seen.' It boasts the best view in New Mexico, the oldest church in the USA and graceful pottery emblazoned with precise line work that's among the most collectable in the world.

Ascend the mesa on a **guided tour** that begins at cavernous San Estevan Mission, built under the worst circumstances possible. Acoma earned Oñate's wrath when the Indians killed several Spanish soldiers robbing their stores. According to oral history, every man over 25 had one foot cut off, leaving women and children to build the mission. Encoded in the geometry of its construction, however, are ratios sacred to the old ways.

The tour takes you through the village, where about 100 residents still live without electricity or running water. After you wander past stands selling pottery and snacks, you can either descend via shuttle or walk the old footpath. Take the path.

Sky City Casino and Hotel (Map p64; ☎ 552-6123, 888-759-2489; www.skycitycasino.com; I-40 exit 102; s/d $61/66; ⓟ ☒ ☒ ☒), right off the interstate, is elegant (for a casino) and alcohol-free, with nice new rooms and free transportation for guests to Sky City.

8am-5pm daily) has three of the most intriguing (and shadeless) hikes anywhere, past some 15,000 ancient pieces of art etched into the rocks.

Take to the skies in a hot air balloon with **Discover Balloons** (Map p58; ☎ 842-1111; www .discoverballoons.com; 205C San Felipe NW; $150). Make reservations at least two days in advance for the rides, which include champagne.

FESTIVALS & EVENTS

The Friday *Albuquerque Journal* and *Alibi* both have weekly events listings.

Gathering of Nations Powwow (☎ 836-2810; www.gatheringofnations.com; late Apr) It's the biggest event in Native America, with folks coming from all over the continent for a week of dancing, drumming, art shows and the Miss Indian World election.

Albuquerque Gay/Lesbian/Bisexual/Transgender Pride (☎ 873-8084; mid-Jun) It's all-inclusive.

New Mexico State Fair (☎ 265-1791; www.nmstatefair.com; late Sep) Food, music, prize livestock, juried art shows, rodeos and creaky carnival rides – you'll have fun.

International Balloon Fiesta (Map p64; ☎ 821-1000, 800-422-7277; www.aibf.org; early Oct) You just haven't lived until you've seen a three-story-tall Tony the Tiger land in your hotel courtyard, which is exactly the sort of thing that happens all over town during this two-week extravaganza. Yeah, everything's packed and parking is horrible, but being on the ground during Mass Ascension, with hundreds of colorful balloons fluttering and inflating all around you like living, breathing beings – it's so worth it. And being in the air? It's great!

SLEEPING

Albuquerque has about 150 hotels, all of which are full during the International Balloon Fiesta and the Gathering of Nations. Make reservations early. The **Visitors Bureau** (p58) has information and links to many more options, and many local B&Bs participate in the **New Mexico Central Reservations Line** (☎ 766-9770; 800-466-7829).

Budget

Inexpensive motels line Central Ave, concentrated around the I-25 on-ramp and

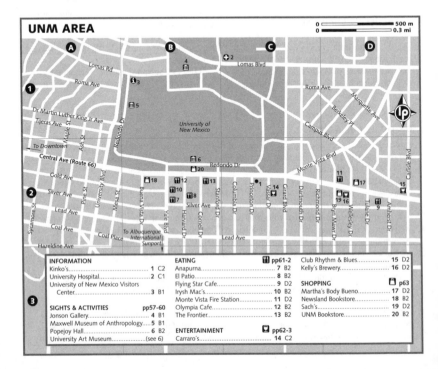

UNM AREA

INFORMATION		EATING	pp61-2	Club Rhythm & Blues	15 D2
Kinko's	1 C2	Anapurna	7 B2	Kelly's Brewery	16 D2
University Hospital	2 C1	El Patio	8 B2		
University of New Mexico Visitors		Flying Star Cafe	9 D2	SHOPPING	p63
Center	3 B1	Irysh Mac's	10 B2	Martha's Body Bueno	17 D2
		Monte Vista Fire Station	11 D2	Newsland Bookstore	18 B2
SIGHTS & ACTIVITIES	pp57-60	Olympia Cafe	12 B2	Sach's	19 D2
Jonson Gallery	4 B1	The Frontier	13 B2	UNM Bookstore	20 B2
Maxwell Museum of Anthropology	5 B1				
Popejoy Hall	6 B2	ENTERTAINMENT	pp62-3		
University Art Museum	(see 6)	Carraro's	14 C2		

east of Nob Hill. You can score a room in the $20 to $30 range, but trust your gut – some are pretty sleazy.

Route 66 Hostel (Map p58; ☎ 247-1813; 1012 Central Ave SW; dm $14, d $20-30; P ⊠ 🐾) With discounts for HI-AYH members, this hostel is clean, festive and conveniently located between downtown and Old Town.

Monterey Motel (Map p58; ☎ 243-3554; 2402 Central Ave SW; s/d $45/55; P ⊠ 🐾) Enjoy great rooms (all of which are nonsmoking) and being close to downtown.

Hiway House (☎ 268-3971; 3200 Central Ave SE; s/d $35/40; P ⊠ 🐾 🍽) Between UNM and Nob Hill, this place has an excellent Korean barbecue joint onsite.

Also recommended is primitive **camping** ($3) at Sandia Crest (p68), or you can enjoy hot showers at **KOA Albuquerque Central** (☎ 296-2729, 800-562-7781; Juan Tabo Blvd; campsite/RV $22/31, Kamping Kabin $40-50). **Turquoise Trail Campground** (p67), in Cedar Crest, is more scenic, and **Sandia Mountain Hostel** (p67), 15 minutes from town, also allows camping.

Mid-Range

The best bets for mid-range accommodations are the endless **chain motels** that hug I-25 and I-40. I-25 exit 227A and I-40 exit 155 are good bets, as is the airport area.

Best Western Rio Grande Inn (☎ 843-9500, 800-959-4726; 1015 Rio Grande Blvd NW; s/d $99/109; P ⊠ 🐾 🍽), south of I-40 and convenient to Old Town, has large, Southwestern-style rooms and lots of little amenities. **Hotel Blue** (Map p58; ☎ 924-2400; www.thehotelblue.com; 717 Central Ave NW; s/d $79/89; P ⊠ 🐾) has fewer frills but is right downtown.

Top End

La Posada de Albuquerque (☎ 242-9090, 800-777-5732; www.laposada-abq.com; 125 2nd St NW; d $80-160; P ⊠ 🐾) This 1939 downtown landmark offers fine rooms, a relaxed bar with weekend jazz, and a classic coffee shop.

Hyatt Tamaya (☎ 867-1234; www.tamaya.hyatt .com; 1300 Tayuna Trail; d from $180; P ⊠ 🐾 🍽) Hidden in the desert landscape of Santa Ana Pueblo, with expansive views, this luxurious property has three pools, three restaurants and a small spa.

Böttger-Koch Mansion (Map p58; ☎ 243-3639, 800-758-3639; www.bottger.com; 110 San Felipe St NW;

d incl breakfast $140-250; P ⊠ 🐾) The most deluxe of several Old Town area B&Bs, this huge Victorian is all antiques and elegance.

EATING

Albuquerque offers the region's widest variety of international cuisines while serving up some of the best New Mexican food anywhere. It's not a foodie destination like Santa Fe, and many restaurants geared to tourists are less than outstanding. Instead head to any of the modest, family-owned joints serving excellent and authentic local cuisine or to the cluster of colorful and (mostly) inexpensive restaurants centered on Nob Hill and around the university.

Downtown & Old Town

The plaza is surrounded with pleasant eateries serving decent food at premium prices (the cost of convenience). Consider walking a few blocks for a better selection.

Garcia's Kitchen (Map p58; ☎ 842-0273; 1736 Central Ave SW; mains $2-8; 🕑 6:30am-10pm) Homemade specialties – including excellent carne adovada, stuffed sopapillas and five-star breakfasts – make this an Albuquerque classic.

Church St Cafe (Map p58; ☎ 247-8522; 2111 Church St NW; mains $5-10; 🕑 8am-4pm Sun-Wed, 8am-8pm Thu-Sat) It's delicious, historic and the exception to the plaza rule. Try the Albuquerque roast beef, a French dip with green chile on a flour tortilla.

M&J Sanitary Tortilla Factory (Map p58; ☎ 242-4890; 403 2nd St SW; mains $3-8; 🕑 9am-4pm Mon-Sat) This is where Mayor Chavez took President Clinton to schmooze, so you know it's got great New Mexican grub – plus fresh tortillas to go.

Artichoke Café (Map p58; ☎ 243-0200; 424 Central Ave SE; mains $9-20; 🕑 11:30am-2:30pm Mon-Fri, 4:30-9:30pm Mon-Sat) Elegant and unpretentious, this popular bistro does creative gourmet cuisine considered among Albuquerque's best.

UNM Area & Nob Hill

In the grand tradition of university neighborhoods, this is the best area for cheap, healthy and vegetarian meals.

Irysh Mac's (Map p60; ☎ 265-5597; 110 Yale Blvd SE; 🕑 8am-midnight Mon-Sat, 9am-10pm Sun) Excellent lattes, pastries and other light snacks are complemented with live local music most nights – they put a sign out front if there's a gig.

The Frontier (Map p60; ☎ 266-0550; 2400 Central Ave SE; mains $3-7; ☼ 24hrs) Get in line for enormous cinnamon rolls and the best huevos rancheros ever. The food, people-watching and Western art collection are all outstanding.

Anapurna (Map p60; ☎ 262-2424; 2201 Silver SE; mains $3-5; ☼ 7am-8pm daily) This awesome vegetarian café has some of the best food in town, including delicately spiced ayurvedic delights that even carnivores love, plus *real* chai.

Flying Star Cafe (Map p60; ☎ 255-6633; 3416 Central Ave SE; mains $5-9; ☼ 6:30am-11pm daily) With innovative entrees and gourmet sandwiches plus a cheerful, always-packed dining room, this local favorite is exactly the wrong place to skip dessert – in fact, try two.

El Patio (Map p60; ☎ 268-4245; 142 Harvard Dr SE; mains $4-8; ☼ 11:30am-10pm daily) Relax on the patio where guitarists sometimes strum, and enjoy tasty New Mexican dishes.

Olympia Cafe (Map p60; ☎ 266-5222; 2210 Central Ave SE; mains $4-8; ☼ 11:30am-9pm daily) This isn't just the best Greek food in town – it may be the best Greek food anywhere (yes, including Greece).

Monte Vista Fire Station (Map p60; ☎ 255-2424; 3201 Central Ave NE; mains $14-20; ☼ 11:30am-2:30pm & 5-10:30pm daily) Enjoy upscale Southwestern-influenced cuisine served up in a pueblo-revival–style fire station (the pole's still there). The upstairs bar and patio are fine places to relax and mingle.

Metropolitan Albuquerque

The most famous restaurant in town (High Finance; p68) requires a tram ride from the base of the Sandias; the following fine choices aren't quite that far off the beaten track, however.

Loyola's Family Restaurant (☎ 268-6478; 4500 Central Ave SE; mains $3-8; ☼ 6am-2pm Tue-Sun) Pure Route 66 style, Loyola's has been serving fine, no-frills New Mexican fare since before there was even a song about the Mother Road.

Los Cuates (☎ 255-5079; 5016B Lomas NE; mains $5-9; ☼ 11am-9pm daily) Lines are often out the door for huge plates of high-quality New Mexican cuisine. Los Cuates changed ownership recently, but the food is still first-rate.

Que Huong (☎ 262-0575; 7010 Central Ave SE; mains $4-8; ☼ 10am-9pm daily) Vietnamese restaurants cluster beneath the enormous Paul Bunyan statue atop May Café, but come here (next door) for authentic Saigon-style dishes.

El Norteño (☎ 256-1431; 6416 Zuni Rd SE; mains $4-9; ☼ 7am-9:30pm daily) Mexican – not New Mexican – cuisine is the thing here, with fantastic pollo norteño, chicken mole and cabrito al horno (oven-roasted goat).

Quarters (☎ 843-7505; 801 Yale Blvd SE; mains $6-18; ☼ 5-9pm daily) The best barbecue in town is slow-roasted at this dark little place.

ENTERTAINMENT

Pick up an *Alibi* for the hottest spots and best shows in town.

Bars & Clubs

Downtown has a great bar scene, starring **El Rey** (Map p58; ☎ 764-2624; 624 Central Ave SW), a fabulous venue for local and national rock, blues and country acts. The retro-modern **Launch Pad** (Map p58; ☎ 764-8887; 618 Central Ave SW) is the hottest stage for local live music.

Sauce/Liquid Lounge (Map p58; ☎ 242-5839; 405 Central Ave NW) is a hip little lounge with great pizza and an NYC feel, while **Anodyne** (Map p58; ☎ 244-1820; 409 Central Ave NW) is another stylish spot featuring pool tables and overstuffed chairs.

Another cluster of nightclubs in Nob Hill includes the piano bar at **Martini Grille** (☎ 255-4111; 4200 Central Ave SE) and **Club Rhythm and Blues** (Map p60; ☎ 256-0849; 3523 Central Ave NE), which brings in national acts. **Kelly's Brewery** (Map p60; ☎ 362-2739; 3226 Central Ave SE) has patio dining, beer and live bands on weekends; **Carraro's** (Map p60; ☎ 268-2300; 108 Vasser Dr SE) is a popular place to relax with brews, pool, pizza and pals.

Practice your two-step at **Caravan East** (☎ 265-7877; 7605 Central Ave NE), or catch live country music at **Midnight Rodeo** (☎ 888-0100; 4901 McLeod Rd NE).

A plethora of gay and lesbian nightclubs include the venerable **Albuquerque Mining Company** (☎ 255-4022; 7209 Central Ave NE) and hipper **Pulse** (☎ 255-3334; 4100 Central Ave SE).

Performing Arts

Popejoy Hall (Map p60; ☎ 277-4569; cnr Central Ave & Cornell St), at UNM, and the historic **KiMo Theater** (☎ 848-1370, 764-1700 for tickets; 423 Central Ave NW) are the two primary venues for theater, dance and symphony orchestra performances.

Sunshine Theater (☎ 764-0249; 120 Central Ave SW) stages alt-rock shows, while **The Pit**

(☎ 925-5626) and **Tingley Coliseum** (☎ 265-1791) host hair bands and teen divas.

Other recommendations are:

Musical Theater Southwest (☎ 262-9301; $10) Stages six Broadway musical productions each year.
New Mexico Ballet Company (☎ 292-4245; $5-25; Oct-Apr) The state's best ballet.
New Mexico Symphony Orchestra (☎ 881-8999; $15-40) Performs at venues all over town, including the zoo.
La Compañía de Teatro de Albuquerque (☎ 242-7929) Theater in Spanish, English and sometimes both.

SPECTATOR SPORTS

Albuquerque Isotopes (☎ 924-2255; www.albuquerque baseball.com) Yes, the city's new baseball team really was named after an episode of *The Simpsons* in which America's favorite TV dad tried to keep his beloved Springfield Isotopes from moving to Albuquerque. It didn't work, and now the 'Topes sell more merchandise than any other minor (and most major) league team. They sometimes win, too.

Albuquerque Scorpions (☎ 265-1791; www .scorpionshockey.com) Tingley Coliseum hosts this ice hockey team as well as the **State Rodeo** (☎ 873-7770; www.nmstatefair.com), held during the State Fair in September.

UNM Lobos (☎ 277-4569; www.unm.edu) The football team packs The Pit, but it's the women's basketball and volleyball teams that carry the banner to playoffs and national championships.

SHOPPING

For a wide selection of Native American crafts, stop by the **Palms Trading Post** (Map p58; ☎ 247-8504; 1504 Lomas Blvd NW) or **Gus's Trading Company** (Map p58; ☎ 843-6381; 2026 Central Ave SW). **Silver Sun** (Map p58; ☎ 242-8265; 2042 South Plaza NW) is a reputable spot for turquoise.

If you're feeling saucy, head to Nob Hill, where a strip of hip stores includes **Martha's Body Bueno** (Map p60; ☎ 255-1122; 3105 Central Ave NE), specializing in handmade beauty supplies and lingerie couture, and **Sachs** (Map p60; ☎ 286-1661; 3112 Central Ave SE), catering to your leather and piercing needs.

GETTING THERE & AWAY
Air

Albuquerque International Sunport (Map p64; ☎ 244-7700; www.cabq.gov/airport; 2200 Sunport Blvd) This ridiculously named airport is New Mexico's largest, served by 12 airlines, nine car rental companies, and private shuttles that run from the Sunport and downtown Albuquerque to Santa Fe and points north. These are all covered in the Transport chapter.

Bus

Albuquerque Bus Transportation Center (Map p58; 300 2nd St SW) It's home to Greyhound (☎ 243-4435, 800-231-2222) as well as TNM&O (☎ 243-4435, 806-763-5389), both of which offer direct service to Santa Fe ($10) and Taos ($24) several times daily.

Train

Albuquerque Amtrak Station (☎ 842-9650, 800-872-7245; 214 1st St SW) Amtrak's Southwest Chief stops here, running daily trains between Chicago and Los Angeles with stops in Lamy and Las Vegas, New Mexico.

GETTING AROUND
To/From the Sunport

The Sunport is served by the No 50 SunTran bus. **Airport Shuttle** (☎ 765-1234) and **Sunport Shuttle** (☎ 883-4966, 866-505-4966) both run between the Sunport and Albuquerque addresses 24 hours a day.

Bus

SunTran (☎ 843-9200; www.cabq.gov/transit; adult/child $1/35¢; ☺ 6am-9pm) The public bus system covers most of Albuquerque on weekdays, major tourist spots daily. Three **trolleys** (adult/child $1/35¢; ☺ 7am-7pm daily) serve downtown, Central Ave and Nob Hill.

Bicycles

Parks and Recreation (☎ 768-2453; www.cabq.gov/bike) Contact this agency for a free map of the city's elaborate system of bike trails. All SunTran buses are equipped with front-loading bicycle racks.

Old Town Bicycles (Map p58; ☎ 247-4920; 2412 Central Ave) rents road bicycles ($12-20/day) and mountain bikes ($20-25/day), with reduced rates for long-term rentals.

Taxi

In general you must call for a taxi, though they do patrol the Sunport, Amtrak and bus station. Rates are $2.25 to start the meter, then $2 per mile.

Yellow Cab (☎ 247-8888, 800-657-6232)
Albuquerque Cab (☎ 883-4888)

ALBUQUERQUE AREA

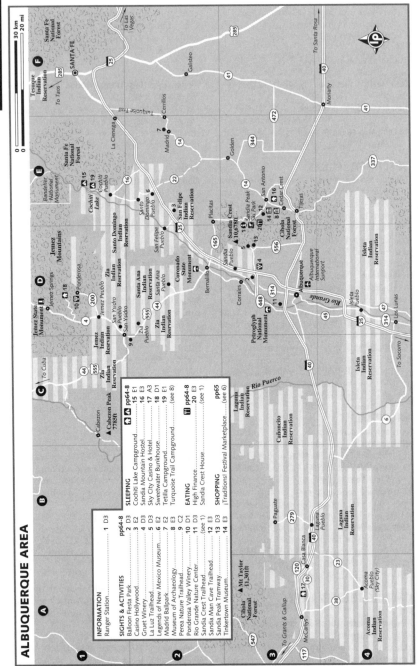

ALBUQUERQUE TO SANTA FE

There are three main routes connecting New Mexico's two major cities: a speedy hour along semiscenic I-25; at least 90 minutes on much lovelier NM 14, the Turquoise Trail; or the day (or better, two-day) meander through the stunning Jemez Mountains.

INTERSTATE 25

It's a one-hour straight shot to Santa Fe, but it's easy to stretch out if you're on vacation.

Sandia Pueblo

Sandia Pueblo (Map p64; ☎ 867-3317; www .sandiapueblo.nsn.us; I-25 exit 234) opened one of the first casinos in New Mexico and subsequently used its wealth to successfully lobby for legislation preventing further development of Sandia Crest, their old sacred lands, appropriated by Cibola National Forest.

The new **Sandia Casino** (☎ 765-7500, 800-526-9366; www.sandiacasino.com) is one of the nicest and boasts an elegant outdoor venue, **Sandia Casino Amphitheater**, hosting everything from symphony orchestras to boxing matches to Bill Cosby.

Bien Mur Marketplace (☎ 821-5400, 800-365-5400; www.bienmur.com; 100 Bien Mur Dr NE; ⏰ 9am-5:30pm Mon-Sat, 11am-5pm Sun), across the road from the casino, claims to be the largest Native American–owned trading post in the Southwest, which is probably true. The tribe invites visitors to **Marketfest** here in late October, when Native artists show their stuff, as well as the **June 13 Feast Day**, with Corn Dances.

Coronado State Monument

After exiting I-25 onto US 150, you'll pass **Coronado Campground** (☎ 980-8256; US 150; campsite/RV $8/18), with shelters for shade and $4 showers, on the way to the **ruins of Kuau'a** (☎ 867-5351; US 150; admission free; ⏰ 8am-5pm Wed-Sun). It's not exactly Chaco Canyon, but the murals are pretty spectacular: various deities are depicted growing corn, bringing rain, and munching plants that appear suspiciously hallucinogenic. The murals have been artfully restored inside the visitors center and cool underground kiva.

Santa Ana Pueblo

Santa Ana Pueblo (Map p64; ☎ 867-3301; www .santaana.org; US 150) is *posh*. No joke. It boasts two great **golf courses** (☎ 867-9464, 800-851-9469; www.santaanagolf.com; $32-100): the **Santa Ana Golf Club**, with three nine-hole courses, and extravagant **Twin Warriors Golf Club**, with 18 holes and waterfalls.

Nearby is Albuquerque's premier fine dining restaurant, **Prairie Star** (☎ 867-3327; Tamaya Blvd; mains $16-22; ⏰ 5:30-9pm Tue-Sun), with dishes like bison tenderloin in horseradish aioli, all served in a romantically appointed historic adobe, with sunsets overlooking the Sandias.

Santa Ana Star Casino (☎ 867-0000; US 150) has a staggering buffet, 36 lanes of bowling and the opportunity to challenge Rocko the Rooster to a $25,000 game of tic-tac-toe (he's good, though). And the tribe is working with Hyatt to open a full-scale resort onsite, complete with a spa.

Stables at Tamaya (☎ 771-6037) offers trail rides and lessons ($25-80) through the bosque, into which the pueblo has recently pumped millions of dollars for cleanup and restoration. And, lest you forget that this is not Beverly Hills west, there are **Corn Dances** on June 24 and July 26.

Legends of New Mexico Museum

At **!Traditions! Festival Marketplace** is the state's newest independent museum (Map p64; ☎ 867-8600; Budaghers exit off I-25; adult/child $5/free; ⏰ 10am-5pm Tue-Sat, 1-5pm Sun). Spotlighting the state's most famous visitors and residents – from Billy the Kid to Bill Gates, the Roswell aliens to Popé and Smokey Bear – well, when they say it's a tribute to multiculturalism, they mean it.

San Felipe Pueblo

Though best known for the spectacular **San Felipe Feast Green Corn Dances** on May 1, this conservative Keres-speaking pueblo (Map p64; ☎ 867-3381; I-25 exit 252; photography forbidden) now has a couple more claims to fame.

Casino Hollywood (Map p64; ☎ 867-6700; 877-529-2946; www.sanfelipecasino.com; I-25 exit 252) isn't just for gambling – this themed venue takes full advantage of its location to pull in acts like Los Lobos and Julio Iglesias.

Even better, the pueblo recently opened **Hollywood Hills Speedway** (Map p64; ☎ 867-6700, 877-529-2946; www.hollywoodhillsspeedway.com; I-25 exit 252; adult/child $10/free), a ³/₈-mile clay track that hosts primarily sprints, plus a few stock car races. In addition to the May 1 dances, visitors are also invited to the June 29 **San Pedro Feast Day** and October **Arts & Crafts Fair**.

Santo Domingo Pueblo

Long a seat of pueblo government – the All Indian Pueblo Council (p29) still meets here annually – this is the tribe of Catiti, a hero of the Pueblo Revolt who led the Keres-speaking pueblos to victory. The original city was later torched, twice, but survivors moved here, on Hwy 22 about 6 miles northwest of I-25 exit 259.

The nongaming pueblo (Map p64; ☎ 465-2214; Hwy 22; ☼ 8am-dusk) has a small **museum** in the gas station and several **galleries and studios** at the pueblo itself, most fronting the plaza in front of pretty 1886 **Santo Domingo Church**, with murals and frescos by local artists. The tribe is most famous for heishi (shell bead) jewelry, as well as the

---

DETOUR: JEMEZ MOUNTAIN TRAIL

Exit I-25 at US 550 (formerly NM 44) and roll past Santa Ana Pueblo for a passionless 25-mile stretch of scrub to San Ysidro, perhaps stopping to stretch your legs in the pretty Rio Salado wetlands along 2-mile **Perea Nature Trail.** Then head north on NM 4 into paradise.

You'll first pass **Zia Pueblo** (Map p64; ☎ 867-6013; US 550), where the state's official symbol (p87) was first designed; it's famed for its August 15 Feast Day, Christmas Buffalo and Crow Dances. Detour, perhaps, to **Ponderosa Valley Winery** (Map p64; ☎ 834-7073; www.ponderosawinery.com; ☼ 10am-5pm Mon-Sat, noon-3pm Sun) for a bottle of Late Harvest Riesling or Pinot Noir.

Jemez Pueblo's Walatowa Visitors Center (Map p64; ☎ 834-7235; US 550; ☼ 8am-5pm daily) is excellent and houses the **Museum of Pueblo Culture** (adult/child $3/2), a **US Forest Service** desk and a gift shop selling CDs by the pueblo's own Grammy-nominated Black Eagle Singers. Across the road, **Jemez Red Rocks** hosts arts and crafts stands on summer weekends, plus a powwow in late May.

That's about when you enter the **Jemez Mountains** proper. A ragged of expanse of moody tufa grays and cool evergreens rising from the brilliant red desert, this is all that remains of the world's largest volcano – they've found pieces of it in Texas. Wind through sculpted formations and melting ruins of abandoned pueblos along the Jemez River, fed by snowmelt and hot springs bubbling up from the still-molten heart of this strange and beautiful wilderness.

The pretty village of **Jemez Springs** was built around a cluster of the springs, as was the ruined pueblo at **Jemez State Monument** (Map p64; ☎ 829-3530; NM 4; adult/child $3/free; ☼ 8:30am-5pm Wed-Mon). You can experience the waters yourself at rustic **Jemez Springs Bath House** (Map p64; ☎ 829-3303; 62 Jemez Springs Plaza; www.jemezspringsbathhouse.com; $10-15/hour; ☼ 10am-7:30pm Mon-Fri, 9am-9pm Sat & Sun), with private tubs, massages and more.

For maps to wilder springs, stop into the **Forest Service Office** (☎ 829-3535; 051 Woodsy Ln; ☼ 8am-4:30pm Mon-Fri). **Spence** is the closest springs to the road, with nudists and riff-raff galore (leave nothing valuable in the car); **McCauley's** lukewarm waters end a shady 2-mile hike to the right, and hard-to-reach **San Antonio** (bring your mountain bike) is the best of the bunch.

Stay at one of several **campsites** ($8) nestled along the river, or at solar-powered and ultra-rustic **Sweetwater Bunkhouse** (Map p64; ☎ 834-7908; 2.2 miles off NM 4; dm $20; P ✕), signed from the highway.

Giggling Star Cabins (☎ 829-9175; www.sulphercanyon.com/giggle; NM 4; $99-145 P ✕ ✕) has lovely lodging plus its own private springs, while **Laughing Lizard Inn** (☎ 829-3108; www.thelaughinglizard.com; NM 4; d low/high $55/70; P ✕ ✕) has great rooms and an attached **café** (creative mains $5-11; ☼ 8:30am-8:30pm Tue-Sun) with live music on weekends. There are a handful of restaurants in Jemez Springs, including a good deli and festive saloon.

Definitely take time out to inspect **Soda Dam,** a warm waterfall that's enveloped boulders with bizarre mineral deposits, and **Battleship Rock,** a dramatic trailhead and fishing spot.

Continue on NM 4 past awe-inspiring **Valles Caldera** (☎ 829-3535; www.fs.fed.us/r3/sfe), once the heart of the volcano, then Baca Ranch, and only recently opened to unguided hiking. Then it's **Bandelier** (p136) and **Los Alamos** (p132), where you'll rejoin civilization once again.

huge **August 4 Corn Dances** and a Labor Day weekend **Arts and Crafts Fair** that attracts folks from all over the state.

Cochiti Pueblo

About 10 miles north of Santo Domingo on NM 22, or 18 miles west of I-25 on NM 16, Cochiti Pueblo (☎ 465-2244) is known for its arts and crafts, particularly ceremonial bass drums. This is where Helen Cordero came up with those storyteller dolls, and today ceramicists like Victor Ortiz exhibit ironic modern interpretations of the old arts at Robert Nichols Gallery (p110) in Santa Fe.

Several stands and shops are usually set up around the plaza and 1628 mission, and dances are held on the July 14 **Feast Day of San Buenaventura** and at Christmas. There's no photography allowed here, but snap away at **Pueblo de Cochiti Golf Course** (p89), considered the state's most challenging, or no-wake **Cochiti Lake** (day-use $3), favored by boaters and swimmers. **Cochiti Lake Campground** and **Tetilla Campground** (Map p64; ☎ 465-0307; NM 22; tent/RV sites $8/12), on opposite sides of the lake, aren't the state's most scenic but they have boating access.

Kasha-Katuwe Tent Rocks National Monument

This is a must. Well-signed from NM 22 and co-managed by the pueblo and BLM, this bizarre and beautiful geological formation of tent-shaped hoodoos can be explored along **Cave Loop Trail**. But the real treat is **Canyon Trail**, an easy and spectacular 2-mile roundtrip, threading a narrow 30ft-tall canyon with walls so close together that you can touch both sides. The steep final leg climbs to a perfect vista overlooking the odd landscape.

THE TURQUOISE TRAIL

The Turquoise Trail has been a major trade route since at least 2000 BC, when local artisans began trading Cerrillos turquoise with communities in present-day Mexico. Today it's the scenic back road between Albuquerque and Santa Fe, lined with quirky communities and other diversions that you'll want to explore.

Cedar Crest

Tinkertown Museum (Map p64; ☎ 281-5233; www.tinkertown.com; 121 Sandia Crest Rd; adult/child $3/1; ☺ 9am-6pm daily Apr-Nov) Just a bit up Sandia Crest Rd (NM 165), this is the most highly recommended excursion in this book. Woodcarver and wisdom collector Ross J Ward built this inspiring assortment of detailed towns, circuses and other scenes that come alive with a quarter, surrounded with antique toys, junque and suggestions that you eat more mangoes naked. The *Theodora R*, a 35ft yacht that sailed around the world, and 'Boot Hill' are highlights but are just part of one truly revelatory experience.

The nearby **Museum of Archaeology** (Map p64; ☎ 281-2005; 22 Calvary Rd, off NM 14; adult/child $3/2; ☺ noon-7pm daily May-Oct) has an 'archaeological site' outdoors (kids dig this) and local Indian artifacts inside. They also run the adjacent **Turquoise Trail Campground** (campsite/RV/rustic cabins $13/22/$50-100; [P]), with hot showers and cool shade.

Sandia Mountain Hostel (Map p64; ☎ 281-4117; 12234 N Hwy 14; campsite/dm/d $8/14/32; [P] [X] [R]) is a great independent hostel, with passive solar-designed common areas and cabins, five friendly donkeys and lots of classic cars (in various states of disrepair) on the expansive and woodsy grounds. Give them a day's notice and they'll pick you up at the end of the SunTran line in Albuquerque.

Stop at one of several restaurants in town and spend the rest of the day exploring Sandia Crest (p68), or continue up the Turquoise Trail, which winds through **Golden**, with an art gallery and lots of gorgeous desert scenery.

Madrid

A bustling company coal-mining town in the 1920s and '30s, Madrid (pronounced *Maa*-drid) was all but abandoned after WWII. In the mid-1970s, the company's heirs sold lots off cheap to tie-dyed wanderers who have built a thriving arts community with galleries and wacky shops. It's not nearly as mellow as you'd think, attracting more bikers than New Agers, but that's just part of the appeal.

The **Old Coal Mine Museum** (☎ 438-3780; 2846 NM 14; adult/child $4/1; ☺ 9:30am-5pm, shorter winter hours – call ahead) preserves plenty of old mining equipment, pretty much right where the miners left it, and hosts the **Madrid Melodrama and Engine House Theatre** (www.madridmelodrama.com; adult/child $10/4 incl marshmallows; ⏰ 2pm & 8pm Sat, 2pm Sun May-Oct) starring a steam locomotive and lots of Wild West desperados, scoundrels and vixens.

Or chat up the modern-day versions at the 1919 **Mine Shaft Tavern** (☎ 473-0743; 2846 NM 14; mains $5-8; ⏰ noon-11pm), with live music on weekends and the 'longest stand-up bar in New Mexico,' built in 1946 and Madrid's favorite attraction ever since. **Mama Lisa's Cafe** (☎ 471-5769; NM 14; snacks $3-7; ⏰ 10am-5pm Fri-Sun) serves good quesadillas and a great red chile chocolate cake.

There are a couple of nice B&Bs in town: one above **Java Junction** (☎ 438-2772; www .java-junction.com; 2855 NM 14; d $69; P ✗ ❂) and **Madrid Lodging** (☎ 471-3450; www .madridlodging.com; 14 Opera House Rd; d $85-105; P ✗ ❂), down the street.

Just north of town, **Madrid Ballpark** (Map p64) hosts wild musical festivals and gatherings like the Gypsy Festival, with fire-eaters and fortune-tellers – you get the idea. Follow the VW buses and bring plenty of water.

Cerrillos

A photographer's dream, with unpaved streets navigating an adobe Old West town relatively unchanged since the 1880s, this is the home of the first mine in North America, built to extract turquoise around AD 100.

Cerrillos Turquoise Mining Museum & Petting Zoo (☎ 438-3008; 17 Waldo St; $2; ⏰ 9am-5pm usually). This top-drawer roadside attraction packs five rooms with mining equipment dating to 3000 BC, plus bottles and

---

DETOUR: SANDIA CREST

Albuquerqueans always know which way is east thanks to 10,678ft Sandia Crest, sacred to Sandia Pueblo and well-named for both its wavelike silhouette and the glorious pink (sandia is Spanish for 'watermelon') its granite cliffs glow at sunset. There are three ways to the top.

Beautiful 8-mile (one-way) **La Luz Trail** (FR 444; parking $3) is the most rewarding, rising 3800ft from the desert, past a small waterfall to pine forests and spectacular views. It gets hot. **Sandia Peak Tramway** (Map p64; ☎ 856-7325; www.sandiapeak.com; Tramway Blvd; adult/child $15/10; ⏰ 9am-9pm daily), the world's longest at 2.7 miles, is the most extravagant route; you can hike up and take the tram down, trekking 2 more miles at the bottom on Tramway Trail to your car.

Finally you can drive, via NM 14, making a quick detour to Tijeras and the **Sandia Ranger Station & Tijeras Archaeological Site** (Map p64; ☎ 281-3304; 11776 Hwy 337; ⏰ 8:30am-5pm daily) for backcountry camping permits, maps, and hiking information, plus a 1-mile stroll through the unreconstructed ruins of a small pueblo.

Jump back on NM 14, then make a left onto Sandia Crest Rd (NM 165), stopping at **Tinkertown Museum** (p67) before heading up the mountain. The road is lined with trailheads and picnic spots (a daily $3 parking fee covers all of them), and low-impact **camping** ($3) is allowed by permit throughout Cibola National Forest. The choices are endless, but don't skip the easy 1-mile roundtrip to **Sandia Man Cave**, where the oldest human encampment in North America was discovered in 1936. Bring a flashlight.

At the top of the mountain, another **ranger station** (Map p64; ☎ 243-0190; NM 165; ⏰ 9:30am-sunset daily May-Oct) offers nature programs four times daily; **Sandia Crest House** (Map p64; ☎ 243-0605; NM 165; mains $3-5; ⏰ 9:30am-sunset daily), in the same building, serves burgers and snacks. This is the jumping-off point for exquisite **Sandia Crest Trail**, which heads 11 miles north and 16 miles south with incredible views; hike north along the ridgeline as long as you'd like to appreciate the best of them.

Take the trail 2 miles south, past **Kiwanis Cabin** rock house, to the tram terminal and **High Finance** (Map p64; ☎ 243-9742; mains $8-26; ⏰ 11am-9pm daily), with mediocre food and more fabulous views.

This is also the site of **Sandia Peak Ski Park** (☎ 242-9052, 800-473-1000; www.sandiapeak.com; lift tickets adult/child $37/28; ⏰ 9am-4pm daily Dec-Mar & Jun-Sep), a smallish but scenic ski area that hasn't seen much snow the past few years. In summer, the park rents **mountain bikes** ($32/38 incl lift tickets) for blazing those downhill runs; note that bikes aren't allowed on the tram.

antiques excavated from an abandoned area hotel, Chinese art, pioneer-era tools and anything else the owners thought was worth displaying. For $2 more you can feed their goats, llamas and unusual chickens.

Continue north on NM 14 until you hit I-25. You can continue on Cerrillos Rd for the last strip-mall– and budget-hotel–lined 7 miles to downtown Santa Fe, or jump on I-25 north for five minutes and take San Francis Rd into town.

Santa Fe

CONTENTS

Artsy and aloof, ancient and tranquil, this town has as many nicknames as personalities. It is the oldest state capital, administrating aspen-fringed peaks, sculpted sandstone deserts and the fertile Rio Grande Valley since before the Pilgrims set sail. It is the City of Holy Faith, where Franciscan friars and their flocks found God in the same. It is the City Different, attracting artists for a century with a quality of light and life unlike any other, and Fanta Sé, where collectors come to gather their work. And, of course, it's good old Santa Fake, with city statutes requiring those adobe exteriors packed with souvenirs for the tourists who love them.

Some say Santa Fe has given up too much of herself to those concha-clad crowds who meander, enchanted, through her narrow gallery-lined streets. But it's just not true. This high desert enclave, her growth long limited by a lack of precious water, remains a beacon of progressive thought and creative culture, committed to the arts like nowhere else and still holding reverent those rituals forgotten by most of this world long before you were born.

Eclectic shrines of mud and straw, with histories both bloody and proud, now house museums and galleries honoring impossibly beautiful creations. There are festivals for art and soul, trails into mountains held sacred for millennia, and houses of worship embracing seekers of every stripe.

Sitting on a portico overlooking the plaza, you may feel a primeval anticipation as summer storm clouds gather. 'Every day I pray for rain,' says one Native refrain, and the manifold deities populating this place may well comply. And after the cooling showers pass, rainbows arcing above now shimmering streets, you'll agree that this is no ordinary destination.

HIGHLIGHTS

- **Museum Hill** Native and Spanish history plus folk art from everywhere else (p79)
- **Institute of American Indian Arts** Exceptional, eclectic Native American art (p80)
- **10,000 Waves** The next best thing to natural hot springs (p99)
- **The Awakening Museum** A single, spectacular masterpiece (p81)
- **Maria Benitez Teatro Flamenco** A moving intensity of dance (p108)
- **Santa Fe Opera** Arias under the stars (p108)
- **Shidoni** Sculptures in their natural habitat (p110)
- **Canyon Road** Acres of fine art (p82)
- **Dale Ball Trails** High desert scenery, right in town (p87)
- **La Fonda** Great art, great stories and spectacular sunsets (p97)

| TELEPHONE CODE: **505** | POPULATION: **65,100** | ELEVATION: **7200FT** |

ORIENTATION

Built long before cars were an issue, downtown Santa Fe, bounded by St Francis Dr to the west and horseshoe-shaped Paseo de Peralta on all other sides, seems to the recent arrival like a warren of narrow, confusing streets, which become narrower and more confusing the closer you get to the plaza. The plaza is most easily accessible via the well-signed turnoff from St Francis Dr.

If you get lost driving in this area, your best bet is to find Paseo de Peralta, which will return you to car-friendly St Francis Dr no matter which way you turn, then follow the signs for another try.

Both Cerrillos (pronounced ser-ree-yos) Rd and St Francis Dr exit I-25 and then intersect at the southern end of downtown, forming a triangle. Cerrillos Rd is a 7-mile, neon-lit strip of motels and businesses, while St Francis Dr takes you more directly to the plaza. Connecting these two main drags are Rodeo Rd, heading west to the airport; St Michael's Dr, with annoying on-ramps; and Cordova Rd, which is very close to downtown.

St Francis Dr becomes US 84/285 north of Santa Fe, connecting the city to Española and points north. Cerrillos Rd is the northernmost stretch of NM 14, also called the Turquoise Trail (p66); you can continue south on Cerrillos Rd past I-25 for the scenic back road to Albuquerque. I-25 South is the fastest route to Albuquerque, while I-25 North actually takes you southeast to Las Vegas, New Mexico.

Paseo de Peralta is the hub for other major roads. Old Santa Fe Trail (which becomes Old Pecos Trail) heads south to I-25 and the old road to Las Vegas. Bishops Lodge Rd (also called Washington Ave; just look for the pink Scottish Rite Temple) runs north to Shidoni and Tesuque, eventually joining US 84/285, or you can make an almost immediate right from Bishops Lodge Rd onto Hyde Park Rd (NM 475, also called Artist Rd) for well-signed access to Hyde Park and Ski Santa Fe.

The train station on Guadalupe St is easily accessible from the plaza on foot but handles primarily tourist excursions and only very limited service connecting to Amtrak. The main train station is 18 miles east in Lamy and is served by a shuttle from Santa Fe

(p113). The bus station is centrally located but miles from the plaza on St Michael's Dr, while the airport is closer to the Cerrillos Rd exit off I-25 than downtown. Both are served by Santa Fe Trails buses.

Maps

The visitors centers stock several free maps, most of them cutesy and advertising-based. If you plan to explore, invest in Rand McNally's *Santa Fe/Taos Local Street Detail* folding street map ($4; it's the green one) with insets covering Española, Las Vegas and Los Alamos. There are several others, available at any gas station, which are almost as good.

Rand McNally also publishes the exhaustive atlas *Albuquerque, Santa Fe & Taos StreetFinder,* but go for the locally produced *Horton Family Map,* a slightly thinner black-and-white book of street maps covering the area.

If you plan to get out into the wilderness, the *New Mexico Road & Recreation Atlas* is indispensable; if you're only going to dip your toes into the great outdoors, the excellent *Highroad Map of North Central New Mexico* is a great, if somewhat outdated, folding map covering Northern New Mexico.

Travel Bug (below) has every map you want or need, including USGS and custom hiking maps, aerial photography, and lots of travel guides.

INFORMATION
Bookstores

Travel Bug (Map pp76-7; ☎ 992-0418; www .mapsofnewmexico.com; 328 S Guadalupe St) With guidebooks to most of the planet and maps covering every inch of New Mexico, this place rules. It may be moving, so call ahead.

Ark Bookstore (☎ 988-3709; 133 Romero St) This place is out to enlighten, covering all your spiritual needs from chakra to chakra.

Garcia Street Books (Map p83; ☎ 986-0151; 376 Garcia St) Shelves packed with heavily illustrated art and architecture books plus lots of rare and unusual offerings could have you perusing for hours. Next door, **Downtown Subscription** has the best newsstand in town.

Photo-Eye Books & Prints (Map p83; ☎ 988-5152; www.photoeye.com; 376 Garcia St) In the same shopping center as Garcia Street Books, Photo-Eye claims (and it's probably true) to stock more photography books than anyplace else in the USA.

Leo's Art Books (Map pp76-7; ☎ 989-7554; 225 Montezuma Ave) Leo has an enormous selection of new and used art books, from verbose histories to sumptuous coffee-table tomes.

Blue Moon Books & Vintage Video (Map pp76-7; ☎ 982-3035; 329 Garfield St) Just try to find a better

collection of new and used New Mexicana, psychedelia, wackidelia and otherwise obscure books anywhere else. Even better, you can rent foreign, artsy, insane and even a few mainstream videos ($4) without membership or ID.

Collected Works Book Store (Map pp76-7; ☎ 988-4226; 208B W San Francisco St) Walls lined with literature, New

SANTA FE IN...

TWO DAYS

After breakfast at Cafe Pasqual's, take in the plaza – it's required, particularly the excellent offerings of the Museum of New Mexico nearby: visit the Museum of Fine Arts (art!), stop at the Palace of the Governors (history!), then inspect the Native American jewelry out front (shopping!). All your official tourist duties are over, and it's not even noon.

Head out on the Walking Tour of Santa Fe, wandering elsewhere if the mood strikes – the route is a suggestion, not an itinerary. Pick up a *Reporter* to see what's on. If nothing strikes your fancy, head to the La Fonda Belltower Bar and watch the sun set.

The next morning, it's up and at 'em with breakfast at Tia Sophia's or coffee at the Aztec. Make reservations at 10,000 Waves, then catch the M-line to Museum Hill, with many options for cultural enrichment – just don't skip the Folk Art Museum. Can't get enough art? Then it's Canyon Rd. Reached art saturation? Then it's the Dale Ball Trails. You've been on your feet for two days, so relax in a hillside hot tub at 10,000 Waves and watch the moon rise over Santa Fe.

THREE DAYS

After two days of wandering the streets of Santa Fe, it's time to get out of town. Hop onto US 285/84 north, pulling over for the photo op at Camel Rock. Take 502 toward Los Alamos, stopping at San Ildefonso Pueblo for fine art and the Maria Poveka Martinez Museum.

Cruise through Los Alamos, aka the Atomic City, pausing at the free Bradbury Museum to learn all about WMDs – it's a blast. Then it's onto Bandelier National Monument for a hike into history and a climb to Ceremonial Cave. Wind your way back past Los Alamos, but veer off 502 onto NM 30 to Española instead, watching the sun set over Black Mesa. Dine on a budget at Angelina's or go all out at El Paragua.

Are you so enchanted that you want to move here? Of course you are. But you'll need money: stop at Cities of Gold Casino and/or Camel Rock Casino and take your best shot. Then it's back to Santa Fe, where you can count your riches or, alternately, spend your last quarters on a brew at the Cowgirl Hall of Fame.

FOUR DAYS

Follow the two-day schedule, but skip 10,000 Waves and catch a show at the Paramount instead. You're headed for the real thing, baby. Wake up, grab coffee and magazines at Downtown Subscription and hit the road. First, brunch at Angelina's in Española. Mmm...chile. Grab some local produce from a roadside stand and keep on to Ojo Caliente Mineral Springs.

Test all the springs and get a massage, then head past El Rito, on the back road to Abiquiú. If you've got the equipment, crash at Rio Chama Campground, 12 miles down CR 151, which will take you an hour. Buy some honey from the Benedictine Monks, then hike, fish and relax.

Forgot your tent? Throw your stuff in a room at the Abiquiú Inn and head to Ghost Ranch. The museums are fine, but you must do Chimney Rock, playing 'Name That O'Keeffe Painting' as you take in the views. The winner gets dinner at the inn.

The next morning, make the detour to San Ildefonso, the Bradbury Museum and Bandelier. And it's back to Santa Fe, perhaps for one last sunset from the Belltower Bar.

SANTA FE

Mexicana and lots of maps make this a fine place to pick up a quality vacation read.

Borders Books & Music (Map pp76-7; ☎ 954-4707; 500 Montezuma Ave) The big chain entry features an expansive selection of Southwestern reading; there's an even larger **branch** (Map p75; ☎ 474-9450; 3513 Zafarano Dr) off Cerrillos Rd.

Emergency

Fire, Police, Ambulance Immediate Dispatch (☎ 911)
Police – non-emergency (☎ 955-5080)
St Vincent Hospital Emergency Room (Map p75; ☎ 820-3934; 455 St Michael's Dr)
Fire & Ambulance Dispatch (☎ 955-5144)
NM Poison Control Center (☎ 800-432-6866)
Santa Fe Rape Crisis Center (☎ 986-9111)
Crisis Response of Santa Fe (☎ 820-6333)

Internet Access

Santa Fe Public Library (Map pp76-7; ☎ 955-6781; 145 Washington Ave) Make reservations for a free half hour of Internet access; if you have to wait, the Cross of the Martyrs (p75) is just a few blocks away.

CD Café (Map pp76-7; ☎ 986-0735; 301 N Guadalupe St) Bonus: you can have coffee and a veggie wrap, or listen to CDs while you surf for $10 per hour.

Internet Resources

City of Santa Fe (http://sfweb.ci.santa-fe.nm.us) This is the city's official website, with information on public transportation and more.

Visit Santa Fe (www.visitsantafe.com) This online guidebook has easy-to-navigate links and reviews.

Santa Fe (www.santafe.org) Definitely on the New Agey side, this site is designed for visitors planning trips for business or pleasure.

Santa Fe EZ (www.santafeez.com) It's pretty basic, but offers comprehensive links to just about every single thing Santa Fe.

Santa Fe Always Online (www.sfaol.com) Articles and links, some of them useful, are just gravy; **Stan's Tuesday Walks**, chronicling Stan's early morning strolls, are what make this a must-click.

Media

PUBLICATIONS

In addition to several lots of free tourist publications available at the visitors centers, including three beautiful gallery guides, there's plenty of great writing and photography lying around.

Santa Fe New Mexican (www.santafenewmexican .com) Santa Fe's daily record has water stats, tourist information, fishing reports and a Saturday 'Directory of Faith Communities' with rundowns on everything from Episcopalian services to Dances of Universal Peace. On Friday, it publishes *Pasatiempo*, a pullout arts and entertainment insert with comprehensive events listings.

Santa Fe Reporter (www.sfreporter.com) This saucy free weekly comes out on Wednesday, with all the events listings, reviews, clever columns and spicy articles you need. The website is frustrating, however.

The Fringe (www.thefringemagazine.com) The newest freebie is mostly a festive, frivolous and funky fashion rag that looks like it might try to take on the *Reporter* one of these days.

Santa Fean (www.santafean.com; $5) Glossy and beautifully illustrated, this monthly magazine has outstanding writing that focuses on the posh side of Santa Fe, including art, history, dining and shopping plus exhaustive listings of events and gallery openings.

Santa Fe Trend (www.santafetrend.com; $5), is a bi-annual 'source for living well,' that aims for an even more exclusive audience.

New Mexico (www.nmmagazine.com; $5) Covering the entire state, it's worth picking up for 'One of Our Fifty is Missing,' a monthly feature relating tales of compatriots unclear about what country New Mexico is in.

Other free monthlies available all over town include *THE magazine*, with arts coverage including reviews of galleries, artists and openings; the *El Dorado Sun* (www.eldoradosun.com), with lefty and green news; *broad issues*, published quarterly by and for the Warehouse 21 crowd (p107); and *The Light*, a sort of New Age publication with the great Dear Louise Hay column, all printed in biodegradable ink.

RADIO

KANW 89.1 FM NPR plus New Mexican and Mexican music.
KUNM 89.9 FM NPR, Native American programming and student DJs spinning wild and free – great stuff.
KSFR 90.7 FM Santa Fe Public Radio: wacky music, lots of jazz and lefty talk radio.
KSLQ 91.5 FM Christian.
KBOM FM 94.7 FM Oldies.
KSFQ 101.1 FM Classic rock.
KIOT 102.5 FM Classic rock with a longer play list.
KTZO 103.3 FM Alternative rock with a six-song play list.
KBAC 104.1 FM Radio Free Santa Fe: great alternative music, but indeed owned by ClearChannel (sigh).
KTEG 104.7 FM Head-banging alternative top 40.
KKOB 770 AM Sanctuary for Michael Savage fans trying to resist the sudden urge to recycle.

(Continued on page 78)

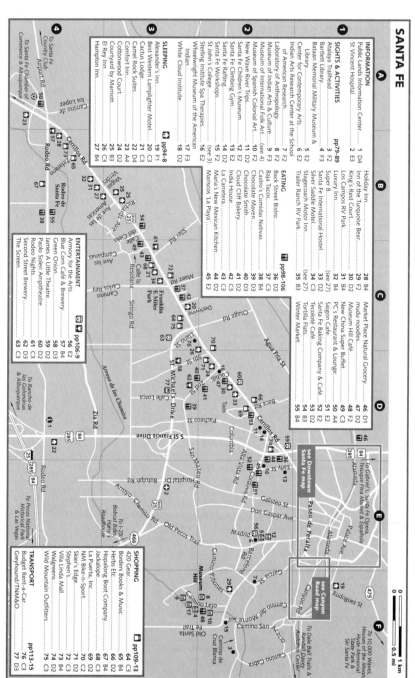

SANTA FE

DOWNTOWN SANTA FE

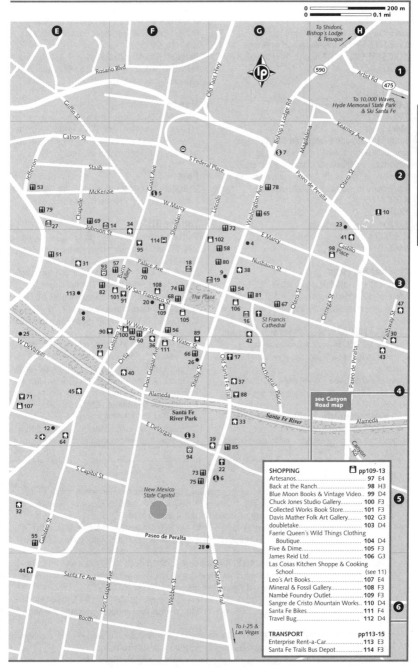

(Continued from page 74)
KSWV 810 AM Mexican and Tex-Mex.
KDCE 950 AM Mariachi, Norteño and Tex-Mex.
KVSF 1260 AM Country oldies and lefty talk radio.
KTRC 1400 AM Local talk radio (there's some weird stuff on this one).

TELEVISION
KASA 2 FOX.
KOB 4 NBC.
KNME 5 PBS.
Santa Fe Community Television 6 or 8 The local community access station is worth watching for the performance art, spiritual talk shows and, best of all, Seven Days in Santa Fe, the *Reporter* rundown on local happenings and area events (5:30pm Fri & Sun).
KAOT 7 ABC.
KRQE 13 CBS.
KAPX 14 Family programming.
KWBQ 19 WB.
KASY 50 UPN.

Medical Services
St Vincent's Hospital (Map p75; ☎ 983-3361, emergency 955-3934; www.stvin.org; 455 St Michael's Dr) This is the major full-service hospital for northern New Mexico.
La Familia Medical Center (☎ 989-5934, emergency 982-4425; 1035 Alto St) You'll wait in line for quality care, paid up-front on a sliding scale, if you don't have insurance.
Planned Parenthood (☎ 982-3684; 514 Oñate Pl) Make an appointment for women's reproductive health services.
New Mexico Alternative Health Center (Map pp76-7; ☎ 983-3003; 436 Cerrillos Rd) Chinese medicine, acupuncture homeopathy, midwifery and more are available.

Walgreens (Map p75; ☎ 982-4643; 1096 S St Francis Dr) This all-night pharmacy has **another location** (☎ 474-3507; 3298 Cerrillos Rd) that's convenient to the budget hotel strip.
Herbs etc (Map p75; ☎ 888-694-3727; 1345 Cerrillos Rd) Natural medications are available here in both packaged formulas and bulk.

Money
It's a tourist town, and all-too-convenient ATMs are everywhere. **Wells Fargo** (Map pp76-7; ☎ 984-0424; 241 Washington Ave), like most area banks, changes foreign currency.

Post
The **Main Post Office** (Map pp76-7; ☎ 988-6351; 120 S Federal Place) is convenient to the plaza.

Tourist Offices
Visitors Center (Map pp76-7; ☎ 827-7336; 491 Old Santa Fe Trail; ☽ 8am-5pm daily) Housed in the historic 1878 Lamy Building (site of the state's first private college), this friendly place has flyers, information, a hotel reservation line, free coffee and even free Internet access on one slow computer. There's a much smaller, but more convenient, **visitors center** (Map pp76-7; ☎ 955-6200, 800-777-2489; 201 W Marcy St; ☽ 8am-5pm Mon-Fri) at the Sweeney Convention Center.
Santa Fe Chamber of Commerce (Map p116; ☎ 983-7317; www.santafechamber.com; 8380 Cerrillos Rd; ☽ 8am-5pm daily) Inconveniently located at the Cerrillos exit from I-25, in the Premium Outlet Mall, this office has information geared toward residents and visitors.
Public Lands Information Center (Map p75; ☎ 438-7542, 877-276-9404; www.publiclands.org; 1474 Rodeo Rd; ☽ 9am-4:30pm Mon-Fri) Come here first for comprehensive information about all state and national

---

RESEARCHING SANTA FE

In this city, where everything is 'the oldest,' genealogists, historians and the merely curious enjoy access to some unusual resources. The Museum of New Mexico operates four free, nonlending libraries, each jam-packed with dusty treasures for those willing to look.

Angélico Chávez History Library (Map pp76-7; ☎ 476-5090; 120 Washington Ave; ☽ 1-5pm Mon-Fri) More than 500,000 historic photos and images plus maps, land grants and other original documents chronicle the state's Hispanic history.

Museum of Fine Arts Library & Archives (Map pp76-7; ☎ 476-5061; 107 W Palace Ave; ☽ 8:30am-4:30pm Mon-Fri) Tons (literally) of information on New Mexico artists collected since 1917 are archived with 5000 tomes pertaining to the state's creative culture.

Laboratory of Anthropology (Map p75; ☎ 476-1264; Camino Lejo; ☽ 10am-noon & 1-5pm Mon-Fri) On Museum Hill, this collection of 25,000 books and 8000 photos concentrates on Native American history.

Bartlett Library (Map p75; ☎ 476-1210; Camino Lejo; ☽ 10am-noon & 1-5pm daily) Photos, archives, audiotapes and more than 15,000 books cover the world's folk art traditions.

parks, national monuments and BLM lands; hunting, fishing and backcountry camping permits; up-to-date information on trails, roads and closures (a list is posted on the door); and a wide selection of books and maps.

New Mexico State Parks (Map pp76-7; ☎ 827-1470; www.nmparks.com; 141 E DeVargas St; ☺ 8am-4pm Mon-Fri) This office has information on all state parks and recreation areas, but they can't reserve campsites.

SIGHTS

The biggest news in Santa Fe is the completion of **Museum Hill**, with four excellent museums, a research library and recommended café, all linked by a sculpture-lined trail. Almost 3 miles southwest of the plaza, it would be silly to walk this far, so take the M Line – a Santa Fe Trails (p114) bus geared toward visitors – that winds through historic neighborhoods.

Most museums and other attractions offer discounts to senior citizens as well New Mexico residents, at least on certain days of the week.

Museum of New Mexico

A collection of four very different **museums** (☎ 827-6463; www.museumofnewmexico.org; $7 for one museum, $15 for a four-day pass to all four, children under 16 free; ☺ 10am-5pm Tue-Sun), two of them on Museum Hill, also offer seminars, musical events and a variety of guided tours with historic or artistic focuses, many designed for children. Both the Palace of the Governors and Museum of Fine Arts, the two located on the plaza, are free on Friday from 5pm to 8pm. All the museums have fabulous gift shops.

PALACE OF THE GOVERNORS

Begin your voyage into Santa Fe's rich past right here (Map pp76-7; ☎ 476-5100; www.palaceof thegovernors.org; 105 E Palace Ave), built in 1610 as the Casas Reales (Royal Houses) and home to 60 state governors before becoming a museum in 1909.

This is where Spanish colonists waited out the Pueblo Revolt of 1680, and where Governor Lew Wallace wrote part of *Ben Hur* right inside. This is also where the first director, Jesse L Nusbaum, displayed the first public collection of Native artifacts west of the Mississippi, an exhibit that's been reinstalled alongside many other treasures: a state seal made entirely of recycled hardware and cutlery, religious items brought by early Jewish settlers, 400-year-old Spanish armor and the impressive Segesser Hide Paintings, which portray a bitter 1720s battle between Spanish and French-Indian coalition forces.

Volunteers lead free, highly recommended **palace tours** throughout the day; call ahead for exact times. Volunteers also lead downtown **walking tours** (p91).

The **Portal Program** (www.newmexicoindianart .org) allows artisans with tribal enrollment to sell jewelry and art in front of the palace. It's a tradition that began in the 1880s, when Tesuque artisans began meeting the train with all manner of wares; today up to 1200 members representing almost every New Mexico tribe draw lots for 76 spaces beneath the vigas each morning; the rest fan out across downtown to ply their work.

MUSEUM OF FINE ARTS

Brush up on your knowledge of New Mexico's manifold artists and art movements at the country's oldest contemporary arts museum (Map pp76-7; ☎ 476-5072; 107 W Palace Ave). The 1917 building is itself among the finest examples of pueblo revival architecture anywhere and served as a starting point from which architects like John Gaw Meem (p81) would go on to transform the city.

With more than 20,000 pieces – including collections of the Taos Society of Artists (p151), Santa Fe Society of Artists, Los Cincos Pintores and other legendary collectives – it's a who's who of the geniuses who put this dusty town on par with Paris and New York. Docents, who give **tours** (☺ 1:30pm daily), are far less likely to roll their eyes than gallery owners while you're learning to appreciate the state's finest offerings.

The museum also hosts chamber music concerts from July through August in **St Francis Auditorium**, an elegant venue designed to look like the interior of a Spanish mission.

MUSEUM OF INDIAN ARTS & CULTURE

Impressive displays, almost installation art pieces, were designed by Diné (Navajo), Hopi, Apache and Pueblo tribal members for this excellent museum (Map p75; ☎ 476-1250; www.miaclab.org; Camino Lejo). Exhibits draw you through 10,000 years of Indian history, from efficient hide tents perfect for the nomadic lifestyle and adobe apartment complexes that grew along with regional agriculture, to modern, HUD-approved hogans with pre-fab kitchens stocking Navajo tacos and government-issued 'Wheat Square Cereal.' The juxtaposition of centuries is jarring.

Your introduction to Native America comprises incredible art, from the ancient and antique to 1960s psychedelic, including instruments, jewelry and an 1885 traditional Navajo blanket emblazoned with steam trains. There's also a great display on the WWII code talkers.

All the exhibits are accompanied by informative and sometimes sobering testimonials from the elders who have lived through so many changes. It's a must. There are guided **tours** (10:30am, 1:30 & 3pm daily).

MUSEUM OF INTERNATIONAL FOLK ART
Prepare to have your mind blown: no craft was too colorful, no medium too wacky, no object too insane to have been considered collectible by the eccentric Alexander Girard, who donated his cultural treasure trove to found this wonderful museum (Map p75; 476-1200; www.moifa.org; Camino Lejo).

More than 100,000 objects pack the place, arranged without regard for time or place but rather by the spirit of the piece. The beadwork of Victorian England is alongside that of West Africa; castles of Mexican tin preside over townships of Chinese ceramic; rooms and rooms of outrageous crafts and toys hail from scores of countries. Kids go crazy (or catatonic) at the sight.

'The whole world is my hometown,' Girard would often quote, a sentiment every wanderer understands. Excellent traveling exhibitions are shown in galleries adjacent to those celebrating Native American and Hispanic crafts, but don't miss Lloyd's Treasure Chest, downstairs, where out-of-rotation pieces are stored. There are also guided **tours** (10:15am & 2pm daily).

Other Museums
GEORGIA O'KEEFFE MUSEUM
Possessing the largest collection of the master painter's work in the world, this museum (Map pp76-7; 946-1000; www.okeeffemuseum.org; 217 Johnson St; $8, free for students & 5-8pm Fri; 10am-5pm Sat-Thu,

10am-8pm Fri) will move even the most casual O'Keeffe (p125) fans. Her thick brushwork and luminous colors don't always come through on the peeling posters you've kept since college; relish them here firsthand.

You'll recognize some of the canvasses straight away: *Abstraction White Rose* (1927) and *Jimson Weed* (1932) are practically cultural icons. And if you've already visited Abiquiú (p125), O'Keeffe's home for half a century, you'll marvel at how her artistic vision was able to render the area's ghostly intangibles, woven into landscapes and bones.

Docents lead free **tours** (four daily), and for $5 you can rent an audio guide.

INSTITUTE OF AMERICAN INDIAN ARTS MUSEUM
Primarily showing work by students and faculty of the esteemed four-year Institute of American Indian Arts, this revealing museum (Map pp76-7; 983-8900; www.iaiancad.org; 108 Cathedral Place; adult/child $4/2; 9am-5pm daily) also features the finest offerings of Native artists from tribes across the USA. It's eclectic: traditional weavings, basketry and jewelry are juxtaposed with more modern statements, like instructor Charlene Teters' stark red-and-black image of President Bush as General Custer, complete with Apache helicopters in the background.

The work can be uneven – this is a student gallery, after all – but much of it is spectacular, and all offer insight into the evolution and integration of classical techniques and symbolism into a contemporary culture, consciously developing on its own terms. The attached **Allen Hauser Art Park** also has sculptures by Michael Naranjo (p120) and others. The five-star gift shop features work by alumni plus plenty of Native kitsch.

WHEELWRIGHT MUSEUM OF THE AMERICAN INDIAN
Another Museum Hill entry, this collection (Map p75; 982-4636, 800-607-4636; www.wheelwright.org; 704 Camino Lejo; donations appreciated; 10am-5pm Mon-Sat, 1-5pm Sun) offers three galleries packed with rotating exhibitions of Native American art, both historic and modern.

The eight-sided Hogan-style structure once housed a collection of Navajo ceremonial art, though most was eventually returned to the tribe. Many events are geared toward kids, including free storytelling by area elders and the All Children's Powwow, held in October, designed to introduce kids to Native culture.

MUSEUM OF SPANISH COLONIAL ART

Museum Hill's newest and smallest entry (Map p75; ☎ 982-2226; www.spanishcolonial.org; 750 Camino Lejo; $6/3 adult/child; ☉ 10am-5pm Tue-Sun), in one of John Gaw Meem's finest buildings, traces the history of Spanish New Mexico. Straw appliqué, a craft popular among gold-poor settlers who still wanted their religious objects to gleam, joins jewelry and other treasures that made the three-year trip from Spain, as well as contemporary pieces like Nicolás Herrera's *Y2K Death Cart*, a motorcycle-riding skeleton

The surreal collection of santos, retablos and bultos includes not only New Mexican examples, but also pieces from Spain, Brazil, Mexico and many other countries. There are guided **tours** (☉ 10:30am & 2:30pm).

BATAAN MEMORIAL MILITARY MUSEUM & LIBRARY

A labor of both love and war, this unusual collection of military mementoes (Map p75; ☎ 474-1670; 1050 Old Pecos Trail; by donation; ☉ 9am-4pm Tue, Wed & Fri, 9am-1pm Sat) began in 1947 as a display in the state capitol honoring the 'Battling Bastards of Bataan.'

Today the museum occupies the former home base of the NM 200th Coast Artillery,

captured when the Japanese invaded the Philippines in 1942, and the very last unit to surrender. Some 70,000 POWs, most Filipino, were forced to walk the brutal, 75-mile Bataan Death March. Of 1800 mostly Hispanic New Mexicans stationed in Bataan, only 900 returned.

In addition to exhibits that tell their story, interesting examples of psychological-warfare leaflets from WWII to the first Gulf War plaster the walls, along with an amazing collection of military patches. Uniforms, weaponry and other gear date as far back as the Spanish conquest. It's the old photos and letters, however, that really hammer the point home.

THE AWAKENING MUSEUM

This isn't a museum so much as a shrine (Map pp76-7; ☎ 989-7636; www.theawakeningmuseum .com; 125 N Guadalupe St; adult/child $3/free; ☉ 10am-6pm daily). Some 8000 sq ft of mahogany panels, originally covering the interior of a West Virginia gymnasium, are emblazoned with artist Jean-Claude Gaugy's roughly hewn, gem-toned figures. Thirteen years of his life were poured into this chronicle of the Passion of Christ, the State of Grace and the Book of Revelations, all of them exploding around you. There is no crucifixion here, only resurrection. And you can touch it.

A recommended audiotape explains the imagery in detail, while **Gaugy Gallery** *(Continued on page 84)*

JOHN GAW MEEM *By Bridgette Wagner*

The father of pueblo revival style, architect John Gaw Meem was instrumental in building Santa Fe. Meem came, like so many others, to convalesce from tuberculosis, then fell in love with 'those graceful little mud houses everybody lives in.' After his recovery he left to study architecture, returning two years later to open up shop.

Only a few years had passed since the city had passed the controversial 1912 adobe-only building laws. Meem took the side of the preservationists and developed architectural designs and methods based on pueblo architecture. He got a few jobs designing homes, including that of writer Mary Austin, but it was the 1928 commission for Maria Vilura Conkey that ignited his career. By combining the vigas, beams and rounded corners of the Spanish pueblo revival with the brick cornices, white painted windows and tall posts of the Territorial Revival, Meem inspired a renaissance in Southwestern architecture.

Meem was contracted to design the Laboratory of Anthropology, refurbish La Fonda Hotel and build the Museum of Spanish Colonial Art in Santa Fe, Fuller Lodge in Los Alamos, and more than 35 buildings at UNM's Albuquerque campus. His projects also included restoring the missions at Laguna and Santa Ana Pueblos. Meem's architectural elements have since become popular throughout the Southwest, but remain quintessentially Santa Fe style.

EXPLORING CANYON ROAD

Once a footpath used by Pueblo Indians, then the main street through a Spanish farming community, Canyon Rd began its current incarnation – as art gallery central – in the 1920s: artists led by Los Cincos Pintores (p32) moved in to take advantage of the cheap rent.

Believe it or not, this opulent stretch of painstakingly remodeled adobes was, until rather recently, the 'hood. Kids of struggling single moms leveraged out 20 years ago still can't go into excellent **Nüart Gallery** (☎ 988-3888; www.nuartgallery.com; 670 Canyon Rd), now specializing in magical realism, without telling tales of Gormley Market, where they used to buy 10-cent candy.

Today it's a can't-miss attraction: 90+ galleries at the epicenter of the nation's healthiest art scene display rare Indian antiquities, Santa Fe School masterpieces and wild contemporary work. It's a little overwhelming, but sooth your battered brain with the requisite wine and cheese on Friday, at 5pm or so, when glittering art openings clog the narrow street with elegant art collectors (and those cheese-filching starving artists).

Here are just a few favorites on the strip, and check the Shopping section (see p109) for more. A handful of upscale restaurants and a couple cool coffee shops (p99) will sustain you on this most inspiring of hikes, but don't expect to find parking. Bring your walking shoes (and credit cards), and get ready to be blown away.

J Mark Sublette: Medicine Man Gallery (☎ 820-7451; www.medicinemangallery.com; 200 Canyon Rd) It's got more Maria Martinez (p119) pottery than her San Ildefonso museum, quality antique retablos, Navajo blankets and $5000 kachinas, plus artwork by seminal Western landscape artist Maynard Dixon.

Altermann Galleries (☎ 820-1644; www.altermanngalleries.com; 203 Canyon Rd) This is the classic venue for legendary Southwestern fine art – cowboys, Indians and landscapes from (art) household names like Fredric Remington, Kim Wiggins and Charlie Russell.

Adobe Gallery (☎ 955-0550; www.adobegallery.com; 221 Canyon Rd) This gallery includes pieces by the 'Five Matriarchs' of the pueblo pottery renaissance: Maria Martinez, Margaret Tofoya, Maria Nampeyo, Lucy Lewis and Helen Cordero, among many other famed Indian artisans.

Pachamama (☎ 983-4020; 223 Canyon Rd) From $5 milagrosas to $50,000 santos and retablos, there's something for everyone in this vibrant collection of Latin American folk art.

Minkay Andean Art (☎ 820-2210; www.minkay.com; 223 Canyon Rd) Andean textiles and art are eclipsed by the outlandish work of Nicario Jimenez, whose obsessively detailed sculptures, populated by saucy subjects rendered from potato paste, are in the permanent Museum of Folk Art (p80) collection.

Hahn-Ross Gallery (☎ 984-8434; 409 Canyon Rd) You'll be floored by this carnival of color: Jose Rodriguez' surreal portraits, Dirk Kortz' meditations on violence and religion, and owner Elizabeth Hahn's vividly colored animals – amazing.

Carol LaRoche Gallery (☎ 982-1186; www.laroche-gallery.com; 701 Canyon Rd), Children are entranced by the engaging wolves, tigers and other engaging animals ready to stare you down.

Canfield Modern Art (☎ 988-4199; 414 Canyon Rd) It's modern art – the challenging kind, which can be a little unnerving – from top Taos and Santa Fe artists of the post WWII era.

Economos (☎ 982-6347; 500 Canyon Rd) This is where museums come to purchase fantastic examples of retablos, ancient Native American art, pre-Columbian Mexican pieces and much, much more, all crammed onto two huge floors aswirl with history.

Pushkin Gallery (☎ 982-1990; www.pushkingallery.com; 550 Canyon Rd) Owned by the family of poet Alexander Pushkin, this gallery shows Russian masters including Nikolai Timkov and Vasily Golubev, who are outshined by newcomer Alexy Smirnov Vókressensky; museum-quality Orthodox icons and lacquer boxes are also on display.

Alene Lapides Gallery (☎ 944-0191; 558 Canyon Rd) Amazing New Mexican contemporary artists, including Marcia Meyers, James Harvard and wildlife photographer Peter Beard, show their weird and wonderful work here.

Zaplin-Lampert Gallery (☎ 982-6100; www.zaplinlampert.com; 651 Canyon Rd) The renowned collection of Santa Fe and Taos School masters is nothing short of phenomenal – check out the Gene Kloss prints. Downstairs, **Frank's Annex** sells less expensive (say, $1200-6000) pieces by the same big names.

Studio of Gian Andrea (☎ 982-0054; 626 Canyon Rd) Religious iconographer, sculptor and ceramicist Drew Bacigalupa has been working and showing in these funky digs since 1956, shaking his head at the other upscale offerings and saying, 'Sometimes I feel like I've seen 50 Canyon Roads.' But a piece of the past lives on right here.

Kania-Ferrin Gallery (☎ 982-8767; 662 Canyon Rd) Though pottery has enjoyed a renaissance, Native American basketry is rare – but not here. Antique and high-quality basketry from 1870–1940, from the Southwest and Pacific coast, are on display.

Chiaroscuro Gallery (☎ 986-9197; 708 Canyon Rd) This sophisticated and often abstract collection, starring painter Kevin Sloan, who tattoos the harshest human experiences with dignity in the defense of innocence, features modernism in every medium.

Artisan Santa Fe (☎ 751-0802; www.artisan-santafe.com; 717 Canyon Rd) If this top art-supply shop's selection of oils, pastels, watercolors and canvases was good enough for Georgia O'Keeffe, it's good enough for you.

Turner Caroll Gallery (☎ 986-9800; 725 Canyon Rd) From Richard Campiglio's wacky takes on Dutch hyperrealism to Michael Berg's amusing and incredible figurative sculptures, this is fine art with a fabulous sense of humor.

The Stables (821 Canyon Rd) This cool collection of studio/galleries is where you can still see artists at work: standouts include the **Japanese Tea House** (☎ 983-9426) with excellent and affordable hand-thrown pottery, and the amazing **Ed Larson Studio,** with illustrated political poetry and the biggest, bestest fish around, all right under the sign reading, 'Jesus said buy folk art.'

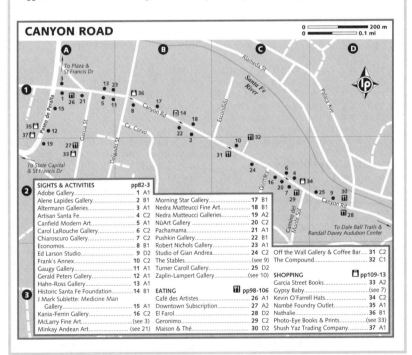

CANYON ROAD

0 — 200 m
0 — 0.1 mi

SANTA FE

(Continued from page 78)
(Map p83; ☎ 984-2800; 418 Canyon Rd) has more examples of this fine artist's work.

SANTA FE CHILDREN'S MUSEUM

Reward younger kids for suffering through that scenic walking tour by bringing them here (Map p75; ☎ 989-8359; www.santafe childrensmuseum.org; 1050 Old Pecos Trail; adult/child $4/3; ☺ 10am-5pm Mon-Sat, noon-5pm Sun) to hang out with locals they can relate to. Giant bubble makers, craft stations and climbing equipment are great for working off all that excess energy, and even more opportunities for play exist outside.

The museum runs daily two-hour **programs** (☺ usually 10am or 2:30pm), led by local scientists, artists and teachers, which take on subjects like solar energy and printmaking. Staff occasionally offer hiking trips and overnight activities.

EL MUSEO CULTURAL DE SANTA FE

Founded on the site of the Santa Fe Railyard in 1998, this kid-friendly spot (Map pp76-7; ☎ 992-0591; www.elmuseocultural.org; 1615B Paseo de Peralta; admission free; ☺ 1-5pm Tue-Fri, 10am-5pm Sat) is a museum, gallery, performance space and community arts center designed for area Hispanic youth. With exhibits by internationally known artists and others still in grade school, plus all manner of displays geared toward home-schooled kids, this is a great place to introduce your own children to la cultura nuevomexicana. The huge warehouse space hosts art openings, live music and theater.

HISTORIC SANTA FE FOUNDATION

On the site of El Zagúan (Map p83; ☎ 983-2567; www.historicsantafe.com; 545 Canyon Rd; donations appreciated; ☺ 10am-4pm Tue-Sun), an expansive territorial-style mansion purchased in 1849 by Anglo entrepreneur James Johnson, this unassuming little museum on Canyon Rd has a few interesting exhibits – old photos, potsherds and whatnot. The expansive gardens outside are also worth a look.

RANCHO DE LAS GOLONDRINAS

About 15 miles south of downtown Santa Fe, in the town of La Cienega, this grassy oasis has been a popular overnight for weary travelers for at least 10,000 years, and many of the historic structures housing

this living-history museum (☎ 471-2261; www .golondrinas.org; 334 Los Pinos Rd, La Cienega; adult/child $5/2, more during some events; ☺ 10am-4pm Wed-Sun Jun-Sep) were built by Spanish explorers who fortified the area in 1625.

The 200-acre preserve has rescued dozens more original Spanish buildings from the bulldozers of progress and brought them from all over the Southwest for respectful renovation. Volunteers use centuries-old equipment to re-create colonial life, and blacksmiths, weavers and lots of cuddly livestock – including rare Churro sheep sheared annually at the Spring Festival, in early June – keep the kids entertained.

Special events include Civil War reenactments, a popular Wine Festival in July and a Harvest Festival in October with dancing, grape crushing, an arts market and more. Kids aged seven to 12 and accompanying adults can go on **Josefina's guided tours** (☎ 471-2261; $20; dates vary), which include snacks and craft making. To get here, take I-25 south from Santa Fe to exit 276, making a hard right at NM 599; the route is well signed.

HISTORIC LINE CAMP GALLERY & HUICHOL INDIAN MUSEUM

About 15 miles north of Santa Fe, this bizarre gift shop and museum (Map p116; ☎ 455-3600; www.tribesgallery.com; US 84/285; $1; ☺ 10:30am-6pm Tue-Sun) claims the largest collection of Huichol Indian art in North America: *Nearika,* unbroken strands of colorful yarn coiled into tales of life and death, and *chaquira,* sculptures of animals covered in tiny, obsessively patterned beads, are said to depict the understandably bizarre dreams of the 'People of Peyote.' Westerners didn't encounter the tribe, which lives in a remote region of the Sierra Madre, until the 1930s.

The small museum has a video as well as artifacts, including clothing, musical instruments, old photos and art, but the most impressive pieces are on sale in the gallery.

Churches

The original Spanish settlers drawn to the City of Holy Faith were a devout bunch, and Santa Fe boasts many of the nation's oldest and finest Catholic churches, many with miracles adorning their rich histories.

ST FRANCIS CATHEDRAL

Archbishop Jean-Baptiste Lamy had a dream to build a French Romanesque cathedral (Map pp76-7; ☎ 982-5619; 213 Cathedral Place; admission free; ☽ 6am-6pm daily; mass 7am & 5pm Mon-Sat, 8am, 10am & noon Sun; confession 3-5pm Sat) worthy of any archdiocese back in Europe, right here in Santa Fe. From 1869 to 1886, imported artists and architects (Lamy wasn't too fond of local retablo-style decor) erected one of the city's most enduring symbols.

The archbishop, buried beneath the altar, didn't survive to see its completion; indeed, original plans called for spires that have yet to be added. Massive bronze doors chronicle the centuries (and martyrs) of New Mexican Catholicism, and above them, the tetragrammaton, reading 'JHVH,' honors the area's Jewish community.

The cathedral was built on the site of the small, adobe **Our Lady of the Rosary Chapel**, extant on the northeast side of the cathedral, honoring the USA's Oldest Madonna, 'La Conquistadora,' declared New Mexico's Patron Saint in 1770. Originally brought from Mexico in 1625, the statuette was rescued shortly before the Pueblo Revolt of 1680 by Josefina Lopez, who abandoned her own possessions and carried the effigy all the way to El Paso.

After negotiations with Pueblo leadership were resolved in 1692, DeVargas led some 70 families on the arduous trek back home. Upon hitting La Bajada, the steep escarpment that still overheats cars on I-25, the caravan got stuck. Hopeless and cold, DeVargas made a vow: if the Virgin would just get his oxen moving, he'd build her a chapel in Santa Fe. Almost immediately, his charges were released from the mud.

During Fiestas (p92), La Conquistadora is still carried in procession around the old city. The rest of the year she resides, surrounded by fine retablos, in the cathedral. The small **Archdiocese of Santa Fe Museum** (☎ 983-3811; 223 Cathedral Pl; donations appreciated; ☽ 9am-4pm Mon-Fri) has more information, and there are pleasant gardens out back.

LORETTO CHAPEL

This small Gothic chapel (Map pp76-7; ☎ 982-0092; www.lorettochapel.com; 207 Old Santa Fe Trail; $2; ☽ 9am-6pm daily summer, 9am-5pm daily winter),

modeled after Sainte Chapelle in Paris, was also commissioned by Archbishop Lamy. But when architect Projectus Mouly (hired after his father, the original architect, went blind) began 'courting' the archbishop's niece-in-law, well, the chapel was left without an architect. And a staircase. And so the Sisters of Loretto prayed to St Joseph, patron of carpenters, for divine intercession, or at least something to replace the darned ladder.

Sure enough, a mysterious man with a burro, T-square and hammer appeared, asking for two tubs of water and perfect solitude. The sisters complied, and using neither nails nor any obvious support structure, the white-haired stranger completed the famously graceful spiral staircase. Then he disappeared. Of course.

Today **St Joseph's Miraculous Staircase** is popular among tourists and wedding photographers, but regular services are no longer held here. The adjacent gift shop is packed with Catholic kitsch.

SAN MIGUEL MISSION

Enter through the gift shop to experience what's probably *not* quite the oldest church in the USA (Map pp76-7; ☎ 983-3974; 401 Old Santa Fe Trail; $1; ☽ 9am-5pm Mon-Sat, 10am-4pm Sun; mass 5pm Sun), as the folks down in Acoma (p59) will explain. Still, the adobe walls of this house of worship have watched Santa Fe grow since 1610.

Tlaxcalan Indian servants brought here by Fray Alonso de Benavidez constructed the church atop even older Native structures; this is also where, according to legend, the 1680 Pueblo Revolt began with the burning of its original patron saint.

Artistic treasures abound, including the 17th-century statue of St Michael and an intricate 1789 reredo, but the most famous artifact is the **San Jose Bell**, cast in the 14th century in Andalusia, Spain.

SANTUARIO DE GUADALUPE

This humble adobe chapel (Map pp76-7; ☎ 988-2027; 100 Guadalupe St; admission free; ☽ 9am-4pm Mon-Sat) looks much as it did when it was built between 1776 and 1796 but has actually gone through several transformations since then. You can see photos of its previous and very different facades, as well as what remains of the original, 200-year-old adobe walls, in the tiny **museum**. It's the oldest shrine to the Virgin of Guadalupe in the USA.

The star attraction is the amazing **altar piece**, brought here from Mexico City by José de Alzíbar in 1783.

CROSS OF THE MARTYRS

More a quick climb than religious shrine, the cross (Map p76; Paseo de Peralta btwn Marcy & Otero Sts) was erected to commemorate the 21 Franciscan friars who lost their lives in the Pueblo Revolt of 1680. Historic plaques explain 400 years of Santa Fe history, and the view from the top really makes you appreciate those adobe-only laws.

Other Attractions

INDIAN ARTS RESEARCH CENTER AT THE SCHOOL OF AMERICAN RESEARCH

Make reservations to tour this vaulted collection (Map p75; ☎ 954-7205; www.sarweb.org/iarc/iarc.htm; 660 Garcia St; $15 tour; ☒ 2pm Fri) of more than 11,000 Native American artifacts, much of it pre-colonial, including textiles, baskets, jewelry and lots of pottery. It's not really displayed for public consumption, which makes the tour through the climate-controlled collection that much more interesting; you'll be surrounded by shelves packed with remnants of a time long past. The **gift shop** (☒ 8am-5pm daily) has an outstanding collection of books by associates and faculty members.

SITE SANTA FE

Enormous, whitewashed spaces (Map pp76-7; ☎ 989-1199; www.sitesantafe.org; 1606 Paseo de Peralta; adult/child $5/3, admission free Fri; ☒ 10am-5pm Wed-Sun, 10am-7pm Fri) are perfect for radical installation pieces (for example, gigantic, plastic-extruding 'art-making machines') and painters who love a large scale. The hybrid museum-gallery space offers **guided tours** (☒ 6pm Fri, 2pm Sat & Sun) and hosts wine-splashed openings, artist talks, movie screenings and performances of all kinds. It's the ultimate cure for Canyon Rd overkill.

NEW MEXICO STATE CAPITOL

Inside the Zia-shaped (check out the inlaid marble floor) 'Roundhouse' (Map pp76-7; ☎ 986-4589; cnr Paseo de Peralta & Old Santa Fe Trail; admission free; ☒ 8am-5pm Mon-Fri) is one of the best art collections in New Mexico – and it's free!

There are **guided tours** (10am & 2pm), or you can grab a flyer with a bare-bones self-guided tour at the visitors desk, then peruse hundreds of sculptures, paintings and photos by the state's best- (and least-) known artists.

PLANETARIUM

Take advantage of the area's altitude and aridity at the Santa Fe Community College Planetarium (☎ 428-1777; Richards Dr; adult/child $5/3), which holds indoor programs investigating everything from dark matter to archeoastronomy (the study of celestial mythology, popular among Geminis) in the planetarium, and outdoor tours of the skies outside after dark. Programs and times vary, so call ahead.

ACTIVITIES

You could easily spend a week or three exploring the museums, churches, galleries and shops of Santa Fe, and you'd have a fabulous vacation. But some would argue that you had missed the best part.

Hiking

The **Public Lands Information Center** (p78) has information on area hikes, including a free copy of *Day Hikes Closest to Santa Fe*, compiled from Craig Martin's *Bike & Hike* column in the *New Mexican*. Also check out *Day Hikes in the Santa Fe Area*, published by the **Sierra Club** (☎ 983-2703; 621 Old Santa Fe Trail); hours and events vary, but schedules for guided day hikes and other activities are posted outside. Several multiuse trails are listed below, under Mountain Biking.

RANDALL DAVEY AUDUBON CENTER

Protecting 135 acres along the acequias of Santa Fe Canyon, just 3 miles north of the plaza, this preserve's **visitors center** (☎ 983-4609; 1800 Upper Canyon Rd; trail-use $1; ☒ 9am-4pm Mon-Fri, 8am-5pm Sat & Sun) has information on the juniper and piñon forest's coyotes, bobcats and other wildlife. It's close to the trailhead for the half-mile interpretive **El Temporal Trail** and the 3-mile roundtrip **Bear Canyon Trail**, which leads into the steep-sided canyon itself.

Guided tours are also available at the 1847 **Randall Davey Home** ($5; ☒ 2pm Mon), with a small but excellent collection of Spanish art and antiques. Plus, there are 1½-hour

guided bird walks and nature walks (admission free; 🕑 some Sat mornings); call in advance.

DALE BALL TRAILS

A great opportunity for day hikers and intermediate mountain bikers (the switchbacks can be challenging, particularly the South Trails), the recently constructed **North and South Dale Ball Trails** (☎ 827-7173) run more than 20 miles to circumnavigate some of Santa Fe's most exclusive neighborhoods, eventually winding past the 'no trespassing' signs to views of unspoiled mountains and deserts. Trails range from several 3-mile loops to a 1500ft climb to Picasho Peak. Eventually the trail hooks into **Atalaya** and **Windsor Trails** (p88), creating an unparalleled opportunity for urban adventure, just a 10-minute bike ride from the plaza.

To get here, follow Upper Canyon Rd north to the well-signed parking lot at Cerro Gordo Rd, or follow Hyde Park Rd and make a left on Sierra del Norte, then park on your right.

HYDE MEMORIAL STATE PARK

Eight miles north of Santa Fe, New Mexico's highest state park (9400ft) offers several hikes through its 350 acres of aspen and pine. The **visitors center** (☎ 983-7175; 740 Hyde Park Rd; day use $4) has information and is close to the trailhead for 3-mile **Hyde Park Circle Trail**, with a 1000ft elevation gain to views of the Sangre de Cristos.

Chamiza Trail Loops begin about 1 mile southwest of the visitors center, following a picturesque canyon to join up with the Windsor Trail after 3 miles; you can hike 5 miles to Big Tesuque campground (p95) for a 1400ft elevation gain and more aspen views.

Bear Wallow Trail begins just north of the visitors center, at the parking lot on the northern edge of the park, and is the first leg of the Triangle Trails, joining Windsor and Borrego Trails for what could be a 4-mile loop or a serious 8-mile hike into the wilderness.

BISHOP'S LODGE RESORT & SPA

This luxury resort (p98) sits astride 450 acres of classic high desert piñon forest, with spectacular views from the 7700ft crest, and graciously allows free public access to scenic trails, many of which are tame enough for smaller kids. The staff do ask that you check in at the lodge (hey, there's a shooting range out there), where they'll give you maps and trail information.

Skiing

Sure, Taos Ski Valley gets all the glory, but **Ski Santa Fe** (Map p116; ☎ 982-4429, snow report 983-9155; www.skisantafe.com; lift tickets adult/child $44/32; 🕑 9am-4pm daily Thanksgiving-Easter) delivers you to the highest skiable peak in the state – 12,003ft. The setting atop the Sangre de Cristos is breathtaking, the runs

---

ZIA SUNSET?

It's on the flag. It's on the license plate. Heck, it's the 'o' on the sign at that sleazy motel where you'll never stay again. It's the ubiquitous Zia sun symbol, sacred to Keresen-speaking Zia Pueblo, where the pot emblazoned with the emblem was first found.

New Mexico adopted the Zia as its state symbol in 1925, inspired by its four-fold meaning: the four directions, the four seasons, the four times of day and the four ages of man – well, according to the pamphlet describing the Zia-shaped state capitol, anyway. Zia Pueblo elders have no comment.

They have, however, made one thing very clear: 'The people of Zia were never compensated or consulted about the use of the Zia sun symbol,' Zia Governor Amado Shije told the state legislature in 1999, adding that the sign had been 'diminished by its casual use.' The tribe then requested $74 million in compensation, $1 million for every year the Zia had been in official use.

The battle raged quietly for three years, reaching a temporary stalemate in 2001, when legislators formed a committee to discuss the issue further. In the meantime, you can still pick up key chains, shot glasses and other Zia-covered kitsch anywhere, or even fly here in a Zia-clad plane.

Southwest Airlines actually approached Zia Pueblo in 2000 with a request to use the sacred symbol. And, after making a hefty donation to the pueblo's college fund, the company was granted not only permission, but also a prayer by Zia elders when the plane was commissioned. It's just amazing what respect for culture – and copyrights – will get you.

are challenging and, best of all, it's only 16 miles from downtown Santa Fe.

With 44 runs, a 1600ft vertical drop and about 225 inches of snow per year, this is serious skiing – and unlike in Taos, snowboarders are welcome. Ski Santa Fe has restaurants, equipment rentals, and lessons for all ages and abilities plus package deals that include accommodation in Santa Fe, lessons and/or equipment. **Chipmunk Corner** (☎ 988-9636), near the lifts, offers daycare for kids from three months to four years old, but make reservations in advance.

Alpine Sports (Map pp76-7; ☎ 983-5155; 121 Sandoval St; ☀ 7:30am-6pm winter, 9:30am-6pm other seasons), one of the USA's top ski shops, rents ski packages (regular/high-performance $12/35) and snowboards ($22); **Skier's Edge** (Map p75; ☎ 983-1025; 1836 Cerrillos Rd) also rents packages for skiers ($16), snowboarders ($27) and kids ($11). **Cottam's** (☎ 982-0495; Hyde Park Rd), on the way to the slopes, has the best prices on packages (adult/child $10/8), and also rents snowblades ($20) and snowshoes ($10).

If you prefer cross-country skiing, **Norski Trail**, about a mile past the Aspen Vista Picnic Ground in Hyde State Park, has almost 3 miles of free, volunteer-maintained trails with the same great views.

Roadrunner Shuttle (☎ 424-3367; one-way/ roundtrip $15/20; ☀ 8am & 11:30am) runs buses from the plaza and some larger hotels to the ski area twice daily in winter.

Mountain Biking

Sun Mountain Bike & Coffee Shop (p114) has information about trails throughout the region, rents bikes and can drop you off at trailheads. Santa Fe Area Mountain Bike Trails, by Craig Martin, is another good source for trail info. Here are a few to get you started:

Atalaya Trail (Map p75) This popular trail leaves from the first St John's College parking lot for a 7-mile loop that will have you gasping – if not from the climb to the top of 9121ft Atalaya Mountain, then from the views. Note that the trail gets packed with hikers, dog walkers and stoned liberal arts students as sunset approaches.

Windsor Trail (Map p116) This 10-mile trail for intermediate bikers is one of the most renowned treks in the state; though hard-core folks may find it overrated, the scenery – particularly in the fall and winter – is outstanding. The route begins at Little Tesuque in Hyde

Park and climbs steadily upward to serve as the spine of several other multiuse trails, including the bike-friendly Chamiza Loops.

Tesuque Peak Rd (Map p116; Aspen Vista Trail) Beginning at Aspen Vista Picnic ground in Hyde Park, this 6-mile abandoned dirt-logging road makes a nontechnical but steep (2200ft) ride to eagle-eye views of the Sangre de Cristos and Santa Fe. It's also open to hikers, horses and llamas.

Santa Fe Rail Trail (Map pp76-7) Beginning at the Santa Fe Rail Depot, this 18-mile trail follows the rail line clear to Lamy. The trail is unpaved until you hit Agua Fria St, then paved the rest of the way, though mountain bikers can take a dirt turnoff at the intersection with US 285 to avoid following a CR 33 into Lamy.

Rafting

Santa Fe's white-water rafting outfits are headed to Pilar (p131) for the renowned Class IV **Taos Box**, an adventure for folks 12 and up; and the Class III **Racecourse**, which is fine for active kids over six. The Class III **Rio Chama** is often rafted as a multiday trip with camping supplies and food included. The day trips, through dramatic Rio Grande Gorge, are great excursions and are easily arranged from May through October through two major Santa Fe outfitters:

New Wave River Trips (Map p75; ☎ 984-1444, 800-984-1444; www.newwaverafting.com; 1101 Cerrillos Rd) Stay cool on day trips through the Rio Grande Gorge (adult/ child $47/44 half day, adult/child $77/70 full day) or Taos Box ($100), or go for a three-day Rio Chama float ($360). Bonus: you can take on the white-water in a 'funyak,' an inflatable kayak that leaves the driving up to you.

Santa Fe Rafting (Map p75; ☎ 988-4914, 800-467-7238; www.santaferafting.com; 1000 Cerrillos Rd) Right next door to New Wave and offering similar trips for similar prices, it's been keeping the competition honest for more than 15 years.

Rock Climbing

Santa Fe Climbing Gym (☎ 986-8944; 825 Early St; adult/child $12/6; ☀ 5-10pm Mon-Fri) has two floors of indoor climbing, rents and sells gear and guidebooks and can offer personal tips about area outdoor climbing opportunities if you're ready to hit the rocks.

Top outdoor sites close to Santa Fe include The Overlook, in White Rock's Overlook Park (p134), with more than 30 routes scaling the basalt cliffs; Las Conchas and Cochiti Mesa Crags, administrated by the Jemez Ranger Station (p66); and throughout the Sandia Mountains (p68). For information on more opportunities for adventure, pick up a copy of *Rock Climbing New Mexico & Texas*, by Dennis R Jackson.

If you don't feel comfortable climbing on your own, Arroyo Seco's **Rock Climbing Adventures** (p154) offers instruction and guided climbs.

Fishing

New Mexico's truly outstanding fishing holes are better accessed from Taos (p153) and the Enchanted Circle, but there are plenty of opportunities around Santa Fe, including Abiquiú and Nambé Lakes and Rio Chama. You'll need a license (p45).

In addition to a wide selection of gear, the **High Desert Angler** (Map pp76-7; ☎ 988-7688, 888-988-7688; www.highdesertangler.com; 435 S Guadalupe St; ❤ 10am-6pm Mon-Sat low season, 8am-6pm Mon-Sat & 8am-4pm Sun high season) offers three-hour introduction courses ($95), guided excursions to private streams (s/d $275/300) and a variety of multiday trips. The shop will also supply independent souls with rod, reel, waders and a one-day license for $25.

Golfing

With 300 days of sunshine, even Nader voters can't always resist a round of golf in this thirsty state, particularly considering these fine greens, generally available from 7am until dusk daily.

Marty Sanchez Links (☎ 955-4400; 205 Caja del Rio Rd; $10-30) Just 20 minutes from Santa Fe, nine- and 18-hole courses have great views, gray-water systems and some of the best golfing in New Mexico.

Santa Fe Country Club (☎ 471-0601; Airport Rd; weekday/weekend $25/35) This semiprivate club welcomes visitors to its green, gray-watered haven, just 2 miles west of Cerrillos Rd, with one caveat: the restaurant is for members only.

Pueblo de Cochiti (Map p116; ☎ 465-2239; 5200 Cochiti Hwy; $14-30) Cochiti Pueblo's (p67) offering, about 45 minutes from Santa Fe, may be the most challenging course in the state.

Other Activities

Genoveva Chavez Community Center (☎ 955-4000 ext 4001; Rodeo Rd; adult/child $4/3; ❤ 6am-6pm Mon-Fri, 8am-8pm Sat, 10am-6pm Sun) offers several services, including a heated indoor pool, hot tub, sauna, weight room and year-round ice-skating rink as well as a variety of yoga and fitness classes.

There are four other **public pools** (☎ 955-2511; adult/child $2/1) in town, including another indoor pool at **Fort Marcy** (☎ 955-4998; 490 Washington Ave; adult/child $2/1; ❤ 6am-8:30pm Mon-Fri, 8am-6:30pm Sat, noon-5:30pm Sun).

YogaSource (Map pp76-7; ☎ 982-0990; www.yogasource-santafe.com; 1/4 classes $14/50; 518 Old Santa Fe Trail; ❤ 8am-9pm Mon-Thu, 8am-5pm Fri-Sun) can stretch your horizons with five different styles of yoga and classes for every level.

Broken Saddle Riding Company (☎ 424-7774; www.brokensaddle.com; 1/3 hours $40/70; 26 Vicksville Rd; ❤ 8am-sunset daily) offers day-trip **horseback rides** at Bishop's Lodge (p98) and in Cerrillos (p68) as well as sunset ($60) and moonlight ($70) options; also check out **Galarosa Stables** (☎ 466-4654; www.galarosastables.com; 2 hours $60; NM 41 S).

Skater dudes and dudettes can check out the ramps during daylight hours at the **Skateboard Park** (Map pp76-7; ☎ 955-2100; 302 W DeVargas St) and **Franklin E Miles Park** (1027 Camino Carlos Rey).

SANTA FE WALKING TOUR

Begin at the **Palace of the Governors (1)** for a crash course in Santa Fe history – you'll appreciate the city even more. Peruse the Native American jewelry out front, then do the obligatory circuit around the plaza, taking careful note of the difference between Santa Fe–style fashions displayed in the windows and what actual Santa Feans, playing hackeysack outside, are wearing.

Head east on Palace Ave to the **Museum of Fine Arts (2)** – ah, pueblo revival architecture! Across the street, the 1890 **Delgado House (3)**, at 124 Palace Ave, is an even older example. Step into the museum for artistic inspiration, then continue east, with a quick detour down Burro Alley to the **French Pastry Shop (4)** for a quick pick-me-up.

Return to and cross Palace Ave to Grant St, making a left onto Johnson St, continuing past the **O'Keeffe Museum (5)**. More art, perhaps? A block farther, the **Awakening Museum (6)** is a much shorter (and cheaper) commitment and has comfy seats for relaxing while you take in a single, phenomenal masterpiece.

Make a left onto Guadalupe St, noting the occasional brick building (this area predates the adobe-only laws), and cross the Santa Fe River. The **Santuario de Guadalupe (7)** is on your right, the **Cowgirl Hall of Fame (8)** is on your left – which feminist icon would you prefer to explore? Continue to Garfield St, noting the old train station and **Tomasita's (9)**, both historic and delicious.

Pick up some unusual vacation reading at **Blue Moon (10)** or a new-to-you outfit at **Faerie Queen (11)**, and make a left on Sandoval. Tired? Make a quick left onto Aztec St, where the **Aztec Café (12)** provides quality people-watching over coffee or a snack.

Continue up Sandoval and make a left on Alameda, following the river east to the Old Santa Fe Trail (which isn't really the Santa Fe Trail, they just called it that). Make a left anyway, and if you can't make it to Taos, snap a picture of the **Inn at Loretto (13)**; the folks back home won't know the difference.

In the mood for a miracle? The **Loretto Chapel (14)** has a nice one. Or make a right onto Water St, then a left onto Cathedral Place. Other choices: **St Francis Cathedral (15)** to see **La Conquistadora**, or the **Institute of American Indian Art (16)** for more cutting-edge contemporary work.

Tired again? This is an excellent place to end the tour, backtracking to **La Fonda (17)**, where you can relax atop the city at the **Belltower Bar**, with the second best view in town.

Hardier souls can make a right onto Palace Ave, popping in to take a look at **Sena Plaza** and perhaps make reservations at the **La Cantina (18)**, then make a left on Otero St for **Back at the Ranch (19)**, where fabulous boots fill just one of several upscale shops.

Take a shortcut across the empty lot out back to Castillo Place, then make a left on Paseo de Peralta, crossing the road to the **Cross of the Martyrs (20)**. Climb the steep hill, reading the plaques for more history, and enjoy the best view in town from the top.

The entire walking tour is about 2½ miles and, with time for enjoying some of

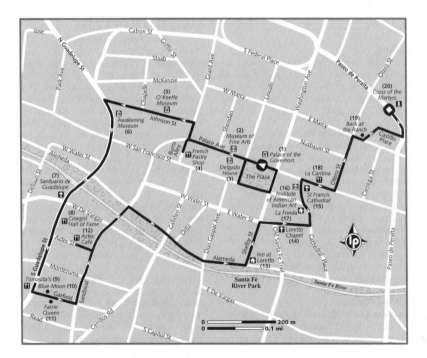

the recommended stops, could take two to four hours.

COURSES

One of the best excuses to spend time in Santa Fe – and away from the plaza – is by enrolling in a course. Check out the several **culinary schools** (p51) offering classes, or attend one of these:

Santa Fe Workshops (☎ 983-1400; www.santafe workshops.com; Mt Carmel Rd) Get in touch with your inner Ansel Adams at week-long photography and digital imagery workshops (classes $500-2500). Meals and lodging are available for an extra fee.

Santa Fe School of Weaving (Map pp76-7; ☎ 982-6312; www.sfschoolofweaving.com; 614 Paseo de Peralta) Danish-born and Israeli-trained weaver Miriam Leith-Espensen teaches small classes usually in four half-day sessions ($200-250 excluding materials).

White Cloud Institute (☎ 471-9330; www.whiteclo udinstitute.com; 1807 2nd St) If your aura's feeling a little off, try a two-day seminar ($150-250) covering everything from sexual quigong to Zen shiatsu.

Santa Fe Executive Aviation (p92) Learn to pilot a Cessna ($100/hour), or go one better and take a lesson in a Mig 15 ($1000-$1700/hour).

SANTA FE FOR CHILDREN

Check *Pasatiempo* (p74) for its 'Bring the Kids' column, with a rundown on area events for children.

The **Santa Fe Children's Museum** (p84) is wonderful, with interactive and educational activities for kids up to 10 or so. Kids of all ages shouldn't miss the amazing **Museum of International Folk Art** (p80); for more color, including some you can take home, a shopping trip to **Jackalope** (p112) is most definitely in order.

Expose your children to the diversity of cultures Santa Fe is so proud of: **El Rancho de las Golondrinas** (p84) shows off Spanish Colonial history made real, while **El Museo Cultural de Santa Fe** (p84) has artwork and other exhibits by kids and for kids.

The **Santa Fe Opera** (p108) does backstage tours during opera season, free for folks under 17, and a visit to the **Wheelwright Museum of the American Indian** (p80) will introduce them early to Native culture, with events and even an annual powwow designed for children.

Older kids in touch with their inner nerd will enjoy the **Santa Fe Community**

College Planetarium (p86), while eye-rolling teens itching for their first tattoo may prefer all-ages **Warehouse 21** (p107), though you probably won't be invited.

Several hiking trails, particularly those at **Randall Davey Audubon Center** (p86), are perfect for active children; just be sure to coat them with sunscreen and make sure they don't get dehydrated. The **Genoveva Community Chavez Center** (p89) has a heated indoor pool and ice-skating rink if the weather's not cooperating.

Most restaurants, except for seriously upscale offerings, are happy to host your kids, and most have special menus – but only the **Cowgirl Hall of Fame** (p107) has a playground *and* a full bar.

Had a growth spurt? Gussy up the kids' wardrobes at glittering **Gypsy Baby** (Map p83; ☎ 995-8030; 708 Canyon Rd), or try **doubletake** (p111) if you'd rather send them to college.

If you want to get out on your own, **Magical Happenings Babysitting** (☎ 982-9327) can have sitters stay with your kids in your hotel room; it's $15 an hour for one child, with a four-hour minimum, and reservations should be made in advance, particularly during the high season.

TOURS
Walking Tours
Palace of the Governors (Map pp76-7; $10; ☑ 10:15am Mon-Sat Apr-Oct) Knowledgeable Museum of New Mexico docents lead 1¾-hours tours that can be somewhat customized, depending on the group, around downtown Santa Fe. Meet at the Blue Gate on Lincoln Ave at 10am.

Aboot About Historic Walks (☎ 988-2774; www.abootabout.com; $10, under 12 free; ☑ 9:30am & 1:30pm daily) Tours begin at the Hotel St Francis and El Dorado, and cover the plaza, St Francis Cathedral, Loretto Chapel and more. The same company runs **Aspook About Walks** ($10; ☑ 5:30pm Mon, Tue, Fri & Sat), which includes ghost stories, as well as the **Loretto Line** (adult/child $12/6; Apr-Oct), an open-air bus tour of the downtown area and historic neighborhoods.

Stephanie Beninato Southwest Tours (☎ 988-8022; www.swguides.com; $18) Make reservations for in-depth custom tours of Santa Fe's Jewish historical sites, haunted places, hidden gardens and even former brothels.

Vehicle Tours

Santa Fe Southern Railway (Map pp76-7; ☎ 989-8600, 888-989-8600; www.sfsr.com; 410 S Guadalupe St) Though the Santa Fe Railroad doesn't run through town, several scenic train rides use the old spur line to take you past the Galisteo Basin and to the fairly ghostly town of Lamy. The four-hour day trip (adult/child $32-55/18-42) is the most popular run, and there are several themed trips like the Barbecue Train (adult/child $50-80/30-65), with live music and a campfire.

Custom Tours by Clarice (☎ 438-7116; www.santafecustomtours.com; $10; ☼ 9am, 11am, 1pm, 3pm & 5pm daily) In addition to the standard 1½-hour tours of Santa Fe sites, including stops at several art galleries, this company arranges group tours of art studios, Bandelier and Taos Pueblo. There's also a Sunset Tour for Lovers ($350) with champagne atop a mountain, after which they'll even arrange your entire wedding at an area chapel ($1000-8000), including flowers, food and a pastor.

Fiesta Tours (☎ 983-1570; 118 Old Santa Fe Trail; adult/child $7/4; ☼ 11am, 1pm & 3pm daily throughout the year, more often in summer) Hop on an open-air bus at the corner of Old Santa Fe Trail and Water St for a one-hour tour of the city, taking in the cathedral, plaza, Canyon Rd and historic neighborhoods of Santa Fe.

Great Southwest Adventures (☎ 455-2700; www.swadventures.com; $45-95) Need to get out of town? Enjoy a guided day trip to Bandelier, Abiquiú, Pecos National Historical Park, or along the High Road to Taos. The company also does guided hikes and can arrange ski trips, opera nights and more.

Outback Tours (☎ 820-6101, 888-772-3274; www.outbacktours.com) Appreciate nature from Taos ($96) to Jemez ($85) to Abiquiú ($85) in an open-air Jeep! You can get out and hike, too.

Santa Fe Executive Aviation (☎ 471-2700, 800-757-9030; www.santafeexecutive.com; 405A Airport Rd; $50) Take a 45-minute 'Discovery Flight' in a Cessna, or learn to fly one yourself at the aviation school.

FESTIVALS & EVENTS

Check the *Pasatiempo* insert in the Friday *New Mexican*, the *Santa Fe Reporter* and all the other freebies (p74) for rundowns on area happenings, including the locations of Friday night art openings, usually held between 5pm and 7pm.

February

ARTfeast Edible Art Tour (☎ 982-1648, 988-2515; $25; late Feb) Art, jazz and plenty of wine bring out locals and tourists alike to sample gourmet cuisine. Proceeds buy art supplies for Santa Fe schools.

June

Pride on the Plaza (www.santafehra.org; mid-June) Drag queens, parades, floats, a **film festival** (☎ 988-5225), music, comedy and more; area bars and restaurants throw special bashes for a full week when everyone flies the rainbow flag.

Rodeo de Santa Fe (☎ 471-4300; www.rodeodesantafe.org; $8-30; late June) For more than half a century, wranglers, ranchers and cowpokes, along with plenty of rhinestone cowpersons, have been gathering to watch those bucking broncos, clowns in barrels, lasso tricks and fancy shooting. A pre-Rodeo parade takes it all downtown.

July

Spanish Market (☎ 982-2226; www.spanishmarket.org; late July) Traditional Spanish colonial arts, from retablos and bultos to handcrafted furniture and metalwork, make this juried show an artistic extravaganza, second only to Indian Market. Another Spanish Market is held in early December at the Sweeny Convention Center.

August

Santa Fe Indian Market (☎ 983-5220; www.swaia.org; weekend after third Thu in Aug) This world-famous event, sponsored by the Southwest Association for Indian Arts, packs the plaza with the finest Native American artisans from all over North America, who must go through a rigid qualification process just to exhibit at the juried show. Events like the **Native Cinema Showcase Film Festival** (www.ttpix.com) and tours of studios, galleries and museum archives run throughout the week. Rooms are packed, parking is horrible, snooty jet-setters snag all the best tables and it's all worth it, at least once in your life – you won't see art like this at your local museum. Get there Friday or Saturday to see pieces competing for the prestigious top prizes (they get snapped up by collectors), but Sunday is when you can bargain.

September

Santa Fe Fiestas (☎ 988-7575; www.santafefiesta.org; first week in Sept) Though it technically begins the first Thursday of September with Zozobra (p93), two full weeks of events celebrating the

September 4, 1692, resettlement of Santa Fe include concerts, a carnival at the Rodeo Grounds, parades involving pets, floats, Don Diego DeVargas and the Procession of La Conquistadora. It all ends on Sunday with a mass at St Francis Cathedral and a candlelight procession around town.

Santa Fe Wine & Chile Fiesta (☎ 483-8060; www .santafewineandchile.org; late Sept) It's a gourmet's fantasy fiesta, with wine tastings and fine cuisine; dinner events ($45-150) sell out early.

December

Las Posadas (December 24) All Santa Fe is illuminated with farolitos as Mary and Joseph make their way around the plaza (and you'll have almost as much luck scoring a last-minute hotel room as they did) while carolers and

---

FEATURE: ZOZOBRA

Have you had a lousy year? Death, divorce, lost friends, lost jobs? Dry your eyes and put on your party clothes, for it is to bid such sorrows farewell that the Santa Fe Fiestas' monumental centerpiece will be sacrificed in fireworks and flames.

Fiestas started out as a solemn affair, begun in 1712 to commemorate the city's 1692 resettlement after the Pueblo Revolt. New Mexico's future patron saint, La Conquistadora, led the procession, followed by a mass for Don Diego DeVargas, the hero who had recently passed on.

Fast forward to the 1920s: Santa Fe, now a bustling community of 8000 or so, is home to not only a rollicking Spanish scene and traditional Native quarter, but also a recent influx of some conspicuously eccentric Anglo artists.

Festivities like La Fonda's rooftop Fiesta Ball, presided over by local royalty costumed as the King and Queen of Spain, have been joined by the Surrealist Ball, with outfits almost as fine – but weirder. The Historical Parade, in honor of DeVargas and the Reconquista, is now followed by the Hysterical Parade, featuring dancing underpants and unsubtle political commentary.

Artist Will Shuster and fellow members of Los Cincos Pintores decided in 1926 that something was needed to bring all these celebrations together. Taking a cue from the Yaqui Indians of Mexico, who stuff an effigy of Judas with fireworks to dispel their woes, they built a 6ft-tall puppet in a field where the library now stands.

Poet Witter Bynner led a mob of fiesta-goers to the park and began the chant as dark-robed Kiwanis set torches at its base. When that first Zozobra – loosely translated from Spanish as 'the gloomy one' – went up in shocking green flames, the crowd went crazy. It was a hit.

Today the scene is set at Fort Marcy Park, where some 30,000 people gather each year beneath 50ft-tall Old Man Gloom's accusing glare. His moans and groans, audible all over town, condemn the crowd for their failures and sins, and with the help of puppeteers the wood-and-canvas giant points out each shortcoming and demands accountability.

As dusk becomes pitch black, the crowd begins to chant: 'Burn him! Burn him!' The hillsides, packed with people who refused to pay the entry fee, echo their cries with gusto. Ghosts – the year's sorrows – mill about at Zozobra's feet. Then in prances the fire dancer, his wand ablaze, reprising a role created by ballet maestro Jacques Cartier in 1936.

The small red figure leaps closer, the chanting crescendos to a frenzy, Old Man Gloom gesticulates wildly, and at least a couple of people pass out. 'Burn him! Burn him!' The dancer teases and taunts, tempting all hell to break loose. Finally, *finally,* with an impossible blast the wand takes its prey, and an eruption consumes the massive creature, all Santa Fe lending voice to the roar.

And that, folks, is what you call catharsis.

All bitterness is burned away by the inferno, fueled by police reports, divorce papers and paid-off mortgages, and four days of Fiestas have most officially begun. La Conquistadora is prepared for her procession, floats both historical and hysterical roll out, and the plaza sees no peace for the rest of the weekend.

Once Fiestas are over and you shake off that much-deserved sleep, it's the first day of the rest of your life. All those dramas and traumas? Forgotten. Your sins? Forgiven. Your hangover? Well, have some menudo. The eternal soap opera of life will continue unabated, but this dawn (or afternoon, as the case may be), your soul is as fresh as the day you were born.

revelers chow biscochitos, drink hot chocolate and make merry.

SLEEPING

Standards are high in Santa Fe, and even the barest-bones budget options (most of which line Cerrillos Rd between I-25 and downtown) are clean, safe and in conformity to Southwestern-style specs; many include a continental breakfast with lots of preservatives.

During the summer and Christmas, and in particular during Indian Market and on Opera nights, expect to pay premium prices for rare rooms; make reservations well in advance. Also note that prices do not include the whopping 11.7% hotel tax.

RESERVATION SERVICES

All Santa Fe Reservations (☎ 474-5557, 877-737-7366; www.all-santafe.com; 3600 Cerrillos Rd, ste 207A) With this service, you can choose among 100 hotels, motels and B&Bs plus car rentals, airport shuttles, ski packages and more.
New Mexico Lodging Association (www.nmhotels.com) Search by city or region, cost and amenities.
New Mexico Bed & Breakfast Association (☎ 800-661-6649; www.nmbba.org) More than a dozen Santa Fe B&Bs plus others all over the state.
Santa Fe Stay (☎ 820-2468, 800-995-2272; www.santafestay.com) Stay in someone else's personally decorated home.

Kokopelli Property Management (☎ 988-7244, 888-988-7244; www.kokoproperty.com) Luxury (read: expensive) abodes in the city and country.

Budget

HOTELS & MOTELS

Cactus Lodge (Map p75; ☎ 471-7699; 2864 Cerrillos Rd; d $32-48; P ⊠) Sure, it's a little on the shabby side, but rooms in this town just don't get any cheaper than this, folks.

Luxury Inn (Map p75; ☎ 473-0567; 3752 Cerrillos Rd; d/ste low $35/55, d/ste high $80/125; P ⊠ ⊠ ⊠) Some huge suites at this fine, independently operated entry have kitchenettes.

King's Rest Court (Map p75; ☎ 983-8879; 1452 Cerrillos Rd; d low/high $36/45; P ⊠) Some of the clean enough, spacious rooms have red shag carpeting.

Cottonwood Court (Map p75; ☎ 982-5571; 1742 Cerrillos Rd; s/d low $36/45, s/d high $55/65; P ⊠) This pleasant, if a bit rundown, option is perfect for folks who consider mismatched furniture 'character.'

Silver Saddle Motel (Map p75; ☎ 471-7663; www.motelsantafe.com; 2180 Cerrillos Rd; s/d low $40/45, s/d high $60/65; P ⊠ ⊠) One of the rustic subjects of the 1988 documentary film *Motel*, this is your best budget bet: inspired Southwestern comfy-rustic decor, including some pet-friendly rooms with attractively tiled kitchenettes, a good location (for Cerrillos Rd) and lots of kitschy appeal.

Super 8 (Map p75; ☎ 471-8811; www.super8.com; 3358 Cerrillos Rd; d low/high $40/90; P ⊠ ⊠) This

---

GAY & LESBIAN SANTA FE

Visitors familiar with Santa Fe's reputation as one of the most gay- and lesbian-friendly destinations in the country might be surprised to find that there's no gay neighborhood, no real gay clubs – not much at all to serve the high proportion of gay and lesbian residents, which by some estimations make up 25% of the city's population. But there's simply no reason to segregate.

'Santa Fe is very open, very accepting – the best thing is that you can just come here and be yourself,' explains Inn of the Turquoise Bear (p97) co-owner Ralph Bolton. 'There's no gay area because nothing's gay, and nothing's straight.'

There is an excellent celebration, **Pride on the Plaza** (p92), with a fabulous parade, and a couple of clubs (Swig and The Paramount; p107) are sometimes labeled gay, though in reality they cater to party people of every taste. The tourist board has never even bothered to market Santa Fe to gays and lesbians for a reason – they just don't think about it.

Long before Witter Bynner and domestic partner Robert Hunt were hosting foreign dignitaries and movie stars at their opulent bashes, Santa Fe was a place where folks from the surrounding communities could come to be themselves, something that's even truer today. What all this adds up to is an absolutely normal vacation – your visit will be much like anyone else's. And, depending on where you're from, that might be the biggest attraction of all.

excellent budget option is a great deal on rooms that are actually much nicer than those in many 'luxury' properties near the plaza.

Travelodge (Map pp76-7; ☎ 982-3551, 800-578-7878; 646 Cerrillos Rd; s/d low $49/59, s/d high $79/89; P ⊠ ⚃ ⚄) Ignore the cigarette burns in the clean, acceptable rooms and enjoy the walk to the plaza

Budget Inn (Map pp76-7; ☎ 982-5952; 725 Cerrillos Rd; s/d low $54/58, s/d high $82/90; P ⊠ ⚃) It's basic, clean and just a short hike from all the action on the plaza.

HOSTELS

Santa Fe International Hostel (Map p75; ☎ 988-1153, 984-0317; santafehostel@quest.net; 1412 Cerrillos Rd; nonmember/AYH member dm $14/15, s/d with shared bathroom $25/35, s/d with private bathroom $33/43; P ⊠ ⚃ ⚄) A cherry tree shades the outdoor patio and grill, and many of the just slightly tatty rooms, with both private options and sex-separated dorms, feature murals done by visiting artists. Add a free continental breakfast, open kitchen, linens and no lockout, and it all adds up to one fine hostelling experience.

CAMPING & RV PARKS

Sadly, the in-town options do not accept tents, including gravelly **Los Campos** (Map p75; ☎ 473-1949, 800-852-8160; 3574 Cerrillos Rd; RV $25-35; P ⚄ ⚄) and much more pleasant and shady **Trailer Ranch** (Map p75; ☎ 471-9970; www.trailerranch.com; 3471 Cerrillos Rd; RV $25-32; P ⚄ ⚄).

Eleven miles southeast of town, off exit 290 from I-25 North, **KOA** (☎ 466-1419, 800-562-1514; www.koa.com/where/nm/31159.htm; Frontage Rd; campsite/RV $25/32, Kamping Kabin $39-42; P) does have campsites and lots of amenities, while nearby **Rancheros de Santa Fe Camping Park** (☎ 466-3282, 800-426-9295; Frontage Rd; campsite/RV $22/32; P) has nice views and a convenience store. Both are open March through November.

Hyde Park Rd (NM 475) to Ski Santa Fe has four beautiful campsites, all with trail access, running water and grills, and you can get a hot shower at **Fort Marcy** (p89) at the bottom of the hill. The USFS operates **Black Canyon** (☎ 982-8674; campsites $10), closest to town, with fir trees and a pretty stream. **Big Tesuque Campground** (☎ 982-8674; campsites free), at 9700ft, has great views of the aspens.

Hyde Memorial State Park (☎ 838-7175, reservations 877-664-7787; www.icampnm.com; campsites/RV $14/10; May-Sep), in between Black Canyon and Big Tesuque, operates **Little Tesuque Campground**, better for campers, and **Hyde Memorial State Park RV Campground**, with full hookups.

Mid-Range

In this price range you've got all sorts of options, from basic rooms right downtown to full suites, complete with dining room, a short drive away. Though Santa Fe is small, keep in mind that parking near the plaza can be frustrating. But it may be well worth the commute.

B&BS

Many mid-range Santa Fe B&Bs forgo a full, hot breakfast, instead dishing up 'expanded continental' cuisine, usually along the lines of homemade granola, fresh fruit and fancy pastries or pancakes.

Inn on the Paseo (Map pp76-7; ☎ 984-8200, 800-457-9045; www.innonthepaseo.com; 630 Paseo de Peralta; d low $79-139, d high $89-179; P ⊠ ⚃) A great deal on pretty, unpretentious rooms hung with modern art, right across from the Cross of the Martyrs (p86), includes one tiny room the staff may make a deal on.

The Madeleine (Map pp76-7; ☎ 986-1431, 888-321-5123; www.madeleineinn.com; 106 Faithway St; d shared bathroom $70-95, d private bathroom $130-180; ⊠ ⚃ ⚄) This is the full B&B experience, with Victorian architecture, Queen Anne antiques, decadent homemade snacks and lovely gardens, even private cottages. The less expensive rooms are tiny but just as sweet.

Camas de Santa Fe (Map pp76-7; ☎ 984-1337, 800-632-2627; 323 E Palace Ave; d $80-145; ⊠ ⚃) It's set up like a hotel but run like a B&B; some spacious rooms (one with shared bath) come with gas fireplaces.

El Paradero (Map pp76-7; ☎ 988-1177; www.elparadero.com; 220 W Manhattan Ave; r low $85-125, r high $95-160; P ⊠ ⚃) Interesting for its architecture alone – the historic building's brick facade predates the city's adobe-only laws – this very traditional B&B has small but airy rooms plus suites with TVs and kitchenettes, and a lovely courtyard.

Alexander's Inn (Map p75; ☎ 986-1431, 888-321-5123; 529 E Palace Ave; d $85-130, casita $150-240; ⊠ ⚃) In a historic neighborhood five blocks from the plaza, this beautiful 1903 Arts and Crafts home is decorated for a frilly romantic escape, while casitas (small houses; some are located several blocks away) boast fireplaces and full kitchens.

El Farolito (Map pp76-7; ☎ 988-1631, 888-634-8782; www.farolito.com; 514 Galisteo St; without fireplace $150-170, with fireplace $175-220; P ✕ ✖) Intimate and elegant, each comfy adobe casita (some including patios) comes with a stocked fridge, VCR and all the amenities you expect from a fine B&B.

HOTELS

Comfort Inn (Map p75; ☎ 474-7330; 4312 Cerrillos Rd; d low/high $60/120; P ✕ ✖ ✚) It's got more character (and perhaps a little more grunge) than other chains; some rooms have fireplaces and/or kitchenettes.

Sleep Inn (☎ 474-9500, 888-675-2422; www .santafesleepinn.com; 8376 Cerrillos Rd; d $60-74; P ✕ ✖ ✚ ✚) It's miles from the plaza, but right off I-25.

Best Western Lamplighter Inn (Map p75; ☎ 471-8000, 800-767-5267; www.bwlamplighter.com; 2405 Cerrillos Rd; s/d low $60/70, s/d high $110/130; P ✕ ✖ ✚) The often oddly shaped rooms of this aging but very well-maintained hotel include refrigerators and coffeemakers.

Holiday Inn (Map p75; ☎ 473-4646; www .holidayinn.com; 4048 Cerrillos Rd; d $69-109; P ✕ ✖ ✚ ✚) This good-quality chain hotel features a fabulous indoor/outdoor pool.

Hampton Inn (Map p75; ☎ 474-3900, 800-426-7866; www.hamptoninn.com; 3625 Cerrillos Rd; d low/high $70/110; P ✕ ✖ ✚) Room access is through the lobby, making this average chain hotel a good pick for folks who like more security.

Courtyard by Marriott (Map p75; ☎ 473-2800, 800-777-3347; www.marriott.com; 3374 Cerrillos Rd; d/ste low $80/100, d/ste high $140/190; P ✕ ✖ ✚) Much more attractive than the average Cerrillos Rd entry, this very professional, businesslike and amenity-laden hotel has onsite bar and restaurant plus free shuttles downtown.

Hotel St Francis (Map pp76-7; ☎ 989-5700, 800-529-5700; www.hotelstfrancis.com; 210 Don Gaspar Ave; d low/high $92/122, ste $205-380; P ✕ ✖ ✚) Built as a luxury hotel in 1923, this great deal on plaza-side accommodations is elegant in a decadently decrepit sort of way. Basic rooms are small but you can upgrade for a few dollars, and the lovely lobby does a famous afternoon tea.

Hotel Santa Fe (Map pp76-7; ☎ 800-825-9876; www.hotelsantafe.com; 1501 Paseo de Peralta; d/ste low $99/189, d/ste high $169/279; P ✕ ✖ ✚ ✚) Mah-waan mah-waan (that'd be Tiwa for 'welcome') to one of the best deals on resort-style accommodations downtown. Picuris Pueblo (p130) operates this pretty adobe, decorated with Pikuri art, several blocks off the plaza – the hotel runs free shuttles, but it would probably be easier to walk. Amenities include a small spa and onsite **Amaya Cafe** (dinner $14-25, other meals $6-10; ☺ 7-10:30am, 11:30am-2pm, 5:30-9pm daily), which does a good buffalo burger plus lots of veggie- and game-focused dishes. Rooms are pretty basic, but ski packages and better suites with fireplaces sweeten the deal.

Old Santa Fe Inn (Map pp76-7; ☎ 995-0400; 800-745-9910; www.oldsantafeinn.com; 320 Galisteo St; d low $109-159, d high $200-249; P ✕ ✖) Smallish rooms, some with fireplaces and including breakfast, are nicely decorated in this nondescript place just blocks from the plaza.

Inn of the Governors (Map pp76-7; ☎ 982-4333, 800-234-4534; www.innofthegovernors.com; 101 W Alameda; d low/high $139/179; P ✕ ✖ ✚ ✚) Somewhere between hotel and B&B, this pleasant property has cramped but elegant rooms, suites with fireplaces, a full breakfast included, the popular **Del Churro Saloon** (snacks $4-8; ☺ 11:30am-midnight daily, bar until 1:30am daily) and a perfect location, just steps from the plaza.

Radisson (☎ 992-5800, 800-333-3333; www .radisson.com; 750 N St Francis Dr; d low/high $150/180; P ✕ ✖ ✚) Not the plushest place in Santa Fe, the Radisson's real claim to fame is hosting Maria Benitez Teatro Flamenco (p108).

Las Brisas (Map pp76-7; ☎ 982-5795, 800-449-6231; lasbrisas@cybermesa.com; 624 Galisteo St; s/d $155/185, ste $175-330 P ✕ ✖) Individually owned and decorated accordingly, these expansive condo-style lodgings mean it when they say 'full kitchen.' They're popular with the opera crowd.

MOTELS

Stagecoach Motor Inn (Map p75; ☎ 471-0707; 3360 Cerrillos Rd; d $78-150; P ✕ ✖) Heaps more character than most Cerrillos Rd entries, this nice spot has huge, beautifully decorated rooms and a shady courtyard and includes breakfast.

El Rey Inn (Map p75; ☎ 982-1931, 800-521-1349; 1862 Cerrillos Rd; d $72-119, ste $109-225; [P] [X] [⊠] [⌖]) It's a 'le classic courtyard' hotel, with super rooms, great pool and even a playground for the kids scattered around five acres of greenery – and there's even a huge continental breakfast. Highly recommended.

Santa Fe Motel & Inn (Map pp76-7; ☎ 982-1039, 800-930-5002; www.santafemotelinn.com; 510 Cerrillos Rd; low/high $79/130; [P] [X] [⊠]) With far more stylish rooms (some with fireplaces) than the exterior would indicate, even better weekly rates make this a great deal. Kitchenettes run about $15 extra.

Garrett's Desert Inn (Map pp76-7; ☎ 982-1851, 800-888-2145; www.garrettsdesertinn.com; 301 Old Santa Fe Trail; d $84-104, ste $111-131; [P] [X] [⊠] [⌖]) The location of this typical Cerrillos Rd hotel, plopped down next to the plaza and sprayed with stucco, makes the basic rooms and spacious suites attractive.

Camel Rock Suites (Map p75; ☎ 989-3600, 877-989-3600; www.camelrocksuites.com; 3007 S St Francis Dr; ste low/high $69/109; [P] [X] [⊠]) Sure, it's like vacationing in a gated community right off I-25, but huge suites – apartments, really – with full kitchens, dining room, fold-out sofas and more make this place a fantastic deal. You can arrange free shuttles downtown.

RESORTS
Sunrise Springs (Map p116; ☎ 471-3600, 800-955-0028; www.sunrisesprings.com; 242 Los Pinos Rd; d low $79-139, d high $110-285; [P] [X] [⊠] [⌖]) Fifteen minutes from town on the road to Las Golondrinas (p84), this is a true hippie haven – the Grateful Dead stayed here! Stay in smallish, Zenned-out rooms with balconies but no TVs, or new casitas with kitchenettes, side dens and enclosed patios. Then wander the pretty, high desert grounds, with a ceramics studio, Japanese tea room and spa. The onsite **Blue Heron Restaurant** (☎ 428-3600; 7:30-10am daily, 11am-2pm & 5:30-9pm Wed-Sun) dishes up vegetarian delights like blue corn–encrusted tofu, or try the duck spring rolls and a nice New York strip. This place is chill.

Top End
B&BS
Inn of the Turquoise Bear (Map p75; ☎ 983-0798, 800-396-4104; www.turquoisebear.com; 342 E Buena Vista St; d $100-315; [P] [X] [⊠]) Surrounded by an acre of sculpted gardens, this is the expansive adobe party palace built by local legend Witter Bynner and domestic partner Robert Hunt. It's now a fantastic B&B with authentic ambiance and all the modern amenities, plus an extravagant, allegedly continental breakfast served in the cozy common areas. It is, as always, straight-friendly but remains a cozy place for gays and lesbians to relax into historic Santa Fe, and the inn can arrange commitment ceremonies and weddings in the gardens. Sunset refreshments, a festive common area and individually decorated rooms make this one highly recommended splurge.

Grant Corner Inn (Map pp76-7; ☎ 983-6678, 800-964-9003; www.grantcornerinn.com; 122 Grant Ave; d low $130-270, d high $145-310; [P] [X] [⊠]) The elaborate, gourmet **breakfast** (included with room, nonguests adult/child $12/6; 8am-10:30am Mon-Sat, 8am-2pm Sunday; reservations required) is alone worth the trip – and has been voted among the best in Santa Fe – but comfortable, antique-filled rooms and every adorable amenity invite you to stay a while.

Inn of the Five Graces (Map pp76-7; ☎ 992-0957; www.fivegraces.com; 150 E DeVargas St; d $295-450 incl breakfast; [P] [X] [⊠]) This exquisite, hidden gem has, hands down, the most romantic rooms in town. Sumptuous suites are decorated in a lavish Persian-hippie fusion theme, complete with fireplaces, beautifully tiled kitchenettes and a courtyard behind the river-rock walls, all of which could transform an ordinary luxury vacation into an upscale gypsy adventure.

HOTELS
La Fonda (Map pp76-7; ☎ 982-5511, 800-523-5002; www.lafondasantafe.com; 100 E San Francisco St; d low/high $219/259, ste $289-529; [P] [X] [⊠] [□] [⌖]) More than just another stylish pueblo-revival hotel, the original 'Inn at the end of the Santa Fe Trail,' which claims to have been here since 1610, is an institution. Its eclectic art collection adorns boutiques, restaurants and bars, including one atop the Belltower (p106), with the best sunsets in town. The lobby is alive with folks selling jewelry, reading tarot cards, strumming guitars and enjoying life – all of which makes up for the smallish, sometimes weird rooms.

El Dorado Hotel (Map pp76-7; ☎ 995-4544, 800-955-4455; www.eldoradohotel.com; 309 W San Francisco St; d $169-289, ste $309-1000, casita $200-409;

⒫ ⊠ ⊠ ▣ ⊠) Uncompromising luxury – a rooftop pool and hot tub, boutiques galore, kiva fireplaces in many flawlessly appointed rooms, glittering ski and 'romance' packages ($245-1150) and the decadent Old House Restaurant (p104) – make this a rewarding spot to treat yourself. Bargain on weekdays, when the usual clientele is stuck overseeing oil fields back in Houston.

Inn of the Anasazi (Map p76-7; ☎ 988-3030, 800-688-8100; www.innoftheanasazi.com; 113 Washington Ave; d low $199-399, d high $289-469; ⒫ ⊠ ⊠) World-class luxury accommodations come compact in this elegant, Navajo-themed property. The gas fireplaces, the excellent Anasazi Restaurant (p101) and pricey packages (like a picnic lunch at Canyon de Chelly: $5150 including airfare) make this Santa Fe's ultimate upscale retreat.

Inn at Loretto (Map pp76-7; ☎ 988-5531, 800-727-5531; www.hotelloretto.com; 211 Old Santa Fe Trail; d low/high $160/360, ste $350-$2500; ⒫ ⊠ ⊠ ▣ ⊠) It looks like Taos Pueblo – gorgeous – and is filled with obsessively luxurious rooms and suites, as well as **The Restaurant** (mains $8-30; ◷ 7am-3pm & 5:30-10pm daily), known for its steak and seafood. The premium property offers a variety of package deals with area museums and cooking schools, as well as the onsite **SpaTerre** (p99).

La Posada de Santa Fe (Map pp76-7; ☎ 986-0000, 800-727-5276; www.laposada.rockresorts.com; 330 E Palace Ave; d low $199-299, d high $299-379, ste $339-659; ⒫ ⊠ ⊠ ⊠) Sprawled across six shady acres a few blocks from the plaza (shuttles are complimentary), this luxury property includes elegantly furnished adobe casitas with gas fireplaces, and more historic (and smaller) rooms in the Staab House, some with views. Onsite **Avanyu Spa** (p99) and the highly regarded restaurant, **Fuego** (dinner $28-32, other meals $7-17; ◷ 7am-2:30pm & 6-9pm daily), are both fabulous, while the cigar-friendly **Staab House Lounge** (◷ 11:30am-midnight daily) is a local favorite for its leather-chaired ambiance and single malt scotch.

RESORTS

Houses of the Moon (☎ 982-9304; www.tenthousand waves.com; 3451 Hyde Park Rd; d $190-265; ⒫ ⊠ ⊠) These beautiful freestanding accommodations are walking distance to the hot tubs at adjacent 10,000 Waves (p99). Spend $20 more and upgrade to even more spacious and serene casitas, which indulge the spa's Japanese Zen theme with low furniture, rice paper screens, tea sets and other relaxing touches, including the famed mountainside hot tubs. The wheelchair-accessible Tsuki suite, with a full kitchen, is a contender for nicest room in Santa Fe. Make reservations two months out.

Bishop's Lodge Resort & Spa (Map p116; ☎ 983-6377; 800-732-2240; www.bishopslodge.com; 1297 Bishops Lodge Rd; d low $149-279, d high $299-429, ste $279-1500; ⒫ ⊠ ⊠ ▣ ⊠) Only 3 miles from the plaza but surrounded with 450 acres of almost untouched piñon wilderness, this family-friendly spot is a different world. Huge rooms and casitas – many with patios, kitchenettes, fireplaces and more – are designed for luxury 'cowboy style.' **SháNah Spa & Wellness** (p99) relaxes harried parents, yoga classes and horseback rides keep the teens happy, and there's a supervised playground and kid's camp for the little ones. There's even a fishing pond, and excellent **Las Fuentes** (p105) restaurant will clean and cook your catch. Add miles of trails and free shuttles downtown, and this is one fabulous vacation.

EATING

With more restaurants per capita than any other city in the USA, Santa Fe is a serious foodie destination, on par with New York or San Francisco in terms of gustatory excellence. Many restaurants start strong, then start cutting corners as the reality of high rents set in. If a place smells like its star has fallen, move on.

The neighborhoods described are fairly subjective: **Plaza & Canyon Rd** covers the downtown area bounded by the Santa Fe River, Guadalupe St and Paseo de Peralta; **Guadalupe St Area** runs from Guadalupe St to the Capitol, including parts of Cerrillos Rd; **Cerrillos Rd** covers the strip south of Guadalupe St plus side streets; and **Metropolitan Santa Fe** covers everything else.

Check for reviews in the *Santa Fe Reporter,* which often has coupons for area eateries, or the free monthly the *Local Flavor,* with reviews and news about area restaurants. The **Santa Fe Restaurant Association** (www.santaferestaurants.net) publishes a free booklet with sparkling reviews of members and has a searchable index online.

Plaza & Canyon Road

BUDGET

Yes, you can fortify yourself on Canyon Rd without breaking the bank. **Café des Artistes** (Map p83; ☎ 820-2535; 223B Canyon Rd; mains $4-8; ◷ 8:30am-5pm) serves up French inspired dishes, like flaky almond croissants and brie-and-berry salads, on the sunny patio, while **Off the Wall Gallery & Coffee Bar** (Map p83; ☎ 983-8337; 616 Canyon Rd; snacks $3-7), in a wonderful gallery with affordable arts and crafts plus some of the cleverest menorahs you'll ever see, does prepared sandwiches, noodles and pastries.

Maison & Thé (Map p83; ☎ 466-3272; 821 Canyon Rd; snacks $3-9; ◷ 8am-5pm daily), in the Stables studio complex (p83) at the end of Canyon Rd, will replenish your energy with rare and exotic teas in an outdoor rock garden.

Burrito Company (Map pp76-7; ☎ 982-4453; 111 Washington Ave; fast food $3-9; ◷ 7am-5pm daily) This popular plaza-side favorite lets you spend more money on art and enjoy budget blue-corn enchiladas and chorizo burritos that can compete with the best of 'em.

Carlos' Gosp'l Café (Map pp76-7; ☎ 983-1841; 125 Lincoln Ave; mains $3-9; ◷ 8am-10:30pm Mon-Fri, 11am-3pm Sat & Sun) Chill with hipsters and mellow businesspeople listening to gospel tunes in the sunny courtyard while enjoying vegetarian hangover stew or the Alice B Toklas turkey-Swiss sandwich.

Downtown Subscription (Map p83; ☎ 983-3085; 376 Garcia St; snacks $2-7; ◷ 7am-7pm daily) Excellent coffee, 31 types of tea, pastries and a few savory offerings are complimented by a

SANTA FE

RELAX INTO MAÑANA TIME

Visitors from faster-paced places (just about everywhere) sometimes feel frustrated with New Mexico's relaxed approach to life: 'Isn't this restaurant supposed to be open on Tuesdays? We had reservations! What do you *mean*, they've gone fishing?'

OK, it's time to head to a spa, where you can indulge in treatments ranging from hot-stone massages to blue-corn facials, or just soak your cares away. Many of the following and other spas have accommodations that offer spa packages.

10,000 Waves (☎ 982-9304; www.tenthousandwaves.com; 3451 Hyde Park Rd; communal tubs $14, private tubs $20-27 per person; ◷ 9:15am-10pm Wed-Mon, 4-10pm Tue) It's true Japanese style, with landscaped grounds concealing 10 attractive tubs in smooth Zen design: some with waterfalls, cold plunges, hot and dry saunas, and two swimsuit-optional tubs, one of which is reserved for women (◷ noon-8pm daily). You could also indulge in herbal wraps, salt glows, facials and several different massages, or even stay a while in the Houses of the Moon (p98).

Ojo Caliente (p124) About an hour north of Santa Fe, this is Mother Nature's original New Mexico spa, where stressed-out Comanche and Pueblo Indians have been soaking for millennia. Massages, facials and other spa treatments are just dessert.

ShaNah Spa & Wellness (Map p116; ☎ 974-2624; www.bishopslodge.com; 1297 Bishops Lodge Rd; ◷ 7am-8pm daily) Enjoy the view with an outdoor massage, overlooking the piñon forested property of Bishop's Lodge (p98). Outdoor hot tubs and dosha-balancing Ayurvedic treatments designed to stimulate your third eye make this a fine place to regenerate.

Avanyu Spa (Map pp76-7; ☎ 954-9630; 330 E Palace Ave; ◷ 7am-8pm daily) This swanky spot, with a Southwest-meets-Beverly-Hills feel, at La Posada de Santa Fe (p98) offers 16 massages, seven facials and a variety of wraps, glows and waxes. Get there early and steam a while.

SpaTerre (Map pp76-7; ☎ 988-5531; 211 Old Santa Fe Trail; ◷ 9am-9pm daily) Inside the Inn at Loretto (p98), this spiritually aware spa has Native American–themed decor and exotic offerings like the Balinese massage followed by a yogurt bath.

Sterling Institute Spa Therapies (☎ 984-3223; www.thesterlinginstitute.com; 513 Camino de los Marquez; ◷ 9am-6pm Mon-Sat) Deluxe offerings like the facial involving 23-carat gold (it conducts electricity!) and exotic wraps using products from Egypt, Hungary and Morocco, among others, make this indulgence at its finest.

Santa Fe Massage (☎ 995-5105; www.santafemassage.com; ◷ 9am-9pm daily) These folks have small spas scattered around town, but the real draw is that they'll come to any area hotel for an in-room massage.

SANTA FE

truly spectacular newsstand and flagstone patio, just a few blocks off Canyon Rd.

Tia Sophia's (Map pp76-7; ☎ 983-9880; 210 W San Francisco St; mains $3-7; ☼ 7am-1:55pm Mon-Sat) The plaza workforce joins collectors-in-the-know over this top spot's fabulous lunch specials and other great New Mexican offerings.

Longevity Café (Map pp76-7; ☎ 986-0403; 133 Water St; mains $3-8; ☼ 11am-midnight Mon-Sat, 11am-7pm Sun) Tucked away in Plaza Mercado, this Zen-friendly joint serves Chinese elixirs that fortify your chi, jing, immune system and sex life, plus vegan and vegetarian options like seaweed salad and curried tofu with organic veggies. Astrologers and tarot card readers are often on hand.

Upper Crust Pizza (Map pp76-7; ☎ 982-0000; 329 Old Santa Fe Trail; mains $6-7, pizza $10-24; ☼ 11am-11pm daily) Relax on the patio or in the cozy interior over pizza piled with pesto, piñon or even pepperoni, considered by many to be Santa Fe's best. The sausage roll is a staff favorite.

MID-RANGE

Plaza Café (Map pp76-7; ☎ 982-1664; 54 Lincoln Ave; dinner $8-30, other meals $6-11; ☼ 7am-9pm daily) Serving hearty meals since before the roads were paved, this Formica-furnished 1918 establishment still makes one of the best breakfasts around, great New Mexican food (they're 'not responsible for chile that is too hot') and a mean gyro. Finish off with one of the pies or cakes on display, and consider giving your favorite New Mexico politician a ring (numbers are posted) to let them know what you think.

Cottonwood Café (Map pp76-7; ☎ 983-1615; 132 Water St; mains $7-11; ☼ 9am-6pm daily) Downstairs and downscale from its famed sister restaurant, the Coyote Café (p101), this unpretentious pub welcomes budget gourmets to sample Mark Miller's cut-rate creations, from steak burritos to green chile potato chowder. Kids love the blue corndog while adults appreciate the full bar, serving the Coyote's signature cocktails.

Paul's (Map pp76-7; ☎ 982-8738; 72 W Marcy St; lunch $6-8, dinner $14-20; ☼ 11:30am-2:30pm & 5:30-9pm nightly) This definite date spot has ambiance more suited to the top-end category. A nightly $22 prix-fixe menu adds an award-winning chocolate ganache and appetizer to entrees like pecan-crusted baked salmon.

The Shed (Map pp76-7; ☎ 982-9030; 113½ E Palace Ave; lunch $6-9, dinner $9-18; ☼ 11am-2:30pm & 5:30-9pm nightly) Superb New Mexican cuisine has been served here since 1953. Order anything – it's all fantastic – but get it red. With an order of calabasas on the side and the rich chocolate mocha cake for desert, you'll be set.

India Palace (Map pp76-7; ☎ 986-5859; 227 Don Gaspar Ave; mains $8-13; ☼ 11:30am-2:30pm & 5-10pm daily) Cloth napkins and stemware add ambiance, but it's the recommended lamb sagwala, baingan bartha (tandoori eggplant) and buffet lunch ($9) that pack those pretty tables with locals and tourists who just can't choke down another burrito.

Cafe Pasqual's (Map pp76-7; ☎ 983-9340; 121 Don Gaspar Ave; dinner $18-21, other meals $8-14; ☼ 7am-3pm & 5:30-9pm daily) Make reservations for dinner if you'd like, but definitely wait in line to enjoy the famous breakfasts, including huevos motuleños, featuring eggs with black beans, sautéed bananas, feta cheese and more; tamale dulce, a sweet corn tamale with fruit, beans and chocolate; or the enormous Durango ham-and-cheese omelet. It's all served up in the festive, if claustrophobic, interior. Jump ahead in line by sitting at the community table, where tourists and locals mix it up daily.

La Plazuela (Map pp76-7; ☎ 982-5511, 800-523-5002; lunch $10-13, dinner $16-23) Make reservations to dine on roasted quail with pistachio stuffing, chipotle-glazed filet mignon and other gourmet goodies at this lovely spot in the painted-glass heart of La Fonda.

Pink Adobe (Map pp76-7; ☎ 983-7712; 406 Old Santa Fe Trail; mains $12-24; ☼ 11:30am-2:30pm Mon-Fri, 5:30-10pm daily) A Santa Fe classic, the Pink Adobe and neighboring Dragon Bar (p106) have been packing 'em in since 1944 with hearty and hailed cuisine like enchiladas and steak Dunigan (cooked with green chile), the signature dish.

TOP END

This is the seat of state government, and lobbyists lather up their prey over thick steaks and single malt scotches at myriad places, including **The Bull Ring** (Map pp76-7; ☎ 983-3328; 150 Washington Ave; lunch $9-15, dinner $21-37; ☼ 11:30am-11pm Mon-Fri, 4-11pm Sat & Sun), serving aged Angus in either the Naugahyde dining room or rustic saloon, and **Rio Chama** (Map pp76-7; ☎ 955-0765; 414 Old Santa Fe Trail; lunch $8-15, dinner

$20-32; ☺ 11:30am-5pm daily), featuring fine meaty fare and the recommended Chama chile, done up Texas-style with huge hunks of steak, available a bit more cheaply at the bar.

Palace Restaurant (Map pp76-7; ☎ 982-9891; 142 W Palace Ave; lunch $8-14, dinner $20-25; ☺ 11:30am-3pm Mon-Sat, 5:30-10pm daily) Over-the-top, plush red decor pays homage to former owner Doña Tules (p102), while equally rich deserts, lamb and veal dishes prepared with Italian flair – including the famed pansotti al prosciutto and a Caesar salad mixed tableside – attract a similarly ostentatious clientele.

Anasazi Restaurant (Map pp76-7; ☎ 988-3236; 113 Washington Ave; dinner $27-33, other meals $8-12; ☺ 7am-2:30pm, 5:30-10pm) This upscale, Navajo-themed entry, where local meat and produce are combined to create a great duck hash at breakfast and award-winning soups and the recommended sautéed red lentils any time. Impress your date with a fine desert or, better, a room at the adjacent Inn of the Anasazi (p98).

La Casa Sena (Map pp76-7; ☎ 988-9232; 125 E Palace; lunch $7-12, dinner $21-27; ☺ 11:30am-3pm & 5:30-10pm daily) Housed in an 1880s-era adobe fronted by an idyllic patio, this restaurant serves four-star gourmet cuisine with Southwestern flair, like the trout baked in adobe with asparagus-leek risotto, with a choice of 1100 wines (no, that's not a typo) with which to wash it down. It once housed the legislative assembly when an 1892 fire tore through the old capitol; it's still favored by politicians and foodies alike.

La Cantina (Map pp76-7; ☎ 988-9232; 125 E Palace; mains $13-25; ☺ seatings at 6:30pm & 8pm daily) Expect an abbreviated menu of La Casa Sena's finest. Make reservations for this serious visitor magnet with one huge bonus: the waitstaff gets dressed up and sings show tunes!

Ore House (Map pp76-7; ☎ 983-8687; 50 Lincoln Ave; lunch $8-13, dinner $18-26; ☺ 11:30am-10pm daily) Folks willing to further indulge their inner tourist should also stop here for a balcony overlooking the plaza, 66 different margaritas and excellent, if slightly overpriced, food.

Coyote Cafe (Map pp76-7; ☎ 983-1615; 132 Water St; mains $21-42; ☺ 6-9pm daily) Chef Mark Miller ascended to superstar status years ago, and his high-quality interpretations of New Mexican cuisine – try the buttermilk corncakes with chipotle prawns or pecan-wood grilled rib chop – remain a highlight of any foodie's visit.

O'Keeffe Café (Map pp76-7; ☎ 946-1065; 217 Johnson St; lunch $9-20, dinner $16-32; ☺ 11am-10pm daily) An elegant eatery with shaded patio dining, this fine café boasts an exceptional wine list and exquisite, mostly organic entrees like chicken roulade with porcini mushrooms and quail marinated in local honey, all right next to the O'Keeffe Museum (p80). The café also does wine tastings and classes on occasion.

Café Paris (Map pp76-7; ☎ 986-9162; 311 Burro Alley; lunch $8-10, dinner $21-25; ☺ 11:30am-2:30pm & 5:30-9pm Tue-Sun) Fine French cuisine, from chicken cordon bleu to a recommended seafood crêpe, has won the hearts of critics, but it's the **French Pastry Shop** (☺ 6:30am-5pm), next door on the pedestrian-only street, that brings in hedonistic locals intent on sweet indulgence.

SantaCafé (Map pp76-7; ☎ 984-1788; 231 Washington Ave; lunch $8-20, dinner $19-24; ☺ 11:30am-2pm Mon-Sat, 6pm-close daily) Chef David Sellars is practically an international celebrity for dishes like goat cheese–stuffed free-range chicken with confit tamales (get the green chile mashed potatoes on the side), served in an 1850s adobe built by the infamous Padre Gallegos. Lunch is a deal, the wine list flawless and the dining room historic – perfect.

El Mesón (Map pp76-7; ☎ 983-6756; 213 Washington Ave; tapas $2-6, entrees $18-22; ☺ 5-10pm Tue-Sun) This beautiful restaurant, famed for its paella (try the vegetarian 'de la Huertas') and list of fine Spanish wines, even has a communal table where solo travelers can find conversation. **¡Chispas!** is known for excellent tapas, live music Wednesday evening and **flamenco** ($5; ☺ 8pm first Sat of month).

El Farol (Map p83; ☎ 983-9912; 808 Canyon Rd; lunch $6-14, dinner $25-50; ☺ 11:30am-late) Billed as the 'oldest bar in Santa Fe,' built in 1835, this cool, dark adobe features music Wednesday through Saturday, murals by artist Alfred Morang (painted in the 1950s to pay off his tab) and delicately spiced paella. It's all about the tapas, however: come here for small dishes like quesode cabra (baked goat cheese), boqueroñes (white Spanish anchovies) and the gambas de ajillo (garlic sautéed shrimp). Make reservations to enjoy three tapas of your choice while taking in the **flamenco** ($45; ☺ 7:30pm first and third Wed of month).

The Compound (Map p83; ☎ 982-4353; 635 Canyon Rd; lunch $12-20, dinner $24-31; ☺ noon-2pm Mon-Fri, 6-9pm daily) Eat in the historic James Beard house or on the sun-drenched patio. The emphasis here is on fresh fish, beautiful salads and clean Mediterranean flavors. It's relaxing, elegant and boasts one of the best green chile cheeseburgers in town, which could be washed down with one of at least 10 fine wines available by the glass. This is a truly grand place for Canyon Rd adventurers to rest their weary tootsies.

Geronimo (Map p83; ☎ 982-1500; 724 Canyon Rd; lunch $13-20, dinner $27-36; ☼ 11:30am-2:15pm & 6: 30-9:30pm Tue-Sun) The most exclusive (and perhaps overrated) dining experience in town can be had by the roaring fire in this 1756 adobe on Canyon Rd.

Guadalupe Street Area
BUDGET
Whole Foods Market (Map pp76-7; ☎ 992-1700; 753 Cerrillos Rd; ☼ 7:30am-10pm, deli 11am-9pm) A shrine to the organic economy's success in a capitalist world, this expansive store has all things natural, including an outrageous deli and salad bar plus enough free samples that you won't even bother with the rest. **MarketPlace Natural Grocery** (Map p75; ☎ 984-2852; 913 W Alameda; ☼ 7:30am-9pm Mon-Sat; 9am-8pm Sun) is the smaller, locally owned version.

Santa Fe Farmers Market (Map pp76-7; ☎ 983-4098; www.farmersmarketsnm.org/santafe; cnr Cerrillos Rd & Guadalupe St; ☼ 7am-noon Sat & Tue Apr-Nov) Local produce, much of it heirloom and organic, is on sale at these spacious new digs alongside homemade goodies, inexpensive food and a fair number of arts and crafts. **Winter Market** (Map p75; 1614B Paseo de Peralta; ☼ 9am-1pm Sat Nov-Apr) is held at nearby El Museo Cultural de Santa Fe.

Chicago Dog Express (Map pp76-7; ☎ 984-2798; 600 Cerrillos Rd; fast food $2-5; ☼ 7:30am-4pm) This usually packed joint serves a mean breakfast burrito topped with good chile, plus dogs galore (yes, even a veggie version); patio seating only.

Bert's Burger Barn (Map pp76-7; ☎ 982-0215; 235 N Guadalupe St; fast food $2-5; ☼ 7am-8pm daily) Despite its grubby veneer, this humble outlet has a devoted following on par with any four-star restaurant for its burgers and carne adovada.

Sage Bakehouse (Map pp76-7; ☎ 820-7243; 535C Cerrillos Rd; sandwiches $3-6; ☼ 7am-5pm Mon-Sat) Coffee, pastries and light lunches are served on a pleasant patio, or while watching bakers pull out the excellent pecan-raisin and extra-sour sourdough bread.

Dave's Not Here (Map pp76-7; ☎ 983-7060; 1115 Hickox St; mains $3-7; ☼ 11am-9pm daily) On the wrong side of the tracks, this relaxed restaurant dishes up justly famed rellenos, burgers and great cake just a bit off the beaten path – follow Paseo de Peralta across St Francis where it becomes Hickox St.

DOÑA TULES: CARDSHARK AND KINGMAKER

According to legend, Maria Gertrudis Barceló was born the peón (indentured servant) of a wealthy Taos family in the early 1800s. After a short marriage to a local miner, the red-haired, cigar-smoking beauty found herself broke and on her own in Santa Fe. She may have sold soap on the plaza, or perhaps La Tules (her nickname, 'The Reed') capitalized on her historically notable assets as a consort to wealthy politicos.

This much is known: the popular fashion plate (remembered for her heavy jewelry and plunging necklines) opened a gambling hall on Palace Ave, where she dealt 40-card monte and entertained an opulent clientele. Among her regulars was Governor Armijo, known for his good looks, high taxes and blatant corruption during the chaotic decades of Mexican rule. The two were romantically linked, but her alleged affections did not compromise her political savvy.

Already friendly with Anglos who frequented her sala, she was contacted in 1846 by US General Stephen Kearny, on his mission of Manifest Destiny: the Americans were coming. Irritated by Armijo's mistreatment of the poor – the class she had risen from – Doña Tules threw in her lot with the USA, loaning Kearny money and even warning him of subterfuge that threatened his tenuous occupation.

Upon her death in 1852, her will requested an elaborate funeral, more appropriate for nobility than a somewhat scandalous former servant. But the church opened its doors to Santa Fe's hostess with the mostest, and the eulogy may well have been given by the bishop himself.

To learn more of Doña Tules' story, or just get a sense of bodice-ripping old Santa Fe, check out *The Wind Leaves No Shadow*, by Ruth Laughlin. Or just stop by Palace Restaurant (p101), on the site of Tules' old sala, for a toast.

Paramount Pizza (Map pp76-7; ☎ 955-1590; 331 Sandoval; ☺ 11am-midnight Sun-Tues & Thu, 11am-2:30am Wed, Fri & Sat) Enjoy New York–style pizza by the slice ($3) or pie ($10-20) plus salads and sandwiches. The staff deliver or serve you at the Paramount Theater and Bar B (p107).

Bumble Bee's Baja Grill (Map pp76-7; ☎ 820-2862; 301 Jefferson; fast food $3-9; ☺ 11am-9pm daily) It's got a drive-thru, but come inside this bright spot and dress the excellent fish tacos, asparagus burritos and grilled chicken quesadillas at the salsa bar – and don't skip the Mexican espresso brownie for desert.

Cleopatra Cafe (Map pp76-7; ☎ 820-7381; 418 Cerrillos Rd; mains $4-9; ☺ 11am-8:30pm Mon-Sat) Hidden away in the Design Center, this Mediterranean eatery has two types of falafel (Egyptian, with favas, or Lebanese, using more common chickpeas) and a great chicken kabob.

Aztec Café (Map pp76-7; ☎ 820-0025; 317 Aztec St; sandwiches $6; ☺ 7am-7pm winter, 7am-dark summer) This cozy café keeps the tattoos-and-climbing-gear crowd caffeinated and fed with sandwiches, ice cream and malteds served beneath local art that pales in comparison to the fabulous people-watching.

Zia Diner (Map pp76-7; ☎ 988-7008; 366 S Guadalupe St; mains $6-9; ☺ 11am-10pm daily) Voted 'Best Comfort Food' by locals, this cozy diner is known for its meatloaf, liver and onions, and homemade pies. Have a beer and watch pink-haired hipsters and graying progressives coo over their blue-plate specials (served weekdays only).

MID-RANGE

Cafe Oasis (Map pp76-7; ☎ 983-9599, delivery 660-5913; 526 Galisteo St; mains $6-11; ☺ 9:30am-midnight Sun-Thu, 9am-2am Fri-Sat) Feel the love over organic, free-range entrees like lamb burgers and curried tempeh served in super groovy theme rooms decked out in original art, or on the totally mellow patio out back. There's live music – accordions, chanting, whatever – Thursday through Sunday starting around 7pm, with no cover.

Tomasita's (Map pp76-7; ☎ 983-5721; 500 S Guadalupe St; mains $6-12; ☺ 11am-10pm Mon-Sat) Locals hate to admit it, but they love this tourist standby for its outstanding green chile, served atop excellent burritos, enchiladas and the huge $10 blue-plate specials, served weekdays only. It's raucous

– perfect for families hauling even the most exuberant kids.

Saveur (Map pp76-7; ☎ 989-4200; 204 Montezuma; mains $8/pound; ☺ 8am-4pm Mon-Sat) Basically a foodie's dream salad bar, this innovative entry serves everything from mixed greens to steamed fish and noodle salads, buffet style. Bonus: at 3pm, soups and salads go for 30% off, and 50% off at 3:30pm.

Banana Café (Map pp76-7; ☎ 982-3886; 329 W San Francisco St; mains $8-12; ☺ 11am-2:30pm & 4-9pm daily) Finally Santa Feans and tourists over the green chile thing can enjoy fabulous Thai cuisine – you can't go wrong with curries or seafood at this beautifully decorated spot.

Santa Fe Bar & Grill (Map pp76-7; ☎ 982-3033; 187 Paseo de Peralta; mains $6-11; ☺ 11am-10pm daily) OK, so it's not in a historic adobe; it's at convenient DeVargas Center (p112). But the patio overlooking a parking lot and sleek interior are packed with people listening to live acoustic guitar and grubbing on Southwestern-style salads, big plates of ribs and recommended red chile onion rings.

Cowgirl Hall of Fame (Map pp76-7; ☎ 982-2526; 319 S Guadalupe St; mains $8-13; ☺ 11am-2am Mon-Fri, 8:30am-2am Sat, kitchen closes at 11pm) Winning both Best Bar and Best Place for Kids in a local survey, thanks to the great playground outside and live music after 9pm (p107), this place has fabulous food, too – try the salmon tacos, butternut squash casserole or anything mesquite grilled – all served with Texas caviar (black-eyed pea salsa) and wacky Western-style feminist flair.

Andiamo! (Map pp76-7; ☎ 995-9595; 322 Garfield St; mains $8-20; ☺ 5:30-10pm nightly) Hipsters to hippies will tell you, this is more than just another extensive, award-winning wine list and fresh and fabulous antipasto, pan-seared pork tenderloin, grilled polenta with goat cheese and tiramisu. It's an excuse to dress up (or down), to see and be seen, and to face a packed house –make reservations.

TOP END

Shohko Cafe (Map pp76-7; ☎ 983-7288; 321 Johnson St; rolls $4-12, mains $9-17; ☺ 11:30am-2pm & 5:30-9pm daily) It's the biggest and best sushi bar in town (yes, there is a Santa Fe roll, with cream cheese and, shockingly, green chile) and serves up bento boxes at lunch and teriyaki dishes for those folks who don't do raw fish.

SANTA FE

Tulips (Map pp76-7; ☎ 989-7340; 222 N Guadalupe; mains $18-32; ⏰ 6-10pm Tue-Sun) California-French cuisine and the perfect accompanying decor make you feel like you're in Napa Valley – or Provence. Dining rooms are intimate and the menu is short, fabulous and changes often. Make reservations and prepare to linger.

Vanessie of Santa Fe (Map pp76-7; ☎ 982-9966; 434 W San Francisco St; mains $12-20; ⏰ 5:30-10:30pm daily) You don't really come to Vanessie for the food, though it's fine, with meaty dishes served à la carte and sides that vegetarians could potentially make a meal out of. No, the attraction here is the piano bar, featuring blow-dried lounge singers who bring Neil Diamond and Barry Manilow classics to life in their own special way.

Old House Restaurant (Map pp76-7; ☎ 988-4455; 309 W San Francisco St; mains $23-30; ⏰ 5:30-10pm daily) The El Dorado Hotel's (p97) flagship restaurant has won every award around with Southwestern-style gourmet grub like the red pepper soup, aged Angus beef and the signature warm liquid-center chocolate cake. It boasts more wines by the glass than anywhere else in town.

Cerrillos Road
BUDGET
Chocolate Smith (Map p75; ☎ 473-2111; 1807 2nd St; ⏰ 10am-5pm daily) Handcrafted dark chocolate, made in small batches and mixed with organic ingredients like green chile and piñon, make this little shop worth the drive.

La Carretera (Map p75; ☎ 471-3678; 2900 Cerrillos Rd; mains $2-8; ⏰ 10am-10pm daily) This hidden gem, adjacent to the Days Inn, does Salvadoran baked goods, including excellent and authentic pupusas (like a thick, savory, stuffed corn tortilla) plus plenty of other Central American treats.

Baja Tacos (Map p75; ☎ 471-8762; 2621 Cerrillos Rd; fast food $2-6; ⏰ 7am-9pm Mon-Sat, 8am-8pm Sun) Grab New Mexican classics – including an extensive vegetarian menu and good carne adovada – inside the cramped interior or at the drive-thru. Bonus: the amazing mural outside, *Her Story is a Part of Our History*, by noted area artists Julia Coyne and Amberleigh, uniquely depicts Santa Fe's cultural heritage, showing San Ildefonso potter Maria Martinez (p119), flamenco maestra Maria Benitez (p108) and painter Georgia O'Keeffe (p125).

Tecolote Café (Map p75; ☎ 988-1362; 1203 Cerrillos Rd; mains $4-8; ⏰ 7am-2pm daily) Start your morning with the sheepherder's breakfast (new potatoes, chile and onions topped with eggs and cheese), excellent eggs Benedict (it's the best Hollandaise sauce in town) or any other equally enormous entrée at the finest hole-in-the-wall on the strip.

Tortilla Flats (Map p75; ☎ 471-8685; 3139 Cerrillos Rd; mains $4-12; ⏰ 7am-9pm daily) Don't be fooled by the chain-style exterior; this recommended spot is known for its roast beef quesadillas, lavishly overfilled vegetarian burritos and the ridiculously huge carnita ranchera omelet, topped with potatoes, cheese, shredded beef, avocado and more.

New China Super Buffet (Map p75; ☎ 438-9777; 3006 Cerrillos Rd; buffet lunch/dinner $6/8; ⏰ 11am-9pm daily) Of Santa Fe's endless selection of Chinese buffets, this one – with a sushi bar (tip the chef a dollar or two extra and he'll treat you right) – is the best.

Back Street Bistro (Map p75; ☎ 982-3500; mains $7-8; 513 Camino de Marquez; ⏰ 11am-2:30pm Mon-Sat) It's hidden in a big blue warehouse a block from St Francis and within view of Lowes, but driving around a bit is worth the search for gourmet soups (try Santa Fe onion, with green chile) and corned beef sandwiches.

MID-RANGE
Santa Fe Baking Company & Café (Map p75; ☎ 988-4292; 504 W Cordova Rd; mains $3-10; ⏰ 6am-6pm Mon-Sat, 6:30am-4pm Sun) This lively local spot for a quick sandwich on homemade bread just rocks.

Maria's New Mexican Kitchen (Map p75; ☎ 983-7929; 555 W Cordova Rd; mains $6-11 ⏰ 11am-10pm Mon-Fri, noon-10pm Sat & Sun) Huge portions of New Mexican standards, prepared with locally grown ingredients and topped off with great natillas (a type of custard), would make this 1952 Santa Fe standby a winner anyway, but with more than 100 margaritas ($5-50, made with lemon, not lime, thank you very much), it's a must.

India House (Map p75; ☎ 471-2651; 2501 Cerrillos Rd; mains $7-13; ⏰ 11:30am-2:30pm Mon-Fri, 5-10pm daily) Excellent lamb sagwala, lamb-stuffed keema nan and everything vindaloo are fabulous, or just show up for the abundant lunch buffet ($7), one of the best deals in town.

Saigon Cafe (Map p75; ☎ 988-4951; 501 W Cordova Rd; mains $7-10; ⏰ 11am-9pm Mon-Sat) Lauded as the best Asian food in all Santa Fe, the options include huge portions of Vietnamese hot and sour soup, vermicelli salad and chow fun, all enthusiastically recommended.

Mariscos 'La Playa' (Map p75; ☎ 982-2790; 537 Cordova Rd; mains $7-16; ☯ 11am-9pm Wed-Mon) Mexican-style seafood, including justly famed ceviche, cocteles and caldo 'El Mejor' – a soup with shrimp, octopus, scallops, clams, crab and calamari – all go well with an agave wine margarita.

Cloud Cliff Bakery (Map p75; ☎ 983-6254; 1805 2nd St; mains $6-10; ☯ 7am-5pm Mon-Fri, 8am-3pm Sat & Sun) Slip on your Birkenstocks and drop by for a loaf. Rainbow trout wraps, grilled polenta breakfasts, soups and sandwiches are served alongside organic wines and microbrews, with plenty of lefty commentary and sometimes live music in the evening.

mudu noodles (Map p75; ☎ 983-1411; 1494 Cerrillos Rd; mains $11-17; ☯ 5:30-9pm Mon-Sat) Pan-Asian, often organic delights like salmon dumplings, Vietnamese spring rolls and tofu laksa inspire lines out the door of this lovely spot; the noodles (of course) and specials are always recommended, and almost everything has a vegan version.

Metropolitan Santa Fe
BUDGET
Castro's Comidas Nativas (Map p75; ☎ 438-0146; 3512 W Rodeo Rd; mains $3-7; ☯ 11am-9pm Mon-Sat) Order basic, 'ranch-style' New Mexican cuisine at the counter, decorated with lowrider cars and Homies figures, then kick back and enjoy burritos, enchiladas (get the red chile) and the best menudo in town, served all day. It's *so* worth the drive.

Bobcat Bites (☎ 983-5319; 420 Old Las Vegas Hwy; burgers $5; 11am-7:50pm Wed-Sun) Also worth the drive – from Albuquerque – this place serves arguably the best green chile cheeseburgers in town at this relaxed roadhouse beneath the neon sign.

Museum Hill Café (Map p75; ☎ 820-1776; 720 Camino Lejo; mains $6-8; ☯ 9am-5pm Tue-Sun, lunch 11am-3pm Tue-Sun) Despite having a captive audience on Museum Hill (p79), the café serves excellent Navajo tacos, salmon in papillote and quesadillas de dia.

PC's Restaurant & Lounge (Map p75; ☎ 473-7164; 422 Airport Rd; mains $6-8; ☯ 11am-2:30pm & 5:30-9pm Tue-Sat) Naugahyde booths surround tables groaning beneath huge servings of excellent,

no-frills stuffed sopapillas and enchiladas, best washed down with pitchers of beer.

Chocolate Maven (Map p75; ☎ 984-1980; 821 W San Mateo; mains $5-9; ☯ 7am-5:30pm Mon-Fri, 9am-3pm Sat & Sun) Sit down to white tablecloths and stemware, and watch through windows as bakers work while you enjoy their incredible pastries, crème brulée French toast or a variety of gourmet sandwiches.

Tesuque Village Market (Map p116; ☎ 988-8848; cnr Bishops Lodge Rd & NM 591; dinner $7-14, other meals $4-9; ☯ 7am-10pm daily) In the upscale village of Tesuque (sometimes described as 'the Beverly Hills of Santa Fe'), grab gourmet groceries or an excellent lunch – from Frito pies to steak fajitas – and enjoy them on the pleasant porch outside.

MID-RANGE
Harry's Roadhouse (☎ 989-4629; 96B Old Las Vegas Hwy; dinner $8-15, other meals $5-8; ☯ 7am-10pm daily) The attractive setting and elegant cuisine far surpass what the prices imply, and dishes like Moroccan vegetable stew over couscous, turkey meatloaf and Cajun blackened catfish are overshadowed only by the specials. Excellent stuff.

Gabriel's (☎ 455-7000; US 84/285; lunch $6-8, dinner $11-16; ☯ 11:30am-9pm daily) The beautiful interior, hung with art by Miguel Martinez, and scenic patio are both fabulous spots to enjoy fresh guacamole, made to order right at your table, excellent New Mexican cuisine and the best ribs ever. Plan to drop by if you're headed to the flea market or points north.

TOP END
315 (☎ 986-9190; 315 Old Santa Fe Trail; lunch $11-18, dinner $18-25; ☯ 11am-2:30pm Mon-Sat, 5:30-9pm daily) Just outside the area demarcated 'downtown,' you'll enjoy some of the city's finest cuisine (including delicacies like white truffle flan and veal scaloppini with morels). But the real draw is the wine list, which is showcased on Wednesday Wine Nights ($55-70), when knowledgeable sommeliers pour vintages according to themes. Make reservations.

Las Fuentes (Map p116; ☎ 983-6377, 800-732-2240; 1297 Bishops Lodge Rd; dinner $24-35, other meals $9-16; ☯ 6:30am-10pm daily) The Bishop's Lodge (p98) restaurant serves light, often vegetarian cuisine alongside game dishes, including roasted venison and lacquered wild salmon.

There's live Latin jazz Thursday through Saturday evenings, but its claim to fame is the outrageous Sunday brunch ($30 with champagne).

ENTERTAINMENT

Santa Fe may be world-renowned for its upscale performing arts scene, but the same isn't really true for its nightlife. But there are several excellent, and odd, venues worth checking out, and the music scene has some pretty outstanding entries. Pick up a copy of the *Reporter* (p74) or *Pasatiempo* (p74) for listings of area events, and be daring. This is a creative community, and sometimes the wackiest offerings will prove the most worthwhile.

Bars & Pubs

Belltower Bar (Map pp76-7; ☎ 982-5511; 100 E San Francisco St; 4pm-sunset Mon-Thu, 2pm-sunset Fri-Sun May-Oct) Atop La Fonda, the tallest building in town, enjoy a cold beer or killer margarita while watching one of those patented New Mexico sunsets. In the lobby, **La Fiesta Lounge** (mains $10-23; 11am-11:30pm daily) serves the same great margaritas alongside good New Mexican cuisine, including a popular lunch buffet ($9), and features live music almost nightly.

Dragon Bar (Map pp76-7; ☎ 983-7712; 406 Old Santa Fe Trail; pub grub $8-24; 11:30am-2am daily) Stop and sit for a spell in this warm and weathered adobe, which has provided shelter, sustenance and stiff drinks to conversationalists since WWII. There's live music – usually flamenco guitar, Latin jazz or the like – almost nightly, starting around 9pm.

Blue Corn Café & Brewery (Map p75; ☎ 438-1800; 4056 Cerrillos Rd; mains $6-15; 11am-10pm daily) This cavernous brewpub has won awards for its Atomic Blonde Ale and Cold Front Coffee Stout, served alongside tapas, burgers and Chuy's chalupas. There's a smaller outpost at **Plaza Mercado** (Map pp76-7; ☎ 984-1800; 133 Water St).

Evangelo's (Map pp76-7; ☎ 983-9014; 200 W San Francisco St; noon-1:30am Mon-Sat, noon-midnight Sun) It's rowdy, it's smoky, and one of these days the floor is probably going to cave in during a packed classic rock show: in short, it's the perfect escape from plaza couture. Drop in, put on some Patsy Cline and grab a draft beer. You'll have a blast.

Second Street Brewery (Map p75; ☎ 982-3030; www.secondstreetbrewery.com; mains $6-10; 11am-11pm daily) After a hard day hiking (or just shopping for hiking equipment), stop by this microbrewery and pair a Cream Stout or Otowi Pale Ale with fish and chips or the Danish bleu and walnut salad. There's often live music in the evenings.

Green Onion (Map p75; ☎ 983-5181; 1851 St Michael's Dr; pub grub $5-10; 11am-11pm Mon-Sat, 11am-9:30pm Sun) When you just want a beer and a good red chile cheeseburger, this dark and convivial spot will set you up.

Live Music

In addition to perusing the *Reporter* and *Pasatiempo*, log on to **Mitch's New Mexico Music Portal** (www.nmmusic.com), with links to

---

QUEST FOR THE BEST MARGARITA

Nothing goes better with New Mexican cuisine than a good margarita, but who mixes the best? In an effort to answer this important question, Museum of New Mexico docents and margarita connoisseurs Mike and Anita Stevenson laboriously compiled this list of top tipples while testing **The Shed's** (p100) outstanding runner-up for the title.

- **La Fonda** (p97) High quality entry gets extra points for the people-watching.
- **Maria's** (p104) With more than 100 varieties, you can test these lemon-juice-only, all-agave concoctions all night long – or until you pass out.
- **Rancho de Chimayó** (p128) Great margaritas, or try a Chimayó cocktail, with homegrown apple cider and crème de cassis.
- **El Paragua** (p124) Wash down Española's finest chile rellenos with the excellent house offering.
- **Adobe Bar** (p164) Top off your Taos adventure with live music and the perfect margarita.

mp3s, for profiles on local artists who play everything from country and mariachi to funk and punk.

Cowgirl Hall of Fame (p103; cover $1-5) In addition to being a fine and rustic-with-a-vengeance venue for catching live shows (despite the name, rarely country), this spot also has microbrews, great food and nonsmoking events.

El Paseo Bar & Grille (Map pp76-7; ☎ 992-2848; 208 Galisteo St; pub grub $5-8; ⌚ 11:30am-1:30am Mon-Sat, 11:30am-midnight Sun, kitchen closes at 11pm) This seemingly sedate wood-paneled pub with microbrews, cigars and green chile cheese steak sandwiches is another excellent place to catch a show.

Catamount (Map pp76-7; ☎ 988-7222; 125 E Water St) It's got pool tables, a nice dark bar and a brighter patio, and there's almost always live music downstairs.

The G-Spot (Map pp76-7; ☎ 982-1851; 311 Old Santa Fe Rd; mains $6-9, cover varies; ⌚ 11am-2am daily) Adjacent to Garrett's Desert Inn (p97), this popular bar with an outdoor patio is the place for Latin jazz, flamenco, mariachi and more in the evening.

Warehouse 21 (Map pp76-7; ☎ 989-4423; www.warehouse21.com; 1614 Paseo de Peralta; cover $5-10) This all-ages club and art center, in a 3500-sq-ft warehouse, is the perfect alcohol-free venue for edgy local bands, plus a fair number of nationally known acts, or for showing off the latest in multihued hairstyles. Download mp3 recordings of recent shows for a preview.

Paolo Soleri Amphitheatre (Map p75; ☎ 989-6318; 1501 Cerrillos Rd) This amazing outdoor venue, designed by Italian arcologist (that's architect plus ecologist, which equals some seriously bizarre buildings) Paolo Soleri, hosts great music festivals like Reggae Sunsplash, as well as hip musicians including Ani DiFranco, Blues Traveler and Morrissey. The sunset over Soleri's strange angles alone is worth the ticket price.

Dance Clubs

The Paramount (Map pp76-7; ☎ 982-8999; www.theparamountnightclub.com; 331 Sandoval; cover varies) This place not only has a dance floor where you can actually shake it to reggae (www.brotherhoodsound.com), Trash Disco and local hip-hop DJs ChicanoBuilt (p108), but it also hosts national recording artists, musical theater like the rock opera *Hedwig*

and the Angry Inch, and jazz and acoustic performances. The adjacent **Bar B** (⌚ 5pm-2am nightly) is more relaxed, with work by local artists hanging from the wall, chandeliers hanging from the ceiling, local performers of the highest caliber, and karaoke nights known to degenerate into impromptu comedy routines.

Swig (Map pp76-7; ☎ 955-0400; 135 W Palace Ave; tapas $13-20; ⌚ 5pm-2am) OK, so there's not really much of a dance floor (and the scantily clad male go-go dancers take up much of it), but with killer DJs imported from all over the country, lots of fancy martinis, a dress code reading 'appropriate attire' (translation: white hot) and some seriously groovy South Beach–style surroundings, it's just got that vibe. Swig is owned by the same folks as Geronimo (p102), so you know the Asian-fusion tapas are good, but in these outfits, who can afford a non-martini calorie?

Zia Diner (Map pp76-7; ☎ 988-7008; 366 S Guadalupe St; cover varies; ⌚ 11pm-2am Thu-Sat) Santa Fe's favorite diner just started cashing in on the growing dance scene with a late-night all-ages club. It has potential.

Rodeo Nights (Map p75; ☎ 473-4138; 2911 Cerrillos Rd; ⌚ 6pm-1:30am daily) It's so big and so packed that it may be a little daunting if you're not already hip to the two-step scene. But it's still the best dance floor in town, with live music almost nightly, including ranchero and salsa.

Performing Arts

This is Santa Fe's pride and joy: a truly world-class collection of fine performers and venues showcasing their talents in music, theater and dance. The Opera may be the belle of the ball – clad, most assuredly, in sparkling denim – but culture junkies flock here in July and August to immerse themselves in chamber music, flamenco and more. *Four Seasons Santa Fe* (www.santafeevents.org) maintains an exhaustive listing of highbrow events.

This is also Santa Fe's headache: you'll have to be quick on the ticket line to score coveted seats, and securing rooms and tables takes similar stamina. Many locals just give up and take a two-month vacation. Others, however, pink hair and all, can be found in the standing-room-only section for every last opera.

SANTA FE

SANTA FE

ARTISTS

Santa Fe Opera (Map p116; ☎ 986-5900, 800-280-4654; www.santafeopera.org; standing room $8-15, seats $20-130; late Jun-late Aug) Many come to Santa Fe for this and this alone: An architectural marvel, with views of wind-carved sandstone wilderness crowned with sunsets and moonrises, and at center stage (and what a stage!) internationally renowned vocal talent performing humanity's masterworks of aria and romance. Best of all, you can wear jeans – just try *that* in New York City.

The show begins two hours before the curtain rises, when the traditional **tailgate party** – a college football ritual rendered glamorous in true Santa Fe style – gets started in the parking lot. Bring your own caviar and brie, make reservations for the buffet dinner and tour ($40) or have a caterer – several customize the menu to the opera's theme – pour the champagne. **Shuttles** (p113) run to and from the event for about $20 from Santa Fe, $30 from Albuquerque.

Seats come equipped with translations in English and Spanish, but the standing-room crowd is on their own. Children under five can attend special youth performances, but otherwise leave the toddlers at home and enjoy – this is truly one of the world's finest offerings. **Backstage tours** (adult/child $5/free; ⊙ 1pm Mon-Sat Jul & Aug) offer opportunities to poke around the sets, while special events, for children and grownups, offer insight into the world of fine music

---

CHICANOBUILT

In the mood for some Latino hip-hop and wild thumping mixes that really work the crowd? Want to dance all night long? Then check out ChicanoBuilt, featuring some of the most popular DJs in town: DJ Rockwell, King George and Automatic, as well as Joe Ray Sandoval, a poet and performance artist who foments **Poetry Allowed,** with slam-style readings for la Raza. And la Raza packs The Paramount and venues all over Aztlán when this eclectic collection of lyrical mix masters takes the stage. Dress to impress and get ready to jump.

Log onto the website (www.chicanobuilt.com) for a calendar and to download mp3s.

Santa Fe Chamber Music Festival (☎ 982-1890; www.sfcmf.org; admission free to $50; Jul & Aug) This is the other big cultural event, known for filling elegant venues like the Lensic and Wheelwright Museum with Schubert, Mozart and other classic concertos. But it's not just world-class acts like violinist Pinchas Zukerman and composer Chan Kan Nin defining the season; nope, top-notch jazz and Portuguese Fado are also on the menu, available for lunch during the popular noon performances at stunning St Francis Auditorium.

Maria Benitez Teatro Flamenco (☎ 955-8562, 888-435-2636; www.mariabenitez.com; $18-42) Perhaps the best flamenco troupe in North America, Maria Benitez and a host of intensely focused and festively garbed protégées have earned every accolade with their impressive performances of the ultimate Spanish dance. They perform June through September at the Radisson (p96) and occasionally at other venues around town and the USA. Can't get enough flamenco? **El Farol** (p101; $45 with three tapas) stages performers from the National Institute of Flamenco on the first and third Wednesday of the month, while **El Mesón** (p101; $5 cover) has flamenco on the first Saturday of the month.

Santa Fe Desert Chorale (☎ 988-2282, 800-244-4011; www.desertchorale.org; $15-50, some free events) Vocal ensembles and chamber choruses perform everything from classical music to Gregorian chants in July, August and during the winter holidays at venues including St Francis Cathedral and Loretto Chapel.

Santa Fe Stages (SFS; ☎ 982-6683; www.santafestages.org; $15-50) Bringing an eclectic and increasingly impressive program of modern and traditional dance, performance art and theater to the Lensic and Armory for the Arts, SFS offers a limited number of $8 tickets to folks willing to get in line by 10am on the day of the performance.

Santa Fe Symphony & Chorus (☎ 983-3530, 800-480-1319; www.sf-symphony.org) From September to May, top musicians heat up venues like the Lensic with classical performances.

Santa Fe Shakespeare Company (☎ 982-2910; www.festivalsantafe.org/shakes.html; adult/child $20/12, some free shows) This troupe performs the best of the bard and other plays including puppet shows and outdoor events with free seating at St John's College, the Lensic, Armory for the Arts and other venues statewide

VENUES

Lensic Performing Arts Theater (Map pp76-7; ☎ 984-1370; www.lensic.com; 1050 Old Pecos Trail) This 1931 Moorish-revival movie house is now Santa Fe's premier, and intimate, 850-seat venue, hosting the Santa Fe Chamber Music Festival, Santa Fe Symphony and many national acts. **Lannan Reading & Conversation** (☎ 986-8160; www.lannan.org; adult/child $6/3; ☯ 7pm Wed) stages readings, which tend to focus on cultural and particularly Native American issues, by local and internationally renowned poets and writers.

Center for Contemporary Arts (Map p75; CCA; ☎ 982-1338; 1050 Old Pecos Trail; adult/child $8/5) The CCA screens old and/or artsy films plus a popular film noir festival. Weekends may stage art openings and live performances, including **Theater Grottesco** (☎ 474-8400; www.theatergrottesco.org; $5-20), a highly recommended avant-garde troupe worth seeking out here or at other venues around the state and nation.

Santa Fe Playhouse (Map pp76-7; ☎ 988-4262; www.santafeplayhouse.org; 142 E DeVargas St; $8-15; ☯ 8pm Thu-Sat, 2pm Sun) Local actors have been putting on plays, including the annual *Fiesta Melodrama* (with audience participation!), in this historic adobe since 1922. The Sunday matinee is 'pay what you wish.'

The theater also hosts several other troupes, including the **Southwest Children's Theatre** (www.southwestchildrenstheatre.com; tickets $5) featuring daytime plays for kids and by kids (plus a few childish adults).

James A Little Theatre (Map p75; ☎ 827-6760; 1060 Cerrillos Rd) At the New Mexico School for the Deaf, this unpretentious venue hosts notional acts like Dar Williams and kd lang, performances by Albuquerque's **Ballet Theatre of New Mexico** (p63) and random offerings including the Los Alamos National Laboratory (LANL; ☎ 505-667-7000) **Frontiers in Science Public Lecture Series** (www.lanl.gov/science/fellows/lecture.shtml; admission free), a program that covers everything from astronomical phenomena to particle acceleration.

Armory for the Arts (Map p75; ☎ 984-1370; 1050 Old Pecos Trail; $6-15) Primarily a spot where community players and local teens stage favorites like *Fame,* this spot also host much bigger events.

Cinemas

In this notoriously artsy town, even Santa Fe's mainstream theaters screen art flicks and foreign films. Of course, you can still catch summer swashbucklers too.

UA DeVargas 6 (Map pp76-7; ☎ 988-2775; 564 N Guadalupe St; adult/child $8/5, matinee $6) Conveniently located at DeVargas Center (p112), this theater shows mainstream movies and a few artsy offerings. **UA South 6** (☎ 471-6066; 4250 Cerrillos Rd) screens a similar cinematic selection at Villa Linda Mall (p112).

The Screen (Map p75; ☎ 473-6494; www.thescreen.csf.edu; 1600 St Michael's Dr; adult/child $8/5) Only challenging and artsy independent films are shown at this small College of Santa Fe theater.

Jean Cocteau Theatre (Map pp76-7; ☎ 988-2711; www.transluxmovies.com; 418 Montezuma Ave; adult/child $8/6, matinee $5) Check out a selected independent flick here with a coffee from the onsite café or with that special someone (or with kids who might get a little crazy) in the VIP room ($3 extra).

St John's College Film Society (Map p75; ☎ 984-6158; www.sjcsf.edu/comcal/films1.htm; 1160 Camino de Cruz Blanca; $2; ☯ 7pm Wed) With wacky double features and cartoon intros, this is your best budget bet.

SHOPPING

You could spend weeks shopping in Santa Fe, and some people do. The focus, of course, is art, from Native American jewelry to wild contemporary paintings. This is one of the three top markets in the USA – New York City is first, while Los Angeles and Santa Fe are in a dead heat. And no, that's not per capita, that's total sales.

The most famous strip of galleries lines Canyon Rd (p82), and downtown is packed with fine art. The two biggest shopping extravaganzas are the juried shows of **Spanish Market** and **Indian Market** (p92), but these award-winning artisans – many of them driving buses and waiting tables, lest you think their pieces are overpriced – show in galleries throughout the year.

But that's just the beginning. Shopping around here isn't about conspicuous consumption, unless you want it to be. It's more like an open-air museum, displaying unique, antique, imaginative and inspiring objects found nowhere else.

SANTA FE

Contemporary & Fine Art

With far bigger budgets than any museum, collectors have helped concentrate some of the world's finest art into Santa Fe's strollable adobes. Gallery owners know they won't make much money off of the casually clad tourists – they send photos of their work directly to the mansions of serious investors – so don't worry about a hard sell. Top galleries are more like storage units, or advertising, and a public service for the rest of us. Besides, they know some of you just won't be able to walk away from that glorious Baumann print.

Gerald Peters Gallery (Map p83; ☎ 954-5700; www.gpgallery.com; 1011 Paseo de Peralta) Santa Fe's preeminent restaurant and real-estate tycoon Gerald Peters began dealing art in college and parlayed his hobby helping artsy friends survive into an empire: La Casa Sena and Blue Corn Café are just a few of his properties. And this gallery, two blocks from Canyon Rd, carries a collection of fine art that few museums can touch, with all the Southwest masters: Jozef G Bazos, Nicolai Fechin, Charlie Russell, Edward Borein, Woody Gwyn and many, many more. The back room has treasures the Museum of Fine Arts can't even afford, so check it out.

Nedra Mateucci Galleries (Map p83; ☎ 982-4631; www.matteucci.com; 1075 Paseo de Peralta) The Taos Society is on display at this top gallery, including the best work of Joseph Henry Sharp, Ernest Blumenschein, and the rest of the gang. In the beautiful gardens out back, sculptures crafted by Native American masters Allan Hauser and Michael Naranjo (p120), as well as Doug Hyde and *Vietnam Women's Memorial* designer Glenna Goodacre, can be seen and touched. Other highlights include actual 1870s 'ledger drawings,' created by Native Americans in custody of the US Army; original work by Georgia O'Keeffe, Peter Hurd and Raymond Johnson; and the best bathroom in Santa Fe. A must.

Shidoni (Map p116; ☎ 988-8001; 1510 Bishops Lodge Rd; www.shidoni.com) One of Santa Fe's true wonders, two enormous gardens (open Mon-Sat until sunset) are alive with figurative and abstract sculptures – some kinetic, some colorful, and all awe-inspiring – of every medium. This is where architects with attitude find wild centerpieces for their

masterpieces and where locals come just to stroll and see what's new. A foundry demonstrates the art of pouring bronze four times on Saturday, and neighboring **Tesuque Glassworks** (☎ 988-2165) has open studios where you can watch glass being blown. Even folks who yawn at the average gallery should consider this one.

Chuck Jones Studio Gallery (Map pp76-7; ☎ 983-5999, 800-290-5999; www.chuckjones.com; 128 W Water St) You've seen the cartoons, you've gotten the tattoos, so come here and check out original cells and drawings of Wile E Coyote, Marvin Martian and Bugs Bunny, as well as original art by Jones, Dr Seuss and other animation superstars. Please note that the staff *have* heard the 'wrong left turn in Albuquerque' joke before, though they do think it's clever.

Davis Mather Folk Art Gallery (Map pp76-7; ☎ 988-1218; 141 Lincoln Ave) Featuring folk art from New Mexico and Latin America, this place emphasizes brightly colored animals and figurines, including miniscule Mexican wrestlers, lascivious Albuquerque strippers and some excellent chickens with character.

Native American Art

Several galleries specializing in Native arts are listed in the Exploring Canyon Road box (p82). For jewelry, the top spot is in front of the Palace of the Governors (p79). These galleries feature fine offerings you won't find anywhere else:

Shush Yaz Trading Company (Map p83; ☎ 992-0441; www.shushyaz.com; 1048 Paseo de Peralta) If you can't get to Gallup, come here for an amazing collection of fine silver and turquoise jewelry, including a large selection of pawn. Top artists include Lucy Leuppe McKelvey, basket weaver Sally Black, and painter Marvin Toddy, who the staff (astutely) call the 'Norman Rockwell of Navajo painters' for his luminous, almost photorealistic techniques. The kachina selection is something else.

Robert Nichols Gallery (Map p83; ☎ 982-2145; www.robertnicholsgallery.com; 419 Canyon Rd) Contemporary Native American ceramics with a serious sense of humor meld old-school techniques with modern sensibilities: Virgil Ortiz' cleverly tattooed figures, Kathleen Nez' interpretations of classic pottery designs and Diego Romero's unique combination of Liechtenstein-style cartoon irony with hand-built pueblo pottery are just some of the appealing offerings.

Morning Star Gallery (Map p83; ☎ 982-8187; www.morningstargallery.com; 513 Canyon Rd) Of all the Canyon Rd shops dealing Indian antiquities, this is the best: weavings, jewelry, beadwork, toy teepees and even a few original ledger drawings are just some of the stars at this beautiful gallery, which specializes in pre-WWII Plains Indian ephemera. Finer than most museums.

Clothes

A magnet for movie stars and other folks with style to spare, Santa Fe can outfit you in an upscale wardrobe for thousands of dollars – or tens of dollars, if you're willing to buy used.

Back at the Ranch (Map pp76-7; ☎ 989-8110; www.backattheranch.com; 209 E Marcy) You'll get a kick out of this haute bouture, featuring costly and colorful cowboy boots that are more art than craft.

James Reid Ltd (Map pp76-7; ☎ 988-1147, 800-545-2056; www.jrltd.com; 114 E Palace Ave) Buckle up with the best of them here, where Western and contemporary belts, cufflinks and bolo ties are crafted at this renowned workshop.

Kevin O'Farrell Hats (Map p83; ☎ 989-9666; 725½ Canyon Rd) The most stylish way to avoid skin cancer is with one of these custom-fitted (check out the measuring helmet!) hats. In a variety of (mostly Western) styles, bead trimmed, concha studded or as simple as you'd want, all go for between $500 and $900.

Nathalie (Map p83; ☎ 982-1021; www.nathaliesantafe.com; 503 Canyon Rd) Come here for the finest cowboy and cowgirl gear, including gemstone-studded gun holsters, handmade leather and denim couture and lingerie for that saloon girl with a heart of gold.

Sangre de Cristo Mountain Works (Map pp76-7; ☎ 984-8221; 328 S Guadalupe St) You need zipper shorts-pants if you want to fit in around here, along with all things fleece and Gortex, plus backpacks, USGS maps, tents and more. You'll find more of the same at **Wild Mountain Outfitters** (☎ 986-1152, 800-988-1152; 851 St Michael's Dr) in the Candyman Center.

Faerie Queen's Wild Things Clothing Boutique (Map pp76-7; ☎ 983-4908; 316 Garfield St; ☉ 2ish-7pm usually) Couture castoffs and crazy clothes are crammed into this unique boutique.

Whether you're headed to the Opera or the Paramount, the Faerie Queen (Tobi, who also owns Cafe Oasis; p103) will help match a perfect vintage to the occasion.

Hopalong Boot Company (Map p75; ☎ 471-5570; 3908 Rodeo Rd) Secondhand Western wear, including lots of broken-in boots, make this a must for the rhinestone cowperson on a budget.

doubletake (Map pp76-7; ☎ 989-8886; 317, 319 & 320 Aztec St) Used groovy, Western and vintage clothing, jewelry and housewares, plus a wide selection of children's clothing and baby gear, come secondhand but first-class at this conglomeration of three great thrift stores on the corner of Aztec and Guadalupe Sts.

Gifts

Five & Dime (Map pp76-7; ☎ 992-1800; 58 E San Francisco St; ☉ 8:30am-9pm daily) Not just a convenient spot for snow globes, this souvenir shop has a story: in 1997, when Woolworth's – the last useful store on the plaza – closed, it was the end of an era: the Frito pie era. Locals who had been hardening their arteries for years with the cheap treat watched, horrified, as owners gutted the property to make room for even more art galleries. The *New Mexican* got letters. Area Allsups reported corn chip shortages. Pressure mounted. Finally the owners capitulated and opened this shop, selling trinkets, T-shirts and, yes, Frito pies ($4). Of course, they aren't nearly as good

---

FRITOS® PIE

Not everyone can whip up an edible green chile stew (p52), but even die-hard bachelorettes should be able to re-create this classic Santa Fe treat.

Ingredients:

 1 single-serving-sized bag of Fritos® corn chips

 1 can chili con carne (substitute vegetarian chili, if desired)

 Grated cheddar cheese and/or diced onion (optional)

Heat chili on a stove or space heater. Open Frito bag. Pour warm chili into the bag as desired, taking care not to smother the chips entirely. Garnish with cheese and onion. Grab a fork and enjoy!

as the old Frito pies (is anything ever?) but they do the trick.

Jackalope (Map p75; ☎ 471-8539; 2820 Cerrillos Rd) Grab a Radio Flyer wagon before perusing this endless kaleidoscope of kitsch: cow skulls, acres of pottery, kiva ladders, ceramic chickens, stuffed alligators, Navajo pot holders and much, much more make an attraction in itself. Bonus: watch prairie dogs frolic in the piñon enclosure and listen to parents blushingly explain that those roly-poly beasties aren't really fighting, they're…um…in love.

420 Gear (Map p75; ☎ 982-4202; 1964 Cerrillos Rd) When you just can't drink another margarita, stop in here for tobacco accessories, cigarette papers and unusually designed…er…vases that former Governor Gary Johnson (p30) tried to legalize for medicinal purposes, at the very least. But he didn't, so you can't, and it's tobacco-only here and at similar shops throughout the state, or you'll just have to leave.

Mineral & Fossil Gallery (Map pp76-7; ☎ 984-1682, 800-762-9777; 127 W San Francisco St) There weren't any Coelophysis in stock at press time, but dozens of extinct animal parts, from oviraptor's eggs to mammoth's tusks, were on the floor. Amber jewelry, glittering geodes and other natural knickknacks make this a fascinating browse.

Nambé Foundry Outlet (Map pp76-7; ☎ 988-3574; 104 W San Francisco St) Gleaming and elegant, Nambé's signature sand-cast, mysterious-metal-alloy tableware, vases and other lifestyle accoutrements have been winning design awards (and, according to Kansas State University, keeping cut flowers fresher longer) since 1951. You have to at least hold a piece of this stuff, the consummate wedding present, either here or at any of their other outlets, including one near **Canyon Rd** (Map p83; ☎ 988-5528; 924 Paseo de Peralta).

Furnishings

Fans of pueblo revival architecture and Santa Fe style come here to hook up home furnishings not found anywhere else. It's worth a look even if you're not having the mansion redecorated. Most stores will ship your treasures anywhere in the world.

Artesanos (Map pp76-7; ☎ 983-1743; www .artesanos.com; 222 Galisteo St) Tiles from Mexico, Spain, China and elsewhere are the specialty, but you can also find unique ceramic light fixtures, tableware and just about anything else, including kitchen sinks.

La Puerta, Inc (☎ 984-8164; www.lapuerta originals.com; 1302 Cerrillos Rd) After salvaging architectural antiques – doors, windows, decorative trim – from 14 countries, this shop's owners refurbish and rebuild their finds into rustic home furnishings.

Stephen's (☎ 471-0802; 2701 Cerrillos Rd) This is what happens when wacky collectors run out of floor space: They bring their treasures here, from antiquities to junque to some seriously strange art, and put it on consignment. Go nuts.

Markets & Malls

If you aren't satisfied with the fluorescent-lit cornucopia of capitalist detritus that is Wal-Mart, there are plenty of other places ready to fulfill your every desire.

Tesuque Flea Market (Map p116; US 84/285; ☑ 8am-5pm Fri-Sun Mar-Dec) There aren't many fleas at this tony outdoor market, a few minutes north of Santa Fe at Tesuque Pueblo. There are definitely deals on high-quality rugs, jewelry, art and clothing, for significantly less than you'll find them in town, but don't expect to score an old microwave for $5. It's just not that kind of place.

Plaza Mercado (Map pp76-7; ☎ 988-5792; www .plazamercado.com; 112 W San Francisco St) Just steps from the plaza, this swish spot is packed with art galleries, antique stores and Santa Fe–style clothing, some feng shuied to improve your chi, as well as the Longevity Café (p100), with more chi-enhancing opportunities, and a Blue Corn Café (p106), where chi isn't really an issue.

DeVargas Center (Map pp76-7; ☎ 982-2655; www .devargascenter.com; 564 N Guadalupe St) The most useful mall in town, it's got an Albertson's supermarket, the DeVargas 6 Movie Theatre (p109), a post office and a slew of practical stores, from RadioShack to Foot Locker.

Villa Linda Mall (Map p75; ☎ 473-4253; 4250 Cerrillos Rd) Surrounded by chain family restaurants and anchored by four huge department stores, this mall with 80-plus shops could be anywhere in the USA – except it's adobe-colored.

Santa Fe Premium Outlets (Map p116; ☎ 474-4000; 8380 Cerrillos Rd) This anemic entry doesn't even have a Starbucks (heresy!) but brings in the bikers with a Wilsons Leather Outlet, and has a handful of stores selling discount designer duds.

GETTING THERE & AWAY
Air
Santa Fe Municipal Airport (Map p116; SAF; ☎ 955-2908; 2511 Camino Entrada) This tiny airport, primarily a landing strip for private planes, is served only by **Great Lakes Air** (☎ 474-5300, 800-554-5111; www.greatlakesav.com), a United Airlines partner, offering at least six flights a day to Denver ($250-350 roundtrip).

Albuquerque International Sunport (Map p64; ☎ 244-7700; www.cabq.gov/airport; 2200 Sunport Blvd) The region's only major commercial hub is served by nine major airlines and three regional carriers. Shuttles run between the Sunport and Santa Fe several times daily; see the Transport chapter (p191) for more information.

Bus
Greyhound (Map p75; ☎ 471-0008; www.grey hound.com; 858 St Michael's Dr; ☺ 7am-5:30pm & 7:30-9:30pm daily) This busy station runs four buses daily to Albuquerque ($12), some stopping at the Sunport, Denver ($60) and Los Angeles ($70). There are two buses daily to Taos ($15) and El Paso ($15). The Santa Fe Trails (p191) No 5 line runs nearby.

Twin Hearts Shuttle (☎ 800-654-9456; www .twinheartsexpress.com) Shuttles run to the Albuquerque Sunport ($20), Taos ($25), Española ($15), Red River ($35) and Questa ($30) daily; make reservations in advance.

Faust Transportation (☎ 758-3410, 888-830-3410; www.newmexiconet.com/trans/faust/faust.html; ☺ 7am-9pm) Also make reservations for the other shuttle service between Santa Fe and the Albuquerque Sunport ($20), Taos ($25), Taos Ski Valley ($30), Angel Fire ($30) and Red River ($35). This is a favorite of hikers and bikers who need drop-off service.

Car & Motorcycle
Santa Fe is about an hour from either Albuquerque or Las Vegas, New Mexico, on I-25, which also connects the city to El Paso, Texas, and Denver, Colorado. There are two other routes between Santa Fe and Albuquerque: via the Turquoise Trail, which circumvents Sandia Crest from the east for a 1½-hour trip, or the much longer Jemez

Scenic Byway, which brings you here via Jemez Springs, Bandelier and Los Alamos – definitely the scenic route.

St Francis Rd becomes US 285/84 north of town, connecting Santa Fe to Los Alamos and Española, which serves as the hub for roads to Abiquiú, Ojo Caliente and the High and Low Roads to Taos. The Low Road is the fastest, taking about 1½ hours; the High Road will take at least three hours.

Train
Lamy Amtrak Station (Map p116; ☎ 466-4511, 800-872-7245; ☺ 9am-5pm daily) Lamy, 18 miles southeast of Santa Fe, is the closest stop for the Southwest Chief, which runs between Chicago and Los Angeles daily. **Lamy Shuttle** (☎ 982-8829; $16) runs between Santa Fe and Lamy with prior reservations.

Santa Fe Southern Railway (p92) Though geared toward tourists, you can purchase an inconvenient one-way train ticket to Albuquerque ($19) along the spur railway. Note that you'll have a two-hour wait in Lamy, and there's a 10-hour layover in the other direction. And there's not one whole heck of a lot going on in Lamy.

GETTING AROUND
To/From the Airport
Santa Fe Trails (see below) runs Bus No 1 between SAF and the plaza every half hour.

Roadrunner Shuttle (☎ 424-3367; one-way/ roundtrip $12/20) This shuttle meets every incoming flight to SAF and can drop you off at several locations around town.

Twin Hearts Shuttle (☎ 800-654-9456; www .twinheartsexpress.com; one-way $20) This shuttle provides transportation between Santa Fe and the Sunport, as well as other destinations.

Sandia Shuttle Express (☎ 474-5696 Santa Fe, 243-3244 Albuquerque, 888-775-5696; www.sandiashuttle.com; one-way/roundtrip $23/43; ☺ 7am-6pm Mon-Fri, 7am-5pm Sat & Sun) This bus offers service from the plaza and Santa Fe hotels (with confirmed reservations) 13 times daily to the Sunport and the UNM area.

Herrera Santa Fe Shuttle Coach (☎ 888-833-2300; one-way/roundtrip $21/38; ☺ 8am-8pm daily) This shuttle provides service to and from the Sunport.

Bicycle

Santa Fe is relatively flat – perfect for two-wheeling around or exploring the myriad trails. A couple caveats: altitude and heat conspire to fell unprepared newbies. Drink plenty of water and don't overexert yourself. Bike lanes are rare and drivers notoriously distracted. Be careful out there!

Santa Fe city ordinance states that bicycles must have a license plate, an attached bell or horn and a front-mounted lamp when riding at night. Bicyclists must follow the same traffic laws as automobile drivers. To find out about getting a license, good for one year, call ☎ 955-5751.

Sun Mountain Bike & Coffee Shop (Map p76; ☎ 982-8986; www.sunmountainbikeco.com; 102 E Water St; ⏰ 9am-5pm Mon-Sat, 10am-4pm Sun) In addition to renting bikes (full/half day $26/20) and trailers for the kids, this shop will drop you off at trailheads throughout Northern New Mexico (up to $50) and can organize bicycle tours with advance notice. Tip: caffeinate and carbo-load at the adjacent coffee shop first.

Santa Fe Bikes (☎ 988-3377; 607 Cerrillos Rd; ⏰ 7:30am-6:30pm winter, 9am-6pm summer) Not far from the plaza, rent bikes (full/half day $35/25) as well as skis ($20/day) and snowboards ($25/day) in season, or grab all those outdoor extras you need. **NM Bike-n-Sport** (☎ 820-0809; www.nmbikensport.com; 1829 Cerrillos Rd; ⏰ 9:30am-5pm Mon-Sat) rents bikes for similar prices.

Bus

Santa Fe Trails (☎ 955-2001; http://sfweb.ci.santa-fe.nm.us/public-works/busschedules; one-way adult/child $1/50¢, day pass $2; ⏰ 6am-11pm Mon-Fri, 8am-8pm Sat, 10am-7pm Sun with limited service) Santa Fe's rapidly improving public transportation system offers nine routes covering most of the city, with downloadable (and easy to find around town) maps, bicycle racks and easy access for wheelchair users. There's also curb-to-curb, on-demand transit for folks with ADA-certified disabilities and anyone older than 60.

However, buses run only from every 15 minutes to every hour, depending on the route. Monthly passes are cheap (adult/child $10/5), and kids under six ride free. The M-Line connects the plaza and Museum Hill via the city's historic districts.

Car

Though the winding streets close to downtown can be confusing (p72), most of Santa Fe is fairly car friendly. One-ways and unpaved roads are common in historic neighborhoods, particularly those east of the plaza, but there's nothing you'd need 4WD for. Note that using a cell phone while driving will get you a $60 ticket in city limits.

There are several rental car places, most of which will deliver the car to you:

Avis (☎ 471-5892, 800-230-4898; www.avis.com; Airport Rd) In addition to the airport location, there's **another office** (☎ 471-0091; 311 Old Santa Fe Trail) at Garrett's Desert Inn.

Budget Rent-a-Car (☎ 984-1596, 800-527-0700; www.budget.com; 1946 Cerrillos Rd)

Enterprise Rent-a-Car (☎ 989-8859; www.enterprise.com; 309 Sandoval St) A convenient location at the Hilton Hotel.

Hertz (☎ 244-7211, 800-654-3001; www.hertz.com; Airport Rd) In addition to the airport location, there's **another office** (☎ 982-1844; 100 Sandoval St) at the Hilton.

Thrifty Car Rental (☎ 474-3365; www.thrifty.com; 2865 Cerrillos Rd) Rent cars and electric bicycles.

PARKING

Parking is a nightmare during high tourist season, with a paltry 900 spaces available in over-packed public lots around the plaza running as high as $6 an hour. A better plan is to park several blocks from the plaza and hoof it. Parking tickets run $5, $25 for parking in a loading zone and $100 for parking in a handicap spot. Folks with handicap placards, however, can park for free. You have 15 days to pay your tickets, after which fees double and a warrant is issued.

Walking

Walking is by far the quickest, easiest way to get around downtown. But, though the city was designed for pedestrians, and city officials have flirted with the idea of making the plaza pedestrian-only, drivers still dominate the roads. Note that Santa Fe has one of the highest rates of traffic deaths in the country, and outside the main tourist area, a crosswalk does not legally give you the right of way. Make eye contact with drivers and yield to cars, even if you feel like you really shouldn't have to.

Taxi

Capitol City Cab (☎ 438-0000) Santa Fe's only cab company operates around the clock. Flagfall is $2.50 (50¢ extra for every minute kept waiting), $1.50 for each extra person and $2 per mile.

Luxury Limousines (☎ 890-6620, 877-232-5466) Cruise Santa Fe rock star–style with a stretch SUV or a more traditionally elongated Lincoln Towncar.

AROUND SANTA FE

The remarkable region surrounding Santa Fe is home to countless villages where Spanish is still preferred over English as well as the six Tewa-speaking pueblos of the Rio Grande, artist collectives, the birthplace of the atom bomb and one town straight out of the Wild West.

However, it is the ethereal landscape of mesas and canyons – bathed in colors that deepen as you climb toward the sun from the glowing golds and pinks of the windswept piñon desert to the volcanic greens and grays of the richly forested mountains – that are the most enduring attraction.

NEARBY PUEBLOS

A quick glance at any map reveals the region north of Santa Fe to be the heart of Pueblo Indian lands. The **Eight Northern Pueblos** (Eight Northern Indian Pueblos Council, Inc; ENIPC; ☎ 852-4265, 800-793-4955) all lie with 40 miles

---

VISITING NATIVE AMERICAN PUEBLOS

Imagine, for a minute, that your neighborhood is a rare example of a culture all but destroyed and now globally respected for its art, architecture and spirituality. Your suburban split-level ranch home, your grandmother's souvenir spoon collection and your macaroni-and-cheese dinner are all objects of mystery and intrigue.

Take it further. Picture packs of sunburned tourists parading across your lawn, asking what that plastic Santa Claus on your roof is all about, peeking in your windows and taking pictures of your kids. Welcome to life at the pueblo in high tourist season.

Pueblo Indians have opened up their world to visitors in a way that not many people would be willing to do – it's sort of the opposite of the gated-community mentality. You're a welcome guest, but don't wear it out. Courtesy, respect and a little knowledge go a long way, as does keeping your kids off the walls. Here are a few tips on how not to be a touron:

- You must buy a permit, usually at the Governor's Office, to take photos, sketch pictures or use a video camera, all of which are generally forbidden inside churches and on feast days – and always ask before you photograph a person.

- Remember that these are sovereign nations and usually forbid alcohol. Give tribal police the same respect you would any other law enforcement officer (technically, they have broader powers), and obey all posted driving and parking rules.

- Never *ever* go into kivas or cemeteries, and don't wander into churches or people's homes uninvited.

- Don't pester folks about their religion and traditions, or expect them to be in war paint, feathers or whatever you saw on TV.

- A ceremonial dance is a prayer, not a performance: Turn off your cell phone and remain silent and respectful throughout (but feel free to 'shh' your fellow tourists), give the dancers and singers their space and don't clap afterward, which is about as appropriate as applause after Mass.

- Most businesses, including gas stations and galleries, are closed on that pueblo's feast days.

- If a guided tour is available, take it. If not, stick to obviously public areas and businesses.

- Pueblos can and will close with just a few hours notice for religious purposes, and even calling ahead can't guarantee access. If you're unlucky enough to have this happen to you, no amount of complaining is appreciated or is going to change their minds.

SANTA FE

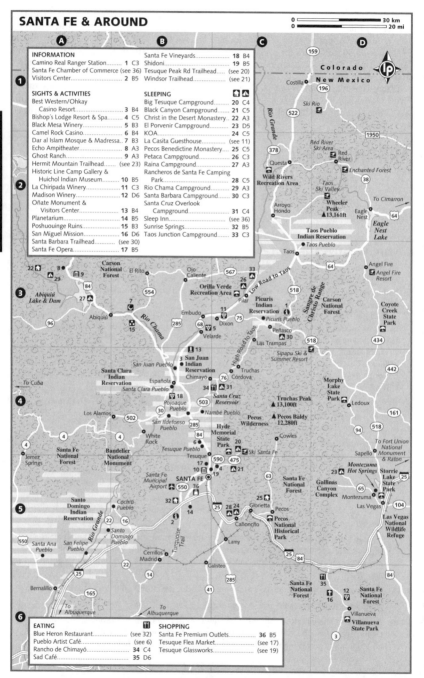

SANTA FE & AROUND

0 —————— 30 km
0 —————— 20 mi

INFORMATION
Camino Real Ranger Station......... **1** C3
Santa Fe Chamber of Commerce (see 36)
Visitors Center............................ **2** B5

SIGHTS & ACTIVITIES
Best Western/Ohkay
Casino Resort......................... **3** B4
Bishop's Lodge Resort & Spa...... **4** C5
Black Mesa Winery..................... **5** B3
Camel Rock Casino..................... **6** B4
Dar al Islam Mosque & Madressa.. **7** B3
Echo Ampitheater....................... **8** A3
Ghost Ranch.............................. **9** A3
Hermit Mountain Trailhead....... (see 23)
Historic Line Camp Gallery &
Huichol Indian Museum........... **10** B5
La Chiripada Winery.................... **11** C3
Madison Winery......................... **12** D6
Oñate Monument &
Visitors Center....................... **13** B4
Planetarium............................... **14** B5
Poshuouinge Ruins..................... **15** B3
San Miguel Mission..................... **16** D6
Santa Barbara Trailhead........... (see 30)
Santa Fe Opera.......................... **17** B5

Santa Fe Vineyards..................... **18** B4
Shidoni..................................... **19** B5
Tesuque Peak Rd Trailhead..... (see 20)
Windsor Trailhead.................... (see 21)

SLEEPING
Big Tesuque Campground............ **20** C4
Black Canyon Campground........ **21** C5
Christ in the Desert Monastery.. **22** A3
El Porvenir Campground............. **23** D5
KOA.. **24** C5
La Casita Guesthouse.............. (see 11)
Pecos Benedictine Monastery.... **25** C5
Petaca Campground.................... **26** C3
Raina Campground..................... **27** A3
Rancheros de Santa Fe Camping
Park....................................... **28** C5
Rio Chama Campground.............. **29** A3
Santa Barbara Campground........ **30** C3
Santa Cruz Overlook
Campground............................ **31** C4
Sleep Inn............................... (see 36)
Sunrise Springs......................... **32** B5
Taos Junction Campground........ **33** C3

EATING 🍴
Blue Heron Restaurant............. (see 32)
Pueblo Artist Café.................. (see 6)
Rancho de Chimayó.................... **34** C4
Sad Café.................................... **35** D6

SHOPPING 🛍
Santa Fe Premium Outlets.......... **36** B5
Tesuque Flea Market................ (see 17)
Tesuque Glassworks................ (see 19)

of Española, some of which is on long-term lease from Santa Clara Pueblo. The eight tribes are connected linguistically – six listed below speak Tewa, while Taos (p166) and Picuris (p130) use somewhat similar Tiwa – and together publish the excellent free *Eight Northern Indian Pueblos Visitors Guide,* available at any area visitors center.

Each pueblo is independently governed, and visitors will find that each is unique. From isolated Picuris Pueblo's magnificent scenery and Nambé's outdoor recreation to Pojoaque's casino and strip, the tribes have developed their resources and tourist infrastructure quite differently.

Many operate casinos, usually several miles from the main pueblo, which are generally open 8am to 4am Monday to Thursday morning, then stay open 24 hours through Sunday. Slots, craps, poker, shows and endless buffet tables are the big draws, but unlike casinos in Las Vegas, Nevada, there's usually a gift shop selling high-quality pottery and other work by local artisans.

The pueblos themselves aren't really tourist attractions – they're towns, with schools, modern houses, post offices and whatnot. They are certainly a must-see, as you'll learn (or unlearn) a lot about Native culture, and area artists in particular appreciate the traffic. Just respect the residents as they go about their day (p115).

Begin by purchasing the required camera permits from either the visitors center, if there is one, or Governor's Office, where staff may be able to point you toward galleries, guided tours and other areas of interest, if they aren't too busy. **Ancient Storyteller Tours** (☎ 753-6901; ancientstorytellers@yahoo.com; PO Box 1979, Española, NM 87532) offers custom tours of the pueblos as well as Bandelier and other ruins, and will also arrange pottery demonstrations, feast meals and classes.

Tesuque Pueblo
☎ 505 pop 450 elevation 6000ft

A temporary encampment since at least AD 700, Tesuque Pueblo was probably founded as a permanent village in the early 1200s by settlers from abandoned Chaco Canyon. By 1541 the city-state comprised six towns and welcomed Coronado on his quest for gold. Spanish-Tesuque relations

deteriorated, however, as Catholic priests began punishing, with increasing severity, those who continued practicing Native religions.

Shortly before the Pueblo Revolt of 1680, the Spanish captured two Tesuque messengers. Elders, suspecting a security breach, ordered the assassination of a priest, a diversion that successfully convinced Spanish strategists to misdirect their troops. The war was won but at great cost, in large part because of this extreme tactic. And when DeVargas returned in 1692 with promises of peace, residents wisely abandoned their homes for two years.

Like most area tribes, heavy taxes, European diseases, and poverty resulting from lost lands and resources continued to devastate the Tesuque population until WWII. Since then they've been slowly rebuilding their culture and infrastructure.

In addition to famed **Camel Rock**, an odd and aptly named geological formation right off US 84/285, encircled by a short trail, the pueblo operates the **Tesuque Flea Market** (p112), **Camel Rock Suites** (p97) in Santa Fe, and **Camel Rock Casino** (Map p116; ☎ 984-8414, 800-462-2635; www.camelrockcasino.com; US 84/285), a swanky spot featuring the recommended **Pueblo Artist Café** (buffet adult/child $7/5; ❧ 10am-midnight daily), with a top-notch buffet serving Native and New Mexican foods. There's also an intimate, if not opulent, venue where fun B-list acts like Bob Newhart and the Smothers Brothers play, plus a **free shuttle** (❧ 10am-midnight daily) from the plaza in Santa Fe – just call and they'll pick you up in a half hour.

Though a few art studios open for tours in the summer, there's not much to see in the pueblo itself, on the other side of the highway, particularly since the noted **Church of San Diego** burned down in 2002. Want to help rebuild it? Call the **Governor's Office** (☎ 995-7728; Tesuque Plaza; ❧ 9am-5pm Mon-Fri) for information on volunteering to lay some adobe. Photography is not allowed.

Pojoaque Pueblo
☎ 505 pop 350 elevation 7000ft

Pojoaque has been the site of permanent habitation since about AD 500 and was a bustling commercial center of several villages by the time Coronado cruised

SANTA FE

SANTA FE

through. Between the Pueblo Revolt and Reconquista, however, the once-populous tribe was reduced to a handful of families.

That was just the beginning: after resettlement, water shortages and disease, including the smallpox epidemic of 1890, decimated the tribe. In 1915 the pueblo was temporarily abandoned, and in 1933 reinstated with just 40 members and 12,000 acres, making it the smallest in the Eight Northern Indian Pueblos Council (ENIPC).

Since then, however, the tribe has taken full advantage of its location at a crossroads between Santa Fe, Los Alamos and Española to rebuild its former prominence – not to mention political pull. In the late 1990s former Governor Jacob Villareal jumped into traffic and threatened to shut down US 285/ 84, on Pojoaque land, if the state legislature didn't ratify certain gaming contracts. The contracts were ratified rather quickly.

A business park, buffalo reintroduction program and **Poeh Cultural Center** (☎ 455-3334; www.poehcenter.com; 78 Cities of Gold Rd), with a noted arts school for Native Americans, have been joined by a huge strip of tax-free businesses, including a fun **Sports Bar** (☎ 455-3105; Cities of Gold Rd; ☷ 10am-2am daily) with video slots and gambling on horse and dog races.

The Cultural Center will also house **Poeh Museum** (scheduled to open in 2004), an imposing adobe that is already home to a huge collection of art and artifacts, primarily from the six Tewa-speaking tribes. Other exhibits will trace area history through the Tewa worldview, as well as showcasing contemporary artists.

The **visitors center** (☎ 455-9023; 96 Cities of Gold Rd; ☷ 9am-5pm Mon-Sat, 10am-4pm Sun) has a great selection of pottery, arts and crafts, and flyers and information about **Towa Golf Resort** (☎ 455-9000; www.towagolf.com; $25-50), with greens known for their great views.

Cities of Gold Casino (☎ 455-3313, 800-455-3313; www.citiesofgold.com; Cities of Gold Rd; r $89), the name of which should be your first clue that you might not find the riches you seek, is a huge place with plenty of razzle dazzle. There's also a **free shuttle** (☎ 455-4253; ☷ 10am-midnight) to Santa Fe, plus rooms that need remodeling and the obligatory buffet.

Skip the buffet (unless it's seafood Friday; adult/child $13/10) and cross the highway to **Roadrunner Cafe** (☎ 455-3012; US 284/85;

mains $2-8; ☷ 6am-9pm daily), beloved by its devoted trucker clientele for the enchiladas, stuffed sopapillas and big breakfasts.

The **Governor's Office** (☎ 455-3901; 17746 US 285/84; ☷ 9am-5pm Mon-Fri) has been actively spearheading a cultural revival since 1973, including Tewa-language programs, and reviving several dances long unpracticed, including those on the **December 12 Virgen de Guadalupe Feast Day**.

San Ildefonso Pueblo

☎ 505 pop 650 elevation 6000ft

Founded in the 1300s by settlers who had abandoned Bandelier in the wake of a long-term drought, San Ildefonso is perhaps the easiest and most interesting of the pueblos to explore independently. Black Mesa, a stronghold successfully used during the Reconquista to negotiate for better peace treaty terms with DeVargas, rises resolutely in the distance and is off-limits.

The helpful **visitors center** (☎ 455-3549; Hwy 502; admission $3, photo/video/sketching permits $10/20/ 25; ☷ 8am-5pm daily), with a few small displays of tribal art and artifacts, has maps outlining a walking tour through the compact plaza, which features an attractive church and kiva, plus several excellent art studios.

San Ildefonso has been at the forefront of the Native American pottery and arts revival for half a century. The most famous artisan was Maria Martinez; a few pieces of her coveted black-on-black pottery are at the **Maria Poveka Martinez Museum** (admission free; ☷ 8am-4pm Mon-Fri), along with work by other pueblo artists. For a preview, check out former governor and artist John Gonzalez' website (www.sanildefonso.com).

During WWII three-quarters of San Ildefonso land was appropriated for the Manhattan Project (p132). The tribe is currently working with Los Alamos and the Department of Energy (DOE) to preserve historic sites that may be open for tours one day. Visitors are welcome to come to the **January 23 Feast Day** and **corn dances** held throughout the summer. For information not directly related to tourism, contact the **Governor's Office** (☎ 455-2273).

Nambé Pueblo

☎ 505 pop 600 elevation 6200ft

Just the drive into the Pueblo of Nambé, through dramatically sculpted, multihued sandstone, is fantastic. NM 503, which leaves US 285/84 just north of Pojoaque to head into hills speckled with piñon, makes for a scenic addition to the High Road to Taos (p127).

Perhaps because of the isolated location (or inspirational geology), Nambé has long been a spiritual center for the Tewa-speaking tribes, a distinction that attracted the cruel attentions of Spanish priests intent on conversion by any means necessary. After the Pueblo Revolt and Reconquista wound down, Spanish settlers annexed much of their land.

Nambé's remaining lands, however, have a couple of big attractions; the loveliest are two 20-minute hikes to **Nambé Falls** (day use $5). The steep upper hike has a photogenic overlook of the falls, while the easier lower hike along the river takes in ancient petroglyphs.

The most popular attraction, however, is **Lake Nambé** (ranger station ☎ 455-2304; Hwy 101; day use $10, no motors; ☪ 7am-7pm April-Oct), created in 1974 when the US dammed the Rio Nambé, flooding historic ruins but creating an important reservoir that attracts boaters and trout lovers.

The **Governor's Office** (☎ 455-2036; Hwy 503; photo/video permits $10/15; ☪ 9am-5pm Mon-Fri), right on the attractive plaza, can arrange tours of the tribe's **buffalo range**, but the ranger station is better equipped for visitors overall. The pueblo has several excellent artists who sell from their homes; the most famed Nambé potter is Lonnie Vigil, coauthor of *All That Glitters: The Emergence of Native American Micaceous Art Pottery in Northern New Mexico,* with Duane Anderson.

Events open to the public include a **July Arts and Crafts Fair**, the **October 4 San Francisco de Asis Feast Day** and a **December 24 Catholic Mass and Buffalo Dance**.

You can **camp** (campsite/RV $20/30) in the shady valley at the trailheads, or head up NM 503 to **Santa Cruz Lake Overlook Campground** (Map p116; ☎ 758-8851; Hwy 503; Apr-Oct; campsites $7), which isn't shady but has a lovely view and some nice trails. Another option is to continue past Cundiyo to **Santa Cruz Lakeside Campground** (Map p116; ☎ 758-8851; Hwy 503; Apr-Oct; campsites $9), with lake access and 6 miles of trails.

Santa Clara Pueblo
☎ 505 pop 2600 elevation 6800ft

The ancestors of this bustling pueblo probably arrived in the area around 1200, along with those of Jemez Pueblo (p66), building a permanent settlement on the

---

MARIA MARTINEZ : A RENAISSANCE IN BLACK

The pride of San Ildefonso Pueblo and probably the USA's most famous potter, Maria Antonia Montoya (1887–1980) was born into a time when Native pottery was a dying art, the lovely but labor-intensive ceramics increasingly abandoned for inexpensive, mass-produced cookware. As a child, however, Maria carefully studied the work of her aunts, master potters Martina Montoya and Nicolasa Peña Montoya. She soon became adept at creating smooth and utilitarian vessels, which were then generally traded for food or labor.

In 1909 her husband, Julian Martinez, was hired to help excavate nearby ruins. Archaeologist Dr Edgar Lee Hewitt asked Maria to reproduce some of the effects on found pottery shards here. After much experimentation, she and Julian were able to adapt techniques used in Santa Clara Pueblo's black pottery, creating matte-on-gloss designs that depicted ancient symbols like the *avanyu* (horned water serpent).

The unique pieces won multiple awards at the first Santa Fe Indian Market (p92) in 1922. After the Otowi Bridge connected the pueblo to Santa Fe in 1924, folks from all over the country started coming to San Ildefonso to shop, transforming the subsistence-economy pueblo into a vibrant arts center. When her vessels earned accolades at the 1934 Chicago Worlds Fair, Maria became world famous. Today work by Maria and Julian, their son Popovi Da, and other family members can command tens of thousands of dollars.

Maria, by Richard L Spivey, is a lavishly illustrated chronicle of her life and art, and *Maria Montoya Martinez: Master Potter,* by Maria's close friend Elsie Karr Kreischer, tells the ceramicist's story for children.

shores of the Rio Grande in the 1300s. They had an elaborate agricultural economy and welcomed the Spanish settlers – at first. Later one of the heroes of the 1680 Pueblo Revolt, Domingo Naranjo, would hail from Santa Clara. After the Reconquista, the tribe abandoned the pueblo for several years.

Today the tribe is becoming known and business savvy, and operates the **Big Rock Casino** in Española (p123); it also plans to open the **Black Mesa Golf Course** (☎ 753-7330; $25-50) before this book hits the shelves. The real claim to fame is the pottery, luminous red and black vessels prized by collectors, particularly those of the Santa Clara's three major matriarchs: Christina Naranjo, Mary Esther Archuleta and Margaret Tofoya, the last considered the most important pueblo potter after Maria Martinez.

The **Governor's Office** (☎ 753-7330, photo permit $5; Hwy 30; ☉ 8am-4:30pm Mon-Fri) issues photo permits, but a better first stop for visitors is **Singing Water Gallery** (☎ 753-9663, 800-430-0622; www.singingwater.com; Hwy 30; ☉ 10am-5pm daily), right outside the main pueblo. In addition to representing 213 of some 450 Santa Clara potters, owners Joe and Nora Baca also offer tours of the pueblo ($10), pottery demonstrations ($30) and classes, and can arrange feast meals ($7-12) with 48 hours notice.

They also guide tours ($13) of the pueblo's famed **Puyé Cliff Dwellings**, a remarkably preserved and massive complex of ruins, which has unfortunately been closed since the 2000 Cerro Grandé fire due to conflicts with the DOE and FEMA. Call the gallery or Governor's Office to see if they've reopened. In the past, admission was $6, and the ruins were open 8am to dusk daily.

In the meantime the sprawling village has a huge number of shops and studios selling the pueblo's renowned pottery, including **Toni Roller's Studio & Gallery** (☎ 753-3003; Hwy 30; ☉ 10am-5pm Mon-Sat), owned by Margaret Tofoya's daughter, and a 1918 church. Events open to the public include the **June 13 San Antonio Feast Day** and **August 12 Santa Clara Feast Day**.

Española Transit (p125) serves the pueblo.

San Juan Pueblo
☎ 505 pop 6750 elevation 5600ft

Probably founded in the late 1100s by the people who abandoned Chaco Canyon, San Juan Pueblo has been an important government seat for at least 700 years and may represent an unbroken line of pan-pueblo leadership back to Chaco's heyday.

For centuries it has been the only place where a pan-pueblo war could legally be declared, and then only by a Yunque-Owinge (San Juan native). Most famously, local priest Popé stood here and called for the Pueblo Revolt of 1680, in response to the torture of Indian religious leaders.

THE ARTISTIC VISION OF MICHAEL NARANJO

Despite being the son of noted Santa Clara potter Rose Naranjo, as a young man Michael Naranjo wasn't particularly interested in making art. Besides, there was a war to fight in Vietnam. He went, as so many Native Americans did. And, like so many Americans, the 22-year-old did not come back physically whole: a grenade blinded him and all but destroyed his right hand.

While he was recuperating, a volunteer asked if she could get him anything. He wanted clay. She brought some in, and he began massaging it into forms he'd seen in nature. 'I knew then I could do it,' he told *Veterans Advantage*. 'It was exhilarating.'

When he returned home he told his family that he was moving to Santa Fe to launch a career as an artist. Though worried, they acceded. He learned to survive on his own and developed a sculptural style with clear roots in Native traditions, fluid and elegant forms reminiscent of Santa Clara's finest pottery, all built by hand. His cast bronze figures danced, prayed and thrived – all without eyes. He was soon recognized as one of New Mexico's finest artists.

His powerful work is now on display at the Museum of Fine Arts in Santa Fe (p79) and the Albuquerque Museum's sculpture garden (p57), as well as in the Vatican, White House and elsewhere. You can appreciate the beauty of his sculptures with your eyes, but close them for a moment and touch the pieces. For it is only through your hands that you will truly understand the artistic vision of Michael Naranjo.

Under his generalship, the Spanish were driven back to El Paso for 12 years and were allowed to return peacefully after agreeing to the pueblos' freedom of religion.

San Juan continues to function as a political center and is the seat of the ENIPC. The **Eight Northern Pueblos Council Visitors Center**, scheduled to open before this book goes to print, will offer insight into the formation and function of various Native arts.

Visitors can tour **Bison Park** and the excellent **Oke Oweenge Crafts Cooperative** (☎ 852-2372; Hwy 74; ☯ 9am-5pm Mon-Fri), which sells the pueblo's renowned and very collectible carved red pottery, as well as jewelry and handicrafts. Other attractions include the attractive 1889 **Nuestra Señora de Lourdes chapel** and brick 1913 **San Juan Bautista Church**; most other historic buildings are off-limits, and photography permits must be arranged with the **Governor's Office** (☎ 852-4400; Hwy 74).

Best Western/Ohkay Casino Resort (Map p116; ☎ 747-5695, 877-829-2865; www.ohkay.com; NM 68; d $70-100; ⓟ ⊠ ⊠ ⊠) fulfills all your gambling needs, including spacious new rooms to crash in if you can't stay awake all weekend.

The onsite **Silver Eagle Lounge** serves alcohol and has live music nightly, while the **Harvest Cafe** (mains $1-12, buffet $6-9; ☯ 6:30am-midnight Sun-Thu, 24hrs Fri & Sat) has a great salad bar and $1 breakfast specials. **Ohkay RV Park** (☎ 753-5067; 2016 N Riverside Dr; campsite/RV $10/21), across the highway, also rents fishing tackle ($8-12) for adjacent **San Juan Lakes** (day use $10).

Events open to the public include the **January Basket Dance**, the **February Deer Dance**, the **June 13 Corn Dance**, the **June 24 San Juan Feast Day**, and a series of Catholic traditional dances and ceremonies from December 24 to 26.

Española Transit (p125) buses serve the pueblo.

ESPAÑOLA

☎ 505 pop city 9700/county 43,000 elevation 5578ft
At the heart of the northern Rio Grande

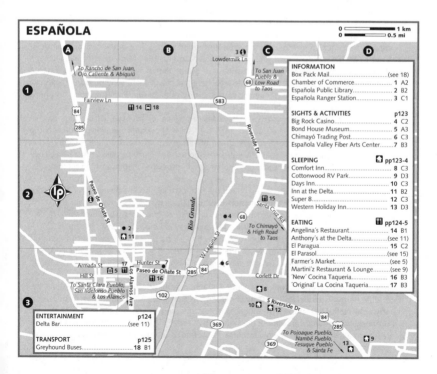

ESPAÑOLA

0 ————— 1 km
0 ————— 0.5 mi

INFORMATION
Box Pack Mail..............................(see 18)
Chamber of Commerce.....................**1** A2
Española Public Library....................**2** B2
Española Ranger Station...................**3** C1

SIGHTS & ACTIVITIES p123
Big Rock Casino.............................**4** C2
Bond House Museum.......................**5** A3
Chimayó Trading Post......................**6** C3
Española Valley Fiber Arts Center.......**7** B3

SLEEPING pp123-4
Comfort Inn..................................**8** C3
Cottonwood RV Park.......................**9** D3
Days Inn......................................**10** C3
Inn at the Delta.............................**11** B2
Super 8.......................................**12** C3
Western Holiday Inn........................**13** D3

EATING pp124-5
Angelina's Restaurant......................**14** B1
Anthony's at the Delta...................(see 11)
El Paragua....................................**15** C2
El Parasol....................................(see 15)
Farmer's Market...........................(see 5)
Martini'z Restaurant & Lounge.........(see 9)
'New' Cocina Taqueria.....................**16** B3
'Original' La Cocina Taqueria...........**17** B3

ENTERTAINMENT p124
Delta Bar....................................(see 11)

TRANSPORT p125
Greyhound Buses..........................**18** B1

Valley, Española was designed for commerce, not postcards. Sure, the setting is stunning, bookended by the Jemez Mountains and Truchas Peak, with the lush farms of the Rio Grande as a dramatic centerpiece, but the city itself feels absolutely no need to gussy itself up for sightseers.

Founded by Don Juan de Oñate in 1598 as the first state capitol, it's sort of the anti–Santa Fe: the adobes are all real, restaurants are authentic and inexpensive, and masterpieces by the city's world-famous artisans are on exhibit at Sonic drive-ins rather than museums.

Most visitors come to Española for the relatively inexpensive lodging and convenient location, which makes perfect sense. As long as you're here, why not have a great meal and enjoy yourself?

Orientation & Information

Española is the all-but-unavoidable gateway to Northern New Mexico, at the crossroads of several major highways: US 84/285 (Santa Fe Hwy) leads southeast to Santa Fe; NM 30 (Los Alamos Ave) runs southwest to Santa Clara Pueblo, Los Alamos and Bandelier; US 84 (Oñate St) heads northwest to Abiquiú and Ghost Ranch; NM 76 (Santa Cruz Rd; High Road to Taos), is the back road to Taos through Chimayó and Peñasco; and NM 68 (Riverside Dr) is the main drag,

---

NEW MEXICO'S LOWRIDING TRADITION

In some circles, Española is more famous for its fine arts tradition than either Taos or Santa Fe. And though it has the name recognition, the entire state of New Mexico has long boasted some of the finest automobile customizers in the world.

The Lowrider Movement began in East Los Angeles during the 1930s, when young Chicanos gave up on assimilation and instead started dressing in zoot suits and customizing their cars quite differently from the racing crowd. 'We lowered the springs in the back,' explained César Chávez. 'Fender skirts. Two sidepipes.' The look was sleek, low-slung sedans, clean and chromed and later customized with wild paint, extravagant interiors and always pure class.

The first New Mexico lowriders began cruising the Española Valley in the 1950s, sweet lows like Ernesto Martinez' white 1949 Chevy and Dennis Martinez' 1949 Mercury with skirts. During the 1960s, when laws against lowered suspensions swept the country, clever cruisers adapted hydraulic pumps that would lift their rides to legal height at the flick of a switch. Soon villages like Chimayó, Truchas, Peñasco and Hernandez were sporting some of the finest lowriders anywhere, and Española was at the center of it all.

Perhaps it's the dry desert air that keeps older cars clean, or perhaps it's the high-paying, technically demanding jobs in Los Alamos – building a show-show quality lowrider can easily top $30,000. Or maybe it's the region's long tradition of Hispanic craftsmanship, the sacred art that is so similarly colorful, or the Hispanic leadership, who are less likely to pass anti-cruising laws. Whatever it is, this relatively poor and unpopulated state produces championship cars that keep Californians and Texans on their toes.

Española's Viejitos car club organized one of the first lowrider shows anywhere in 1975; by this time, lowriding was a statewide phenomenon. In Albuquerque hydraulics entrepreneur Orlie Coca founded *Orlie's Lowriding* magazine, with readers in some 20 countries. The Smithsonian's only lowrider hails from Chimayó, David and Irene Jaramillo's 1969 Ford LTD, 'Dave's Dream.'

And in 1993 (much to the consternation of East Los Angelenos) MTV announced the title Española had been claiming for years, 'Lowrider Capital of the World.' If you want to see why, pick up a copy of *Low 'N Slow: Lowriding in New Mexico,* by Carmella Padilla, Jack Parsons and Juan Estevan Arellano, featuring rides you may catch cruising around town.

Shows usually take place on Sunday around 11am, in parks and parking lots throughout the state. Albuquerque's annual **Rollerz Only Show** (www.rollerzonly.com; $20; June), thrown by one of the country's most influential clubs, is the biggest and best, bringing in cars from all over the Southwest. But on weekend evenings throughout the state, and especially in Española, you'll almost certainly be treated to a lowrider show the old fashioned way, free of charge and on the streets.

heading south to Santa Fe and north as the Low Road to Taos.

The city sprawls, with two major settlements on either side of the Rio Grande, traversed by two bridges (at Oñate St and Santa Clara Bridge Rd). The western, older part of the city has a small historic district and most community services; the east side has more commercial development.

You can pick up maps and flyers at the **chamber of commerce** (☎ 753-2831; www.espanola nmchamber.com; 719 Paseo de Oñate; ☼ 9am-5pm), while the **Española Ranger Station** (☎ 753-7331; 1710 N Riverside Dr; ☼ 7:30-4:30 Mon-Fri) has information on area trails and campsites. The **Chimayó Trading Post** (☎ 753-9414; 110 Sandia Dr), on the National Register of Historic Places, has flyers, maps and free coffee, and can quickly take care of all your souvenir-buying needs.

Española Public Library (☎ 747-6087; 313 Paseo de Oñate; ☼ 9am-6pm Mon-Thu, 9am-3pm Fri & Sat) offers free Internet access. The weekly paper *Rio Grande Sun* (www.riograndesun.com) has community events listings.

Sights & Activities

Española's not what you'd call a tourist trap.

Bond House Museum (☎ 747-8535; 706 Bond St; donations appreciated; call for opening hours) An enormous 1880 adobe with Victorian airs, this newish museum has displays about Española's days as a frontier mercantile community, era antiques and art exhibitions.

Big Rock Casino (☎ 747-0059; 419 N Riverside Dr; ☼ 8am-4am Mon-Thu, 24hrs Fri-Sun) It's rumored by gambling cognoscenti to have the best odds in the state. True or not, it's right

downtown, has a decent restaurant and features a **bowling alley** (games $2-4; ☼ 10am-midnight daily) to amuse the kids while you gamble their college money.

Española Valley Fiber Arts Center (☎ 747-3577; www.la-tierra.com/evfac; 325 Paseo de Oñate; admission free; ☼ 9am-4pm Mon-Sat) This place houses lots of beautiful antique looms and offers demonstrations and classes in weaving, spinning and natural dyes.

Santa Fe Vineyards (Map p116; ☎ 753-8100; Hwy 285; ☼ 10am-5pm Mon-Sat, noon-5pm Sun) This winery makes a good cabernet and port, and you can sample them here for free (it's $5 a flight in the Santa Fe store). But the real reason to come is to meet the notoriously cranky, eye-rolling sommelier.

Oñate Monument and Visitors Center (Map p116; ☎ 852-4639; www.rioarribanm.com; NM 68; ☼ 8am-5pm Mon-Fri) Just north of town, it has flyers galore, an above-average gift shop and a great statue by artist Reynaldo 'Sonny' Rivera of Don Juan de Oñate in full military regalia. In 1998 vandals calling themselves the 'Brothers of Acoma' defaced, or rather defooted, the sculpture in symbolic retribution for the conquistador's allegedly similar treatment of the Acoma Indians (p19). The pueblo, incidentally, claims no knowledge as to the whereabouts of the missing foot, which was replaced but never found. And that's just one more item to keep an eye out for on eBay.

Sleeping

Lodging is inexpensive, and hardy souls can go even cheaper at several semi-sketchy motels clustered in town along NM 68. These seem safer and have basic, clean rooms.

SIKHS IN NEW MEXICO

As you explore the region, you'll often spot people dressed from turban to toe in spotless white. Most are Sikhs, and many are members of Hacienda De Guru Ram Das Gurdwara, in Española. The gurdwara was founded in the 1970s and now has about 150 members; the small golden-domed edifice is one of the US centers for Sikhism, the fifth-largest religion in the world.

You might think these unusually dressed individuals, dedicated to a religion founded in Medieval India, would have a hard time finding acceptance in largely Catholic New Mexico. There have been occasional cultural conflicts; for example, Sikhs consider carrying a weapon (usually symbolic, like a pocket knife) an obligation of faith – and one that required working closely with local high schools to maintain. But local folks don't bat an eye, as Sikhs have become a respected and downright normal part of Northern New Mexico's cultural landscape.

Cottonwood RV Park (☎ 753-6608; US 84/285; campsite/RV $16/21; P) Just south of town, park your tent or RV, then enjoy your complimentary margarita at festive **Martini'z Restaurant & Lounge**, where you register.

Ranchito San Pedro B&B (☎ 753-0583; www .janhart.com; SR 581; d $50-85 incl breakfast; P ⊠ ⊠) Call for directions to this adobe, dog-friendly 'art dude ranch' in a surprisingly pastoral neighborhood – about as relaxing as it gets.

Inn at the Delta (☎ 753-9466, 800-995-8599; 304 Paseo de Oñate; r $100-150 incl breakfast; P ⊠ ⊠) Española's finest lodging has stylish, spacious rooms decorated with local art and adobe-toned ambiance to spare.

Super 8 (☎ 753-5374; 811 S Riverside Dr; r $45-80; P ⊠ ⊠ ⚲) Just slightly below average.

Comfort Inn (☎ 753-2419; 604-B Riverside Dr; r $40-80; P ⊠ ⊠ ⚲)

Days Inn (☎ 747-1242; 807 S Riverside Dr; r $40-85; P ⊠ ⊠)

Western Holiday Inn (☎ 753-2491; 1215 S Riverside Dr; r $45-60; P ⊠ ⊠ ⚲) Almost charming, and definitely the best of the bunch.

Eating

If you want lard-free Nouveau Mexican tapas, your best bet is Santa Fe. But when you're hankering for hearty family recipes perfected over 400 years of working with ingredients grown right here, come on up to Española.

Farmers Market (Calle Don Diego; ⊙ noon-dusk Mon Jun-Oct) Local produce, live entertainment and lots of food stands make this an event. Produce stands also set up daily along Riverside Dr in season.

'Original' La Cocina Taqueria (☎ 753-3486; 310 Old Los Alamos Hwy; mains $3-6; ⊙ 7am-1:30pm Mon-Fri) This beloved hole in the wall does legendary stuffed sopapillas, while the **'New' Cocina Taqueria** (☎ 753-3016; 411 Santa Clara Bridge Rd; mains $6-14; ⊙ 11am-8:30pm daily) has nicer digs and a bigger menu, including a great fajita salad.

Angelina's Restaurant (☎ 753-8543; 1226 N Railroad Ave; mains $6-11; ⊙ 7am-9pm daily) Sit down at this popular and delicious local favorite for the finest organic lamb burritos anywhere or any of the other New Mexican specialties – but get 'em red.

Anthony's at the Delta (☎ 753-4511; 228 Paseo de Oñate; mains $9-17; ⊙ 5-9:30pm daily) Enjoy upscale steak and seafood in elegant Southwest style here or at the adjoining **Delta Bar** (⊙ 2pm-close), with a less expensive bar menu featuring killer ribs.

El Paragua (☎ 753-3211, 800-929-8226; NM 76; lunch $6-9, dinner $9-20; ⊙ 11am-9pm daily) Make reservations on weekends for one of the state's best restaurants, with a perfect margarita, Spanish Old West ambiance, and

---

DETOUR: OJO CALIENTE

Ojo Caliente means 'hot eye' in Spanish, a reference to the geothermal springs bubbling up throughout the region. **Ojo Caliente Mineral Springs** (☎ 800-222-9162; 50 Los Baños Dr; www.ojocalientespa.com; rooms s/d $70/95, cottages s/d $85/120; P ⊠ ⊠), 18 miles north of Española, has five of them, plus a charmingly tattered, family-owned resort with pleasant if not luxurious rooms and casitas. The onsite **Artesian Restaurant** (mains $5-15; ⊙ 7:30am-2:30pm & 5-9:30pm daily) prepares organic and local ingredients with aplomb, including fresh trout encrusted with pine nuts in a cilantro-jalapeño butter.

The springs, considered sacred by Pueblo Indians, are an unusual trick of hydrogeology: each of the beautiful pools is fed by a different water source with different mineral contents. The Lithia spring has a kick – bring a bottle so you can take some home. Drop by for a visit (weekday/weekend $10/14) and consider indulging in one of the spa treatments ($20-330), a yoga class ($8/10 guests/ visitors) or a hike along one of their trails.

Other accommodations within walking distance include the **Inn at Ojo Caliente** (☎ 583-9131; Los Baños Dr; s/d $85/95 incl breakfast; P ⊠ ⊠), with a Ping-Pong table and nicer rooms than the resort; and **Lomita Motel** (☎ 583-2109; Hwy 285; without/with kitchenette $50/65; P ⊠), perhaps a bit dingy but with spacious and relaxing rooms and porches. There are also a couple of restaurants in town, including the **Mesa Vista Cafe** (☎ 583-2245; Hwy 285; mains $2-7; ⊙ 7am-9pm daily), serving New Mexican diner food with lots of veggie options and a recommended red chile cheeseburger.

chile rellenos, enchiladas and camarones borrachos you'll be daydreaming about for years. The adjacent **El Parasol** (☎ 753-8852; mains $2-8) is a revered taco stand.

Rancho de San Juan (☎ 753-6818; www.rancho desanjuan.com; Hwy 285; prix fixe $55; d $175-575; P ⊠ ⊠) This gourmet restaurant is the best excuse to dress up in Española, featuring four-star dishes with a nod to New Mexican classics, at two nightly seatings. The property also has first-class accommodations including a spa, as well as a **sandstone shrine** carved into a nearby mesa that's well worth the $3 admission.

Getting There & Around
Greyhound stops at **Box Pack Mail** (☎ 753-4111; 1227-A Fairview Ln; ⏰ 6:30a-5p Mon-Sat), across the street from Angelina's Restaurant, with twice daily bus service to Taos ($10), Santa Fe ($8) and Albuquerque ($16). **Española Transit** (☎ 753-2176; one-way $1; ⏰ 7am-6:30pm daily) covers the city with service to the Greyhound bus station, San Juan and Santa Clara Pueblos, and connections with Los Alamos Bus System (p136).

ABIQUIÚ
☎ 505 pop 550 elevation 6800ft
Less a visit to town than an excursion through a muted dreamscape, this is New Mexico at its most ethereal, a multihued land of striking silhouettes and tiny settlements, where spiritual types of every stripe have gathered in collective awe. You've seen the pictures of Rio Chama, flat-topped Pedernal Mountain and so many other landmarks in hazy pastel, courtesy of famed former resident Georgia O'Keeffe. Come experience this place for yourself, and do consider staying the night.

Orientation & Information
Abiquiú stretches for about 20 peaceful miles along US 84, from the intersection with Hwy 554 (18 miles north of Española) to Ghost Ranch. There's no city center (although Bode's Mercantile serves the purpose), no public transportation and no chamber of commerce, though you can download maps and other information at www.digitalabiquiu.com.

Sights & Activities
Georgia O'Keeffe House & Studio Tour (☎ 685-4539; www.abiquiuinn.com/tour.html; $22; Tue, Thu & Fri Apr-Nov) Make reservations months in advance to tour the home and studios of the artist who illuminated Abiquiú's quiet beauty with her own intensity of color and form. Fans will recognize the house (where

---

GEORGIA O'KEEFFE *By Bridgette Wagner*

Although classically trained as a painter at art institutes in Chicago and New York, 21-year-old Georgia O'Keeffe was always uncomfortable with traditional European style. For four years after finishing school, she did not paint, and instead taught drawing and did graphic design.

However, after studying with Arthur Wesley Dow, who shared her distaste for the provincial, O'Keeffe began developing her own style. She drew abstract shapes with charcoal, representing dreams and visions, and eventually returned to oils and watercolors. These first works caught the eye of her future husband and patron, photographer Alfred Steiglitz, in 1916.

In 1929 she visited Taos' Mabel Dodge Luhan Ranch and returned to paint the 'The Lawrence Tree,' still presiding over DH Lawrence Ranch (p172). O'Keeffe tackled the subject of the Ranchos de Taos Church, painted by so many artists before her, in a way that had never been considered: only a fragment of the mission wall, contrasted against the blue of the sky.

It was no wonder she loved New Mexico's expansive skies, so similar to her paintings' negative spaces. As she spent more time here, landscapes and fields of blue permeated her paintings. During desert treks, she collected smooth white bones of animals, subjects placed against that sky in some of her most identifiable New Mexico works.

Telltale scrub marks and bristle impressions divulge how O'Keeffe blended and mixed her vibrant colors on the canvas itself. This is in direct contrast to photographs of her work, which convey a false, airbrush-like smoothness. At the Georgia O'Keeffe Museum (p80), you can experience her work firsthand.

SANTA FE

she lived from 1945 to 1984) and the views from it, which have been enshrined in her masterpieces, just about all of them available in poster and book form at the Abiquiú Inn.

Ghost Ranch Living Museum (☎ 685-4333; www.ghostranch.org; US 84) Founded amidst the colorful canyonlands as the former 1766 Serrano Land Grant and later dubbed Rancho de los Brujos (Ranch of the Witches) because of various eerie *X-Files*–style supernatural activity – howling, mud-covered banshees, for example – this Presbyterian retreat offers lodging (p127), classes and other activities for folks of any or no faith.

There are two small museums (adult/child $2/1; 9am-noon & 1-5pm Mon-Sat): the **Ellis Museum of Anthropology**, outlining 12,000 years of human habitation in the area, and the **Ruth Hall Museum of Paleontology**, a cool collection of fossils excavated on the ranch, including a skeleton of Coelophysis, New Mexico's state fossil, which was discovered here. Leave a donation at the trailhead before taking the recommended 4-mile-roundtrip trek into **Box Canyon** or the popular 3-mile-roundtrip to **Chimney Rock**, with views of the Piedra Lumbre basin.

Dar al Islam Mosque and Madressa (Map p116; ☎ 685-4515; www.daralislam.org; Hwy 155; admission free; 8am-4pm Mon-Fri) For a little insight into Islam, drop into this graceful adobe mosque, which conducts classes and outreach program for non-Muslims interested in broadening their horizons. Built by Egyptian architect Hassan Fathy in 1979, the mosque once served an eclectic community of Muslim immigrants, most of whom have since moved away. But the compound, which includes a library and facilities for seminars, lectures and film programs, remains. Take Hwy 554 north from US 84 toward El Rito, cross the Rio Chama, make your first left onto NM 155 and follow it for 3 miles.

The Annual Studio Tour (☎ 685-4454; www.abiquiustudiotour.org; Oct) Every fall you can visit more than 30 local artists' studios and galleries, including the **Magpie Woman Gallery** (☎ 685-4829; US 84), across from Bode's, with handmade deerskin clothing and work by several area artists, as well as **Abiquiú Organics and Folk Art** (☎ 685-4585; NM 68), known for retablos, santos and more; there's also a

farmers market here Monday and Friday afternoons.

Abiquiú Lake & Dam (Map p116; ☎ 685-4371) This fairly scenic reservoir is popular among boaters, campers (see below) and fishers, who come for the trout, kokonee and channel catfish. Ten miles north, you can experience the acoustically impressive **Echo Amphitheater** (Map p116; day use $2 per car), a majestic natural cavern worn into the sandstone, and take to the trailhead for a couple of short hikes. Two miles south of town, an easy 1-mile-roundtrip hike to the **Poshuouinge Ruins** (Map p116) overlook offers a birds-eye view of the Chama Valley and remains of a 700-room pueblo founded at least 600 years ago. The ruins themselves are off-limits.

Sleeping & Eating

Featuring phenomenal camping and other unusual accommodations, Abiquiú is best appreciated as an overnight destination. Many lodging operators offer meals as part of the package, a good idea considering the dearth of dining options.

Raina Campground (Map p116; ☎ 685-4371; reservations 877-444-6777; campsite/RV $5/14; P) Featuring immediate access to Abiquiú Lake and several short hiking trails, this is a fine place to spend the night.

Rio Chama Campground (Map p116; FS 151; campsites free; P) Serene and shady campsites in the canyons along Rio Chama are 12 miles from civilization – well, except ultra-rustic Christ in the Desert Monastery (see below), next door. Two hikes begin at Skull Bridge, located near Big Eddy Picnic Area, about 7 miles from US 84: 12-mile-roundtrip **Ojitos Canyon Trail**, climbing Mesa del Camino, and the **Rio Chama Trail**, which runs 8 scenic miles along the Rio Chama and ends at the monastery.

Christ in the Desert Monastery (Map p116; fax 419-831-9113; www.christdesert.org; FS 151; r $50-75 donation incl 3 meals; P) When you really want to get away from it all, head west from US 84 onto the rough dirt Forest Service Rd 151, then follow it along the meandering Rio Chama for 13 inspirational miles to this isolated Benedictine Monastery. Simple rooms, outrageous trails and peace and quiet – special medallions indicate your silent retreat – include vegetarian meals served without conversation. Chores are requested (not required) and include minding the gift shop or tending the garden.

Ghost Ranch (Map p116; ☎ 685-4333; www.ghostranch.org; US 84; dm with shared bath $42-64, dm with private bath $75, campsites/RV $15/18, all incl 3 meals; P ✗ ✗) When space is available (seminar participants get first dibs), you can get a dorm bed here, including cafeteria-style meals made with locally raised meat and organic veggies grown on the ranch farm.

Las Parras de Abiquiú B&B (☎ 685-4200, 800-817-5955; www.lasparras.com; US 84; d $125 incl breakfast; P ✗ ✗) Primarily a vineyard, Las Parras also features two luxuriously appointed rooms with outstanding art, fireplaces, an outdoor hot tub and lots of little amenities. Top notch.

The Abiquiú Inn (☎ 685-4378, 800-447-5621; US 84; www.abiquiuinn.com; RV $18, s/d $55-100, 4-person casitas $115-145; P ✗ ✗) An area institution, this sprawling collection of shaded adobes is peaceful and lovely, and some spacious rooms have kitchenettes; no tent sites are available. The very professional staff also run the onsite **Abiquiú Cafe** (mains $6-11; ✷ 7:30am-9pm daily). Stick to the Middle Eastern

menu – falafel, dolmas and gyros are all winners – and you can't go wrong.

Independent eateries are in short supply, but **Bode's** (☎ 685-4422; US 84; ✷ 7am-8pm daily), a small grocery store and gas station, has a good **deli** (✷ 8am-3pm daily), while **El Farolito** (☎ 581-9509; Hwy 554, El Rito; mains $3-12), in the village of El Rito (10 miles north of Abiquiú on Hwy 554), serves excellent New Mexican cuisine topped with award-winning green chile.

HIGH ROAD TO TAOS

New Mexico's famed 'High Road to Taos' winds through river valleys, sandstone cliffs and the pine forests of the Sangre de Cristo mountains, connecting villages that until very recently were known for keeping their isolated Spanish-colonial character pristine.

In recent years artists taken by the region's stark beauty (and taking advantage of increasing tourist traffic along the well-publicized route) have moved into these rugged mountains, opening their own studios alongside those famed for Spanish artistic traditions. All provide the visitor ample excuse to stop and explore these

---

SANTUARIO DE CHIMAYÓ

In the days leading up to Good Friday, it seems that all roads leading to **El Santuario de Chimayó** (☎ 351-4889; NM 76; admission free; ✷ 9am-5pm daily; mass 11am Mon-Sat, noon Sun) are lined with pilgrims, many barefoot, some dragging crosses and all in a state of spiritual self-discovery (read: drive carefully).

According to legend, it was during Holy Week in 1810 that Bernardo Abeyto, a Penitente, saw a light shining forth from the earth. When he went to investigate, he found a crucifix bearing the image of Our Lord of Esquipulas, aka the Black Christ, patron saint of a Guatemalan village known for its own healing sanctuary.

Abeyto took the cross to Santa Cruz, where it promptly disappeared, rematerializing back in Chimayó. A second long procession proved just as maddeningly miraculous. Abeyta finally gave up and built a shrine at the santo's chosen spot, where the Santuario stands today.

Other tales tell of hot springs sacred to the Tewa tribes, now dry, their healing powers left behind in the loose earth upon which the Santuario was constructed. Which is really why you're here: sure, it's a beautiful place, graceful and venerable, with five outstanding reredos and a famed bulto of El Señor Santiago, but most folks come for the dirt, known for its healing powers.

Walk past santos of every design, from traditional wooden carvings to black velvet airbrushed paintings, and enter a small room behind the altar. There a modest pit of sand lies open, allegedly on the very spot where the crucifix was found. If you so desire, kneel down and scoop some into your own container (none are supplied), then add it to your bath, rub it onto the worn-out parts of your body, even mix it with water and drink it – but don't treat this miracle lightly. Too many prayers have been answered here, too many wounds healed and good deeds done by whatever power is working through this crowded shrine to consider this place just another roadside attraction.

small villages as you make your way north.

Begin your journey by heading north on St Francis Dr from Santa Fe, where it becomes US 285/84, continuing north past Pojoaque and the left turn to Los Alamos. You can either make a right onto NM 503 toward Nambé Pueblo (p118) to begin your trek, or continue north to Española. In Española, make a right onto NM 76, at the sign to Chimayó, heading east toward the Santuario.

Chimayó
☎ 505 pop 4400 elevation 6200ft

The village of Chimayó, folded into a lush valley surrounded by dramatically sculpted high desert, is striking from above and seems welcoming as you meander its shady streets. Though it has much to recommend it – a famed santuario and a 400-year-old tradition of fine weaving – Chimayó also has a love-hate relationship with the 300,000 camera-snapping tourists who roll through each year. Show respect – and lock your car.

Collectors come for the woven wool tapestries, a tradition of craftsmanship passed down unbroken through generations of families who have raised sheep and grown the plants to make natural dyes for

centuries. The original storefront is century-old **Ortega's Weaving Shop** (☎ 351-4215; NM 76; 9am-5pm Mon-Sat), which seems to have fallen prey to touristitis.

There are several other spots in town for finding that perfect weave, including **Centinela Traditional Arts** (☎ 351-2180, 877-351-2180; www.chimayoweavers.com; NM 76; 9am-6pm Mon-Sat), with 100-year-old looms and great information on Rio Grande weaving online. Weavings run anywhere from $10 for coaster-sized swatches to more than $500 for full-sized wall hangings.

You can learn more about Chimayó's history at tiny **Chimayó Museum** (☎ 351-0945; www.chimayomuseum.org; cnr NM 76 & NM 502), on historic Plaza del Cerró, still fortified by protective adobe structures that now house neat shops. It has exhibits by local artists and a permanent collection of old photos, and runs a **studio tour** in September.

Can't decide whether to stay or weave? Try **Blue Heron Inn** (☎ 351-1158, 877-351-1158; NM 76; d $75-95 incl breakfast; P X), with spacious rooms, kitchen access and weaving and dying classes with advanced arrangements. Call for directions.

The most famous place for dinner is **Rancho de Chimayó** (Map p116; ☎ 351-4444; www.ranchodechimayo.com; d $95-150, mains $8-16; 9am-9pm daily, closed Sun Nov-Apr; P X),

---

PATROCIÑO BARELA: MASTER OF WOOD

His fluid forms, carved from a single piece of wood, are clearly anchored in the santero tradition, but markedly different: this is what art historians now call Barela Style. Patrociño Barela, *Time* magazine's 1936 'discovery of the year,' was lauded worldwide as a genius and master after his rounded and emotional pieces took center stage at a WPA show at New York City's Museum of Modern Art.

Probably born in 1900 (he wasn't sure), Barela worked at steel mills and picked vegetables until moving to Taos in 1930. There, an elderly neighbor asked Barela to repair her San Antonio. He did it with a pocket knife, then carved his own Santa Rita.

Area churches, taken by his heartfelt interpretations of saints and martyrs, began asking him to fill their own altars with his creations. His work caught the attention of New Deal representatives, who trained him for one week – perhaps his only formal education – and began collecting his art for government shows.

Barela never attended those openings in Washington DC, New York City or Paris; he seemed unconcerned with his following among critics and collectors. Instead, he worked in his Taos studio, often donating prized pieces to churches and sanctuaries. Years later, the Smithsonian interviewed him for a retrospective, and asked if he had become wealthy from his renowned carvings. 'No,' he told the interviewer. 'I go to Monte Vista to pick potatoes.'

Both the Harwood and Millicent Rogers museums in Taos have excellent collections of his work, and you'll see his themes echoed among artists and sculptors throughout the state.

serving classic New Mexican cuisine, courtesy of the Jaramillo family's famed recipes, and the perfect margarita. Rooms are fine, but it's the location and old school ambiance that packs 'em in.

Excellent, authentic and ultra-festive **Chimayó Holy Chile Mercadito Milagroso** (☎ 351-4824; NM 76; mains $1-7), across from the Santuario, is far better for your budget, serving great carne adovada and chicharones – exactly what you need after that long pilgrimage.

From the Santuario, NM 76 rises 3000ft as it passes the villages of Córdova, Truchas and Peñasco.

Córdova

☎ 505 pop 400 elevation 800ft

Just off NM 76, carpenters founded Córdova in the 1700s near the site of old Pueblo Qemado. The community of woodworkers established a tradition of carved and unpainted retablos and bultos, created from strikingly grained woods, including juniper, aspen, ash and cedar, carefully pieced together for an unusual effect.

'Córdova-style' pieces, pioneered by masters like José Rafael Oregón and Jose Dolores Lopéz, are now collected by the Smithsonian and other museums. Though much more expensive in Santa Fe, you can find small animals and angels for around $10, while larger and more complex museum-quality pieces – saints and the Tree of Life are the classic subjects – run well over $1000.

Operated by Terry Enseñat Mulert, who carves graceful, traditional bultos in the style of legendary carver Patrocinio Barela (p128), and Paula Castillo, who shows contemporary acrylic paintings and imposing steel sculptures, the unusual **Castillo Gallery** (☎ 351-4067; www.castillogallery.com; Main Rd; 10am-6pm daily) also organizes poetry festivals and other events.

More traditional carvings are sold at the homes of santeras **Gloria López** (☎ 351-4487; Main Rd; 8am-5:30pm daily), who offers one-hour demonstrations ($100, call ahead) in techniques perfected over 54 years of carving, and **Sabanita Lopéz Ortiz** (☎ 351-4572; Main Rd; 8am-6pm daily), great-granddaughter of Jose Dolores Lopéz, who can also arrange demonstrations.

Truchas

☎ 505 pop 950 elevation 8400ft

A case study in rural gentrification (or, more precisely, gallerification), Truchas has become something of an arts center in recent years. A dozen studios now grace the dramatic set of Robert Redford's movie *Milagro Beanfield War,* chosen after camera-shy Chimayó turned down the actor.

Once you come here – and it is a fine detour – you'll understand why creative spirits congregate atop this mesa: Picturesque farms, ancient traditions, and stunning views of 13,100ft Truchas Peak and the wide Española Valley seem made to inspire.

The village still operates according to the bylaws of its 1754 Spanish land grant, forcing lowrider cars to compete with livestock for the narrow road connecting galleries like **The Cordovas Handweaving Workshop** (☎ 689-2437; www.la-tierra.com/busyles; Main Truchas Rd), with unique weavings, and **Hand Arts Gallery** (☎ 689-2441; Main Truchas Rd), featuring work from some 40 area artisans, much of it displayed in the outdoor sculpture garden.

Continue to the end of Main Truchas Rd to the Truchas Peak trailhead (though most hikers begin at Cowles, north of Pecos), where an alpine meadow beneath that granite peak will take your breath away.
Rancho Arriba B&B (☎ 689-2374; www.ranchoarriba.com; Main Truchas Rd; s/d with shared bath $50/70, d with private bath $85 incl breakfast;), in a rustic adobe farmhouse on the edge of Pecos Wilderness, has horses and wood stoves, and will arrange to cook you dinner in advance. **Truchas Farmhouse** (☎ 689-2245; Main Truchas Rd; d $50-90;) is simpler but still nice.

There are no restaurants, but you can grab snacks and beer at **Tofoya's General Store** (☎ 689-2418; Main Truchas Rd; 8am-7pm Mon-Sat, 11am-4pm Sun), serving Truchas since 1915.

Las Trampas

The tiny adobe village of Las Trampas is most famous for outstanding Spanish-colonial architecture, particularly the restored 1760 **San José de Garcia Church** (9am-5pm Mon-Sat Jun-Aug; mass noon first & third Sun), considered among the loveliest in the country. Original carvings and paintings remain in excellent condition, and bloodstains from the Los Hermanos Penitentes are still visible.

SANTA FE

There are few services in town, but you can pitch a tent at **Trampas Diamante** or **Trampas Trailhead** (☎ 842-3292; CR 207; campsites $7), about 5 and 8 miles, respectively, south of NM 76 from the El Valle turnoff, along a rough dirt road.

Peñasco

☎ 505 pop 650 elevation 7452ft

This 250-year-old community of farmers and ranchers is a gateway to the Carson National Forest. Stop into the **Camino Real Ranger Station** (Map p116; ☎ 587-2255; 15160 NM 75; ☽ 8am-4:30pm Mon-Sat) for information on camping, hiking and cross-country skiing.

Sipapu Ski & Summer Resort (Map p116; ☎ 587-2240, 800-587-2240; www.sipapunm.com; NM 518; lift tickets adult/child $33/25; d $24-79, campsites $5-25; P ✗) A cozy, family-operated ski resort about 10 miles south of Peñasco on NM 518 offers 65 acres of powder, 31 trails, a 1055ft vertical drop, and some of the shortest lines and best deals on downhill skiing in New Mexico. It makes a great spot to spend the night year-round.

Serious hikers may want to try the 23-mile-roundtrip **Santa Barbara Trail** to Truchas Peak, which begins at **Santa Barbara Campground** (Map p116; ☎ 587-2255; FR 116), about 9 miles south of Peñasco on a good dirt road. In town, the colorful **Sugar Nymphs Bistro** (☎ 587-0311; NM 75; mains $4-12; ☽ 11:30am-2:30pm & 5:30-7:30pm Thu-Sat, 10am-3pm Sun) offers creative and healthful diner food, great desert and sometimes live theater.

From Peñasco, you can head west on NM 75 to Picuris Pueblo and Dixon; east on NM 518, which will take you southwest to Las Vegas (p138); or north, continuing along the High Road, topping out at 8500ft on US Hill. Continue on to Rancho de Taos, home to famed San Francisco de Asis Church (p152), where you join NM 68, the Low Road to Taos, for the short final leg of your journey.

Picuris Pueblo

☎ 505 pop 339 elevation 7500ft

Once among the largest and most powerful pueblos, the Pikuri built adobe cities at least seven stories tall and boasted a population approaching 3000. After the Pueblo Revolt and Reconquista, when many retreated to Kansas rather than face DeVargas' wrath, the returning tribe numbered only 500. Between the Spanish and Comanches, that number continued to dwindle.

That the tribe has chosen not to open a casino (heck, some feel guilty about selling tax-free cigarettes), and that their remote location puts them well off the beaten tourist trail, make this sleepy pueblo an interesting boondoggle.

The **Governor's Office** (☎ 587-2519; photo/video permits $5/10; ☽ 9am-5pm Mon-Fri) can, with advance notice, help arrange guided tours of the pueblo, including the small buffalo herd, organic gardens, ruins from the old pueblo site and the exquisite 1770 **San Lorenzo de Picuris Church**. The unique tower kiva is off-limits to visitors but makes quite an impression even from the outside.

The tribe is renovating **Picuris Pueblo Museum** (☎ 587-2957), which displays tribal artifacts and local art, as well as **Hidden Valley Restaurant**, with burritos and Native snacks. The Indians plan to reopen these, as well as campsites near their **Tutah Lake fishing pond** (day use adult/child $7/5) by 2004. You can also grab a great sopapilla burger at the nearby **Rio Lucio Cafe** (☎ 587-1725; 1341 NM 75; mains $4-8; ☽ 8am-7pm Sun-Fri).

Picuris is best known for its micaceous pottery, golden-hued, unglazed vessels flecked with gleaming mica that New Mexicans swear are the best pots for simmering beans. Anthony Duran is probably the best-known Picuris potter, but other well-regarded artists include Margaret Archuleta and Caroline Honyumptewa. Most artisans open their studios on weekends.

Events open to the public include the **Tri-Cultural Arts and Crafts Fair**, in mid-June, and the popular **San Lorenzo Feast Days**, August 9 and 10. Featuring food and crafts booths, dances, races and pole climbs – not to mention clowns egging on participants and visitors alike – the feast days are the best time to visit Picuris.

LOW ROAD TO TAOS

If you don't have all day to make the trip between Española and Taos, your best bet is NM 68, a speedy 40-mile trek that would be famous for its views of deeply cut Rio Grande Gorge if it didn't have to suffer comparisons with the spectacular High Road.

Velarde

About 15 minutes north of Española, Velarde has a few produce stands and **Black Mesa Winery** (Map p116; ☎ 852-2820, 800-852-6372; www.blackmesawinery.com; 1502 NM 68; ☯ 10am-6pm Mon-Sat, noon-6pm Sun), where you can enjoy a free seven-vintage flight, including the excellent Coyote Red and wacky Black Beauty, a red wine with chocolate flavoring.

Embudo

☎ 505 pop 725 elevation 5815ft

For a lunch worth planning your trip around, visit New Mexico's first brewpub, **Embudo Station** (☎ 852-4707, 800-452-4707; www.embudostation.com; NM 68; mains $6-20; ☯ 11:30am-9pm Tue-Sun May-Sept, noon-9pm Fri-Sun Oct-Apr; d cabin $100 incl breakfast; P ✂ ✂). Situated along a particularly lovely stretch of the Rio Grande – embudo, Spanish for 'funnel,' refers to the narrow pass – there's a patio perfect for taking in the view, not to mention New Mexico wines and microbrews (try the green chile ale) served alongside gourmet Southwestern cuisine made with local produce and meats smoked right here. The Station also has one very nice cabin for rent and can arrange leisurely two-hour rafting trips ($35 including lunch).

Just up the road, the **Classical Gas Museum** (☎ 852-2995; NM 68; donations appreciated) has no regular hours, but if the gate's open, stop in to see an enormous collection of antique pumps, advertisements, oil cans and more – it's a must. Seriously. Donations support the Dixon Animal Shelter.

Pilar

☎ 505 pop 100 elevation 6400ft

Populated by a small but dedicated community of nature lovers and river rats, the village of Pilar is the gateway to a variety of outdoor adventures, most famously white-water rafting 'The Box,' with Class VI+ rapids best appreciated in May and June (though the season runs April through October), when the water level is higher. There are also mellower floats available from a variety of area outfitters.

Big River Raft Trips (☎ 758-9711, 800-748-3746; www.bigriverrafts.com; cnr NM 68 & CR 570) offers floats, from an all-day experience in The Box ($105) to half-day trips on the Class III Racecourse ($50) and Class III Lower Gorge ($50).

Far Flung Adventures (☎ 776-1443, 800-359-2627; www.farflung.com) offers similar trips as well as options combining rafting with horseback riding ($125), a three-day 'gourmet river trip' ($750) replete with chef-prepared meals, and various kayak trips. Most leave from the **Pilar Yacht Club & Café** (☎ 758-9072; cnr NM 68 & CR 570), which also sells sandwiches and burritos.

DETOUR: DIXON

Snuggled almost invisibly between two beaten paths, Dixon's not a destination many folks take the time to enjoy. Which is a shame, considering the potential for relaxation in this community of artisans, organic farmers and other folks who appreciate the solitude. Stop by the **Library & Community Center** (☎ 579-9181; NM 75; ☯ noon-5p Mon-Sat) for free Internet access, maps and information about area studios and farm tours; there's also an annual studio tour in late fall.

The big draw is **La Chiripada Winery** (Map p116; ☎ 579-4437, 800-528-7801; NM 75; ☯ 10am-6pm daily), which makes many of New Mexico's top-rated wines, including an award-winning Riesling, highly regarded Cabernet Sauvignon and Rio Embudo White.

Pick up locally made food products – think wild cherry–red chile jam – to go with your chosen vintage at the distinctive **Casa de Piedra** (☎ 579-4111; NM 75; ☯ 10am-5pm Tue-Sun), an artists' and growers' cooperative representing some 60 area craftspeople. It's in the historic rock house on the west end of town.

If you find yourself more interested in the rocks than the art, **Harding Mine** (☎ 277-4204), a mile north of town and a place of geological extremes that's open to rockhounds, may be for you.

There are a few B&Bs scattered throughout town, including **La Casita Guesthouse** (Map p116; ☎ 579-4297; www.cyberrentals.com/nm/millenm.html; d $85 incl breakfast, 2 night minimum; P ✂), a peaceful spot lost in the vineyards of La Chiripada.

BLM-administered **Orilla Verde Recreation Area** operates four **campgrounds** (☎ 758-8851; www.nm.blm.gov/tafo/rafting/rio_grande/ovra/ovra_info.html; CR 570; day use $3, campsites with/without shelter $5/7) along the river; **Petaca** (Map p116) is the nicest for tent campers, while **Taos Junction** (Map p116), just across the Taos Junction Bridge, is best for RVs.

The **Rio Grande Gorge Visitors Center** (☎ 751-4899; NM 68; ☼ 9am-5pm daily summer) has information on campsites and area hikes, including the 2-mile **La Vista Verde Trail**, with great gorge views and petroglyphs, and the less-developed 9-mile **West Rim Trail**, popular with mountain bikers. Both begin just past Taos Junction Bridge. **Rio Grande Gorge HI Hostel** (☎ 758-0090; CR 570; dm $14; P ✗) has an open kitchen, and rents boats and bicycles in summer.

Greyhound (☎ 800-229-9424; www.greyhound.com) stops at the Pilar Yacht Club.

You can continue up NM 68 into Taos, or follow CR 570 across the Taos Junction Bridge, which becomes a steep dirt road to CR 567 for about 3 tortuous miles, then intersects a very nice, paved shortcut directly to Ojo Caliente (p124).

LOS ALAMOS
☎ 505 pop 18,365 elevation 7355ft

Since it's in one of New Mexico's most stunning settings at the gateway to the Jemez Mountains, you might expect Los Alamos to resemble a kitschy resort town.

Not even close. Just when you thought the Cold War was over, this 'Atomic City' is still awash in spy scandals and studded with WWII-era military-grade architecture, all centered on secretive Los Alamos National Laboratory (LANL), probably the most sophisticated weapons lab in the world.

This isn't a tourist attraction, it's a scientific experiment. But folks fascinated with that one bright moment when humanity's role on Earth fundamentally shifted – the day we took responsibility for safeguarding life itself – will want to see the birthplace of the nuclear bomb. And, perhaps, purchase a T-shirt.

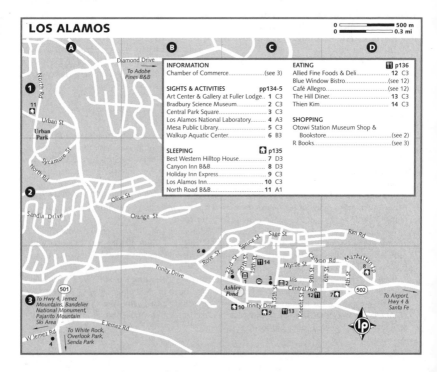

LOS ALAMOS

INFORMATION	
Chamber of Commerce	(see 3)

SIGHTS & ACTIVITIES	pp134-5
Art Center & Gallery at Fuller Lodge..	1 C3
Bradbury Science Museum	2 C3
Central Park Square	3 C3
Los Alamos National Laboratory	4 A3
Mesa Public Library	5 C3
Walkup Aquatic Center	6 B3

SLEEPING	p135
Best Western Hilltop House	7 D3
Canyon Inn B&B	8 D3
Holiday Inn Express	9 C3
Los Alamos Inn	10 C3
North Road B&B	11 A1

EATING	p136
Allied Fine Foods & Deli	12 C3
Blue Window Bistro	(see 12)
Café Allegro	(see 12)
The Hill Diner	13 C3
Thien Kim	14 C3

SHOPPING	
Otowi Station Museum Shop & Bookstore	(see 2)
R Books	(see 3)

History

The secret city was founded by federal order in 1943, after the US military appropriated Los Alamos Ranch Boy's School and its isolated mesa-top location. Here, General Leslie Groves and physicist Robert Oppenheimer assembled an army of top scientists and engineers, furnished them with every possible resource and gave them a single mission: to build an atomic bomb before Nazi Germany.

Brainpower recruited from across the world reported to 109 Palace St in Santa Fe, where they were whisked out the back door and shuttled past menacing guard towers keeping watch over the code-named Manhattan Project. Housing was flimsy, water was scarce and security was tight.

Schoolchildren did not use their last names, scientists did not discuss work with their families and all correspondence was heavily censored. Information was given on a need-to-know basis; few on the project knew exactly how their creation would manifest.

The weapon was a blinding success. On July 16, 1945, the world's first nuclear device detonated at White Sands, a luminous inferno that prompted Oppenheimer to quote the *Bhagavad Gita:* 'I am become death, the destroyer of worlds.' After which he lit another cigarette, having no further incentive to quit.

A month later Hiroshima and Nagasaki were hit hard by the new technology. It was a revelation in warfare: at least 120,000 civilians were killed instantly, more in the following days, prompting Japan to surrender and end WWII. The USA became a world power, the word 'fallout' entered the dictionary, and in 1949 the USSR tested its own nuclear device, getting the Cold War started with a bang.

Los Alamos remained federally owned and operated after the war, restricting visitors and keeping close tabs on residents, including communist party members Ethel and Julius Rosenberg, who were executed in 1953 for espionage. Finally, in 1957 Los Alamos was opened to the public, just like a normal city. Sure.

LANL remains the region's top employer, but it's not just for WMDs anymore: supercomputers, genome decryption and nuclear safety are mentioned in all the brochures. The Wen Ho Lee (p134) debacle, however, made it clear that there's more going on around here than just cutting-edge medical research.

Los Alamos is still recovering from the spy scandal, as well as the devastating Cerro Grande Fire of 2000: a controlled burn went horribly awry, devouring 220 buildings and 43,000 acres of forest surrounding the city and lab. Conspiracy theorists are still

---

NUTS FOR NUKES? LEARN MORE

You may opt to continue worrying rather than learn to love the bomb, but Dr Strangelove himself (the real-life Edward Teller) shows up in most of these books and websites designed to illuminate both the humanity and technology of the nuclear age.

- *"Surely You're Joking, Mr. Feynman!,"* by Richard P Feynman – Witty Nobel Prize–winning physicist remembers the Manhattan Project and the minds that made it all happen.
- *The House at Otowi Bridge,* by Peggy Pond Church – The story of Edith Warner's tea room, where scientists mingled with San Ildefonso Indians.
- *The Making of the Atomic Bomb,* by Richard Rhodes – The best-written, best-researched history of the bomb yet.
- *My Country Versus Me,* by Wen Ho Lee – Lee's side of the story.
- *A Spy Within,* by Lynette Baughman – A fictional detective tracks the real-life spy 'Perseus,' still at large after selling secrets to the Soviets.
- Los Alamos National Laboratories (www.lanl.gov) – The official LANL website.
- Los Alamos Study Group (www.lasg.org) – All the news you can use (and hair you could lose) from folks on the other side of the fence.

speculating about what they might have inhaled along with the smoke.

A sense of pride in Los Alamos' unusual community endures, as evidenced by coffee mugs reading, 'Back off, man – I'm a scientist.' But you wonder if they'd rather be part of a Manhattan-style project to save the world, instead. If only they could get the funding.

Orientation & Information

Built atop a series of slender mesas, Los Alamos would be difficult to navigate even if it hadn't been designed as a military facility. Luckily most attractions are well-signed and located along Central Ave (Hwy 502) between 9th and 20th Sts. The suburb of White Rock is just south of Los Alamos on NM 4.

The **chamber of commerce** (☎ 662-8105, 800-444-0707; www.visit.losalamos.com; 109 Central Park Sq; ☺ 9am-5pm Mon-Fri, 9am-3pm Sat & Sun) has a free map, accommodations listings and pamphlets. The **White Rock branch** (☎ 672-2183; 125 NM 4; ☺ 8am-4pm daily) is more convenient if you just want to skip Los Alamos and head into the forest.

Mesa Public Library (☎ 662-8240; 2400 Central Ave; ☺ 10am-9pm Mon-Thu, 10am-5pm Fri-Sun) offers free Internet access. **R Books** (☎ 662-7257; 111 Central Park Sq), with a coffee bar, and **Otowi Station Museum Shop and Bookstore** (☎ 662-9589; www.otowi.com; 1350 Central Ave) both have wide selections of scientific and historic tomes. The *Los Alamos Monitor* (www.lamonitor.com) is the daily paper.

Walkup Aquatic Center (☎ 662-8170; 2760 Canyon Rd; adult/child $3/2) has showers and an Olympic-sized pool.

Sights & Activities

Los Alamos itself is a sight to behold: chosen for its isolation among mountains and steep canyons, it enjoys stunning views best appreciated at **Overlook Park** in White Rock; they form an impressive backdrop to the military-efficient architecture. WWII buffs may appreciate the almost Soviet-style aesthetic with which this town was thrown together. Everyone else will want to head to **Bandelier** (p136) and the beautiful **Jemez**

WEN HO LEE: INTERNATIONAL MAN OF MYSTERY?

His odyssey began in March 1999, when the *New York Times* published an article alleging that during the mid-1980s, a Chinese-American scientist at LANL had given China information about W-88 miniaturized nuclear warheads. After the story broke, an embarrassed FBI moved quickly, taking Taiwanese-American physicist Wen Ho Lee into custody and grilling him for two days without counsel. Shortly afterward Lee was named primary suspect in the case.

Evidence was largely circumstantial: Lee had visited China in the mid-1980s (with LANL's blessing), worked on a prototype of the W-88 (not the model China supposedly had) and hugged a Chinese scientist (is this illegal?). However, Lee did take top-secret work home on weekends, storing it on his unsecured PC. Even more damning, after failing a polygraph test, he deleted classified files stored on an unclassified section of the LANL computer mainframe.

On December 30, 1999, Lee was placed in solitary confinement, his legs shackled much of the time. Secretary of Energy Bill Richardson stated firmly that 'if anyone puts classified information on unclassified computers, we are going to treat them the same way.' (But when former CIA Director John M Deutch did exactly that, the attorney general declined to prosecute.)

Lee steadfastly maintained his innocence as allegations began to unravel. More than 60 agents assigned to the case found no proof of espionage but learned that many scientists surreptitiously save hours of code decryption each day by keeping classified materials in more easily accessible, unclassified files – hey, they've got deadlines to meet, too.

The government eventually dropped 58 of 59 charges; Lee pleaded no contest to the last – improperly storing sensitive information – and was released after 278 days alone and in chains. 'I am sad that I was induced in December to order your detention,' said Judge James A Parker, who presided over both hearings. 'I sincerely apologize to you, Dr Lee, for the unfair manner you were held in custody.' A week later, the *New York Times* also apologized.

As for Lee, he went home to White Rock, where friends, family and former coworkers quietly celebrated his release.

Mountains (p66) after checking out the two excellent, free museums.

BRADBURY SCIENCE MUSEUM

This outstanding museum (☎ 667-4444; www.lanl.gov/museum; cnr 15th St & Central Ave; admission free; 9am-5pm Tue-Fri; 1-5pm Sat & Sun) is LANL's public face, offering insight into the political and scientific challenges the lab faces in its primary mission of 'ensuring the safety and reliability of America's nuclear weapons.' They don't dumb it down much either, and well-designed exhibits offer serious, though-provoking insight into the architecture of the nuclear age.

Historical exhibits focus on WWII's Pacific Theater, including the Bataan Death March, while scientific displays cover the lab's peacetime projects, including hazardous waste cleanup, supercomputing with the solar-powered Hal 9000 and the problems of keeping our rusty old nuclear stockpile up-to-date, now that testing them is (drat!) illegal.

Buffalo Tours (☎ 662-5711; adult/child $10/5; 1pm Mon-Sat) begins at the museum for 1½-hour tours of Los Alamos' and LANL's history, science and geology.

LOS ALAMOS HISTORICAL MUSEUM

This museum (☎ 662-4493; 2132 Central Ave; admission free; 9:30am-4:30pm Mon-Sat, 11am-5pm Sun) blazes half-heartedly through the pre-WWII era before plunging into an introspective examination of the strange and isolated lives led by Los Alamos scientists during the war, as well as the world's reaction to the Atomic Age they engineered.

Pop culture is a big focus, with *Radioactiveman* comics displayed alongside the controversial mushroom-cloud–shaped birthday cake that commemorated the Bikini Atoll tests. The counterweight to all this kitsch is a wrenching 360-degree photo of Hiroshima, the morning after. In the same historic building, the **Art Center at Fuller Lodge** (☎ 662-9331) hangs work by local and international artists.

PAJARITO MOUNTAIN SKI AREA

Cold fusion still eludes them, but frustrated physicists strap on their skis and get inspired at this small resort

(☎ 662-5725, 888-662-7669; www.skipajarito.com; 397 Camp May; lift tickets adult/child $33/22; 9am-4pm Fri-Sun Dec-Apr), operated by the nonprofit Los Alamos Ski Club. It's got short lines for five lifts, 37 trails and 1400ft of vertical drop, all topped with 125 inches of snow annually – but no snow machines. Call ahead. Pajarito also offers lessons and has a cafeteria.

HIKING

The city's dramatic location above several finger canyons means Los Alamos has more than its fair share of hiking opportunities. Favorites include the steep, 2-mile-roundtrip **Blue Dot Trail**, descending into White Rock Canyon from Overlook Park, and 3-mile-roundtrip, petroglyph-lined **Red Dot Trail**, beginning at La Senda Park. For more area options, check out www.losalamos.com/hiking.

Sleeping

Most visitors are government employees with tight expense accounts and low expectations, and rooms tend to be both threadbare and overpriced. Bargain on weekends.

Holiday Inn Express (☎ 661-1110; 2455 Trinity Dr; d/ste $90/100 Sun-Thu, d/ste $60/70 Fri-Sat; P) is probably the nicest chain offering, with **Best Western Hilltop House** (☎ 662-2441; 800-464-0936; 400 Trinity Dr; r weekends/weekdays $70/80 P) close behind.

WWII buffs will want to stay at **Los Alamos Inn** (☎ 662-7211; 2201 Trinity Dr; d weekends/weekdays $80/90; P), with that sleek barracks styling and authentic cement-block ambiance achieved only during the Manhattan Project's heyday.

Los Alamos has several B&Bs; contact the chamber of commerce for complete listings. They tend to be businesslike affairs serving continental breakfasts. These options include the adequate **Canyon Inn B&B** (☎ 662-9595, 800-662-2565; www.canyoninnbnb.com; 80 Canyon Rd; $65; P) and **North Road B&B** (☎ 662-3678, 800-279-2898; 2127 North Rd; $50/55; P), probably the best deal in town.

Adobe Pines B&B (☎ 661-8828; www.losalamos lodging.com; 2201 Loma Linda; s/d $71/78; P) is an exception, in a pretty adobe overlooking one of the canyons.

Eating

When asked about their favorite spot for an inexpensive meal, residents invariably reply, 'Española.' But there are a few gems on the hill.

Café Allegro (☎ 662-4040; 800 Trinity Dr ste D; ⏰ 7am-5pm Mon-Fri, 8am-2pm Sat) Start your day with a fancy coffee and buttery pastry, or come in for soups and sandwiches at lunch.

Allied Fine Foods & Deli (☎ 662-2777; 751 Central Ave; sandwiches $4-7; ⏰ 7am-6pm Mon-Fri, 7:30am-4pm Sat) Gourmet sandwiches with exotic cheeses and cold cuts are tops, or you could try the recommended sirloin burger.

Thien Kim (☎ 661-4221; 160 Central Park Sq; mains $7-9; ⏰ 11am-9pm Mon-Sat; P) This authentic strip-mall entry serves good pho, bún, and excellent Vietnamese iced coffee.

The Hill Diner (☎ 662-9745; 1315 Trinity Dr; mains $7-9; ⏰ 11am-8pm daily) Physicists and flunkies alike flock to here for the barbecued brisket and big burgers – get mashed potatoes on the side. The diner, decorated with photos of old scientists, specializes in banana cream pie.

Blue Window Bistro (☎ 662-6305; 813 Central Ave; mains $6-19; ⏰ 11am-3pm & 5-9pm Mon-Sat, 8:30am-3pm Sat) Eclectic fine-dining options include Southwest chicken stuffed with bousin cheese and chipotle pesto, then baked in phyllo bread. Saturday breakfasts featuring gourmet pancakes ($6) pack in the engineers.

Katherine's (☎ 672-9661; 121 Longview Dr, White Rock; lunch $6-7, dinner $15-24; ⏰ 11:30am-2:30pm Tue-Fri, 5:30-9:30pm Tue-Sat) This White Rock restaurant, featuring fresh and hearty European gourmet standards in style – anything Italian or involving sausage is a sure bet – is the most elegant way to blow your expense account.

Getting There & Around

You can get here by car from several directions: from Santa Fe and Pojoaque Pueblo on NM 502, and from Española and Santa Clara Pueblo along NM 30, which joins NM 502 for the last stretch up the hill into downtown. White Rock, Bandelier and the museums are all well-signed from this road. The most scenic route, from Albuquerque, is through the Jemez Mountains (p66).

The **Los Alamos Bus System** (☎ 662-2080; www.labus.org; $1-3; ⏰ 6:30am-6pm Mon-Fri) runs buses every half hour throughout Los Alamos County. The airport is no longer offering commercial flights, though this may change in the future. There's a **Budget Rent-a-Car** (☎ 662-1924, 800-527-0700; 1040 Airport Rd) at the airport.

BANDELIER NATIONAL MONUMENT

The reason why Bandelier (Map p116; ☎ 672-3861; www.nps.gov/band; car $10 for 7 days; ⏰ 7am-7:30pm) is so expensive and crowded – some 350,000 people visit the park annually – is because it's incredible. Pale and pockmarked canyon walls plunging into lush, narrow valleys would have marked this land for preservation even without the beautiful and well-preserved Puebloan Indian ruins, occupied between 1150 and 1550. Show up early on weekends to beat the crowds.

NEW MEXICO'S GOLD STANDARD

In 1997 the US Mint decided to mint a new $1 coin depicting Sacagawea, the 15-year-old Lemhi-Shoshone guide who led explorers Lewis and Clark from North Dakota to the Pacific Ocean, carrying her son, Jean-Baptiste, the whole way.

Santa Fe sculptor Glenna Goodacre, who also designed the Vietnam Women's Memorial in Washington, DC, was tapped for the job. Because no images of Sacagawea are known to exist, she chose Randy 'L He-dow Teton, a Shoshone-Bannock Indian and graduate of both UNM and the IAIA, to model in the legend's place. Teton wore an antique doeskin dress, loaned by Morningstar Gallery on Canyon Rd, and a doll strapped to her back.

The new dollar, colored gold to distinguish it from the quarter, is the first coin depicting a mother and child in circulation anywhere. And you can get it – the best deal around on New Mexican art – at any bank or post office. 'It represents all Native American women,' says Teton, now an artist in her own right. 'All women have the dignity of the golden dollar's image.'

More than 70 miles of trails traverse almost 33,000 acres of pine forest. Standouts include the easy 1.4-mile **Main Loop Trail**, past petroglyphs and the Frijoles Ruins, with a worthwhile 2-mile-roundtrip spur out to the skyscraping Ceremonial Cave (the 150ft of ladders may not be suitable for smaller kids). **Falls Trail** offers a 3-mile roundtrip to the Upper Falls, and a steep and recommended 5-mile roundtrip past the Lower Falls to the Rio Grande. In an unattached segment of the park 13 miles north on NM 4, 2-mile **Tsankawi Trail** threads ruins on a path so ancient that it's literally worn into the mesa bedrock.

Hard-core hikers should consider taking the three-day, 28-mile walkabout to **Stone Lion Shrine**, near the ruins of Yapashi Pueblo, an ancestral home of the Chochiti tribe. This is still a sacred site of pilgrimage, so please respect the two ancient carvings of lions, which probably predate Pueblo culture. A free backcountry permit is required for overnight hikes.

Juniper Campground (tent/RV $10) is close to the **visitors center**, which has maps, guidebooks and historical artifacts on display. **Enchanted Lands** (☎ 661-8687; www.enchantedlands.com; $95 per person) offers guided hikes, including transportation from hotels in Santa Fe and Los Alamos, twice weekly in summer and by appointment in winter.

The park is located on NM 4, 12 miles from Los Alamos, and can also be accessed from Jemez Springs (p66).

EAST OF SANTA FE
Pecos National Historical Park
At the gateway to the **Pecos Wilderness**, administered by the Las Vegas Ranger Station and with almost unlimited opportunities for hiking and camping, is this historical park (☎ 737-6414; www.nps.gov/peco; 9am-4:30pm daily), centered on the windswept remains of a well-preserved 700-room pueblo, including a rebuilt kiva and spectacularly dilapidated 1717 mission. All are reached along a 1-mile loop trail from the **visitors center**.

You'll have to make reservations in advance to see the site of the 1862 **Battle of Glorietta Pass**, sometimes called the 'Gettysburg of the West,' though that's a stretch. Union forces cleverly divided a much stronger Confederate contingent

from Texas, retreating from battle as another unit destroyed the Texans' supply lines. This battle ended the South's campaign to take California ports.

Most of the actual battlefield is still privately owned, but the owners do allow a reenactment of the battle in early May, when you can watch history repeat itself in glorious blue and gray.

You'll also need to make reservations to see **Greer Garson Ranch** (☎ 757-6414; adult/child $3/free; Fri), former home of actress Eileen Evelyn Greer Garson, seven-time Oscar nominee and winner for her roll as Mrs Miniver. She earned accolades as an actor in the 1930s and '40s, but after marrying oil tycoon Elijah Fogelson, she relocated here. You'll tour the grounds, an 18-room home and see their Rolls Royce.

The **Pecos-Las Vegas Ranger Station** (☎ 757-6121; Hwy 63; 8am-4:30pm Mon-Fri; Sat in summer) has flyers, free maps and listings for local outfitters that specialize in fishing, horseback riding, rock climbing and other adventures. **Cowles**, about 18 miles north, is where serious hikers begin the ascents of **Pecos Baldy** and **Truchas Peak**.

SLEEPING & EATING
Though there's no camping in the historical park, there are eight developed **campgrounds** (campsite $8-10) in the Pecos Wilderness, most located north of Cowles.

The nearby town of Pecos has several restaurants and accommodations options, ranging from a handful of motels to the **Pecos Benedictine Monastery** (☎ 757-6415; www.pecosabbey.org; Hwy 63; s $50 donation; P), which has small hermitage rooms perfect for the aspiring ascetic.

Villanueva State Park
In a red-rock canyon carved over the millennia by the Pecos River, this disproportionately dramatic state park (Map p116; ☎ 421-2957; Hwy 3; day use $4) has shady **campsites** (reservations ☎ 888-667-2757; www.icampnm.com; campsite/RV $10/14) close to the pretty, 2-mile **Canyon Trail**, which heads out to a rim vista then back along the Pecos River.

To get here, take exit 323 off I-25 and follow Hwy 3 south, through the stunning desert scenery and picturesque Spanish villages of Villanueva and San Miguel, for

12 miles. Stop in at **Madison Winery** (Map p116; ☎ 421-8028; Hwy 3; ☑ 10am-6pm Mon-Sat, noon-6pm Sun) for free samples of the winery's Pecos Wildflower, Flyin' Saucer and other vintages.

Don't miss **Sad Café** (Map p116; ☎ 421-3380; Hwy 3; mains $5-10; ☑ 9am-5pm Wed-Thu, 9am-8pm Fri-Sat), a gourmet anomaly in the middle of nowhere (well, in Ribera, a mile south of I-25) en route to the park. The menu boasts exquisitely prepared dishes made with locally grown and organic produce, courtesy of former New York celebrity chef Benjamin Alexander, who has officially left the rat race. There's often live music on the patio in summer.

Las Vegas
☎ 505 pop 14,565 elevation 6470ft

Las Vegas is quite simply one of the loveliest towns in New Mexico, with a strollable downtown, shady plaza and some 900 gorgeous buildings – most of them not adobe – listed in the National Register of Historic Places. The classic Western

backdrop is the perfect spot for a high noon shootout, an ambiance exploited in cowboy flicks like *Wyatt Earp* and *The Ballad of Gregorio Cortez.*

Home to the Comanche people for some 10,000 years, Las Vegas was founded by Mexico in 1835, just in time to serve as a stop along the Santa Fe Trail and later the Santa Fe Railroad. It quickly grew into one of the biggest, baddest boomtowns in the West.

Those days are gone, but Las Vegas still retains a sienna-tinted elegance and lively social swirl, much of which radiates from the city's two universities. It's also the gateway to two striking wilderness areas: the Pecos Wilderness and Las Vegas National Wildlife Refuge .

ORIENTATION & INFORMATION
Las Vegas is 65 miles east of Santa Fe on I-25 North and about 90 miles south of Angel Fire on Hwy 518. Old Town Plaza lies near the intersection of Hot Springs Blvd, which leads north to Montezuma and the Pecos Wilderness, and Bridge St, which connects

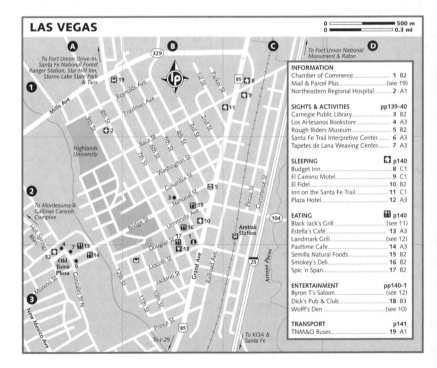

LAS VEGAS

0 —— 500 m
0 —— 0.3 mi

INFORMATION
Chamber of Commerce..................... **1** B2
Mail & Parcel Plus............................(see 19)
Northeastern Regional Hospital..........**2** A1

SIGHTS & ACTIVITIES   pp139-40
Carnegie Public Library...................... **3** B2
Los Artesanos Bookstore.................... **4** A3
Rough Riders Museum......................... **5** B2
Santa Fe Trail Interpretive Center....... **6** A3
Tapetes de Lana Weaving Center........ **7** A3

SLEEPING   p140
Budget Inn......................................**8** C1
El Camino Motel................................**9** C1
El Fidel..**10** B2
Inn on the Santa Fe Trail..................**11** C1
Plaza Hotel.....................................**12** A3

EATING   p140
Black Jack's Grill...........................(see 11)
Estella's Café.................................**13** A3
Landmark Grill...............................(see 12)
Pasttime Cafe.................................**14** A3
Semilla Natural Foods.......................**15** B2
Smokey's Deli..................................**16** B2
Spic 'n Span...................................**17** B2

ENTERTAINMENT   pp140-1
Byron T's Saloon..............................(see 12)
Dick's Pub & Club.............................**18** B3
Wolff's Den....................................(see 10)

TRANSPORT   p141
TNM&O Buses..................................**19** A1

the pedestrian old town to the Grand Ave business district.

The **chamber of commerce** (☎ 425-8631, 800-832-5947; www.lasvegasnm.info; 701 Grand Ave; ☿ 9am-5pm Mon-Fri) has free maps of town, suggested walking tours and the requisite wall of flyers.

Historic **Carnegie Public Library** (☎ 454-1401; 500 National St; ☿ 9am-5:30pm Mon-Sat, 1:30-5:30pm Sun) offers free Internet access. **Los Artesanos Bookstore** (☎ 425-8331; 220 Old Town Plaza; ☿ 11am-3pm Tue-Sat) specializes in antique books and Southwestern themes.

Other services include the **post office** (☎ 425-9387; 1001 Douglas St) and **Northeastern Regional Hospital** (☎ 425-6751; 1235 8th St).

SIGHTS & ACTIVITIES

Las Vegas' main in-town attraction is strolling the beautiful neighborhoods surrounding the plaza and Bridge St.

Rough Riders Museum (☎ 454-1401; 727 Grand Ave; admission free; ☿ 9am-4pm Mon-Fri, 10am-3pm Sat year-round; noon-4pm Sun Apr-Sep) This small but informative museum chronicles the fabled cavalry unit led by future US President Theodore Roosevelt in the 1898 fight for Cuba. More than one-third of the volunteer force came from New Mexico, and here you'll see their furniture, clothes and military regalia.

Santa Fe Trail Interpretive Center (☎ 425-8803; 127 Bridge St; admission free; ☿ 9am-6pm Mon-Sat) The local historical society has finally put its impressive collection on display, including old photos and artifacts from Las Vegas' heyday as a rough-and-tumble trading post along the Santa Fe Trail. Guided tours and lectures are also available.

Tapetes de Lana Weaving Center (☎ 426-8638; www.tapetesdelana.com; 1814 Old Town Plaza; admission free; ☿ 8am-5pm Mon-Sat) This nonprofit rural development project teaches area villagers how to weave and offers visitors the opportunity to watch folks tackle those antique looms. Your purchases help preserve some small, self-sustaining communities.

Montezuma, 5 miles north of Las Vegas on NM 65 (Hot Springs Blvd), is home to rosy, turreted **Montezuma Castle**, a sensational 1886 spa and retreat that now houses United World College. It's closed to the public except on prearranged **tours** (☎ 454-4221 for appointments) or when visiting the **Dwan Light Sanctuary** (☎ 454-4200; admission free; ☿ sunrise-sunset daily), a meditation chamber decorated in prisms and rainbows.

Gallinas Canyon Complex, about 10 miles farther up NM 65, is a green and gorgeous unit of the Santa Fe National Forest, with five campsites and lots of hikes. The classic is the steep, 14-mile roundtrip from El Porvenir Campground to **Hermit Mountain** (Trail 223), where the eccentric Giovanni Maria Angoste performed various miracles in the 1860s. Stop at the **Santa Fe National Forest Ranger Station** (☎ 425-3534; 1926 N 7th St; ☿ 8am-5pm Mon-Fri) for maps and information on this and other recommended hikes.

ON THE SANTA FE TRAIL

Though the Santa Fe Trail (SFT) – linking Franklin, Missouri, to Santa Fe – had been used by Europeans since the 1700s and Native peoples for millennia prior, the Spanish Crown jealously limited the route's use until 1821. When Mexico declared its independence, and finally initiated free trade with the USA, the SFT was legally open for business.

The wisdom of Spain's enforced isolation soon became clear, however, as economic and cultural ties were forged between New Mexico and the United States along the SFT. When General Kearny and US troops marched the 900-mile route in 1846, they were met with little resistance – even open arms – by Santa Feans less than thrilled with the Mexican government.

After New Mexico was ceded to the USA in 1847, American businesspeople, traders and settlers began pouring in, and in 1880 brought with them the Santa Fe Railroad, ending the need for the SFT.

'Rut Nuts' still follow the trail, however, in search of old wagon tracks still embedded in the hardened earth. The Rough Riders Museum has a free flyer with directions to popular ruts, best seen in early morning or late evening. Want to learn more? Log onto the University of Kansas SFT Homepage (www.ku.edu/heritage/research/sft), with links and information.

SANTA FE

Las Vegas National Wildlife Refuge (☎ 425-3581) Take a break from the desert in this wetlands preserve, with a driving loop, nature hikes, lots of rare waterfowl and hunting in September and October. It's located 6 miles southeast of town: take I-25 to exit 345, head east on NM Hwy 104 for 1½ miles, then south on NM Hwy 281 for 4 miles.

Fort Union National Monument (☎ 425-8025; NM 161; $2) History buffs may prefer to take I-25 north to this small park, where a 2-mile interpretive trail guides you past SFT-era wagon ruts and the weathered adobe remains of the Civil War–era fort.

SLEEPING

The startlingly lush countryside makes for great **camping**: try the five relatively undeveloped campgrounds of the **Gallinas Canyon Complex** (campsite $4-10); the sweet spots at **Storrie Lake State Park** (☎ 827-7465, 800-451-2541; campsite/RV $8/14), where you can catch rainbow trout and crappie; or the comfortable **KOA** (☎ 454-0180; campsite/RV/ Kamping Kabin $21/27/38), 4 miles south of Las Vegas on I-25.

El Fidel (☎ 425-6761; 500 Douglas St; d/ste $40/85; P X R) is an elegant, if faded, 1920s belle of a hotel, with character to spare (perhaps too much character for some folks) and a neat lounge with a **coffee bar** (☺ 8am-7pm daily) and pub, the **Wolff's Den** (☺ 6-11pm daily).

There are several budget hotels with classic neon signs and brown carpeting of questionable cleanliness lining Grand Ave north of town, including **Budget Inn** (☎ 425-1456; 1216 Grand Ave; s/d $40/45; P X R R) and **El Camino Motel** (☎ 425-5994; 1152 Grand Ave; s/d $50/65; P X R R). The shady, tasteful exception is **Inn on the Santa Fe Trail** (☎ 425-6791, 888-448-8438; 1133 N Grand Ave; s/d $70/80 summer, s/d $55/65 winter; P X R R), with large, modern rooms (some of which have microwaves and refrigerators).

The historic **Plaza Hotel** (☎ 425-3591, 888-328-1882; www.plazahotel-nm.com; 230 Old Town Plaza; d/ste $100/150; P X R), both storied and spectacular, is housed in an 1882 Victorian edifice complete with antiques, a ghost (former owner Byron T Mills), the solid **Landmark Grill** (mains $9-22; ☺ 7am-2pm & 5-9pm daily) and **Byron T's Saloon** (see Entertainment), the best bar in town. It comes highly recommended.

Star Hill Inn (☎ 425-5605; www.starhillinn.com; Hwy 518; d $165-195, d guesthouse $230-375 incl breakfast), located 13 miles north in the village of Sapello, is a stellar B&B, which includes your choice of telescope and/or an astronomy lesson with every room. There's a two-night minimum.

EATING

Cheap eats and fast food can be found along Mills Ave, but look downtown to find local favorites, most concentrated around the plaza and Bridge St.

Semilla Natural Foods (☎ 425-8139; 510 University Ave; ☺ 10am-6pm Mon-Sat) This natural grocery has organic treats galore, but no real deli.

Estella's Café (☎ 454-0048; 148 Bridge St; mains $4-8; ☺ 11am-3pm Mon-Wed, 11am-8pm Thu-Sat) Devoted patrons treasure this highly recommended local gem for its homemade red chile, menudo and scrumptious enchiladas.

Smokey's Deli (☎ 426-8612; 600 Douglas St; sandwiches $5-10; ☺ 11am-7pm Mon-Fri, 11am-3pm Sat) Featuring deli sandwiches (try the roast beef with green chile) in four different sizes, this self-consciously kitschy place does do malteds in its Happy Days–style setting.

Spic 'n' Span (☎ 426-1921; 715 Douglas St; mains $5-10; ☺ 6:30am-5:30pm Mon-Sat, 6:30am-3pm Sun) This place is cheerful, casual and usually crowded, thanks to a great bakery and better food.

Pastime Cafe (☎ 454-1755; 113 Bridge St; lunch $5-8, dinner $10-18; ☺ 11:30am-2:30pm & 5-9pm Mon-Sat) When you're over burritos, come here to enjoy a gourmet touch to tapas, seafood, organic salads and the recommended chocolate confusion cake.

Black Jack's Grill (☎ 425-6791; 1113 N Grand Ave; tapas $7-10, mains $14-25; ☺ 5-9pm daily) Don't let the location put you off – this handsome, upscale steakhouse comes well recommended by locals for its hearty seafood enchiladas and spicy pork tenderloin.

ENTERTAINMENT

Though the nightlife can't compare with that *other* Las Vegas, convivial places to imbibe include **Byron T's Saloon** (☎ 425-3591; 230 Plaza; ☺ 11am-2am daily), a cozy place that brings live music to the Plaza Hotel

Thursday through Sunday evening, and **Dick's Pub & Club** (☎ 425-8261; 806 Douglas St; ☉ 10am-2am Mon-Sat), where Highland University students pack the two-story nightclub to guzzle more than 30 varieties of beer. Dude.

A fine evening can be had May through September at the **Fort Union Drive-In** (☎ 425-9934; 3300 7th St), New Mexico's last drive-in movie theater.

GETTING THERE & AROUND

Las Vegas is about an hour east of Santa Fe on I-25 and three hours south of Angel Fire and the Enchanted Circle on Hwy 518, which makes for a great trip through backcountry New Mexico, if you've got the time.

AJ Transport Airport Shuttle (☎ 425-7508) runs twice daily between the Plaza Hotel and the Santa Fe Airport (one way $25) and Albuquerque Sunport (one way $45).

TNM&O Buses, serving the Southwest in conjunction with Greyhound, leave for Raton ($30) and Santa Fe ($15) twice daily from the **Mail & Parcel Plus** (☎ 425-8689; 611 Mills Ave) in the Lowe's Shopping Center.

Amtrak (☎ 800-872-7245; cnr Railroad & Lincoln Sts) runs its Southwest Chief between Chicago and Los Angeles through Las Vegas daily; coach tickets to Albuquerque run about $30 (roundtrip $50). **Las Vegas Cab** (☎ 454-1864, 800-884-2599) can take you anywhere in town.

DETOUR: MONTEZUMA HOT SPRINGS

Just past Montezuma Castle on NM 65, headed north from Las Vegas, you'll see a small sign on your right reading 'hot springs.' Pull over, and you'll see the well-maintained (and clothing-optional) **Montezuma Hot Springs** (admission free; ☉ 5am-midnight).

Famed throughout the Aztec Empire (Montezuma was allegedly raised and/or bathed here), these healing springs were most recently developed in the 1880s as part of the Montezuma Castle Resort but have fallen into charming disrepair. The rock and cement ponds are kept clean by the good folks at United World College, who graciously keep them open to the public. The pools range from 98-113°F, perfect for soaking off a long hike through the Pecos Wilderness.

Taos

CONTENTS

Is it the isolated location, at the foothills of New Mexico's mightiest peaks, which once forced the Santa Fe Railroad to bypass this stunning enclave? Or perhaps it's the resolute presence of Taos Pueblo, strong and dignified, still a potent force defining the culture and character of this place. Maybe it's the light, unencumbered by the weight of atmosphere and moisture, and studied in the dreamtime of artists drawn here by the most suspect of coincidences.

Whatever it is, Taos has gathered the most remarkable collection of people to its scenic breast and nurtured them to magnificence far beyond what one would expect from a small mountain village. It's a haven where refugees from the modern world – whether the 16th or 21st century – have collected themselves and called home.

Tourists come here, most certainly, to challenge themselves at one of the nation's top ski resorts, just the tip of a mountain of attractions. Art collectors, movie stars (without makeup, so you probably won't even recognize them) and the merely curious wander the galleries and museums, but Taos doesn't consciously cater to them – it's a bit shocking, this oversight, particularly after a few days in Santa Fe. Then it becomes a relief.

And while the capital's eccentricities sometimes seem a bit contrived, it's as though Taoseños couldn't help themselves, even if they made the attempt. Some have, and failed, then found their peace here. But this is no exile from the concrete and steel of modern society, though it may seem so to those suited and sane. It is its own world, welcoming all those willing to accept it on its own strange terms.

TAOS

HIGHLIGHTS

- **Taos Pueblo** The prettiest city in New Mexico (p166)
- **Taos Ski Valley** Incredible in all seasons (p169)
- **Millicent Rogers Museum** Where kitsch meets fine art (p148)
- **Horseback riding in the Blue Lakes Wilderness** Sacred and scenic (p167)
- **Adobe Bar** Margaritas, music and outstanding people-watching (p164)
- **Wild Rivers Recreation Area** Lonely and beautiful (p174)
- **Rio Grande Gorge Bridge** The best sunset (or sunrise) ever (p152)
- **Solar Survival Tours** Get off the grid (p152)
- **Hiking with llamas** The cuddliest way to camp (p153)
- **Ledoux St** Two top museums and galleries galore (p148)

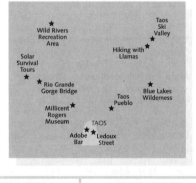

| ■ TELEPHONE CODE: **505** | ■ POPULATION: **6,500** | ■ ELEVATION: **6950FT** |

ORIENTATION

Downtown Taos lies at the northern terminus of NM 68, called Paseo del Pueblo Sur (roughly, 'South Pueblo Road') as it enters the village, and is centered on the intersection of US 64 (which is called Kit Carson Rd as it heads southeast toward Angel Fire) and Paseo del Pueblo Norte ('North Pueblo Road') after seamlessly transitioning from NM 68 (you won't realize you've changed highways) downtown. Together, the paseos are often referred to as Main St.

As you hit Taos coming north from Santa Fe on NM 68, Paseo del Pueblo Sur is lined with budget hotels, chain stores and restaurants. The chamber of commerce is at the intersection of Paseo del Cañon E (Hwy 585), which heads east to bypass the plaza and connect with US 64, the direct route to Carson National Forest campgrounds. Continue north a couple more increasingly gridlocked miles on Paseo del Pueblo Sur into downtown.

One mile north of town, Paseo del Pueblo Norte forks: to the northeast it becomes Camino del Pueblo and heads toward Taos Pueblo, and to the northwest, US 64 continues to the intersection of Taos Ski Valley Rd (NM 150), NM 522 to Questa and, after making a hard left at the stoplight, to the Rio Grande Gorge Bridge. Though just a normal stoplight now, this intersection was once marked by the 'blinking light' and is still sometimes referred to as such.

Maps

Taos is small enough to navigate using the maps provided in this book, but Rand McNally's *Santa Fe/Taos Local Street Detail* folding map, available at most gas stations, has more detail. If you plan to stay a while, grab a copy of the *Horton Family Map*, a black and white book of street maps covering Santa Fe, Española and Taos.

Folks headed to the Enchanted Circle, or anywhere else out of town, should invest in the folding *Highroad Map of North Central New Mexico* at least; real wanderers will want to pick up a copy of the *New Mexico Road & Recreation Atlas*.

Native Sons Adventures (p152) and **Cottam's** (p154) both carry large selections of maps, including USGS topos, highly recommended if you plan to do much hiking or mountain biking in the region.

INFORMATION

Bookshops

Looking for the Barnes & Noble? Tough luck. And there isn't a Starbucks for 70 miles! **Taos Book Shop** (Map p149; ☎ 758-3733; 122D Kit Carson Rd) New Mexicana, Americana, out-of-print books and up-to-date maps are interspersed with neat souvenirs.

Lucille's Book Exchange (Map p149; cnr Camino de la Placita & Ledoux St) Stacks upon stacks of used paperbacks could keep you busy for hours – or years.

Moby Dickens (Map p149; ☎ 758-3050; www.moby dickens.com; 124A Bent St #6) Used, rare, really rare and new classics make this one wonderful wander.

Mystery Ink Bookshop (Map p149; ☎ 751-1092; 121 Camino de la Placita) Get your thrills and chills – and a fair number of children's books, too – at this mystery trove.

Emergency

Fire, Police, Ambulance Immediate Dispatch (☎ 911)

Police (☎ 758-2216; 107 Civic Plaza Dr)

Holy Cross Hospital Emergency Room (Map p147; ☎ 751-5895; 1397 Weimer Rd)

Internet Access

Taos Public Library (Map p149; ☎ 758-3063; 420 Camino de la Placita; ☺ 10am-5pm Mon-Sat) Internet access costs $2 an hour without a library card. You can purchase a temporary (four-month) card without residency for $1 plus a $25 refundable deposit. Sheesh.

Magic Circle Bagels Cyber Cafe (Map p147; ☎ 758-0045; 710 Paseo del Pueblo Sur; snacks $3-6; ☺ 6:30am-3pm Mon-Fri, 7am-2pm Sat-Sun) Three fairly fast computers ($6/hr) go well with lattes, soups and 19 different bagels, right in the Raley's shopping center.

Daylight Donuts (Map p147; ☎ 758-1156; 312 Paseo del Pueblo Sur; ☺ 5:30-11:30am & 4-8pm Mon-Fri). Come for a half hour of free, painfully slow Internet access with coffee, donuts or the Belgian waffle bar.

Island Coffees & Hawaiian Grill (p162) T1 lines ($6/hr) come with Hawaiian decor.

Internet Resources

Also check out the Sights and Sleeping sections of this chapter for more useful Taos websites.

Destination Taos (www.destinationtaos.com) The chamber of commerce posts events listings, tourism and relocation information online.

Taos Guide (www.taosguide.com) Click for an exhaustive list of easy-to-navigate links.

Taos Webb (www.taoswebb.com) Access links and information, including sites covering north-central New Mexico.

Taos Is Art Online (www.taosis.com) Check the schedule of art openings and studio tours, plus links and articles on local galleries.

Taos Link (www.taoslink.com) It's a tad intimidating, with links to every website even remotely associated with Taos.

Media
PUBLICATIONS

There are stacks of free visitors guides designed to show tourists the ropes, available at the chamber of commerce and on racks all over town.

Taos News (www.taosnews.com) This award-winning daily updates its website every Thursday, when it also

---

TAOS IN...

ONE DAY

Get up early and hit the Low Road to Taos, timing it so the sun will filter dramatically into Rio Grande Gorge as you ascend the mountain. Make a quick detour to San Francisco de Asis, gleaming in the sun: photo op! If you're hungry as you roll into town, head to Michael's Kitchen if you just need a pick-me-up, make it Cafe Tazza instead. Thus fortified, it's time to explore. Head toward Ledoux St, perusing the galleries and either the Harwood or Blumenschein museum. Ah, culture. From there, make your way back to the plaza, perhaps getting a tarot-card reading at Inspirations, or popping into La Fonda for a peek at DH Lawrence's Forbidden Art. Then it's back to the car for the quick drive to Taos Pueblo. Grab a camera permit and take the tour, not forgetting to shop. By now, its dinnertime, and that means Orlando's. Don't dally too long – you want to hit the Rio Grande Gorge Bridge as the sun sets. Then it's back to town, for music and a margarita (just one!) at Adobe Bar before returning to Santa Fe.

TWO DAYS

It's an early start on the Low Road to Taos, stopping at Embudo Station to appreciate the river. At San Francisco de Asis, take time to view the miraculous Shadow of the Cross. Cool. Throw your stuff in your hotel room – the Taos Inn, perhaps? – then take time to appreciate downtown and Taos Pueblo properly. At the Blumenschein grab a three-pack of museum passes, as you'll need one for the Harwood and another tomorrow. Wander. Relax. Drink as many margaritas as you'd like. If you can, get up early to watch the sunrise over the Rio Grande Gorge and take the Solar Survival Tour. Return via the Millicent Rogers Museum and have a burrito at Orlando's for lunch. Then it's the High Road south, stopping at La Chiripada Winery for a flight. Make the detour onto Main Truchas Rd, exploring a gallery or two, and at the end of the road do your best Maria von Trapp imitation in the shadow of Truchas Peak. Stop into Cordova for some woodcarvings or Santuario de Chimayó for some dirt, then relax at either Rancho de Chimayó or El Paragua over dinner. Consider one margarita before hitting the road – keeping a sharp lookout for lowriders – on your way back to Santa Fe.

FIVE DAYS

Follow the two-day itinerary, but instead of taking the High Road, wake up late and make reservations at the New Buffalo Inn or Adobe and Stars, and consider renting a tent and fishing pole. Stop into Hacienda Martinez, then head north, lunching in Arroyo Seco while choosing which hike you'd like at Taos Ski Area. Watch the sun set, have dinner, then relax in hot springs or a hot tub before going to bed. Wake up early to begin the Enchanted Circle: pay your respects at the DH Lawrence Memorial, hike or drive the Wild Rivers Recreation Area, then either camp or get a hotel room in Red River. Continue in the morning, stopping to investigate the Elizabethtown Museum, hike Clear Creek Trail in Cimarron Canyon and visit the Vietnam Veterans Memorial. After a long shower in your Taos hotel room, return your camping equipment and check to see what live music is on – at Eske's? The Alley Cantina? The Adobe again? Your call. Wake up late, grab some breakfast and poke around the galleries before hitting the High Road back down the mountain.

publishes the weekly arts and entertainment pullout *Tempo*, with events listings.

Horse Fly (www.horseflyonline.com) A fat, 50¢ politics and arts monthly includes at least three inspired rants about sometimes-Taos-resident Donald Rumsfeld in each edition. Can that guy even get within 100 miles of his vacation home anymore?

Geronimo (www.taoswebb.com/geronimo) This free monthly publication is all about arts and politics, and *Taos Magazine* is a free, almost-monthly glossy with articles on artists and studios.

RADIO & TELEVISION

All television stations and most radio stations are based in Santa Fe and Albuquerque, with a few notable exceptions. You can get National Public Radio (NPR) on KRZA 88.7 FM and 91.9 FM, while KXMT 99.1 FM broadcasts Spanish-language public radio. KTAO 101.9 FM (see below) is a great local station that broadcasts using solar power.

Medical Services

Holy Cross Hospital (Map p147; ☎ 758-8883, emergency 751-5895; www.taoshospital.com; 1397 Weimer Rd) is southeast of town; make a right onto Weimer Road off Paseo del Cañon E.

There's a pharmacy at **Raley's Supermarket** (Map p147; ☎ 758-1203; 1100 Paseo del Pueblo Sur; ☯ 6am-midnight daily).

FEATURE: GOOD DAY SUNSHINE

Just as the Rio Grande Gorge opens up to engulf US 68 for the scenic climb into Taos, your radio will start to sputter – so much for those Santa Fe stations. Don't put on that tired old CD; flip to **KTAO 101.9 FM,** broadcasting shows like 'Trash and Treasures' (where callers describe their wackiest for-sale items), Larry Torres' news and views from Taos Pueblo, and lots of great music, much of it local and the rest leaning toward adult contemporary and folk, though you just never know.

KTAO has been doing it all with solar power since 1991, when station owner Brad Hockmeyer installed 50,000 watts worth of photovoltaic cells atop Mount Picuris. The station broadcasts all that good stuff throughout southern Colorado and Northern New Mexico (well, as long as you're on a mesa), 100% terrorism-, Texas oil- and ClearChannel-free.

The station sponsors events throughout the year, but the biggest bash of them all is the **Solar Music Festival** (p157), held around the summer solstice at Kit Carson Park as a benefit for the **New Mexico Solar Energy Association** (www.nmsea.org). Big-name artists come from all over the world to play the Solar Stage, attracting fans by the thousands – but that's just the beginning.

A free **Solar Village** sets up outside, showcasing everything from the Los Alamos National Laboratory's solar-powered supercomputer to homemade solar cookers, which look like satellite dishes and can do anything from simmer stews to bake bread. Grab a cup of solar-percolated coffee and chat up alternative-energy lovers pitching straw-bale construction, solar cars that fool the UFO-watchers down in Roswell, passive solar design ('used at Taos Pueblo for a thousand years!'), and of course the fine folks from the **Taos Earthship Community** (p152).

You may even spot a protester or two outside the concert carrying signs that ask, 'Solar energy is free, why does this cost admission?' They're the ones to talk to about the radical New Mexico solar scene – folks who seceded from the US government-affiliated Solar Energy Industries Association (www.seia.org) to protest US subsidies of fossil fuel technologies. Ah, Taos, where there's even a counter-counterculture.

Long renowned for its quality of light – though the artists who extolled that virtue probably didn't have anything like *this* in mind – Taos is on the crest of a trend, and indie radio stations and private homeowners nationwide come here to learn more about harnessing all that free sunshine, then dance the night away.

There's even a movement to have Taos designated the 'Solar Energy Capital of the World,' and why not? It's closer to Sol than most spots, and the community has actually bothered to make it work for them. Why not give props to people doing the research now, while there's still some backup when the clouds roll in? It just makes sense, and besides, it's a party. So tune in, turn on (www.ktao.com has streaming audio, too) and drop by – but don't forget your sunscreen.

Want to learn more? Check out *The Passive Solar Energy Book*, Edward Mazria's seminal guide to solar architecture, or the less technically demanding *Rads, Ergs, and the Cheeseburgers: The Kids' Guide to Energy and the Environment*, by New Mexico solar gurus Michael Taylor and Bill Yanda, who has probably intercepted more solar energy than anyone else on Earth with his hand-built adobe greenhouses.

TAOS AREA

0 — 4 km
0 — 2 mi

TAOS

Money

Conveniently located downtown, **First State Bank** (Map p149; ☎ 758-6600; 120 W Plaza) has an ATM and exchanges foreign currency. **Centinel Bank** (Map p147; ☎ 758-6700; 512 Paseo del Pueblo Sur) also exchanges currency and has drive-through ATMs, but it's worth going inside to see *New Mexico Linda*, carved by David Gonzalez, the former Taoseño famous for creating those cute little 'Homies' figurines.

Post

The main **Taos Post Office** (Map p149; ☎ 758-2081; cnr Paseo del Pueblo Norte & Brooks St) is just north of the plaza.

Tourist Offices

Taos Visitors Center (Map p147; ☎ 758-3873; www .taoschamber.com; cnr Paseo del Pueblo Sur & Paseo del Cañon; ⏱ 9:30am-5pm Mon-Sat, open 9:30am-5pm Sun in summer) Stop here first for racks of flyers, a small museum covering Taos Pueblo and the desk for Historic Taos Trolley Tours (p156).

Carson National Forest Supervisor's Office (☎ 758-6200; www.fs.fed.us/r3/carson; 208 Cruz Alta Rd; ⏱ 8:30am-4:30pm Mon-Fri) Just east of the strip, this office has information on hiking, camping, rafting and everything else going on in Carson National Forest.

Bureau of Land Management (Map p147; BLM; ☎ 758-8851, 888-882-6188; www.nm.blm.gov; 226 Cruz Alta Rd; ⏱ 7:30am-4:30pm Mon-Fri) Next door, this office has more information on public lands.

SIGHTS

For a village that gets as much tourist traffic as Taos, there aren't that many sights to see. **Downtown**, a collection of ancient and irregularly shaped adobes centered on the picturesque **plaza**, threaded through by historic **Ledoux St** – at least one bar dates to the 1500s – makes a great wander.

The **Museum Association of Taos** (www.taos museums.org) offers a $20 pass to six area museums (a $37 value), as well as options including a ticket to three museums (adult/child $10/7 or $8/5 for two). All the museums have different hours, themes and single-entry prices.

The area's two top attractions, **Taos Pueblo** and **Taos Ski Valley**, are covered in their own sections later in this chapter.

Harwood Foundation Museum

If the Taos Society of the Arts (TSA) is the village's Barbazon, then this museum (Map p149; ☎ 758-9826; www.harwoodmuseum.org; 238 Ledoux St; $5; ⏱ 10am-5pm Tue-Sat, noon-5pm Sun) is its Louvre. From the grand pueblo revival exterior, one of John Gaw Meem's (p81) earliest works, to touring exhibits that have included Jasper Johns retrospectives, New Mexico's second-oldest museum is about as world-class as it gets in a town this size.

Anyone with a passing interest in New Mexico art will recognize the pieces hanging: John Ward Lockwood's *Portrait of Clyde Lockwood*, Irving Couse's *Cacique* and the largest public collection of bultos carved by Patrociño Barela (p128) anywhere are just a few of the highlights.

If you're already over the TSA theme, fear not: other movements are well represented, with pieces like Cady Wells' abstract impressionist *Penitente Morada* and an entire gallery devoted to the white-on-white work of internationally acclaimed artist and long-time Taos resident Agnes Martin. The upstairs portion of the museum features the work of many Hispanic Works Progress Administration (WPA) artists, with an emphasis on santos, reredos and other sacred art.

Millicent Rogers Museum

See what a top-quality squashblossom necklace is supposed to look like at this jam-packed museum (Map p147; ☎ 505-758-2462; www.millicentrogers.org; Millicent Rogers Museum Rd; adult/child $6/5 ⏱ 10am-5pm daily, closed Mon Nov-Mar), showcasing the collection of oil heiress, fashion designer and Native arts aficionado Millicent Rogers, possessed of a Lauren Bacall–style glamour and *lots* of fantastic jewelry.

The 'Best Dressed List' alumna spent the 1940s and '50s defining Santa Fe style – velvet Navajo shirts and flowing skirts cinched with concha belts, accented with heavy silver bracelets and draped with those necklaces – and she made it work. Then everybody else tried it.

You can see her smashing outfits and endless assortment of accessories here, along with one of the best collections of pueblo pottery in existence. The museum showcases the gleaming Martinez (as in Maria; p119) family collection, plus work by all the important matriarchs: Margaret Tofoya, Christina Naranjo and Mary Esther

Archuleta from Santa Clara, Cochiti's Helen Cordero, and many more.

Spanish artists are also well represented, including Lydia Garcia's reverse-painted glass, bultos by Patrociño Barela (p128) and scores of Virgens, santos, retablos and one very creepy *Carretera de la Muerte con Doña Sebastiana*, by Dolores Lopez.

As you complete your tour de force of New Mexico's finest non-Anglo artists, before exiting to the outrageous museum store (appropriate, considering how this woman could shop), you'll be treated to Rogers' own excellent, if odd, illustrations for Hans Christian Anderson's classic *The Little Mermaid,* as interpreted by one gal who never looked back.

La Hacienda de los Martinez

About 2 miles from downtown, this 21-room adobe fortress (☎ 758-1000; Ranchitos Rd (NM 240); adult/child $5/3; ☯ 9am-5pm) was built to protect an entire community from the Comanche raids of the 1700s and marks the end of the Camino Real, connecting Taos to Mexico City and points south.

Don Antonio Severino Martinez purchased the property in 1804, shortly after peace was made with the Comanches. He continued expanding the edifice to its current girth and raised six children here, including Padre Antonio Martinez, owner of the region's first printing press.

Padre Martinez printed Taos' first newspaper and several textbooks for the

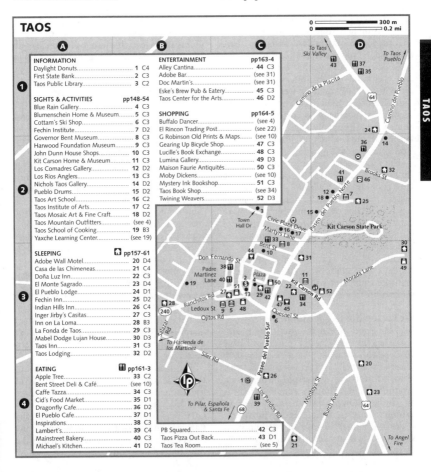

TAOS

0 ————— 300 m
0 ————— 0.2 mi

To Taos Ski Valley
To Taos Pueblo
To Angel Fire
To Pilar, Española & Santa Fe
To Hacienda de los Martinez

Camino de la Placita
Camino del Pueblo
Brooks St
Paseo del Pueblo Norte
Civic Plaza Drive
Kit Carson State Park
Town Hall Dr
Marty's Lane
Bent St
Don Fernando St
Padre Martinez Lane
Plaza
Kit Carson Rd
Morada Lane
Ranchitos Rd (240)
Ledoux St
Ojitos Rd
Quesnel St
Salazar Rd
Siler Rd
Paseo del Pueblo Sur
Los Pandos Rd
Montoya St
Burch Ave

school he founded, but he's remembered best for friction with Archbishop Lamy. *Death Comes for the Archbishop* presents one side of the story – that Martinez and his pals were corrupt – but historians note that Martinez encouraged locals to educate themselves on US property laws, so they wouldn't lose their Spanish land grants. Either way, he's probably the best-loved priest ever to be excommunicated.

Displays at the Hacienda avoid that controversy almost entirely, instead presenting a series of obsessively accurate displays on Spanish colonial life: The walls are whitewashed with *tierra blanca*, a mixture of wheat paste and micaceous clay; the churro wool hangings are colored with vegetable dyes; and corn is explained as a secondary crop, as the growing season is just too short up here to really grow the stuff.

And uncomfortable histories are addressed. Taos was something of a slave-trade center during the 1700s: women and children, one exhibit explains, went for $50 to $100, as they were considered more valuable than 'difficult to handle' adult male Indians, who cost perhaps $20. Some of that probably went on right here, at the hacienda, which might explain those Comanche raids.

The Americans were no improvement. In a reproduced 1851 proclamation by Governor James C Calhoun, all able-bodied males were authorized 'to pursue and attack any hostile tribe of Indians which may have entered the settlements for the purpose of plunder and depredation.' Translation: open season.

Kids will enjoy the fun and oft-tactile displays, but adults who take the time to read the fine print will come away with a sense of history glossed over elsewhere.

Kit Carson Home & Museum

In 1843 professional mountain man and local legend Kit Carson purchased this 1825 adobe sprawler (Map p149; ☎ 758-0505; Kit Carson Rd; adult/child $5/3; 🕙 9am-5pm daily, shorter winter hours) for his 14-year-old bride, Josefa Jaramillo-Vigil. Though remembered as an 'Indian killer' (though, according to exhibits, only in self-defense), he didn't make his name because of his shooting skills. He was an accomplished linguist, fluent in Spanish, English and at least

10 Native tongues, and could facilitate communication in the Southwest's regular Tower of Babel as he scouted the trail ahead.

He was also a staunch supporter of the US government's efforts to annex the territory: Taos is one of two places in the USA where the flag can fly at night legally, as he and his pals guarded it around the clock during the Mexican-American War.

Carson's adventures were legion, but he was shocked to come across Charles Amerille's overwrought thriller, *Kit Carson, Prince of the Gold Hunters*. Who knows what he would have thought about comics like the 1908 *Kit Carson: King of the Scouts*, displayed alongside exhibits that offer a glimpse into his actual life?

Union Blues, lots of guns, a display on Freemasons (he was one, too!) and colonial-era kitsch flesh out the legend. But not too much – some myths just don't need to be debunked entirely.

Blumenschein Home & Museum

This 1797 adobe (Map p149; ☎ 758-0505; 222 Ledoux St; adult/child $5/3; 🕙 9am-5pm daily, shorter winter hours) was the former home of artist Ernest Blumenschein, the painter who accidentally transformed Taos into an art colony one fateful 1898 September afternoon. He and fellow artist Bert Phillips broke a wagon wheel 20 miles north of town, then flipped a coin to see who would go get it fixed. 'Blumy' lost the toss and made his muddy, miserable way into Taos. Then the clouds parted over Taos Pueblo and its awesome backdrop, and that was it.

Phillips relocated to Taos almost immediately, while Blumenschein returned several times to paint the scene, finally moving here for good in 1919. He had to convince his wife and fellow painter, Mary Shepherd Greene, that Taos really wasn't a backwater *per se* and founded the Taos Society of Artists (p151) to prove it.

The period furniture is interesting, but the art is spectacular. Work by all six of the original TSA artists is joined by Mary's detailed illustrations as well as work by later Taos painters: Elmer Turner, Jozef G Bazos, Leon Gaspard, Gene Kloss and many others portray the scene right outside the museum's door.

The **Taos Tea Room** (Map p149; ☎ 751-0211; light lunches $4-7; ☼ 11am-5pm) is planning to move into the museum, and you won't have to pay admission to sample sandwiches, Mexican hot chocolate or high tea ($12; reserve 24 hours in advance).

Fechin Institute

Though he didn't get here until 1927, the year the TSA disbanded, Nicolai Fechin was among the finest artists Taos has ever inspired, and much of his work still hangs at his former home (Map p149; ☎ 758-1710; www.fechin.com; 227 Paseo del Pueblo Norte; $4; ☼ 10am-2pm Wed-Sun) His paintings, drawings and sculptures are in museums and collections worldwide, but this may be the only place you can see his hand-built furniture, carved with a distinctly Russian intent.

Upstairs, his remarkable oil paintings will soon be joined by the collection of Duane Van Vechten, formerly housed at the Van Vechtin-Lineberry Taos Art Museum, now closed. The work of these two impressive talents shares space with Fechin's private collection, including lots of Asian art, and the lovely adobe also hosts occasional chamber music events.

Governor Bent Museum

Not a member of the Museum Association of Taos, this bric-a-brac–packed historic spot (Map p149; ☎ 758-2376; 117 Bent St, adult/child $2/1; ☼ 9am-5pm daily, shorter winter hours) is nonetheless worth dropping by, if only to see the hole in the adobe wall through which the wives of Governor Charles Bent and Kit Carson escaped during the uprising of January 19, 1847.

When the USA annexed New Mexico in 1846, Bent became the first US territorial governor and clearly had no idea what he was getting into. Though locals didn't organize regular troops to resist the incursion, a group of guerillas (or drunks, depending on which historian you talk to) loyal to former Governor Armijo allied with several Indians from Taos Pueblo, although it's unclear if they were acting with the pueblo government's blessing. The details of the attack remain shrouded in history, but while his family escaped Bent was scalped, touching off yet another bloody episode in the European-Native relations.

In addition to the hole in the wall, the museum features lots of animal skulls, stuffed iguanas, mastodon tusks,

---

THE TAOS SOCIETY OF ARTISTS *By Bridgette Wagner*

In 1893 artist Joseph Henry Sharp first visited Taos to produce a group of illustrations depicting the pueblo for publication. Taken with the scene, Sharp spread the word among his colleagues about his 'discovery,' and shortly afterward relocated here permanently.

Ernest Blumenschein, Bert Phillips and many more of his contemporaries followed, and in 1912 they, along with Oscar Berninghaus, Eanger Irving Couse, and Herbert Dunton, established the Taos Society of Artists (TSA). The original six were later joined by other prominent painters including Lucy Harwood, the only female member, and Juan Tafiho Mirabol, a Taos Indian.

Early TSA paintings were inspired by the backdrop of the Sangre de Cristo Mountains as well as the buildings and people of Taos Pueblo. Set against the tonal shapes and neutral colors of earth, human figures act as anchors of color seen nowhere else in the desert. Pueblo architecture, with its golden clusters of block shapes, organic and sculptural, reflecting the high desert light, also appealed to the Taos painters' artistic sensibilities.

The artists' styles were as diverse and experimental as the many philosophies of painting that defined the first half of the 20th century. From Sharp's illustrative and realistic approach and Blumenschein's impressionistic treatment of Southwestern themes to the moody art deco spirit of Dunton's landscapes, the TSA portrayed the same subjects in infinite ways.

Only in later years would the TSA's contribution to modern art's development be fully recognized. Historically the paintings of the TSA are recognized as a visual documentary of Northern New Mexican cultures, which had not yet been so dramatically influenced by the industrial age.

Larger collections of these influential works can be viewed in Taos at the Harwood Foundation and Blumenschein Museum. In Santa Fe, look to the Museum of Fine Arts as well as the Gerald Peters and Nedra Matteucci galleries.

a collection of beer steins, and all sorts of Indian, Aleutian, Spanish and Anglo artifacts not necessarily hailing from the Govenor Bent period.

San Francisco de Asis Church

Four miles south of Taos is this church (Map p147; ☎ 758-2754; St Francis Plaza; donations appreciated; ☯ 9am-4pm), in Ranchos de Taos. Built in the mid-18th century and opened in 1815, the church boasts bulbous buttresses and an unusual grace that has inspired just about every major artist in New Mexico to render it – but you'll have to go around to the back to get the famous view.

Perhaps the most interesting painting is not of the church, but inside: *The Shadow of the Cross*, by Henri Ault, is a miracle that you, too, can witness firsthand ($3). Step into the side room where you'll watch a video, after which the room goes entirely dark. Above Christ's left shoulder, the luminous silhouette of a cross (some folks also see a boat) appears. Evidently, even Ault wasn't sure how it happened.

Rio Grande Gorge Bridge

On US 64 about 12 miles northwest of Taos, this is the second-highest suspension bridge (Map p171) in the USA. Built in 1965, the vertigo-inducing steel spans 500ft across the gorge and 650ft above the river below, and there's a walkway across it all. The views west over the emptiness of the Taos Plateau and down into the jagged walls of the Rio Grande are incredible.

Earthships

Is that Mos Eisley Spaceport, about 2 miles past the Rio Grande Gorge? Nope, it's the world's premier sustainable, self-sufficient community of earthships, and you can see one for yourself on a **Solar Survival Tour** (Map p171; ☎ 751-0462; http://earthship.org; US 64; $5; ☯ 10am-4pm daily).

The brainchild of architect Mike Reynolds, sometimes described as ⅓ visionary, ⅓ entrepreneur and ⅓ cult leader, earthships are a form of biotecture (biology + architecture = buildings based on biological systems of resource use and conservation) that maximizes available resources so you'll never have to be on the grid again.

Walls made of old tires are laid out for appropriate passive solar use, packed with tamped earth, then buried on three sides for maximum insulation. The structures are outfitted with photovoltaic cells and an elaborate gray-water system that collects rain and snow, which filters through several cycles that begin in the kitchen and end in the garden.

Though this is their homeworld, earthships have landed in Japan, Bolivia, Scotland, Mexico and beyond, often organized into little communities like this one, and more are being built using available kits ($10,000-60,000 total cost) every day. You can tour a deluxe version or even stay overnight (p161); if you've already come as far as the bridge, you've got to at least drive by.

ACTIVITIES

Taos is the jumping-off point for an endless variety of outdoor activities, from llama trekking and Nordic skiing to hot air balloon rides. **Taos Outdoor Recreation** (www.taosoutdoorrecreation.com) has an online rundown of all your options.

Native Sons Adventures (Map p147; ☎ 758-9342, 800-753-7559; www.nativesonsadventures.com; 1033 Paseo del Pueblo Sur; ☯ 7:30am-7pm winter, 7:30am-5pm summer) This is your one-stop adventure-tour stop: Rent bicycles (standard/mountain $20/40), take a guided bike tour ($25/hour) or just have guides shuttle you to a trail ($80/shuttle). You might also try a guided ATV tour ($45/hour), a guided hike ($110/day), or a white-water rafting trip ($45-450). In winter you can rent skis, snowmobiles and other equipment. The store also sells just about everything you'd need to strike out on your own, including USGS maps and guidebooks. If Native Sons can't get enough people together to make shuttles to hiking and biking trails cost-effective, contact **Faust Transportation** (p166), who may be able to get you there for less.

Taos Mountain Outfitters (Map p149; ☎ 758-9292; www.taosmountainoutfitters.com; 114 S Plaza) This huge outfitter has everything – including guides, maps and gear – you need to get out and play, with sleeping bags, tents, backpacks, cross-country ski packages and more for rent. The specialty is climbing gear, and staff can point you toward top spots or toward a guide who'll show you the ropes.

Hiking

Start at the **Carson National Forest Supervisor's Office** (p148) or **BLM** (p148), both of which offer information on most area excursions.

Some of the best area hikes are covered in other sections of this book, including **Taos Ski Valley** (p169), with several spectacular and difficult climbs, including the challenging trail to Wheeler Peak; **Wild Rivers Recreation Area** (p174), with a plethora of short hikes into and along the scenic canyon; **Orilla Verde Recreation Area** (p132), with great views of the Rio Grande Gorge; and **Red River** (p175), worth the drive for access to alpine lakes and the longer, prettier trail to Wheeler Peak.

Several folks, including **Oso Negro** (☎ 776-1628; osonegro.freeyellow.com), in San Cristobal, offer guided hikes into the wilderness; Native Sons Adventures (p152) can hook you up with others.

If you enjoy **hiking with llamas** (who'll carry all the water), you're in luck: two outfitters, **El Paseo Llama Trekking** (☎ 800-455-2627; www.elpaseollama.com; half day/full day/overnight $60/80/250) and **Wild Earth Llama Adventures** (☎ 800-758-5262; www.llamaadventures.com; day/overnight $75/250) offer one-day and multiday treks into the Wheeler Peak Wilderness, and llamas love kids. Note that El Paseo lets your tots ride the beasts, while Wild Earth does not.

Fishing & Hunting

Taos is within an hour drive of scores of stocked streams and lakes, some with full wheelchair access and others that require 11-mile hikes. It's all about trout, cutthroat and German brown. Red River and the Rio Grande generally have the best fishing September through April, while Cimarron Canyon State Park and area lakes (some stocked with salmon) are best between May and September. There's more information in the Enchanted Circle section (p170), and you must have a license (p45) to take advantage of all that fish.

Los Rios Anglers (Map p149; ☎ 758-2798, 800-748-1707; www.losrios.com; 126 W Plaza Dr) Make reservations 48 hours in advance for these elite guided fly-fishing trips (s/d half day $175/200, s/d full day $250/300) onto unspoiled private lands threaded with secret sparkling streams. Or do it yourself – they've got all the tackle you could possibly need.

Taos High Mountain Angler (☎ 770-1419; www.high mountainangler.com) leads evening fishing trips ($135) and guided day trips (s/d $185/200) and rents rods and tackle ($12). The shop also produces a line of hand-built rods designed specifically for area streams. In addition to organizing custom fly-fishing trips, **Ed Adams** (☎ 586-1512; www.edadamsflyfishing .com), in Questa, runs trips (s/d $275/300) while maintaining a river schedule and fishing reports online.

Elk herds in New Mexico are thriving! Help stop them, along with mule deer, buffalo, javelina, antelope as well as other tasty critters with **High Mountain Outfitters** (☎ 751-7000; www.huntingnm.com), which also offers bow-hunting; **United States Outfitters** (☎ 800-845-9929; www.huntuso.com); or the **Circle Heart Outfitters** (☎ 377-6396; www.circleheart.com). Guided hunts are usually reserved months in advance and last three to five days. Hunts for elk, buffalo, deer and exotics cost around $1500 to $3000 on public lands (an extra $1000 on private) while javelina, turkey and rabbit hunts run $400 to $1000.

Rafting

White-water rafting in Taos' Class IV 'Box' and mellower Class III Rio Grande Gorge are major summer attractions, attracting a flurry of sunburned and screaming tourists to the put-in at Pilar. The best time to go is in May and June, when snowmelt keeps the rivers rapid, but it's warm enough to enjoy the splash. If you know what you're doing, the **BLM** (p148; www.nm.blm.gov/tafo/rafting/river_segments.html) has information for independent river rats.

Los Rios River Runners (Map p147; ☎ 776-8854, 800-544-1181; www.losriosriverrunners.com; Taos Ski Valley Rd) can take you on a variety of half-day trips including The Box ($95), Lower Gorge ($80), an ultra-mellow float fine for little kids at Orilla Verde Recreation Area ($45), as well as multiday camping and rafting trips on the Rio Grande and Rio Chama.

The Pilar section (p131) lists more opportunities for getting wet, while there's an opportunity for dinner floats at Embudo Station (p131).

Horseback Riding

There are several stables offering horseback rides nearby, including **Taos Indian Horse**

Ranch (p167), which takes you out into the sacred Blue Lake Wilderness of Taos Pueblo.

Rio Grande Stables (☎ 776-5913; www.lajitas stables.com/taos.htm), by the Ski Valley, offers one- to three-hour trips ($35-100), all-day rides (including one to the top of Wheeler Peak) and combination horseback-rafting-camping treks customized just for you. Cieneguilla Stables (☎ 751-2615; melcienguillastables@hotmail.com; rides $30-60), in Pilar, keeps it basic.

Biking

An enormous network of mountain-bike and multiuse trails threads the region of the Carson National Forest between Taos, Angel Fire and Picuris Peak. Pick up maps and information at the Carson National Forest Supervisor's Office (p148).

Standouts include the 9-mile West Rim Trail at Orilla Verde Recreation Area, suitable for strong beginners and intermediate cyclists who enjoy views of Rio Grande Gorge; and storied South Boundary Trail, considered one of the best mountain-bike trails in the nation – a 28-mile ride for experienced bikers with maps and more specific information; talk to Native Sons (p152).

Check the Red River section (p175) for more mountain-biking opportunities, including downhill runs from the top of the chairlift. The 84-mile Enchanted Circle loop makes a fine road-bike circuit, once you've acclimated to the altitude.

In addition to Native Sons, Gearing Up Bicycle Shop (Map p149; ☎ 751-0365; www.gearingup bikeshop.com; 129 Paseo del Pueblo Sur; ☯ 9am-6:30pm daily), just south of the plaza, rents mountain and hybrid bikes (hour/day/week $10/35/110) plus gear.

Skiing

Of course Taos Ski Valley (p169) is the main draw, but check out other nearby ski resorts, including Angel Fire (p178), which has capitalized on Taos' skateboard ban by building some serious shred-worthy runs, including a 400ft half-pipe; Red River (p175), overlooking a friendly resort town and boasting fantastic beginner and intermediate skiing; Enchanted Forest (p175), with 25 miles of groomed Nordic trails; and Sipapu (p130), a small family-owned resort.

Carson National Forest maintains cross-country ski trails, and you can pick up the free guide, Where to Go in the Snow, at the Supervisor's Office (p149). Most trails are concentrated near Questa, Red River and Valle Vidal, but 15 minutes from town on NM 518, the three Amole Loop Trails (cnr NM 518 & Amole Canyon Rd) offer 15 miles of powder to beginning and experienced Nordic skiers.

Cottam's Ski Shop (Map p147; ☎ 758-2822, 800-322-8267; www.cottamsskishops.com; 207-A Paseo del Pueblo Sur; ☯ 7am-6pm daily) rents ski packages ranging from ancient skis and boots from the late 1990s ($15) to modern equipment ($20-25) to the high-performance stuff ($35-40), and sells anything else you'll need. Adventure Ski Shops (Map p147; ☎ 758-1167, 800-433-1321; 1033 Paseo del Pueblo Sur; ☯ 7am-7pm daily) offers similar packages.

Other Activities

Pueblo Balloon (☎ 751-9877; www.puebloballoon.com; $225) This is just one of the area's hot air balloon operators who'll send you up softly, by sunlight or the full moon, then bring you back down for champagne. You've got to do it at least once in your life, so why not over the gash of Rio Grande Gorge?

Night Sky Adventures (☎ 754-2941; www .nightskyadventures.com; adult/child $25/12) Enjoy the altitude and aridity with a guided tour of the crystal-clear cosmos from this Red River ranch.

Taos Country Club (☎ 758-7300, 800-758-7375; 54 Golf Course Dr; $48-63) Take a swing atop greens kept that way entirely through gray-water systems. Bonus: balls go 10% farther here than at sea level.

Rock Climbing Adventures (☎ 776-2222; www .climbingschoolusa.com) Instruction and guided climbs all over area cliffs start at $180 per person, with rates dropping dramatically for couples and groups.

TAOS WALKING TOUR

Start with coffee or a snack at unique Cafe Tazza (1), and consider dropping into the Kit Carson Historic Home (2), across the street. Afterward head southeast, watching for traffic, on Kit Carson Rd. Make a right onto unpaved Morada Ln to the Mabel Dodge Luhan House (3). Take the self-guided tour (ask first), and stop next door to wander the grounds of Lumina Gallery (4). Head back down Morada Ln, cross Kit Carson Rd and follow Quesnel St past galleries and antique adobes galore.

After crossing Paseo del Pueblo Sur, make a quick detour into **Blue Rain Gallery (5)** for a peek at the finest in Native arts, then continue west on Camino del Placita. Take a left on Ledoux St, stopping into the **Blumenschein (6)** and **Harwood (7)** museums, and poke around the fine galleries and bookshops along the way.

Make a right onto Ranchitos Rd, then a left on Doña Luz St; if you need to rest your feet (or brain – too much art can hurt!), grab a snack at either **Mainstreet Bakery (8)** or **Inspirations (9)**, where you might also indulge in a tarot-card reading. Alternately, continue north, making a right on Don Fernando St and left onto Camino Placita, and a quick right to the village's oldest building, now **Alley Cantina (10)**.

After you're sufficiently reinvigorated, wander the plaza, perhaps stopping into La Fonda to take in the **Forbidden Art (11)**, or perhaps purchasing a **Taos snow globe** at one of the souvenir shops. Make your way through the maze of adobe to the well-signed John Dunn House Shops, making sure to search **G Gordon Robinson Maps & Prints (12)**

and **Moby Dickens (13)** for true treasures. Make a right onto Bent St, stopping at the **Governor Bent Museum (14)** to see Taos' most famous hole in the wall.

Continue down Bent St and finish your tour with a well-deserved break (and margarita) at **Adobe Bar (15)**.

This entire walking tour is almost 2 miles, and depending how long you tend to linger over coffee or art, should take two to three hours. You can cut off almost half a mile by skipping the Mabel Dodge Luhan house, but do drop by another time.

TAOS FOR CHILDREN
Tiempo has a 'For Kids' calendar with listings of events and activities, like tales from storyteller **Roberta Courtney Meyers** (☎ 776-2562; ☺ 6pm & 8pm Wed & Sat) at the Fechin Inn (p161), for tots (and parents).

The **Taos Youth & Family Center** (Map p147; ☎ 758-4160; 407 Paseo del Cañon East; $5/child; ☺ 10am-7pm Mon-Fri, 10am-6pm Sat & Sun), has pool tables, toys, a skate park and supervision for kids over eight, but younger children must bring a parent.

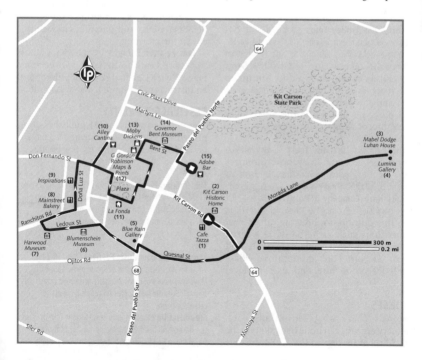

Yaxche Learning Center (Map p147; ☎ 751-4419; www.yaxche.org; 123 Manzanares St) offers classes and wilderness adventures, plus a **Kids Cooking Camp** through the Taos School of Cooking (p53).

La Hacienda de los Martinez (p149) and the **Harwood Foundation** (p148) are both designed with kids in mind; the Harwood Museum offers free children's **programs** (10-11:30am Sat) covering such subjects as retablo making, and has a pamphlet that transforms those TSA paintings into a treasure hunt. **Twining Weavers** (p165) has giant looms and lots of stuffed animals, making it a nice break from boring grown-up galleries.

Shorter, kid-friendly hikes (though they are steep) can be found at **Wild Rivers Recreation Area** (p174), while **llama hikes** (p153) cater to kids. **Los Rios River Runners** (p153) offers an all-ages float, though your teenagers will probably be begging for The Box – 12 and older only. **Taos Ski Valley** (p169) offers lots of resources during the ski season, including pricey day care and full-day lessons that include lunch.

TOURS

Historic Taos Trolley Tours (Map p147; ☎ 751-0366; www.taostrolleytours.com; cnr Paseo del Pueblo Sur & Paseo del Cañon; adult/child $33/10; ☻ 10:30am & 2pm daily) Take a cute red trolley from the visitors center on two different tours: one visits Taos Pueblo, San Francisco de Asis and the plaza (where the trolly will also pick you up), while the other takes in Millicent Rogers Museum and the Martinez Hacienda.

Enchantment Dreams Tours (☎ 776-2562) Storyteller Roberta Meyers customizes tours of Taos with more than a dash of poetic theatrics. Reservations are required.

Taos Herb Company (Map p147; ☎ 800-353-1991; www.taosherb.com; 710 Paseo del Pueblo Sur; $40) In addition to brewing up herbal concoctions such as Yerba de la Negrita shampoo, knowledgeable naturalists lead day-hikes into the mountains, where you'll learn the lore and uses of local plants.

COURSES

Inspired? That's what Taos is all about. Culinary artisans can hone their skills at the **Taos School of Cooking** (p53), while creative souls otherwise inclined are catered to by several fine schools.

Fechin Art Workshops (☎ 776-2622; www.fechin.com; $355) Five days of instruction at Donner Ranch include accommodations, meals and classes focusing on oil painting and landscapes.

Taos Art School (Map p149; ☎ 505-758-0350; www.taosartschool.org; $300-700) Weekend and weeklong classes cover everything from painting New Mexico's churches to making micaceous pottery; there's even a Navajo weaving class held right on the reservation, where you'll stay in a hogan, herd sheep and card wool before even prepping the loom.

Taos Institute of Arts (Map p149; ☎ 800-822-7183; www.taosinstituteofarts.com; 108 Civic Plaza Dr; $420) Four-day courses range from writing workshops to jewelry making, plus lots of painting classes.

Cine-Slam (☎ 758-7859; 7155A NM 518) The Taos Filmmaker's Initiative offers intensive, two-day seminars that cover the ins and outs of film production.

Nichols Taos Gallery (Map p149; ☎ 758-2475; www.nicholsgallery.com; 403 Paseo del Pueblo Norte; $50-400) Prominent area artists give three-hour demonstrations and painting classes, usually in the morning.

Taos Aviation Services (☎ 737-0505; www.taosaviation.com) Learn to fly your own personal plane: Rent a Cessna 172XP ($85/hour) and an instructor ($30/hour), and you're off.

FESTIVALS & EVENTS

The visitors center (p148) publishes comprehensive listings, while *Tiempo* keeps tabs on current events. Here are a few biggies:

April

Taos Talking Pictures (☎ 751-0637; www.ttpix.com; $10/event; mid-Apr) Independent films, including lots of Hispanic, Native American and teen offerings, are interspersed with seminars and workshops.

May

Taos Jazz & Latin Music Festival (☎ 758-2052; www.taosjazzfest.org; pass $75, one show $25; early May) Two weeks of internationally acclaimed jazz artists from all over the world, plus lots of chill events to celebrate them.

Memorial Day (Last Mon in May) Mount Old Glory on the Harley and head to the Memorial Day Motorcycle Day Rally in Red River, then fly those colors proudly as you cruise past the Vietnam Veterans Memorial ceremonies.

June

Angel Fire Kite Festival (☎ 800-446-8117; mid-June) Bring your own kite, buy one there or just relax and watch the world whirr by.

Taos Poetry Circus (☎ 758-1800, 877-203-0520; www.poetrycircus.com; early Jun) It starts with poetry and music at Taos Pueblo, then moves on to more readings, workshops and slams, but it all comes down to the World Heavyweight Championship Poetry Bout: there can be only one. Which rhymes with fun. So get your iambic pentameter in gear and come on up!

Zoukfest World Music Festival (☎ 751-3512; www .zoukfest.com; $40; late Jun) Musicians and tunes from every continent collide in a cavalcade of performances all over town.

Solar Music Festival (☎ 800-732-8267; www.solar musicfest.com; Kit Carson Park, 1/3 days $20/65, kids under 10 free; late Jun) This three-day festival (p146) features exhibits, camping and a solar stage packed with performers like Michelle Shocked, Los Lobos and Harry Belafonte.

July

Independence Day (Jul 4) Sparks fly over Taos Ski Area and Eagle Nest Lake.

Taos Pueblo Powwow (☎ 758-1028; www.taospueblo .com; Taos Pueblo Rd; $15; second week in Jul) Plains and Pueblo Indians gather in for dances, workshops and even feathers as this centuries-old tradition continues.

Wings over Angel Fire (☎ 800-446-8117; late Jul) It's got hot air balloons, vintage planes, air shows, skydivers and lots of people not paying attention to where they're going.

Los Fiestas de Taos (☎ 800-856-1516; last weekend in Jul) In honor of not one but two patron saints, Taos fiestas are twice the fun.

White Cloud Stampede (☎ 800-992-7669; www .emanuelli.com/taosmarathon; late July) Only the toughest survive this marathon run to the top of Wheeler Peak.

September

Taos Story Telling Festival (☎ 758-0081; mid-Sep) Tellers of tales come to Taos for three days of yarn-spinning action.

December

Christmas Holidays (late Dec) Dances at Taos Pueblo, mass and Las Posadas at San Francisco de Asis Church, Christmas carolers and bischochitos all over downtown, and farolitos everywhere help keep everyone's spirits bright.

SLEEPING

Taos has two serious tourist seasons: ski season, which runs from Thanksgiving through March with lulls in early December and mid-January, and the summer season, from late May through October, when the rest of the Southwest is unbearably hot. Christmas holidays are the real spike, so make reservations early – and don't expect a bargain.

Also check in the Arroyo Seco and Arroyo Hondo sections, both about 15 minutes from downtown, for other options, including the **Abominable Snowmansion HI Hostel** (p168).

RESERVATION SERVICES

There are more than 100 hotels, lodges and B&Bs in the region, not to mention scores of available vacation homes, so try these reservation services if nothing here strikes your fancy:

Accommodations Taos (☎ 800-257-7720; www .accommodationstaos.com) B&Bs, hotels, cabins and lodges in Taos, Red River and Angel Fire.

Taos Vacation Rentals (☎ 800-788-8267; www .taosvacationrentals.com) Vacation homes in and around Taos.

Taos Property Management (☎ 758-7150, 800-480-7150; www.taospropertymanagement.com) Even more vacation homes, with much better weekly and monthly rates.

Ski Central Reservations (☎ 776-9550, 800-238-2829; www.taosskicentral.com) Lodging in the Ski Valley and Taos, too.

Budget

Though there are no hostels right in town, the **Abominable Snowmansion HI Hostel** (p168) in Arroyo Seco and **Rio Grande Gorge HI Hostel** (p132) in Pilar are just a few minutes away by car. The strip south of town along Paseo del Pueblo Sur serves as Taos' Cerrillos Rd, lined with budget hotels and chains that may be your best bet during high tourist seasons. Rooms are clean and basic, breakfast is continental and decor usually involves yellowing RC Gorman prints.

HOTELS & MOTELS

Sun God Lodge (Map p147; ☎ 758-1716, 800-821-2437; www.sungodlodge.com; 919 Paseo del Pueblo Sur; d low/ high $45/60; Ⓟ ⊠ 🐾) The nice-enough adobe rooms arranged around a green courtyard are a little threadbare but original.

Hacienda Inn (Map p147; ☎ 758-8610, 800-858-8543; 1321 Paseo del Pueblo Sur; d $45-65; Ⓟ ⊠ 🐾)

TAOS

This family-owned and -operated entry has clean and spacious rooms arranged around a nice enough courtyard.

Budget Host Inn (Map p147; ☎ 758-1667, 800-323-6009; 1798 Paseo del Pueblo Sur; d low/high $48/64; P ⊠ ⠿) Much better rooms than you'd expect from the exterior of this somewhat inconveniently located hotel come with fridges and coffee makers.

Adobe Wall Motel (Map p149; ☎ 758-3972; 227 E Kit Carson Rd; d $56-66; P ⊠) For almost 100 years, this shady courtyard motel has been setting up travelers in big, slightly tattered rooms with wonderful fireplaces.

Super 8 (Map p147; ☎ 758-1088, 800-800-8000; 1347 Paseo del Pueblo Sur; $55-70; P ⊠ ⠿) Basic, average and absolutely acceptable – your bill is also frill-free.

Days Inn (Map p147; ☎ 758-2230; 1333 Paseo del Pueblo Sur; d $50-65, ste $75 incl breakfast; P ⊠ ⠿) The suites are designed more as bunkrooms for skiers than for families, sleeping six comfortably rather than providing an extra room, but overall this well-maintained entry is a great budget choice.

El Pueblo Lodge (Map p149; ☎ 758-8700, 800-433-9612; www.elpueblolodge.com; 412 Paseo del Pueblo Norte; d low/high $54-89; P ⊠ ⠿ ⠿) Right downtown, with big, clean rooms, some with kitchenettes and/or fireplaces, a pool, hot tub and fresh pastries in the morning – what's not to love?

CAMPING & RV PARKS

In-town campsites are fine but nothing to write home about, especially considering the wealth of verdant options surrounding the village. The **Orilla Verde Recreation Area** (p132), **Taos Ski Area** (p169), **Wild Rivers Recreation Area** (p174) and the stretch of US 64 between Taos and Angel Fire (p178) all offer excellent campsites within an hour's drive. Note that the snow doesn't melt completely until May at the earliest.

Taos Valley RV Park & Campground (Map p147; ☎ 758-4469, 800-999-7571; campsite/RV $18/28) Park your RV or snuggle your tent into the chamisa just five minutes from the plaza – and across the street from the Greyhound station.

Budget Host RV Park (Map p147; ☎ 758-1667, 800-323-6009; 1802 Paseo del Pueblo Sur; campsite $17, teepee/RV $25) With gravelly tent sites and fun but basic teepees, this convenient spot caters more to the RV crowd.

Enchanted Moon Campground (Map p147; ☎ 758-3338; www.emooncampground.com; US 64; campsite/RV $14/20) Less convenient – halfway in between Taos and Angel Fire – but far lovelier, this fine spot has a lodge, playground, hot showers and a trout pond, plus lots of shady campsites where you can pretend you're roughing it.

Mid-Range

For these prices, you can either enjoy a spacious, modern room on Paseo del Pueblo Sur or something more historic (read: nice but cramped) downtown. Folks who don't usually like B&Bs should note that many in Taos have private entrances and baths, which gives you the same privacy as a hotel – plus all those cookies and quilts and things.

B&BS

Taos has more B&Bs per square inch than anyplace else in the state, and they go all out. The **Association of Taos Bed & Breakfast Inns** (☎ 800-939-2215; www.taos-bandb-inns.com) lists lots of them, while **Traditional Taos Inns** (www.taos-lodging.com) lists only the most exclusive properties. There are two more excellent mid-range options in the pretty village of Arroyo Hondo, just a few minutes north of town.

Laughing Horse Inn (Map p147; ☎ 758-8350, 800-776-0161; www.laughinghorseinn.com; 729 Paseo del Pueblo Norte; s/d low $58/68, s/d high $98/150, ste $100-150; P ⊠) Narrow adobe rooms are furnished with chile-shaped Christmas lights, piñon incense, hand-hewn furniture – it's how Taoseños actually live! The communal atmosphere continues with a hot tub under the stars, kitchen privileges and a huge penthouse, and the whole vibe reminds you why you travel in the first place.

Doña Luz Inn (Map p149; ☎ 758-9187, 800-758-9187; www.ladonaluz.com; 114 Kit Carson Rd; $60-130; P ⊠ ⠿) The fabulous location is just the beginning at this historic, 200-year-old inn. Rooms range from the tiny La Luz (guests should be under 6'2") to the three-level Rainbow Room suite, with a hot tub on the rooftop sundeck. All are decorated in colorful Spanish-colonial style, a cheerful clutter of amazing art – lots of it sacred, most of it antique and all of it beautiful.

American Artists Gallery House B&B (Map p147; ☎ 758-4446, 800-532-3041; www.taosbedand breakfast.com; 132 Frontier Ln; d $85-160; Ⓟ Ⓧ Ⓧ) Join George the peacock and lots of cats at this friendly B&B, with Jacuzzi rooms that will blow your mind. All have wood-burning fireplaces, and two are relatively wheelchair-accessible.

Old Taos Guesthouse (Map p147; ☎ 758-5448, 800-758-5448; www.oldtaos.com; 1028 Witt Rd; d $85-160; Ⓟ Ⓧ) Outdoorsy types enchanted with this wilderness wonderland can start here, in spacious, Southwestern-style rooms wrapped around a shady lawn and hot tub, hidden away in a quiet residential neighborhood. The proprietors are seasoned adventurers and can point you toward excursions of every sort, right after breakfast.

Inn on the Rio (Map p147; ☎ 758-7199, 800-859-6752; www.innontherio.com; 910 Kit Carson Rd; d $99-129; Ⓟ Ⓧ Ⓧ). A little over a mile from the plaza, this adobe (part of it 250 years old, the rest built in the 1950s with private entrances) has bright floral murals, pretty Southwestern-style rooms, a small heated pool and excellent biscochitos. The owners are happy to play concierge and hook you up with restaurants and activities.

Mabel Dodge Luhan House (Map p149; ☎ 751-9686, 800-846-2235; www.mabeldodgeluhan.com; 240 Morada Ln; d $85-160; Ⓟ Ⓧ Ⓧ) You may have stayed at plusher B&Bs, but not one with a story like this: The 'Patroness of Taos,' Mabel Dodge Luhan – by equal measures graceful and grand, scandalous and unbearable – built this fabulous mansion to bring in everyone from Emma Goldman and Margaret Sanger to Carl Jung and Ansel Adams for a nice chat. After which they would find somewhere less stressful to stay.

Egos like hers don't go easily, and you may still catch a glimpse (or whiff – they say she wears cinnamon) of the legendary hostess keeping tabs on the old adobe homestead. It's a bit of a walk from the plaza but worth it, and the rooms are weird: the Solarium, with windows painted by DH Lawrence and a 360-degree view of the mountains, is not for shy guests; Tony's Room, designed by Mabel's husband (p160), has a wonderful fireplace and flagstone patio, where he preferred to sleep outside.

Intrigued? Stop by for a self-guided tour through the house and grounds, or sign up for one of the myriad retreats and workshops held here ($400-2500).

Hacienda del Sol (Map p147; ☎ 758-0287; www .taoshaciendadelsol.com; US 64; d $105-215; Ⓟ Ⓧ Ⓧ) The foothills retreat where Mabel Dodge and beau Tony Luhan first shacked up is still one of the most romantic spots in town, with fireplaces, Jacuzzis and those mountains right out back.

HOTELS & MOTELS

Indian Hills Inn (Map p149; ☎ 758-4293, 800-444-2346; 233 Paseo del Pueblo Sur; d low $60-74, d high $69-99; Ⓟ Ⓧ Ⓧ Ⓧ) This inexpensive and independently run option offers pleasant, fairly basic rooms walking distance from the plaza.

Taos Inn (Map p149; ☎ 758-2233, 800-826-7466; www.taosinn.com; 125 Paseo del Pueblo Norte; d $60-225; Ⓟ Ⓧ Ⓧ Ⓧ) Parts of this landmark date to the 17th century, which is why it's on the National Register of Historic Places – and why it's not exactly the plushest place in town. But it's fabulous, despite the gradually settling adobe architecture, with a cozy lobby, heavy wood furniture and a sunken fireplace, plus the classic restaurant Doc Martin's (p163) and lots of live local music at its famed Adobe Bar (p164).

Sagebrush Inn (Map p147; ☎ 758-2254, 800-428-3626; www.sagebrushinn.com; 1508 Paseo del Pueblo Sur; d $70-85 incl full breakfast; Ⓟ Ⓧ Ⓧ Ⓧ) Since 1929 this elaborately arched adobe has been keeping travelers rested and fed, featuring **Los Vaqueros** (mains $11-29; ☺ 5:30-10pm daily) with lots of steak and prime rib, plus an excellent onsite bar (p164) with live music almost nightly.

Comfort Suites (Map p147; ☎ 751-1555, 888-751-1555; http://taoswebb.com/taoshotels/comfortsuites; 1500 Paseo del Pueblo Sur; ste low/high $70/150 incl breakfast; Ⓟ Ⓧ Ⓧ) All accommodations sleep five, at least, and have two TVs – suite!

Quail Ridge Inn (Map p147; ☎ 776-2211, 800-624-4448; www.quailridgeinn.com; d low $69-130, d high $79-230, ste $235-425; Ⓟ Ⓧ Ⓧ) More a comfortable resort than typical hotels, it's got great deals on family-friendly rooms, acres of grassy grounds with tennis courts and pools, onsite dining and drinking, and huge suites geared toward skiers.

Quality Inn (Map p147; ☎ 758-9009, 800-845-0648; 1043 Paseo del Pueblo Sur; d $79-99 incl breakfast; Ⓟ Ⓧ Ⓧ Ⓧ) For an extra $10, you can get a microwave and refrigerator in your room.

TAOS

Holiday Inn Don Fernando de Taos (Map p147; ☎ 758-4444, 800-759-2736; www.holiday-taos.com; 1005 Paseo del Pueblo Sur; low/high $89/114; Ⓟ ⊠ ⊠ ⊠) An enclosed heated swimming pool, plus suites sleeping six with fireplace and fridge, make this a standout entry.

Taos Lodging (Map p149; ☎ 751-1771, 800-954-8267; 109 Brook St; d/f $90/110; Ⓟ ⊠) This is a great deal on spacious 1940s casitas designed to keep the family happy, with kitchenettes, hide-a-beds and other amenities, all built around a cute courtyard just blocks from the plaza.

La Fonda de Taos (Map p149; ☎ 758-2211, 800-833-2211; www.hotellafonda.com; 108 S Plaza; d low $99-119, d high $139-169; Ⓟ ⊠ ⊠) Though it's been completely renovated in upscale (and seemingly upstanding) Southwest style, this plaza-side hotel, formerly owned by notorious playboy Saki Karavas, just can't shake its sexy vibe – even the kiva gas fireplaces in the smallish, sensually angled suites seem like they're up to illuminate no good. Perhaps it's the **Forbidden Art** of DH Lawrence (p155), banned in 1929 Europe and displayed here to consenting adults ($3), depicting, and perhaps inspiring, all sorts of sinful fun.

Top End
Those seeking out the typical presidential suite will need to expand their horizons: Taos' finest options are in a quirky class by themselves and satisfy even the most pampered souls with style to spare.

B&BS
These luxurious retreats include exquisite antiques, evening wine tastings, multicourse breakfasts and all the saltillo-tiled elegance you'd want. Note that nearby Arroyo Seco (p168) offers two of the region's very best properties.

Inger Jirby's Casitas (Map p149; ☎ 758-7333, 866-758-7333; www.jirby.com; 207 Ledoux St; d $175-225 ; Ⓟ ⊠ ⊠) Top contenders for the Best Room in Taos award, these two lofty spaces, decorated by the Swedish artist with a colorful gallery right next door, have full kitchens, great art and grand-slam views. Kids will love the bigger suite, which sleeps four extra comfortably.

TONY LUHAN: UNLIKELY AMBASSADOR OF PUEBLO CULTURE

When hostess extraordinaire Mabel Dodge followed her latest artsy husband to the increasingly hip West, she wasn't exactly intending to stay. Between the villa in Italy and the artist salon in New York City, New Mexico probably seemed like a good place for some downtime. Then she fell in love with Taos. Then she fell in love with Antonio Luhan.

The courtship was brief and intense – despite their respective spouses – and in 1918 the two lovebirds, one a worldly heiress and the other a prominent Taos Pueblo Indian, moved in together; neither came from a culture particularly comfortable with such a romance. While the thrice-married Dodge sniffed unconcerned at the gossips, Tony would spend the rest of his life working overtime as an ambassador between his own Native culture and the eclectic collection of artists and writers he and Mabel would host.

Ansel Adams, Carl Jung, Aldous Huxley, DH Lawrence and others were introduced to Northern New Mexico through the prism of Tiwa philosophy. Luhan's wagon rides and introspective air inspired author Willa Cather to create the character of Eusabio, friend of Lamy in *Death Comes for the Archbishop*. With Georgia O'Keeffe, Luhan formed a special bond, joining her well away from the sometimes hectic salon while she painted in peace.

And in 1922, when federal legislation threatened Taos Pueblo's sovereignty and land, Luhan called in favors. He led his pack of famous friends to battle the bill, which was subsequently struck down in Congress.

Between trips to New York City and Washington, DC, Luhan would return to Taos Pueblo for prayer and rituals that remained more important than any urban enticement beyond the kiva walls. And through 40 years of marriage to his unlikely love, he managed to engender an understanding and respect for Pueblo Indian culture and wisdom among those influential newcomers and their audiences around the world.

Adobe & Pines Inn (☎ 751-0947, 800-723-8267; www.adobepines.com; 4107 Hwy 68; $130-170; P ✗ ✗) The grounds are shady and landscaped with bridges and benches, and the enormous rooms – some with beautifully tiled full kitchens, others with wet bars, and all but one ($100) with fireplaces – feature some of the most fabulous bathrooms ever. Folks who appreciate talaveras (long soaks) have found their B&B.

Inn on La Loma (Map p149; ☎ 758-1717, 800-530-3040; www.vacationtaos.com; 315 Ranchitos Rd; d $125-300 ; P ✗ ✗ 🖳 🖳) A rambling 200-year-old hacienda that's almost as much a resort – pool, Jacuzzi, tennis privileges, in-room massages – as a B&B keeps those personal amenities like hors d'oeuvres in the evening and insider tips coming. Rooms are smallish but very plush.

Casa de las Chimeneas (Map p149; ☎ 758-4777, 877-758-4777; www.visit-taos.com; 405 Cordoba Rd; d $165-325; P ✗ ✗) Lavish is really the only word: Surrounded by flower gardens landscaped almost monthly, this no-holds-barred B&B tucks you into immaculate Southwest-style rooms that go way, *way* beyond saltillos and vigas, then coordinates your vacation to include golfing, hot air balloon rides and three-hour beautification regimes at the onsite spa. Linger over breakfast or the complimentary 'light buffet' dinner while you plan, then get ready to relax movie-star style.

HOTELS & RESORTS

Earthship Rentals (Map p171; ☎ 751-0462; US 64; d/f $130/180; P) Want to experience life off the grid (forgoing TV and phone, of course)? Stay in an earthship (p152), 100% solar powered with a gray-water system, beautifully biotectured interior and reduced rates for multiple-night stays.

Fechin Inn (Map p149; ☎ 751-1000, 800-811-2933; 227 Paseo del Pueblo Norte; d from $114-187; P ✗ ✗) This expansive, swanky and somewhat sterile spot (though the two original Fechins and lobby accented in appropriately carved wood are pretty sweet) may not be a great deal for independent travelers, but if you're planning a business event or upscale retreat, it's got plenty of Taos style plus every facility you'll need, and the staff will work with you on group rates.

El Monte Sagrado (Map p149; ☎ 800-828-8267; www.elmontesagrado.com; 317 Kit Carson Rd; d $300-800;

P ✗ ✗) This brand-new, lavishly decorated eco-resort has bright and cozy themed suites whimsically decorated with Native American, Mexican, Moroccan and Egyptian cultures in mind, all arranged around a 'sacred circle' (actually a flourishing courtyard irrigated with a gray-water system). There's an onsite spa, package deals with the ski valley and lots of other amenities, all as unique and colorful as the festive decor.

EATING

Although there are some quality upscale options around the plaza, that old rule of thumb still applies: The farther you get from the tourist epicenter, the better the food – or at least, the better the deal.

Budget

Raley's Supermarket (Map p147; ☎ 758-1250; 1100 Paseo del Pueblo Sur; ⊙ 6am-midnight daily) It's got groceries, a deli, post office and pharmacy.

Cid's Food Market (Map p149; ☎ 758-1148; 623 Paseo del Pueblo Norte; ⊙ 7:30am-7pm Mon-Sat) If it's local, organic, holistic or just tasty you'll find it at this fabulous natural foods emporium, with a meat department specializing in elk and other game.

Monte's Chow Cart (Map p147; ☎ 758-3632; 402 Paseo del Pueblo Sur; mains $2-7; ⊙ 7am-10pm) Skip the chains and drive through this independently owned joint, with great breakfast burritos and a high-quality chile relleno burrito (ask for the 'Trujillo'), many available as meal deals with fries and a large drink.

The Bean (Map p147; ☎ 758-7711; 1033J Paseo del Pueblo Sur; light meals $4-7; ⊙ 7am-2pm daily) The best lattes in town come with pastries, breakfast burritos and other breakfasty snacks; a **second location** (☎ 758-9918; 900 Paseo del Pueblo Norte; snacks $3-5; ⊙ 6:30am-6pm Mon-Fri, 7am-4pm Sat-Sun), north of town, has a smaller menu but longer hours.

Caffe Tazza (Map p149; ☎ 758-8706; 122 Kit Carson Rd; organic goodies $3-7; ⊙ 6:30am to at least 6pm, until 10pm for events) It's more than just coffee drinks, Taos Cow rBGH-free ice cream and healthy, mostly organic soups, sandwiches and burritos. This place packs its patio and cozy art-lined interior with hippies, hipsters, tarot-card readers, yoga-doers and lots of confused tourists, who then shrug their shoulders and stick around for evening poetry slams and live music.

PB Squared (Map p149; ☎ 758-0240; 122 Paseo del Pueblo Sur; noshes $3-10; ☺ 9am-9pm) Stop at this sweet second-story spot for great meat or veggie rice bowls, breakfast wraps and other 'noshes' when you need more than a snack but not quite a meal. It's an all-ages club in the evening, where new local bands try out their chops free of charge; tips are always appreciated.

Mid-Range

Mainstreet Bakery (Map p149; ☎ 758-9610; Guadalupe Plaza; mains $4-7; ☺ 7:30am-2pm Mon-Fri, 7:30-11:30am Sat & Sun) This bakery's bread and butter is baking for natural grocers, but grab some toast with a side of scrambled tofu or perhaps more traditional (and huge) breakfast treats. Also try the lunch special: a bowl of black beans, green chile, red onions, tomatoes and cornbread.

El Pueblo Cafe (Map p149; ☎ 758-2053; 625 Paseo del Pueblo Norte; mains $4-11; 6am-11:30pm Sun-Thu, 6am-2:30am Fri & Sat) With four wines on tap, great Frito pies and recommended huevos rancheros (the pitched debate about which was better on top, red or green, soon involved every table – go Christmas), and hours perfect for party people, it's no wonder folks love El Pueblo.

Sheva Cafe (Map p147; ☎ 737-9290; 812 Paseo del Pueblo Norte; mains $3-8; ☺ 11am-10pm Sun-Thu, 7:30am-4pm Fri) Unusual Middle Eastern and Central European delicacies include shakshuka (eggs poached with veggies) and borekas (pastries packed with potatoes, veggies, eggs and/or cheese), served up alongside hummus, baba ganoush and the other usual suspects in friendly, hippie-Israeli style.

Michael's Kitchen (Map p149; ☎ 758-4178; 304C Paseo del Pueblo Norte; dinner $8-13, other meals $5-7; ☺ 7am-8:30pm daily) OK, so it's a little touristy. But that doesn't make the gigantic cinnamon rolls any less gooilicious or the huge plates of New Mexican and pork-chops-and-mashed-potatoes-type comfort food any less satisfying. And hidden between the ski bunnies and art collectors are plenty of Taoseños willing to suffer the mob, too.

Inspirations (Map p149; ☎ 751-0959; 114 Doña Luz St; astro meals $5-8; ☺ 9:30am-6pm Mon-Fri, 11am-5pm Sat-Sun) Can't decide what to eat? When's your birthday? Order meals designed for your astrological sign at this New Agey

outpost, with wheatgrass, lattes and the best salad bar in town (☺ 11am-3pm daily). Should your Cancer moon ache for the avocado and cheese sandwich, Gemini sun debate the mezza platter's merits and Taurus ascendant insist on the tempeh burger glazed with peanut sauce, there's still hope: Tarot-card readers ($1/minute) are usually available to assist you in these and other decisions.

Taos Pizza Out Back (Map p149; ☎ 758-3112; 712 Paseo del Pueblo Norte; slices $4-6, medium pie $18-23; ☺ 11am-9pm daily) Enjoy every possible ingredient under the sun (for example, the recommended Vera Cruz has chicken breast and veggies marinated in a honey-chipotle sauce) as pizza pies or slices the size of a small country. This kid-friendly spot has crayons at the table and a great back patio.

Guadalajara Grille (Map p147; ☎ 751-0063; 1384 Paseo del Pueblo Sur; lunch $4-8, dinner $6-13; ☺ 11:30am-9:30pm daily) Right next to the car wash, this Mexican (*not* New Mexican) favorite serves everything from Mazatlan shrimp and fresh oysters to basic but bombastic burritos, with white wine sangria on the side; a **second location** (Map p147; ☎ 737-0816; 822 Paseo del Pueblo Norte; breakfast $5; ☺ 10:30am-9:30pm Mon-Fri, 9am-9:30pm Sat & Sun) doesn't have quite the cachet (or car wash), but does serve the same great food, plus breakfast.

Ginza (Map p147; ☎ 758-7645; 321C Paseo del Pueblo Sur; rolls $4-11, mains $7-14; ☺ 11:30am-2pm Mon-Fri, 5-9pm Mon-Sat) Worth the drive from Santa Fe for sushi fans on a budget, Ginza does double orders of quality nigiri and exotic rolls, plus good Chinese food, but it's the lunch buffet ($7) that's just a spectacular deal – and includes all the sashimi you want! OK, it's mostly tuna, but it still rocks. Order your unagi on the side.

Island Coffees & Hawaiian Grill (Map p147; ☎ 758-7777; 1032 Paseo del Pueblo Sur; mains $6-11; ☺ 8am-9pm Mon-Fri, 10am-9pm Sat & Sun) Surfboards, hula skirts, Kahlua pig and huge burgers that have won (and clogged) the hearts of every service-industry worker on the strip will make you forget that the only thing lacking around here is a beach. Well, an ocean, anyway. It's also got the fastest Internet access in town.

Dragonfly Café (Map p149; ☎ 737-5859; 402 Paseo del Pueblo Norte; mains $5-11; ☺ 7am-3pm daily)

With the atmosphere of an eternal Sunday brunch, this fine spot serves all manner of baked goods and egg dishes, but stars a gravlox (Scandinavian-style salmon) plate and curried chicken salad on excellent bread. For something completely different, try the recommended bibimbop: eggs, veggies and rice with kimchee.

Bent Street Deli & Café (Map p149; ☎ 758-5787; 120 Bent St; dinner $11-19, other meals $3-10; ⏲ 8am-9pm Mon-Sat) Build your own sandwich (or order one of the 21 recommended combinations), grab a side order of cucumber salad or tabouleh, then kick back and enjoy. Dinner is gourmet comfort food and breakfast is grand, but it's really all about the sandwiches.

Orlando's (Map p147; ☎ 751-1450; NM 522; mains $7-11; ⏲ 11am-3pm & 5-10pm daily) This is it, the best New Mexican food in town, period. And of course you've got to somehow get 2 miles north of the plaza to experience it. But those chicken enchiladas, huge burritos, all dressed to perfection and served up in the packed and beautiful dining room – it's worth walking.

Top End

The Apple Tree (Map p149; ☎ 758-1900; 123 Bent St; dinner $13-25, other meals $6-10; ⏲ 11:30am-3pm & 5-10pm daily) It's fancy, taking full advantage of its fabulous location and historic adobe with fine art, candles, a lovely patio, a huge wine list and gourmet twists on New Mexican classics like mango chicken (or tempeh) enchiladas. The real deal is at lunch, when an abbreviated to-go menu wraps up simpler, but still stunning, fare picnic-style for a few dollars less than you'd pay to eat inside.

Trading Post Café (Map p147; ☎ 758-5098; cnr NM 68 & NM 518; lunch $6-9, dinner $7-22; ⏲ 11:30am-9:30pm Tue-Sat, 5-9:30pm Sun) White tablecloths and stemware evoke an ambiance improved only by amazing art everywhere – there'll be no lack of conversation starters, that's for sure – plus a divine torta Cubana and recommended fresh fettuccini alla carbonara.

Zen Ranch (Map p147; ☎ 758-7373; NM 522; lunch $6-11, dinner $12-25; ⏲ 11:30am-9pm Thu-Mon) Next to the Overland Sheep Complex, wander through the landscaped gardens to this upscale spot for Asian food with a twist: kaffir lime and lemongrass salmon,

hot and sour black mussel stew and other divine offerings are all good choices, but just make sure to start with the macadamia nut–encrusted fried tomatoes, served with gingered goat cheese.

Lambert's (Map p149; ☎ 758-1009; 309 Paseo del Pueblo Sur, mains $14-26; ⏲ 5:30-10pm daily) Everyone in town has their favorite dish, which they simply must describe in mouthwatering detail after gushingly recommending this spot as their second-favorite restaurant *ever* (after Orlando's), first if someone else is paying. The seafood paella, red-chile–rubbed buffalo loin, and especially the pepper-crusted lamb get 'em all starry-eyed.

Doc Martin's (Map p149; ☎ 758-2233; 125 Paseo del Pueblo Norte; dinner $14-24, other meals $5-11; ⏲ 7am-2:30pm & 5:30-9:30pm daily) It's won every award, charmed every tourist and been a top spot for locals since Blumenschein came up with the TSA here – so what are you waiting for? Duck tamales, grilled trout primavera, wild mushroom ravioli and spectacular huevos rancheros are just a prelude to the great deserts; try a prix fixe dinner ($18-23) for four courses in heaven.

Stakeout Grill & Bar (☎ 758-2042; 101 Stakeout Dr; mains $16-28; ⏲ 5-10pm daily) Atop Outlaw Hill (yes, there were outlaws here at one point), about 4 miles south of Rancho de Taos on NM 68, this place is perhaps a bit overpriced. But the 360-degree views of Rio Grande Gorge are truly awesome at sunset, and with a wine list like this, you'll still have a marvelous evening.

ENTERTAINMENT

Considering the variety of venues around town – sometimes the best shows are way off the beaten track – the best place to start is **Que Pasa** (Map p147; ☎ 758-7344; www.taosnews.com/calendar/quepasa.shtml; 338 Paseo del Pueblo Sur; ⏲ 10am-6pm Mon-Sat, noon-5pm Sun), a music store that keeps an exhaustive calendar of area events, and sells tickets to most of them. *Tiempo* also has listings.

Pubs, Bars & Live Music

You can often catch live music at restaurants, including eclectic, acoustic and poetic offerings at **Caffe Tazza** (p161), jazz and Latin sounds at **Momentitos de la Vida** (p169) and youthful garage bands who consider Korn classic rock at **PB Squared** (p162).

Adobe Bar (Map p149; ☎ 758-2233; 125 Paseo del Pueblo Norte) It's the packed streetside patio adjacent to the Taos Inn, with some of the state's finest margaritas and an eclectic lineup of great live music like Manzanares and Madi Soto – and there's almost never a cover.

Alley Cantina (Map p149; ☎ 758-2121; www .alleycantina.com; 121 Terracina Lane; pub grub $5-14) It figures that the oldest building in Taos is a comfy bar, built in the 1500s by forward-thinking Native capitalists as the Taos Pueblo Trading Post. Nowadays you can catch live music ranging from zydeco to rock and jazz almost nightly. But don't miss the Cullen Winter Blues band.

Eske's Brew Pub & Eatery (Map p149; ☎ 758-1517; 106 Des Georges Ln; pub grub $6-11; ☙ 11:30am-10pm daily) A half-block south of Taos Plaza, this crowded hangout rotates more than 25 microbrewed ales, from Taos Green Chile to Doobie Rock Heller Bock, to compliment hearty bowls of Wanda's green chile stew and sushi on Tuesday. Live local music, from acoustic guitar to jazz, is usually free but national acts might charge a cover.

El Taoseño Restaurant and Lounge (Map p147; ☎ 758-4142; 819 Paseo del Pueblo Sur; mains $9-22) Mexican and Spanish performers, including mariachi, norteños, flamenco and more, liven up this top spot also loved as a splurge on authentic New Mexican cuisine.

Sagebrush Inn (Map p147; ☎ 758-2254; 1508 Paseo del Pueblo Sur) Live music almost nightly focuses on classic rock and country, which may well lure people onto the dance floor.

Dance Clubs

Fernando's Hideaway Lounge (Map p147; ☎ 758-4444 1005 Paseo del Pueblo Sur) Just because it's a hotel bar (at the Holiday Inn) doesn't keep crowds away from the renowned happy hour or the live DJs spinning hip-hop and dance music on weekends.

Vista Grill (Map p147; ☎ 776-0775; 9 NM 150; mains $14-22, tapas $6-8, cover $5-10; ☙ 5:30-9: 30pm Tue-Sat, noon-9pm Sun, bar open until at least midnight) A trendy place to drink off that bruising 'mogul incident' on the slopes, grab tapas (think goat cheese galette on wilted greens), and enjoy the live music, which ranges from hip hop and Latin jazz to country and Western, in the swinging 'Retro Lounge.'

Performing Arts

Taos Center for the Arts (Map p149; ☎ 758-2052; www.taoscenterforthearts.org; 133 Paseo del Pueblo Norte) In a remodeled 1890s adobe mansion, the TCA stages local and international performances of everything from chamber music to belly dancing to theater.

Taos Chamber Music Group (☎ 758-0150; adult/child $12/8, $15 at door) performs classical and jazz at venues throughout the region, including the Taos Center for the Arts and Harwood Museum. Performances usually start at around 7pm, sometimes opening with a speaker, and local restaurants including the Apple Tree and Doc Martin's offer dinner discounts when you show your ticket, making this a great date-night out.

Metta Project Theater (☎ 751-3349; 114 Alexander St) Local and experimental theater troupes put on shows, usually in winter, at this small community theater.

Cinemas

Storyteller Cinema (Map p147; ☎ 758-9715; 110 Old Talpa Cañon Rd; adult/child $7/5, adult/child matinee $6/3) A few mainstream flicks and lots of artsy ones show at Taos' only movie house, right off Paseo del Pueblo Sur.

Taos Talking Pictures (☎ 751-0637; www .ttpix.com; $7; ☙ 6:15pm & 8:30pm Wed & Thu, 1pm Sat) In addition to the world-famous film festival, this organization sponsors a weekly film series of oddball, artsy and a few semi-mainstream films at the Storyteller Theater.

SHOPPING

Everything that you actually need (Wal-Mart, supermarkets, liquor stores) can be found on Paseo del Pueblo Sur, south of downtown. But everything you want is by the plaza.

Contemporary Art

Most international artists who maintain New Mexico galleries stick to Santa Fe, where they'll get the most traffic. But Taos is just far enough off the beaten path that most work you see here was actually done here.

Twining Weavers (Map p149; ☎ 758-9000; 133 Kit Carson Rd) Dominated by the massive central loom, almost 14ft long and weighing in at 900lb, and often operated by skilled weavers, this shop showcases textiles as high art; one look at Ginger O'Neil's quilts and you'll agree.

Lumina Gallery (Map p149; ☎ 758-7282; www .luminagallery.com; 239 Morada Lane) Currently housed in the former home of Victor Higgins, a Taos School artist, and surrounded by a phenomenal contemporary sculpture garden, this top-flight gallery of mostly New Mexican artists will likely be relocating to Arroyo Seco before this book is off the shelves; give them a call.

Las Comadres Gallery (Map p149; ☎ 737-5323; 228A Paseo del Pueblo Norte) This women's collective of local artists, some of whom are in the Smithsonian and other large museums, show their jewelry, textiles, sculpture and other art right here.

Native American Art

The best spot for good-quality Native American jewelry, crafts and art on any budget is at Taos Pueblo, where you can peruse local work after your tour. But there are lots of fine galleries downtown, including **Pueblo Drums** (Map p149; ☎ 758-7929, 888-412-3786; www.pueblodrums.com; 110 Paseo del Pueblo Norte) with handmade drums by Phillip Martinez, and **Taos Mosaic Art and Fine Crafts** (Map p149; ☎ 758-0166; 216C Paseo del Pueblo Norte), showcasing the outstanding micaceous pottery of Angie Yazzie and others from Taos Pueblo.

Blue Rain Gallery (Map p149; ☎ 751-0066, 800-414-4893; www.blueraingallery.com; 117 S Taos Plaza) Among an excellent collection of museum-quality contemporary Pueblo Indian and other Native art, expect to find the finest paintings, jewelry and baskets – some traditional, some not.

Jewelry

El Rincon Trading Post (Map p149; ☎ 758-9188; 114 Kit Carson Rd) This 1909 shop could be considered an attraction, and there is a free museum in the back with photos, clothing, pipes and beadwork from Taos Pueblo. But the wide variety of treasures for sale – Native American pawn, African beads, Filipino jewelry and more – all brought here by traders who work with those artisans personally to find the very best selection, is unreal.

FX-18 (Map p147; ☎ 758-8590; www.fx18.com; 1018 Paseo del Pueblo Norte) In addition to fine jewelry (including bracelets worn by Taos'

sweetheart, Julia Roberts, in *The Mexican*), grab a Virgin of Guadalupe watch, pocket angels and lots of other fun stuff, about 2 miles north of downtown.

Buffalo Dancer (Map p149; ☎ 758-8718; 103A East Plaza Taos) One of the older outlets for Native American jewelry on the plaza, this place stars Rodney Concha's fine pieces plus other work in silver and semi-precious stones.

Gifts

Taos Gems & Minerals (Map p147; ☎ 758-3910; 637 Paseo del Pueblo Sur) Old-timers come in for the selection of gems, minerals, fossils and jewelry, while the New Agers stop by for particularly effective crystals. Rockhounds all over the state consider this a top shop.

G Robinson Old Prints and Maps (Map p149; ☎ 758-2278; 124D Bent St) The star of the Dunn House Shops carries a unique assortment of original maps of the American West, including railroad, geological and army surveys, plus collectable cartography from all over the world dating as far back as the 1500s.

Maison Faurie Antiquités (Map p149; ☎ 758-8545; 1 McCarthy Plaza) If you're in the market for old medical objects, US military memorabilia or art deco lamps – basically anything that catches the eye of owner Robert Faurie – it's all crammed into this fine spot for poking around.

Treasure Island (Map p147; ☎ 758-5553; 1506 Paseo del Pueblo Sur) Between the artists, eccentrics and movie stars, it's no wonder that Taos has such a fabulous selection of thrift stores – and this one has something for everyone.

GETTING THERE & AWAY
Air

Tiny **Taos Municipal Airport** (Map p147; ☎ 758-4995; Hwy 64) is served by Rio Grande Air (☎ 737-9790, 877-435-9742), which offers three flights to Albuquerque daily, running about $70 one way with two-weeks advance purchase, $125 the same day. The airport primarily serves as a landing strip for personal planes.

Bus

Greyhound (Map p147; ☎ 758-1144; www.greyhound .com; 1386 Paseo del Pueblo Sur) Buses leave the station, next to Guadalajara Grill, twice daily to Santa Fe ($16, 1½ hours) and Albuquerque ($28, 2¼ hours) with stops in Pilar and Española. There's also direct service to Denver ($67). Only the morning run to Albuquerque stops at the Sunport, and both will drop you downtown.

Twin Hearts Shuttle (☎ 800-654-9456; www.twin heartsexpress.com) Shuttles run between Taos and the Albuquerque Sunport ($45), Santa Fe ($25), Española ($15), Red River ($15) and Questa ($15) daily; make reservations in advance.

Faust Transportation (☎ 758-3410, 888-830-3410; www.newmexiconet.com/trans/faust/faust.html; ☽ 7am-9pm) Make reservations for the other shuttle service between Taos and the Albuquerque Sunport ($40), Santa Fe ($25), Taos Ski Valley ($12), Angel Fire ($15) and Red River ($20); this is a favorite of hikers and bikers who need drop-off service.

Car
Taos is about 90 minutes from Santa Fe via the Low Road; and about three hours on the more scenic High Road, though with recommended stops it could easily take all day. It's about three hours to Las Vegas on NM 518.

GETTING AROUND
Though downtown Taos is easily explored on foot, and the Chile Line (see Bus) serves many major sites including Taos Pueblo, exploring the greater area will require either a car or a private shuttle, particularly in summer, when the Chile Line suspends service to Arroyo Seco and the Ski Valley.

To/From the Airport
Faust Transportation and **Twin Hearts Shuttle** (see above) both provide service to and from the Albuquerque Sunport; Faust is your best bet for arranging pickup at the Taos Municipal Airport. There's no public transportation to the airport, but there are two rental car agencies.

Bicycle
Mountain bikes, road bikes and bike racks can be rented through **Gearing Up Bicycle Shop** (p154) and **Native Sons Adventures** (p152). Costs range from $20 to $35 daily, with discounts for long-term rental.

Bus
The **Chile Line** (☎ 737-2606; one way 50¢, day pass $1; ☽ 7am-7pm Mon-Sat) runs north-south along NM 68 between the Rancho de Taos post office and Taos Pueblo every 30 minutes, connecting to Greyhound buses. In winter only, the Chile Line also serves the Ski Valley and Arroyo Seco. All buses are handicap-accessible and have bike racks. You can get passes at the chamber of commerce.

Car
Enterprise Rent-a-Car (Map p147; ☎ 737-0514; Paseo del Pueblo Sur; ☽ 8am-6pm Mon-Fri), just south of downtown, has another location at the **airport** (☎ 737-0514; ☽ 2-8pm Mon-Fri, 9am-3pm Sat & Sun). **Dollar** (☎ 758-3500, 800-800-4000) also has a desk at Taos Municipal Airport. Any of them can arrange to have a car dropped off at your hotel.

Friday Motors (☎ 758-2252; 1040 Paseo del Pueblo Sur) often has better deals.

Taxi
Faust Transportation (☎ 758-3410, 888-830-3410) provides taxi service around town.

AROUND TAOS

TAOS PUEBLO
☎ 505 pop 2200 elevation 7100ft

This is what all that pueblo-revival architecture in Santa Fe wants to be when it grows up: among the first and still the best, beautiful **Taos Pueblo** (Map p147; ☎ tourism office 758-1028, Governor's Office 758-9593; www.taospueblo.com; Taos Pueblo Rd; adult/child $10/5, photography or video permit $5; ☽ 8am-4pm daily, closed for 10 weeks around Feb & Mar) is perhaps the most awe-inspiring image in all New Mexico.

The city's stunning architecture – two five-story complexes in ancient adobe, Who-ma on the north side of red-willow–lined Rio Pueblo, and Whoa-quima to the south, both set against the mightiest peaks of the Sangre de Cristos– have also made it among the most visited spots in the state. Which may explain why residents are so tourist-savvy (or in some cases, tourist-weary).

There's no guesswork involved: follow the signs to the main gate, where you'll get hooked up with passes and permits, then pointed toward the 1850 **San Geronimo Chapel**, home to a lovely Virgin regularly decked out in colors and symbols that reflect the changing seasons. There, guides will begin the tale of Taos Pueblo.

History

Founded about 1000 years ago – anthropologists (and certain folks at Acoma, Taos' friendly rival in the 'oldest inhabited US city' debate) put that date at 800 years ago, but whom are you going to believe? – this northernmost pueblo has long served as a trade and cultural center where Pueblo and Plains Indians could come together.

Captain Fernando Alvarado first visited Taos in 1540, and by 1619 Spanish arrivals had completed the original San Geronimo Chapel, using forced Native labor, of course. Everyone got a new Spanish surname and the Catholic religion, harshly enforced, which did not go over well. So when Popé declared a pan-pueblo war at Santa Clara, Taos was ready to roll.

Military strategists led by Popé, who quickly moved operations to remote and heavily fortified Taos Pueblo, were clever: Using Spanish to communicate with linguistically diverse tribes, and yucca cords with knots untied each morning in a universal countdown, they coordinated the only successful indigenous revolt in North America. And though DeVargas resettled Santa Fe in 1692, Taos held out for four more years.

While periods of civil unrest and sporadic violence followed the reoccupation, it was not until 1847 that political tensions again exploded. Territorial Governor Charles Bent, representing the new US government, was assassinated by a coalition of Spanish and Indian guerillas almost certainly acting independently of the pueblo government.

But Bent was scalped, Taos was blamed and the US Army decided to teach the pueblo a lesson. Some 150 women, children and elders (most soldiers were not there) were burned alive as they huddled inside that first chapel. Today nothing remains but the slowly dissolving bell tower.

Unbowed, Taos remained a political force, spearheading resistance to legislation that would have compromised Indian sovereignty throughout the USA in 1922, and successfully lobbying for the reintegration of Blue Lake, an important and sacred watershed, which was returned to the tribe in 1970 by order of President Nixon. Today about 150 people still live in the main houses, forgoing running water and electricity in order to maintain the city's integrity.

Sights & Activities

Taos Mountain Casino (Map p147; ☎ 737-0777, 888-946-8267; www.taosmountaincasino.com; ☯ 8am-1am Sun-Wed, 8am-2am Thu-Sat) With less razzle-dazzle – not to mention smoke – than some casinos, this cozy alcohol- and cigarette-free spot is one of the nicest places around to blow your cash. Grab some green chile stew or an ice cream cone at surprisingly good **Lucky 7s** (Map p147; snacks $3-5; ☯ 10am-10pm), settle into blackjack or slots, and stay a while. It's served by the Chile Line.

Several craftspeople sell fine jewelry, micaceous pottery and other arts and crafts at the main pueblo, which you can peruse after your tour. You can also grab tacos, chewy horno bread and other snacks ($3-5).

Galleries include **Summer Rain Gift Shop** (☎ 469-9148; North House; ☯ 8am-4pm daily), with corn maidens and local pottery, or **Tony Reyna Indian Shop** (Map p147; ☎ 758-3835; Taos Pueblo Rd; ☯ 8am-noon & 1-5pm daily), just outside the main pueblo, with a vast collection of arts and crafts from Taos and other tribes. Also look under Native American Art in the Taos Shopping section (p164) for more galleries that carry local artists' work.

Taos Pueblo's vast Blue Lakes Wilderness is off-limits to visitors – unless you go on horseback with **Taos Indian Horse Ranch** (☎ 758-3212, 800-659-3210; hoofbeats@laplaza.org; 1½-hr easy rider $45/85, 2-hr experienced rider $115). This unusual outfitter combines basic rides with cultural and historical information. The guides also arrange overnight and multiday pack overnights, which run about $130 a day including food, water and gear, which emphasize wilderness survival from an Indian perspective.

Note that in 2003 the 6000-acre Encebedo Fire raged across pueblo lands, though firefighters managed to stop the blaze before it damaged the main houses and riding trails. They may need volunteers to help reseed the forest; if you're interested, give the tourism office a call.

TAOS

Eating

Tewa Kitchen (Map p147; ☎ 751-1020; Taos Pueblo Rd; mains $5-13; ✆ Wed-Mon 11am-5pm, until 7pm in summer) It's one of the few places in the state where you can sit down to a plate of Native treats like phien-ty (blue corn fry bread stuffed with buffalo meat), twa chull (grilled buffalo) or a bowl of heirloom green chile grown on pueblo grounds.

ARROYO SECO

☎ 505 pop 1150 elevation 7100ft

Ever since urban creep consumed El Prado, it's been up to Arroyo Seco to maintain that hip edge and unprocessed local flavor. And it does, with a groovy plaza, growing art scene and one big hurdle to anyone looking to capitalize on it all: despite the name, it's not the lack of water limiting development, but a high water table that makes wastewater treatment a real pain in the derrière.

So, while anyone hoping to build a big resort is s*** out of luck, you get to enjoy pure, unadulterated high-desert lounging of the very finest sort. There's not much to do right in town, and plenty of ways not to do it.

Sleeping

There's no middle ground in Arroyo Seco, nor are there any bad options.

The Abominable Snowmansion HI Hostel (Map p147; ☎ 776-8298; http://taoswebb.com/hotel/snowmansion; dm $15-22, s/d campsite $12/16, teepee or cabin $34-38, d $42-48; ℗ ✗ ⌨) This HI hostel offers $3 off to members, but anyone can enjoy the cozy lodge, clean (if a tad threadbare) private rooms, a wonderful campground with an outdoor kitchen, fun teepees, surprisingly nice cabins, or just a sweet and simple dorm bed. The communal area centers on a warm gas fireplace and big kitchen, with a pool table and piano to keep the party going. There's no lockout, lots of room to store your ski equipment, and a complimentary breakfast served in the winter months. It's served by the Chile Line in winter only.

Adobe and Stars B&B (Map p147; ☎ 776-2776, 800-211-7076; www.taosadobe.com; d $110-185 incl breakfast; ℗ ✗) Amazing rooms with real fireplaces and private entrances, fabulous mountains visible through huge windows and simply wonderful vibes: this could well be the best B&B in New Mexico. It definitely wins the coveted Best View from the Hot Tub award.

Go even further upscale at gorgeous **Alma de Monte** (Map p147; ☎ 776-2721, 800-273-7203; www.almaspirit.com; 372 Hondo-Seco Rd; d $160-200 incl breakfast; ℗ ✗ ✖), a flawlessly decorated hacienda with spacious, comfortable rooms, amazing mountain views, fireplaces and antiques everywhere, three-course breakfasts and hors d'oeuvres in the evening. Fabulous.

Eating

Once again, you'll either be enjoying life on the cheap or on the credit card; either way you'll be on cloud nine.

CEREMONIAL DANCES OPEN TO THE PUBLIC

Each pueblo invites visitors to some of their dances and events (www.santaana.org/calendar.htm has a complete schedule), and Taos' list is the longest. With the exception of the powwow, these are religious observances, and proper respect is requested.

Turtle Dance (Jan 1)
Deer or Buffalo Dance (Jan 6)
Santa Cruz Dance (May 3) Footraces in the morning and young people dancing
San Antonio Feast Corn Dance (Jun 13)
San Juan Day Corn Dance (June 24)
Taos Pueblo Powwow (second weekend in Jul) The Plains and the Pueblos meet for the biggest bash this side of Albuquerque, and you can even take photos
Santiago Day Corn Dance (Jul 25)
Santa Ana Day Corn Dance (Jul 26)
San Geronimo Feast Days (Sep 29 & 30) Vespers the night before, dancing and pole climbing on the 30th
Procession of the Virgin (Dec 24) Early-evening bonfire procession and traditional dances
Deer or Matchines Dance (Dec 25) Spanish-influenced traditional dances

Abe's Cantina y Cocina (Map p147; ☎ 776-8516; NM 150; mains $3-8; ⊙ 7am-6pm Mon-Fri, 7am-2pm Sat; cantina 10am-close) Predating the hipsters by a decade or three, this small grocery store and deli is renowned for its tamales and cantina, a good place to throw one back and chat up folks.

Gypsy 360° (Map p147; ☎ 776-3166; 'downtown' Arroyo Seco; mains $5-11; ⊙ 8am-4pm Mon-Sat, 9am-3pm Sun) Right on the tiny plaza, with a sundrenched patio and relaxing interior, these folks cater to the traveler in everyone: Vietnamese spring rolls, Japanese sushi, Indonesian satay and beer from all over the world. They're still getting things rolling but plan to have later hours and live music in the very near future.

Momentitos de la Vida (Map p147; ☎ 776-3333; NM 150; mains $19-24; ⊙ 4:30pm-midnight Tue-Sun, bar open until 2am Tue-Sat) Take in the sunset on the expansive patio or relax into the elegant interior, beginning with the Sevruga caviar and perhaps moving on to lobster risotto or grilled habañero prawns. Come on Friday or Saturday to enjoy live jazz while you peruse the wine list.

TAOS SKI VALLEY
☎ 505 pop 56 elevation 9200ft

If you're coming here to ski, you already know what awaits: one of the USA's most challenging mountains, which gets folks from Colorado – heck, even Switzerland – all excited. And jealous. 'It's like looking at a wall when you stand at the bottom,' says one ski bunny, but don't let that stop you. Well, unless you're one of those crazy snowboarders, in which case you're headed to Angel Fire, as they don't appreciate yer kind around here.

Summer visitors to the village, which was once the rough-and-tumble gold-mining town of Twining, will find an alpine wilderness with great hiking and cheap lodging but no public transportation during the off season. There's no gas station or grocery store either.

Skiing
With more than 300 inches of all-natural powder annually, a peak elevation of 11,819ft and a 2612ft vertical drop, seasoned skiers are already stoked that more than half of the ski area's 72 trails are ranked experienced.

Newbies need not be discouraged, however: **Ernie Blake Ski School** (☎ 800-347-7414) is ranked one of the best in the world and offers lessons geared toward kids, adults, experienced skiers just looking to improve, and folks over 50 (taught by instructors over 50). Though packages and multiday options will save you money, two-hour group lessons run $40, private lessons $175.

The Ski Area operates a **chamber of commerce** (☎ 776-2233, 800-992-7669; www.taosskivalley.com) year-round, offering lots of skiing-lodging-dining-lessons packages. Rates for basic lift tickets vary throughout the season (from $19 in early December to adult/child $51/31 over Christmas). Ski week packages, including room, board, lessons and lift tickets, average $1400 per person.

You can rent equipment (adult $23-33, child $13) at the Ski Valley, or stop at **Cottam's Ski Shop** (Map p147; ☎ 776-8719, 800-322-8267; www.cottamsskishops.com; packages $15-40; ⊙ 7am-6pm daily, winter only) in the village; there's another location in Taos. Stick to skis, though – at press time, snowboards were banned on the slopes.

Hiking
This is the high country, and special considerations should be taken before attempting any of the longer hikes. The Questa Ranger Station (p173) and Carson National Forest Supervisor's Office (p148), in Taos, both have maps and other information. Water is generally available year-round but must be treated. Many trails have some risk of avalanche, particularly in the early spring.

If you just want to romp, get tickets for the **chairlift** (adult/child $7/5; ⊙ 10am-4:30pm Thu-Mon late Jun-Sep) at **Taos Ski & Boot Company** (☎ 776-2292; NM 150) in the village, then walk on down the mountain along any of the super scenic and well-marked trails.

Twining Campground is the trailhead for two hikes: the excellent 8-mile-roundtrip to scenic (but fish-free) **Williams Lake**, with opportunities for rock climbing; and the granddaddy of all area hikes, summiting 13,161ft **Wheeler Peak** – and this is the short-and-steep route (for the longer trail beginning near Red River, see p176). It's 16 miles roundtrip, and you could do it in a day but consider camping overnight.

TAOS

Gavilan Trail begins close to Chalets of Taos, following pretty Gavilan Creek for a steep hike (2000ft elevation gain) that opens up into a gorgeous alpine meadow, for a total 7-mile roundtrip. It connects into a trail system accessing Lobo Peak, Flag Mountain and Gold Hill trails.

Italianos Canyon Trail starts next to Columbine Inn and follows the canyon up a newly rebuilt trail that's popular with llama trekkers.

Sleeping & Eating

The conspicuously quaint Village of Taos Ski Valley, a clutch of Tudor-style lodges with rooms sleeping six and cutesy names that unsubtly refer to the actual Alps, operates the **Taos Valley Resort Association** (☎ 800-776-1111; www.visitnewmexico.com), which can reserve rooms year-round.

All the lodges have hot tubs and fireplaces, and many have rooms with kitchenettes, which will save you cash (bring food from Taos). Restaurants that the lodges operate tend to be overpriced and mediocre.

Summer visitors, particularly those with fishing poles, should check out the four tiny **campgrounds** with no fees and no running water (unless you count the trout-packed Rio Hondo, which has to be treated): **Twining** (Map p147), at 9400ft, can get chilly; **Chuchilla** (Map p147) and **Chuchilla Medio** (Map p147) are shady; and **Lower Hondo** (Map p147) is sunnier, with the easiest RV access.

Inn at Snakedance (Map p147; ☎ 776-2277, 800-322-9815; www.innsnakedance.com; NM 150; d summer/winter $75/225 incl breakfast; P 🗶) This huge resort at the bottom of the lifts has a restaurant, bar, in-room massages and lots of other amenities, and it's a much better deal as part of a package.

Amizette Inn (Map p147; ☎ 776-2451, 800-446-8267; www.amizette.com; NM 150; d $59-79 summer, d $99-159 winter incl breakfast; P 🗶) With cabins and your choice of breakfast, this is a sweet spot to light.

Austing Haus B&B (Map p147; ☎ 776-2649, 800-748-2932; NM 150; d $59-85 summer, d $72-145 winter incl breakfast; P 🗶) Two miles from the slope, this claims to be the tallest wood-framed structure in the USA, and definitely has the nicest dining room around.

Columbine Inn (Map p147; ☎ 888-884-5723; www.columbineinntaos.com; NM 150; $59-79 summer,

$89-179 winter; P 🗶) A bit of a sprawler, this pleasant inn would be perfect for that group retreat.

The **Thunderbird Lodge** (Map p147; ☎ 776-2280; NM 150) and **Inn at Snakedance** both have quality sit-down restaurants with gourmet dinners, good burgers and high-energy snacks, but budget skiers should head to **Tim's Stray Dog Cantina** (Map p147; ☎ 776-2894; 105 Sutton Place; mains $3-10) instead, with beer, chile rellenos and a mean breakfast burrito. **Crossroads Pizza** (Map p147; ☎ 776-8866; 6 Thunderbird Rd; mains $10, large pizza $16-20; ☽ 11am-9:30pm daily) delivers.

Getting There & Away

Take Hwy 64 north from Taos to the stoplight and veer right on Hwy 150. The beautiful winding drive follows the Rio Hondo about 20 miles to the village. The **Chile Line** (p166) runs several times daily between downtown Taos and the ski area during winter only.

Both **Faust Transportation** and **Twin Hearts Express** (p166) make runs between the Ski Valley Village and downtown Taos, Santa Fe and Albuquerque several times daily in the winter, and can get you here by arrangement in summer months.

And, while you can't really recommend this in print, note that hitching from Taos to the Ski Valley is common in winter – although you shouldn't do it, because it can be dangerous.

ENCHANTED CIRCLE

Encompassing the alpine highlands that rise to 13,161ft Wheeler Peak, the Enchanted Circle is an 84-mile stretch of highway through a region markedly different from that covered elsewhere in this book. Windswept meadows carpet the rolling steppe, pierced by naked granite scenically draped in pine forests and crystalline lakes: This is marmot country.

Most towns on the circuit (with the notable exception of Questa) are young, founded in the 1880s gold rush by mostly Anglo settlers looking for the mother lode. It never quite panned out, however, and the abandoned mines and ghost towns are highlights of the trip.

Those who remained turned to tourism, opening major ski resorts at Red River and Angel Fire; knickknack shops and adventure tours are probably the other two major employers. If you just do this as a drive, you may be a bit disappointed – folks around here are more likely to compare their rare world to the Bermuda Triangle than the tourist bureau's more evocative moniker. But take time to

explore, and it will be one of the highlights of your trip.

Taos Net (www.enchantedcircle.org) has links to all area visitors centers; these links in turn link to outfitters, hotels and restaurants. Fill your gas tank in Taos, where it's cheaper, and allow at least a full day to make the

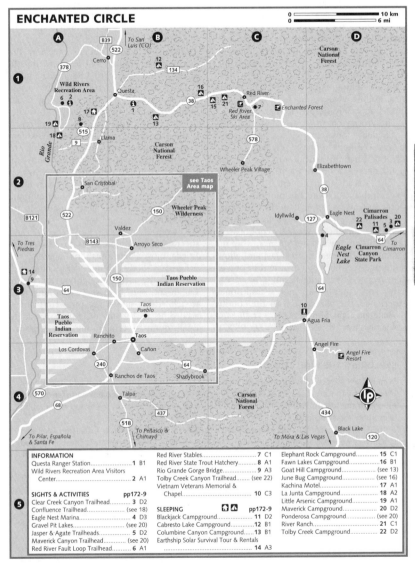

ENCHANTED CIRCLE

journey. Better yet, spend the night along the way.

Arroyo Hondo

This picturesque village, with hot springs secreted throughout the red sandstone cliffs and lush ribbon of farms, is best known to recovering hippies as the home of **New Buffalo Inn** (Map p147; ☎ 776-2015; www.newbuffalotaos.com; d $50 incl breakfast; **P**). Call for directions to the former commune that hosted *Easy Rider* legends Dennis Hopper and Timothy Leary, among many others, as they enthusiastically barreled through the doors of perception. There's evidently *still* a lost stash of long-expired LSD-25, forgotten in a hollow viga somewhere among the sprawling, oddly-shaped adobes.

The groovy common area, stocked with psychedelic books and videos, is attached to very well-kept but basic private quarters, like the Enchantment Room, with vigas (solid, every last one of them) carved fairly legibly to read 'enchantment,' 'peace' and 'joy'; and the Tower Room, featuring a secret hideaway loft just perfect for kids – or anyone who just needs to be alone, man. The current, predictably cool owners can point you toward hot springs, whip up a great mostly-organic breakfast and allow camping, in either your own tent or one of their teepees, by arrangement.

If you prefer a more traditional experience, the oldest B&B in the county is **Mountain Light B&B** (Map p147; ☎ 776-8474; www.mtnlight.com; s/d $65/95 incl breakfast; **P** **X**), featuring two rooms decorated with Central American flair in a lovely adobe about a mile off NM 522 – call for directions and ask for the blue corn waffles at breakfast.

DH Lawrence Ranch & Memorial

A pilgrimage-worthy destination for many reasons, DH Lawrence's former home (Map p147; ☎ 776-2245; www.unm.edu/~taosconf/ranch; admission free; ☼ sunrise-sunset), administered by UNM, allows folks to pay their respects to the famed author of such classics as *Lady Chatterley's Lover,* not to mention the decent pornographer whose pieces are still discretely displayed at La Fonda de Taos.

Lawrence lived here for only a few months from 1924 to '25, chopping wood, hiking trails and (with the help of his wife, Frieda) fighting off the attentions of typist Lady Dorothy Brett and patron Mabel Dodge Luhan, somehow managing to complete the novella *St Mawr* in between. Relax beneath the **Lawrence Tree**, which brings in the O'Keeffe fans (yep, it looks just like her painting) and contemplate what he called 'the best experience he ever had.'

Lawrence returned to Europe in 1925 and succumbed to tuberculosis in 1930. After Frieda moved back to Taos in 1934, she ordered his body exhumed and incinerated, and had the ashes brought to the ranch. Luhan and Brett both showed up uninvited to help scatter said ashes (mrowrrrr) which, according to legend, prompted Frieda to finally dump the remains into a wheelbarrow

---

EXPLORING THE HIGH COUNTRY

Even in New Mexico, this is considered high altitude, with most of the Enchanted Circle at well over 7500ft. The oft-repeated advice to acclimate goes double here, triple if you plan to take on one of the tough but rewarding hikes into the mountains – physical stress and dehydration exacerbate the symptoms.

Unlike in the rest of the state, water is rarely a problem and though it has to be treated, lakes and streams are generally reliable all summer long. Snow melts by June at even the highest developed campgrounds, but tent sites and trails higher than 9000ft may have drifts for another month. Prepare for nighttime temperatures to drop well into the 40s, even in July.

Summer afternoon thunderstorms can be dangerous, and not just because of the potential for hypothermia – you're likely the tallest thing around. You'll probably be able to see storms rolling in from quite a distance, but they move fast – get below the tree line ASAP, even if you only *feel* one coming let alone see one. Pick up appropriate USGS maps, as these paths don't see much traffic, then grab a backcountry permit and register your itinerary at either the Questa Ranger Station (p173) or the Carson National Forest Supervisor's Office in Taos (p148). And don't forget your camera.

full of wet cement, saying, 'Let's see them try to steal this!'

Ascend the meandering paved walkway to the memorial, designed by Frieda's third husband, where the lump of concrete has been inscribed with DHL's initials and pressed leaves. It's heartwarming, with a scandalous giggle, just like Lawrence would have wanted.

The Lama Foundation

This spiritual retreat (☎ 586-1269; www .lamafoundation.org; $25 donation; May-Sep; P) near San Cristobal offers several simple shelters in summer – think outhouses and kerosene lamps – and tent sites available by donation or trade for work. The foundation also offers a variety of classes, including drum making, meditation and yoga.

Call in advance for directions and reservations, and plan to show up on Visitors Sundays, held bimonthly through the summer tourist season, with a vegetarian lunch at 1:30pm.

Questa

☎ 505 pop 2200 elevation 7670ft

Unlike many communities on the Enchanted Circle, Questa has deep roots, not to mention theme-free restaurants and rooms. It's primarily a mining town, thanks to the mountains of molybdenum you'll pass heading west. There's also a good-sized contingent of artists, subsistence farmers and other organic types, and everyone appreciates the view: an alpine bowl glittering with lakes (you can rent ice-skates downtown during winter) and bright wildflowers, spectacularly torn by the great chasm just north.

The **Artesanos de Questa & Visitors Center** (☎ 770-1600; 41 NM 38; 🕐 10am-5pm Thu-Sun) sells work by local artists and can recommend B&Bs. The artisans also hold **Cambalache** (early Oct) nearby, an arts and crafts festival culminating with the burning of el cucui (the bogeyman).

There's not much to do in town, but the visitors center will point you toward pretty St Anthony's Church, local artists' studios and **Red River State Trout Hatchery** (Map p171; ☎ 586-0222; NM 515; admission free), south of town about 2 miles off Hwy 522, which has displays all about trout, plus

lots in the ponds and raceways outside – the kids may appreciate this more than you do.

Kachina Motel (Map p171; ☎ 586-0640; 2306 Hwy 522; s/d $45/65; summer only; P ✗) is cute, clean and pretty basic, while **Sangre de Cristo Motel** (☎ 586-0300; cnr NM 522 & NM 38; d $45-60; P) has a more central location and slightly shabbier rooms, and (the real draw) is open year-round.

There are a handful of restaurants in town, but make a beeline to **Questa Café** (☎ 586-9631; 2422 NM 522; mains $3-9; 🕐 6am-10pm Mon-Sat, 6am-3pm Sun) an expansive diner beloved for its Frito pie, chile-cheese fries (go for red) and homemade deserts. **Paloma Blanca Coffee Shop** (☎ 586-2261; NM 522; snacks $2-5; 🕐 6am-6pm Mon-Sat, later on Tue & Fri) has lattes, pastries, burritos, a rack of tourist flyers and an attached laundromat.

Questa Ranger Station (Map p171; ☎ 586-0520; Hwy 38; 🕐 8am-4:30pm Mon-Fri), about a mile east of Questa, is a must-stop before exploring any of the area wilderness. Folks headed for the Valle Vidal Loop in particular should stop by for up-to-date road and camping conditions. This is also where backpackers should leave their itineraries.

After making the detour to Wild Rivers Recreation Area, you'll leave Questa and enter the **Carson National Forest**, administrated by the Questa Ranger Station. The road follows Red River past a string of beautiful **campgrounds** ($6; May-Oct) with fishing access and some wheelchair-accessible sites:

Cabresto Lake This top fishing and camping spot, just east of Questa on rough FR 134 (make a left just after NM 38 begins and follow the signs for about 10 gravelly miles) has running water and a trailhead for scenic Lake Fork Trail to 11,500ft Heart Lake, where you could also pitch a tent.

Goat Hill It's scenic, with fishing but no running water.

Columbine Canyon This one does have potable water plus access to short, steep Columbine Trail, through canyons and over four bridges, and to 11-mile Rio Hondo & Red River Canyon Trail to Rio Hondo Bridge.

Elephant Rock Fish in both the river and nearby Fawn Lakes, and enjoy running water, too.

Fawn Lakes At 8500ft, it's the highest of the bunch, with running water, fishing at Fawn Lakes and pull-through sites.

June Bug This pretty spot has river fishing and running water.

TAOS

Wild Rivers Recreation Area

They call it 'New Mexico's Grand Canyon,' which may be a bit of a stretch – a bit. But access to two wild rivers instead of a single tamed one, carved into volcanic ash of the deepest gray and surrounded by the dark, piñon-studded plugs of the ancient volcanoes that wrought this lonely place, more than makes up the comparison. And best of all, there are rarely crowds – just try finding this sort of peace on the rim of Arizona's claim to fame.

The **visitors center** (Map p171; ☎ 770-6600; NM 378; day use $3; ✆ 10am-5pm Fri-Sun) has information about the park's five **campsites** ($7), none with running water, and the five hiking trails that drop 800ft from each campsite into the gorge below. **La Junta** has the best view, but **Little Arsenic** is the most coveted, with shade and fresh spring water that should be treated.

Trails descend into another world, perceptibly moister and cooler by degrees even as the vegetation around you erupts into lush green. At the bottom, these trails are connected by the **Confluence Trail**, running from La Junta along the Rio Grande through the cottonwood to Little Arsenic; a rim trail runs along the top. You can camp at the bottom with a permit.

Other, less shady trails investigate the volcanoes, including the 2-mile **Red River Fault Loop** and steep but rewarding 4-mile roundtrip **Guadalupe Mountain Trail**, accessible by a turnoff 2 miles north of the visitors center.

Even if you don't feel like a hike, just driving the scenic 13-mile **Wild Rivers Backcountry Byway** loop allows an impressive and visceral experience. There's plenty of access to phenomenal views, and La Junta provides the perfect spot for a picnic overlooking the confluence of the twin gorges.

DETOUR: VALLE VIDAL LOOP

Those in the mood for a longer drive through the highlands can try the Valle Vidal Loop, which departs the Enchanted Circle in Questa, north on NM 522 past the Wild Rivers Recreation Area, and rejoins the road more traveled in Eagle Nest via US 64, for a 173-mile total trip.

The bulk of the route is impassable during winter, and the washboard gravel road of FR 1950 is no picnic at the best of times – bring a spare tire and don't expect to hit third gear. The northern gate to FR 1950 is closed April 1 to early June for elk calving season, while the southern gate closes January through March to let them winter in peace. The estimated 1800 elk are a major attraction the rest of the year and are best seen in the morning and evening.

Take NM 522 north past the El Rito turnoff, which accesses the elk-infested **Latir Peak Wilderness**, with mesas at 12,000ft and higher, administrated by the Questa Ranger District. Privately owned **Latir Lakes** (☎ 586-0542 for permits), eight alpine gems set into 12,700ft Latir Peak, are worth the hike that begins here.

Farther north the **Urraca Wildlife Area** (☎ 476-8000; www.gmfsh.state.nm.us) has hiking and fishing, while the small town of **Costilla**, 2 miles south of the Colorado border, has a couple of accommodations options. Just out of town, NM 198 loses its cement and heads into the wilderness.

The upshot of the rough access road is that in addition to elk, wildcats and bears roam almost unmolested through what's sometimes called 'New Mexico's Yellowstone.' FR 1950 follows stocked Rio Costilla, a fly-fishers paradise and great place to relax, and opens onto unlimited access to multiday backpacking adventures in both the national forest and privately owned **Rio Castillo Cooperative Livestock Association** (☎ 586-0542), which allows free fishing access during summer and pricey elk hunts in early October.

Continue your journey into the Valle Vidal Unit of Carson National Forest, wending through meadows, forest, more elk, outstanding views of granite peaks and four developed **campgrounds.** McCrystal has nicer shelters, but Shuree is closer to the **fishing pond,** which is the hub of several short trails. Two scenic stops (of many) include **Windy Gap,** a weird geological formation resembling a human-made wall, and **Ring Ranch,** an 1890 home just a short walk from the road.

The route becomes blessedly paved again when you make a left onto US 64 for the drive through Cimarron Canyon State Park (p177) and into Eagle Nest, where you rejoin the Enchanted Circle.

Wild River Tours (☎ 586-1189; www.tournewmexico.net; 195 Cerro Rd) arranges guided hikes (adult/child $50/25) and driving tours (adult/child $120/60) of the area, as well as group camping and expeditions to abandoned area gold mines.

Red River

☎ 505 pop 480 elevation 8750ft

The problem with visiting New Mexico is that it just never seems like…well, a holiday. Sure, there's a small theme park in Albuquerque, and Señor Murphy's in Santa Fe carries handmade fudge. But saltwater taffy? Forget it. And a theme? Unless you consider adobe a theme (and it's taken much too seriously to be considered a fun theme, anyway), you kitsch connoisseurs are straight out of luck.

Then, on the edge of the vast alpine plains, you'll see it, a cluster of cheerfully painted shops and chalets, gleaming in the high desert sun: Red River, ski resort for the masses, decked out in German-peasant style with an Old West theme – you'd think it wouldn't work, but it does. Saltwater taffy? Oh yes. And that's just the beginning.

Red River was founded as a mining town in the late 1800s, and by the early 1900s was a bustling community of hard-drinking gold miners with high hopes, subsequently dashed by difficult-to-process ore. The view kept things cheerful, however, and hangers-on realized that their outdoor paradise might appeal to flatlanders with income.

Six historic buildings, and lots of dilapidated mines, have since been joined by a ski resort, adventure outfitters, ticky-tacky shops galore and, this being New Mexico (though they'd probably side with Texas if it came down to it), art galleries.

ORIENTATION & INFORMATION

The main drag is NM 38, which forks on the western end of town, south to NM 578, which passes the golf course and ends at the trailhead for Wheeler Peak; or north to continue the Enchanted Circle. The entire town is within three blocks of the highway.

The **chamber of commerce** (☎ 754-2366, 800-348-6444; www.redrivernewmex.com; 100 E Main St; ☽ 8am-5pm Mon-Fri) publishes a comprehensive visitors guide and has flyers for every area business plus great information on the surrounding wilderness. If you've come on a weekend, fear not: there are racks of this stuff all over town. There's even a trolley, the **Red River Miner's Transit** (☎ 770-5959; adult/child 50¢/free; ☽ 7:30am-5pm daily), which runs up and down NM 38.

WINTER ACTIVITIES

Red River Ski Area (Map p171; ☎ 754-2223, 800-331-7669; www.redriverskiarea.com; lift tickets adult/child $44/30; ☽ 9am-4pm daily Nov-Mar) More popular with skiers from Oklahoma and Texas than New Mexicans, this resort caters to families and newbies with packages that include lessons and equipment rental. Deals on multiday stays include accommodations at more than 30 area lodges, and your fourth day is usually free. The basic package (adult/child $80/70) includes a lesson, lift ticket and all your gear, and there's an option for **snowboarders** who want to check out Bobcat Terrain Park, specifically designed to lure you east from Angel Fire.

Enchanted Forest (Map p171; ☎ 754-2374, 800-966-9381; www.enchantedforestxc.com; NM 38; adult/child $9/3; ☽ 9am-4:30pm Nov-Mar) More than 25 miles of groomed trails near 9820ft Bobcat Pass make this New Mexico's premier Nordic ski area. The views are spectacular, snowshoeing is encouraged, and special events include the illuminated Christmas Luminaria Tour, Moonlight Ski Tours (the Saturday before a full moon), and Just Desserts Eat & Ski (late February), when you'll ski from stand to stand as area restaurants showcase their sweet stuff. **Miller's Crossing** (☎ 754-2374; 417 W Main St) maintains the trails and rents snowshoes and cross-country skis.

There are several places to rent skis and snowboards too, including **Red Dawg Ski Rentals** (☎ 754-2721, 800-858-8103; Main St) and **Lifts West Ski Rentals** (☎ 754-6609; Main St). For more adrenaline-pumping fun, rent a snowmobile at **Fast Eddie's** (☎ 754-3103; 619 E Main St), downtown, or **Bobcat Pass Wilderness Adventures** (☎ 754-2769; NM 38), just east of town. Both also offer tours ($50-100) of the area's extensive snowmobile trail system, which accesses ghost towns, mining encampments and other unusual stuff. A free map with trail descriptions is available at the chamber of commerce.

SUMMER ACTIVITIES

Frye's Old Town Shootout (Main St; admission free; 4pm Tue, Thu & Sat Jun-Sep) showcases the Second Amendment in all its ten-gallon-hatted, buckskin-jacketed glory as cowboys hold a faux showdown right in the center of town. From there, it's either **shopping**, taking a swing at **Red Eagle Golf Course** (754-6569; 2163 NM 38; $13-25), or heading out into the spectacular wilderness surrounding the strip.

The 2-mile **Red River Nature Trail**, beginning at the covered bridge in Brandenburg Park or the end of Goose Lake Rd, has interpretive plaques about the area's geology and ecosystems.

Take NM 578 into the heart of the Wheeler Peak Wilderness for more challenging options. **Horseshoe Lake Trail** leaves the Ditch Cabin Site for a 12-mile roundtrip to the 11,950ft-high lake with good camping and fishing. **Wheeler Peak Trail** ascends the 13,161ft summit, beginning at 9400ft, via a 16-mile roundtrip direct route, with options for a 19-mile total loop. Allow three days, and contact the Questa Ranger Station before attempting this one. **Lost Lakes** is 4 miles along the trail and makes a great overnight spot with ample fishing opportunities.

The **fishing** here is spectacular, with several lakes stocked with rainbow and German brown trout, as well as Red River itself. **Jeff Fagan** (754-2504; jafffagan25@hotmail.com; half/full day $75/120, each extra person $25) leads guided fly-fishing expeditions and supplies all your gear.

The Ski Area's **Summer Chairlift** (adult/child $8/5, day bicycle pass $15; 10am-3pm), which operates weekends from late May until mid-June, then daily until September, takes you to 10,350ft, where a restaurant, hiking trails and mountain-bike runs begin.

You could also bike the two rough **Jeep trails** into USFS land that access dozens of old mines in various states of collapse. Pick up interpretive flyers at the chamber of commerce, then hike, bike or drive (4WD recommended, particularly in wet weather) **Pioneer Canyon Trail**, along 4-mile FR 485, beginning at Pioneer Rd behind Arrowhead Lodge, and **Placer Creek Trail**, along 4-mile FR 486, just east, beginning at the stream crossing at the end of Goose

Lake Rd and passing fishing ponds, mines and mills.

You can rent Jeeps and ATVs at **Bobcat Pass Wilderness Adventures** (above) and **Red River Mountain Adventures** (754-6363; Main St), both of which can also arrange guided tours for you. Mellower folks might prefer a horseback ride from **Red River Stables** (Map p171; 754-1700; NM 38), just east of town.

SLEEPING

Red River has more than 50 RV parks, lodges, B&Bs and hotels, many of which offer package deals with local outfitters and the Ski Area. Once the snow melts, this is the best place on the Enchanted Circle to bargain for a great room, though most don't have air conditioning (rarely a worry at this altitude, though).

Reservations Unlimited (754-6415; www.red riverreservations.com; d $65-125, f $85-380; P) can arrange stays in vacation homes, cabins and condominiums, while the chamber of commerce has information and links to dozens more options.

River Ranch (Map p171; 754-2293; www .redrivernm.com/riverranch; 1501 W Main St; campsite/RV $16/23, cabins $42-79; P) It may not be quite as scenic as those USFS campgrounds, but it does have hot showers, full hookups, lots of fishing and rustic cabins that sleep up to six, but bring your own bag.

Alpine Lodge (754-2952, 800-252-2333; www .thealpinelodge.com; Main St; d low $40-70, d high $78-139; P) This comfortable chalet has rooms sleeping six or more, plus an onsite **restaurant** (mains $3-7; 7am-2pm daily) that serves the best New Mexican food in town.

Copper King Lodge (754-6210, 800-727-6210; www.redrivernm.com/copperking; Main St; d $43-63, f $84-127; P) Rough-hewn wood, rustic furnishings and a great backyard make these cabins and condos with kitchenettes a great deal.

Carousel House B&B (754-3166, 877-479-0584; www.carouselhousebb.com; 500B E Main St; $85-125 incl breakfast; P) With two pleasantly pastel rooms, a deck and big breakfast, this is the leisurely way to relax between runs.

Lodge at Red River (754-6280, 800-915-6343; www.redrivernm.com/lodgeatrr; Main St; s/d $42/84, f $106-165; P) This huge pre-fab resort hotel has some of the nicest rooms in town, plus an onsite bar and restaurant with fresh trout all summer long.

EATING

Even the grocery store has a Saxon theme: **Der Market** (☎ 754-2974; 307 W Main; ☺ 7am-7pm daily) is not only adorable, it's the best place to resupply in the Enchanted Circle.

Shotgun Willies (☎ 754-6505; cnr Main St & Pioneer Rd; mains $3-10; ☺ 7am-3pmish daily) has enormous artery-clogging breakfast specials for just $4, and barbecue by the pound.

Texas Reds Steakhouse & Saloon (☎ 754-2964; 111 E Main St; steaks $11-24, other mains $5-15) doesn't take reservations, but you can call ☎ 754-2922 to find how many people are waiting for steak, game, burgers and the opportunity to throw peanut shells on the floor. **Timbers** (☎ 754-2769; 402 W Main St; mains $7-22; ☺ 4:30-9pm Mon-Sat) provides even more opportunity to explore the cowboy theme, with a restaurant famed for rib-eye steaks, and summer **Cowboy Evenings** ($45), featuring a wagon ride to the top of Bobcat Pass, where a campfire, chuck-wagon dinner and cowboy poetry await.

If you prefer a little line dancing with your barbecue, Red River is a favorite stop on the country-and-western music circuit. You can catch live acts all over town on weekends, including at **Bull o' the Woods Saloon** (☎ 754-2593; Main St) and **Lonesome Pine Pub** (☎ 754-2488; Main St), among others.

Elizabethtown

Once the Colfax County Seat and a thriving gold-mining community, Elizabethtown is now an empty place with plenty of ghosts, courtesy of boarding-house owner Charles Kennedy. Every budget traveler's worst nightmare was realized as he murdered and robbed his guests, then burned the evidence piece by piece. When Kennedy's wife spilled the beans, they lynched the guy.

Eventually, the mines dried up and folks moved on, but you can still see the melting adobe walls of **Mutz Hotel** reaching into the broad sky, more reminiscent of pueblo ruins than what you'd expect from an Old West ghost town. **Elizabethtown Museum** (☎ 377-3420; NM 38; donations appreciated; ☺ 10am-5pm May-Sep) gives you the perfect excuse to investigate. The small museum is packed with wall-to-wall antiquities, most dating between 1870 and 1915. **Gold Rush Days** (early July) brings out folks in era costumes. The owners will also point you toward the creepy cemetery, old buildings and other areas of interest, and perhaps divulge a few more scary stories.

Eagle Nest

☎ 505 pop 300 winter/500 summer elevation 8382ft

Though it doesn't have Red River's range of services, Eagle Nest is a better lodging choice if you just can't handle the tourist overkill. The mile-long arts-and-crafts strip (US 64; crossed by roads like 'Humbug Dr') makes for a nice stroll, but outdoor access is the real draw.

This mining community, originally called Therma, found quicker ways to get rich shortly after statehood. It became something of a gambling mecca in the 1920s, attracting winners and losers from Santa Fe en route to the Raton racetrack. Gambling eventually lost its allure, and you may be able to spot old slot machines at the bottom of Eagle Nest Lake.

The tiny **chamber of commerce** (☎ 377-9117; 800-494-9117; www.eaglenest.org; Therma Dr; ☺ 10am-4pm Tue-Sat) has piles of information on the Enchanted Circle, Cimarron Canyon State Park and the **Valle Vidal Loop** (p174), which begins here, and the chamber's excellent website has links to the area's six scenic RV parks and other area businesses.

CIMARRON CANYON STATE PARK

Three miles north of Eagle Nest on US 64, this dramatic 8-mile stretch of scenic Cimarron River (Map p171; ☎ 888-667-2757 information, 877-664-7787 reservations; www.nmparks.com; campsite/RV $10/14), hued in pine greens and volcanic grays, encompasses Horseshoe Mine, beaver ponds, lots of wildlife and fishing, and plenty of hikes.

Three developed campgrounds have showers, running water and electrical hookups: **Tolby Creek** is the closest to Eagle Nest, with easy access to 14-mile Tolby Creek Canyon Trail, along old logging roads that would probably make for good mountain biking; **Maverick** abuts the gravel lake pits (prettier than they sound); and **Ponderosa** has access to 10-mile Maverick Canyon Trail.

There's also primitive, five-tent **Blackjack Campground**, with port-o-potties and no running water. It's closest to two of the

TAOS

prettiest hikes in the park: 4-mile-roundtrip **Jasper and Agate Trails**, popular among the horseback set, and lovely 7-mile roundtrip **Clear Creek Canyon Trail**, which follows a mossy little stream punctuated with waterfalls and lined with aspen trees, which makes for a golden-hued hike come September.

Rock climbers can attempt the cliffs at **Cimarron Palisades** close to Palisades Picnic Area (permits required), or just take advantage of the photo op, while **Horseshoe Mine** is just a short walk from the day-use parking lot.

EAGLE NEST LAKE

Spreading across more than 2200 acres, this expansive lake is why most folks are here. Originally dammed by ranchers in 1918 – an impressive job – the lake is now stocked with trout, kokonee and koho salmon, and you can row around and admire the reflection of Wheeler Peak while attempting to catch dinner.

It's not what you'd call a pristine mountain experience, but it's certainly entertaining – especially on July 4, when Eagle Nest explodes a disproportionately large fireworks show over the lake. **Eagle Nest Marina** (☎ 377-6941; www.angelfire-nm.com/cabins; US 64) rents several different kinds of boats ($85-200 per day) and fishing tackle, and sells fishing licenses.

SLEEPING & EATING

D&D Motel (☎ 377-2408, 800-913-9548; 116 Therma Dr; d $45-85, cabin with kitchenette $85-175; **P**) Don't expect another cookie-cutter hotel experience at this wonderful place. The cabins – basically prefab trailers – have been brightly decorated, and the 'large cabin,' which sleeps seven comfortably, is so much like landing in a comfy country home (real country, not B&B mythological country) that you almost expect to find a pot of green beans simmering in the full kitchen.

Laguna Vista Lodge (☎ 377-6522, 800-821-2093; www.lagunavistalodge.com; 51 Therma Dr; d low/high $80/100, f $150-200; **P** ✖) This place has spacious, beautiful rooms and amenities galore, including kitchenettes in the family suites, while the neighboring **restaurant and saloon** (lunch $10, dinner $10-20; ✆ 11am-2am Mon-Sat, noon-midnight Sun) serves burgers, salads and trout.

There are several other restaurants in town, but grab breakfast at **Cowboy's Corner Cafe** (☎ 377-9525; cnr US 64 & NM 38; mains $3-11), serving freedom toast and a variety of egg breakfasts, plus freedom fries alongside the recommended barbecue at lunch. French visitors may want to give this one a miss.

Vietnam Veterans Memorial

This gracefully sculpted memorial (Map p171; ☎ 377-6900; Hwy 64; donations appreciated), overlooking the vast and lonely plains, was the first monument built to honor US troops in Vietnam. Dr Victor Westphall built the shrine in the memory of his son, David Westphall III, who died in battle as hostilities exploded in 1968.

The sanctuary lies just beyond the Huey helicopter parked outside, silently guarding a simple and genuinely moving **chapel**, open 'forever.' It's a place where former soldiers have found solace since 1969, when so many Americans were unable to understand all that they had faced. They still stream in and out, veterans of many wars, stopping to light a candle or study twelve portraits of fallen soldiers, changed monthly for photos donated by families across the country.

The **visitors center** (✆ 9am-5pm daily) has become a museum, hung with the American and South Vietnamese flags, among others. It displays artifacts, exhibits and personal items that attempt to convey the experience of being a soldier, or family member, during that conflict. Doves should note that there's no glamorizing of war in this place. The message board, in fact, reveals quite the opposite.

Angel Fire

☎ 505 pop 1048 summer/2300 winter elevation 8382ft

It's sort of like the lost suburb, centered on massive and media-savvy Angel Fire Resort, which boasts the closest slopes to Taos where you can snowboard. It doubles in size when the snow machines start to hum, and summer attracts baked refugees from lower altitudes.

The **chamber of commerce** (☎ 377-6661; 800-446-8117; www.angelfirechamber.org; 3407 NM 434; ✆ 9am-5pm Mon-Sat) has lots information on area businesses, with a huge rack of flyers available 24 hours from the lobby out front.

SKIING

Angel Fire Resort (Map p171; ☎ 377-6401, 800-931-7001; www.angelfireresort.com; NM 434; lift tickets 1-day adult/child $45/36, 5-day $221/176; ☼ 9am-4pm daily October-March) As if the 2077ft vertical drop and 450 acres of trails weren't enough, the resort recently underwent a massive $40 million retrofit, adding lifts, trails, snowbiking (on bikes with skis), snowskating (on skateboards without wheels) and a whole new ski park just for kids, making this is one serious winter wonderland.

The resort takes full advantage of the Taos Ski Valley snowboard ban with **Liberation Park**, featuring the state's only half-pipe: a Chris Gunnarson–designed, 400ft-long, competition-quality monster, with a wicked 26% grade. You can, like, totally take advantage of all this with the Learn to Snowboard, Keep the Gear deal, including two days of lessons plus boots and board for $249. Dude.

Rent **ski packages** (☎ 800-633-7463; 1-day adult/child $20/13) and snowboards (adult/child $32/28) snowshoes ($12), snow bikes ($35), and just about anything else you might need for fun. You may get better prices on rental equipment from **Bump's Ski Shop** (☎ 800-993-4754; NM 434) or **Ski Tech** (☎ 377-3213; NM 434).

OTHER ACTIVITIES

The resort offers guided **snowmobile** tours, or rent your own and pick up a map to trails at the chamber of commerce.

Valle Escondido Golf Course (☎ 758-3475; NM 64; $40) has the third-highest-altitude 18-hole course in the USA (your ball will fly) where elk come to relax in the early evening – you could consider this a hazard or just play through. **Roadrunner Tours** (☎ 337-6416; www.rtours.com; NM 434; hour/day $25/185 incl lunch) offers horseback rides with add-ons including gold panning, dinner by a campfire, riding lessons or even multiday pack trips and cattle drives ($200-600).

In summer Angel Fire Resort organizes lots of activities for kids (mostly geared to small children and pre-teens) including miniature golf, mountain biking, summer chairlift rides from June through Labor Day, fishing and tubing in private **Monte Verde Lake** (☎ 377-9971), and a 5200ft-long maze where you can lose them for hours. Not long enough? Child care is also available in summer.

The most popular event is **Wings over Angel Fire** (☎ 800-446-8117; 1/3 days $6/10; third weekend in Jul), a three-day hot air balloon festival with an air show, arts and crafts, food stalls and games for the kids. **Balloons and Professional Services** (☎ 377-2477, 888-993-2477; www.bipsnm.com; $150) can take you aloft anytime.

SLEEPING & EATING

There are some 2000 vacation homes in the area, and **Advantage Property Management** (☎ 377-2442, 888-924-2442) can set you up in one. For reservations at lodges, B&Bs and hotels, try **Angel Fire Central Reservations** (☎ 377-3072, 800-323-5793; www.angelfirenm.com/cenres/index.html).

Angel Fire Resort (Map p171; ☎ 377-6401, 800-931-7001; www.angelfireresort.com; NM 434; d summer/winter $90/209, ste summer/winter $120/359; P ✗ ✗ 🖳 🕭) Comprehensive and self-contained, it's got three restaurants, package deals, child care (☎ 377-4213; $50-60 per day) and much more. Summer means empty rooms so bargain. With all the activities for children, it's a good deal for families, especially if the kids need a break from being cooped up in the car.

Elkhorn Lodge (☎ 377-2811; 3377 NM 434; d low/high $79/89, f $135-150; P ✗) has a more central location, decks off all rooms, and suites with kitchenettes that sleep six. **Red Cloud Ranch** (☎ 751-1005; www.redcloudranch.com; NM 434; $125-150 incl breakfast; summer only; P) is a cluster of rustic cabins at the epicenter of a series of hiking and biking trails throughout adjacent Carson National Forest, with a hot tub, trout pond and four-course dinner ($40).

The **Early Bird Café and Bakery** (☎ 377-3992; 3420 NM 434; mains 4-8; ☼ 6:30am-2pm daily) has pastries, big breakfasts and excellent lunch sandwiches. **Rocky Mountain BBQ & Grill** (☎ 377-2765; NM 434; mains $9-12; ☼ 11am-8pm Mon-Sat) is the place to go for barbecued chicken, beef and pork.

The **Roasted Clove** (☎ 377-0636; 48 N Angel Fire Rd; mains $15-28; ☼ 5:30-9:30pm Wed-Mon) is everyone's favorite fine dining: chipotle roasted chicken, forestièrre (sautéed wild mushrooms) and mesquite-grilled filet are just a few of the gourmet dishes that you'll be snarfing with the perfect fine-wine accompaniment.

GETTING THERE & AROUND

Angel Fire is strung out along the northern terminus of NM 434, just south of the intersection with US 64 and the Vietnam Veterans Memorial, beginning a scenic route that could take you through Mora to Las Vegas, a great meander if you've got some extra time. Otherwise, continue on US 64 through the Carson National Forest back to Taos.

The **Magic Bus** (☎ 377-6856; $1-3; 🕗 7:30am-5:30pm Mon-Wed, 7:30am-10pm Thu-Sun winter) has regular winter routes and operates on-demand during summer; currently it can take you as far as the Vietnam Memorial, and there's discussion of reestablishing service to Eagle Nest.

Faust Transportation (☎ 758-3410, 888-830-3410; www.newmexiconet.com/trans/faust/faust.html; 🕗 7am-9pm) offers shuttle service year-round.

Shadybrook & Carson National Forest

Just when the endless vistas of alpine meadows and sheer granite peaks start

getting old, it's back into the forest as US 64 descends from the high plains.

Casitas at Shadybrook (☎ 758-7737; 26219 US 64; d $75-150; Ⓟ ☒ ☒) has one- and two-bedroom suites, lavishly remodeled with saltillo floors, fireplaces and lots of Central American extras; you can fish and hike from the property. **Quina's Shadybrook Cafe** (mains $7-11; 🕗 8am-2:30pm Sun-Thu, 8am-9pm Fri & Sat) has a pleasant porch and dining room where you can sample Quina's Cuban roasted pork and lasagna.

Carson National Forest (Map p171; ☎ 758-6200; www.fs.fed.us/r3/carson) administers most of the final 10 miles back to Taos, with several campsites (and some private cabins) along the way. Sites with drinking water run $6; others are otherwise free.

La Sombra Drinking water, fishing and three RV-friendly sites.

Capulin Pull-through sites for RVs, drinking water and a trail to the 'ice cave,' fronted by a waterfall.

Taos Creek Cabins (☎ 758-4715; US 64; d $90-120; Ⓟ ☒) Beautiful cabins with full kitchens, luxuriously rustic interiors, fireplaces, televisions and decks (but no

---

DETOUR: THE BACK ROAD TO LAS VEGAS

It's off the beaten track, not even ranking as one of New Mexico Tourism's '24 Scenic Byways,' but this lovely route heads south from Angel Fire on NM 434 straight into the Rincon Mountains. Allow at least three hours to watch green fields and ponderosa pine forests trade off beneath the gaze of distant peaks.

You'll pass **Coyote Creek State Park** (☎ 888-667-2757, reservations 877-664-7787; www.nmparks.com; NM 434; campsite/RV $10/14), a tiny but beautiful place boasting the most densely stocked fishing ponds in the state, shady campsites and short trails through the cottonwood and pine.

Continue south through the villages of Guadalupita and El Turquillo to **Alpaca Victory Ranch** (☎ 387-2254; www.victoryranch.com; NM 434; adult/child $3/2; 🕗 10am-3pm Fri-Sun), where you can pet prize-winning alpacas or buy wearables woven from their hair.

Mora is the closest thing to a town around, so stop and grab some sustenance after the intersection with NM 518 at **Hatcha's Cafe** (☎ 387-6034; mains $3-8; 🕗 7am-9pm Mon-Sat), a family-owned New Mexican restaurant with great sopapillas and beer. You can detour along rough, unpaved NM 94 to **Morphy Lake State Park** (☎ 888-667-2757, reservations 877-664-7787; www.nmparks.com; NM 94; campsite $10), with no plumbed water but with a stocked lake and sparkling creek where you can camp and catch dinner.

Continue south on Hwy 518 into **La Cueva,** with a fully operational granary and mill on display at the **Cleveland Roller Mill Museum** (☎ 387-2645; NM 518; adult/child $2/1; 🕗 10am-3pm Sat & Sun May-Oct), featuring photos and artifacts from the adobe edifice's 1850s heyday. Summer visitors can also stop by 30,000-acre **Salman Ranch** (☎ 988-8848; NM 518) and pick raspberries in late August, or purchase jams, fresh produce and snacks all summer long.

From here, the last leg of your journey skirts the **Pecos Wilderness,** taking you through **Sapello** and into **Las Vegas** (p138), where you can catch I-25 for the one-hour straight shot to Santa Fe.

phones), plus a short trail to a waterfall just outside (read: decadent retreat).

Las Petacas RV-friendly with pull-through sites (running water but no hookups), plus fishing the Rio Fernando and hiking the North Boundary Trail to Capulin Canyon.

La Vinateria Drinking water, fishing access on the Rio Fernando and pleasant family sites.

El Nogal No drinking water, but fishing and hiking the 6-mile Devisadero Loop Trail along the ridgeline, or biking South Boundary Trail.

TAOS

Directory

CONTENTS

ACCOMMODATIONS

Accommodations range from the disturbingly downscale (meth labs, prostitutes) to the obscenely luxurious, running $450 or more a night for every possible amenity (Persian rugs, day trips to Canyon de Chelly – by plane). Don't discount B&Bs, practically an art form in both Santa Fe and Taos, where there are good mid-range deals as well as luxury properties – and many rooms even have private entrances like a hotel, so ask. There are also plenty of wackier options, like earthships and old communes, and a decent network of hostels. RV Parks and campsites are plentiful, but keep in mind that nights are cold from October through May.

Lodging isn't cheap, and this book defines budget rooms as under $60 per night, low season; mid-range $60 to $100; and top-end right on up into the stratosphere. Don't be afraid to bargain. If your road karma is good (tipping hotel staff helps) you may be able to talk proprietors down by 30% or more on weekdays and during the off-season, particularly at luxury properties. Too shy? When you're quoted a rate, simply ask,

'Do you have anything cheaper?' AARP, AAA and other discounts are also common, so ask. You can also ask for discounts on multinight stays. One caveat: late summer and the Christmas holidays are high season. Make reservations as far in advance as possible, and expect rates to double.

RVs and Campsites

RV parks, most of which allow tent camping, are plentiful and usually located on the outskirts of town. Campgrounds on public lands generally run $7-10 per night for tent sites and $14-20 with hookups. Not all public campgrounds have running water. Backcountry camping is free, but you must have a permit. The ranger stations administrating each region are noted throughout the text.

The **Public Lands Information Center** (Map p75; ☎ 505-438-7542, 877-276-9404; www.publiclands.org; 1474 Rodeo Rd, Santa Fe; ☼ 9am-4:30pm Mon-Fri) has information on all of them and issues backcountry camping and hiking permits. You can't reserve campsites on federal land, but **New Mexico State Parks** (☎ 888-667-2757, reservations 877-664-7787; www.nmparks.com; Santa Fe; campsite/RV $10/14; ☼ 8am-4pm Mon-Fri) takes reservations for the 29 state parks that allow camping.

Hostels

Hostels are few and far between, but all are festive and fairly well kept, with bunks running about $15 per night, private rooms about $35 a night. None have lockout and all offer full use of kitchen facilities. Those covered in this book are:

Route 66 Hostel (p60) In Albuquerque.
Sandia Mountain Hostel (p67) In Sandia Crest, north of Albuquerque.
Santa Fe International Hostel (p95)
Rio Grande Gorge HI Hostel (p132) In Pilar, south of Taos.
The Abominable Snowmansion (p168) In Arroyo Seco, north of Taos.

Rental Properties

Many people maintain vacation homes near Taos and Santa Fe, which they rent out through various agencies. Rentals range from tiny adobe casitas to huge ranch-style homes, and you'll get better deals by staying a week or more. Some agencies include:

The Management Group (☎ 505-982-2823, 800-283-2211; www.santaferentals.com)
Santa Fe Stay (☎ 505-820-2468, 800-995-2272; www.santafestay.com)
Kokopelli Property Management (☎ 505-988-7244, 888-988-7244; www.kokoproperty.com)

Motels
Motels tend to be well kept and basic, and in ski areas they often have rooms sleeping six, a great deal for a group or family.

Motels are generally less expensive the farther you are from downtown, and often offer a continental breakfast, replete with plastic-wrapped pastries. The cheapest motels, including many on Central Ave in Albuquerque and in central Española, may also serve as flophouses for down-on-their-luck locals. Seasoned budget travelers who don't mind those conditions can get rooms for under $30. Most entries listed in this book run $40 to $80, with prices skyrocketing in high season.

B&Bs
Bed and breakfasts really run the gamut, from glorified hotels costing $60 to $90 to absolutely stunning antique-filled properties, ranging from $80 to $140 and up, with full hot breakfasts, fabulous amenities and refreshments in the evening. The **New Mexico Bed & Breakfast Association** (☎ 800-661-6649; www.nmbba.org) has listings and links for B&Bs all over the state.

Hotels & Resorts
Hotels on the commercial strip, farther from downtown, usually run $60 to $150 a night, but those within walking distance to the plaza are much pricier, ranging from $100 a night right up into the stratosphere.

Invariably decorated in Southwestern style, they often have pools, plus onsite restaurant/bars, coffeemakers in the rooms and a continental breakfast. Kitchenettes and fireplaces are often available for around $20 more, while basic suites run $30 to $50 extra.

Resort-style accommodations, with all that plus pueblo revival architecture, spas, concierges, fireplaces and generally better locations (or shuttles to get you there) tack on an extra $40 – at least – for those amenities. True resorts (those out in the country) can include everything from horseback riding and childcare to natural hot springs. Prices vary widely.

BUSINESS HOURS
Many businesses close on Sunday or keep shorter hours. Small businesses may also close for lunch. Particularly in rural areas, but even in Santa Fe, businesses may close for a day or week unannounced – hey, everyone needs a vacation. Businesses geared to tourism and museums (particularly in Taos) may also keep shorter hours in winter and other off-season periods.

Shops and **galleries** are generally open 9am to 5pm daily, sometimes taking off Sunday or Monday; some galleries keep longer hours Friday evening for art openings. **Bars** are usually open from 11am until 2am Monday through Saturday, closing at midnight Sunday by law.

Restaurant hours vary widely, and many close from 2pm to 5pm – ah, siesta culture. Most restaurants close early, around 9pm or 10pm; even bars close their kitchens at that time.

Indian pueblos may close to visitors with just a few hours notice for religious purposes. **Casinos** are open 8am to 4am Sunday through Thursday, and remain open round the clock from Thursday morning until Sunday night. On feast days, almost all businesses at that particular pueblo are closed.

CHILDREN
New Mexico is an extremely kid-friendly destination. Between the strong Catholic and hippie traditions, most folks are comfortable with rambunctious children just about anywhere. Local parents are quick to recommend sights, activities and restaurants to visitors, so don't be shy. Lonely Planet's *Travel with Children* has lots of tips and advice for keeping kids happy and healthy on the road.

Practicalities
Museums and other attractions generally offer discounts for children (the age

varies widely, however) as well as a range of children's activities. Only the most exclusive restaurants will turn up their noses at kids, and the rest usually have children's menus.

Some B&Bs do not accept children, but this is more the exception than the rule. Call ahead. Many other lodging options have large family rooms and casitas with kitchenettes, hide-a-beds and even playgrounds outside. In larger cities, services will send sitters to your hotel room; check the yellow pages.

The **Childcare Provider Hotline** (☎ 800-691-9067; www.newmexicokids.org) is primarily geared toward residents but has listings of accredited providers and other information. Breast feeding is legal and, in general, acceptable throughout New Mexico.

Keep in mind that children are more sensitive to sunburn, dehydration and altitude sickness than adults: Slather them with sunscreen and make sure they wear hats and are getting enough liquids. Allow them to acclimate for a few days before taking on any serious activities. Ensure that they stay well away from sick or dying animals, particularly groundhogs and other rodents, many of which carry diseases.

Sights & Activities

Every newspaper and free weekly includes listings for children's events and activities. Pick up the free monthly *New Mexico Kids!* (www.newmexico-kids.com), with information on kids' stuff in Albuquerque and throughout the state, and the quarterly *Tumbleweeds*, covering Santa Fe and the surrounding area. Brief rundowns of attractions geared toward kids are included in the Santa Fe (p91) and Taos (p155) chapters.

New Mexicans take pride in their tricultural community, and showcase Native American culture, Hispanic history and Anglo arts with a focus on inclusiveness and understanding, making it a great place to inoculate your children against small-mindedness while they're still small.

Outdoor activities are another highlight: between the rafting trips through the canyon lands, oddball opportunities like llama excursions and hot air balloon rides, and short hiking trails that feature not only wildlife, but petroglyphs and caves,

your child will remember this vacation for a long time.

CLIMATE CHARTS

Don't like New Mexico weather? Just wait a minute. This is a land of extremes, and in fall or spring, you may have snow on the ground in the morning and T-shirt weather by afternoon. Even summer visitors should bring jackets. For more information, check out the When to Go section (p9) in the Getting Started chapter.

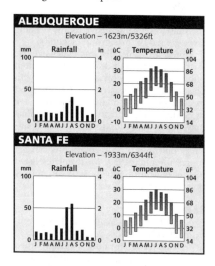

DANGERS & ANNOYANCES
Crime

New Mexico ranks near the bottom of US states in personal income, yet it attracts wealthy tourists who often flash their cash around. You do the math.

Yep, New Mexico ranks second in the USA for overall crime, first in burglary. Sure, you'll be helping support the local economy if you park your gear-packed car in an isolated spot (this most definitely includes trailheads) or carry all your cash in a cute handbag, but why not buy more art instead? Keep the car clean, and stash emergency money and credit card contact information somewhere other than your wallet, perhaps in your luggage or under the seat of your car.

Rio Arriba County, just north of Santa Fe, has the highest rate of heroin overdose in the country. While the situation is improving, don't count on criminals to be predictable, just desperate. And though Chimayó and Española get most of the press, drug addiction and the attendant criminal activity is a statewide problem. Stay alert.

Weather
Desert temperatures are extremely variable, easily dropping 40°F when the sun goes down. Carry an extra layer when hiking, even in summer. Don't underestimate the effects of dehydration: you may not realize how much you're sweating (it evaporates quickly) and become disoriented. Folks have died getting lost on a day hike. Bring and drink a gallon of water per person, per day.

Thunderstorms roll in regularly, but not exclusively, on summer afternoons, when you should try to be below the tree line at higher elevations. And even if you haven't had a drop of rain, a wall of water can come barreling down a dusty arroyo with little or no warning. Never camp in anything resembling a waterway, no matter what the forecast.

Wildlife
Scorpions and tarantulas in this region are not deadly, though they do leave nasty welts. More worrisome are potentially deadly (particularly for kids) black widow and brown recluse spiders, both of which enjoy outhouses and other shady spots. If bitten, get to a doctor.

Rattlesnakes, with diamond-shaped markings, easily have enough venom to kill. They enjoy sunbathing on rocks and roads on chilly mornings, when you're most likely to surprise them. Generally they strike only when threatened, so just give them their space. If bitten, refer to the Health chapter for first-aid instructions, and get to a hospital as quickly as possible.

Black bears can be pesky but are smart enough not to bother you. If you see one up close, back away slowly, speaking softly, to let them know you mean no harm. Pack up all foodstuffs when you leave a campsite, and don't leave any food, toothpaste or other tasty-smelling treats in the tent.

Wildfires
Between the drought, the piñon bark beetle and long-term fire suppression, New Mexico is currently undergoing a massive ecosystems overhaul, courtesy of Mother Nature and morons who flick cigarettes out of cars. Wildfires over the past few years have been devastating.

The **National Interagency Fire Center** (www.nifc.gov) has up-to-date information on wildfires and regions affected. While you're unlikely to be surprised by a fire, don't discount that plume of smoke on the horizon. And for heaven's sake, make sure your campfire is absolutely, 100% completely out.

DISABLED TRAVELERS
Although laws requiring all businesses to be wheelchair-accessible are in place, centuries-old areas like downtown Santa Fe and Taos still have some prohibitively narrow sidewalks and doorways. Steps are being taken, if slowly, to live up to regulations.

Public parking is free for anyone with a disabled placard. Most better hotels maintain at least one wheelchair-accessible room, and guide dogs are welcome at all businesses. Some B&Bs keep pets and livestock, and while legally bound to accept your well-behaved pooch, owners may be uncomfortable with how their own animals will act. Call first.

The Governor's Committee on Concerns of the Handicapped (☎ 505-827-6465, 800-552-8195, TTD 505-827-6399; www.state.nm.us/gcch; 491 Old Santa Fe Trail ste 117) has a semi-useful (but it has potential) online guide to the region, and three free pamphlets that can be mailed to you: *Access New Mexico* and *Access Santa Fe*, listing businesses with accessibility details, and *Directory of Recreational Activities for Children with Disabilities*, with information on amusement parks and camping. The New Mexico State Parks TTD is ☎ 505-827-7465.

New Mexico's **Adaptive Ski Program** (☎ 505-995-9858; www.adaptiveski.org), at Santa Fe Ski Basin and Sandia Ski Park, offers lessons including special equipment, if required, for folks with a wide range of disabilities. Make reservations two weeks in advance for lessons ($40-60).

Wheelchair Getaways (☎ 505-247-2626, 800-642-2042; www.wheelchairgetaways.com), located in Albuquerque, rents wheelchair-accessible vans.

DISCOUNT CARDS

Many motels and hotels offer discounts to holders of **AAA** (p194; ☎ 800-874-7532; www .aaa.com) and **AARP** (p181; ☎ 800-424-3410; www.aarp.org) cards, while **student IDs** can often score you savings at attractions.

Traveler Discount Guide (☎ 800-222-3948; www.roomsaver.com) Available at any visitors center or by mail, coupons offering substantial savings on chains hotels are also downloadable.

New Mexico Department of Tourism (www .newmexico.org) Order a free visitors guide and New Mexico Discount Card, with deals on more than 400 businesses.

FESTIVALS & EVENTS

New Mexico loves a good party, and special events involving everything from upscale wine tastings and studio tours to motorcycle rallies and exploding 50ft-tall puppets are just part of the fun. See p92 for schedules of larger events in Santa Fe, p156 for Taos and p60 for Albuquerque. Newspapers, visitors guides and free weeklies provide much more comprehensive listings.

FOOD

New Mexican cuisine is a highlight of any visit, and the Food & Drink chapter (p47) has a rundown on all the delicious dishes waiting in store. You can fill up at budget spots for $3 to $8, while mid-range restaurants serve quality cuisine in the $8 to $15 range. Top end spots start at $15 for dinner, but often serve the same fine food far more cheaply at lunch.

GAY & LESBIAN TRAVELERS

Gays and lesbians can travel more openly in Northern New Mexico than almost anywhere else in the country, though sadly, hate crimes are not unknown, so consider refraining from public displays of affection in quiet neighborhoods after dark, particularly in rural areas. Neither Taos nor Santa Fe (p94) has a real 'gay scene,' but Albuquerque has a few gay and lesbian bars, and the Nob Hill area has a cluster of gay-friendly businesses. But the region is so integrated that establishing gay neighborhoods has never really been necessary.

New Mexico boasts the most comprehensive legal protection in the country for gays and lesbians, going so far as to guarantee equal treatment not only for sexual orientation but also sexual identity, unique in the USA. The free monthly *Out! Magazine* (www.outmagazine.com) maintains a great website with listings and links. There are several organizations with more information:

Coalition for Equality in New Mexico (☎ 505-424-7161, 888-304-2366; www.coalitionforequalitynm.org)
Albuquerque Lesbian and Gay Chamber of Commerce (☎ 505-243-6767)
Parents, Families and Friends of Lesbians & Gays (☎ 505-424-8951; www.pflag.org)

HOLIDAYS

Religious holidays – Christmas and Easter – see some businesses close for a week, about how long it takes to walk to Chimayó.

New Year's Day January 1
Martin Luther King Jr Day Third Monday in January
Presidents' Day Third Monday in February
Easter A Sunday in March or April
Memorial Day Last Monday in May
Independence Day July 4
Labor Day First Monday in September
Columbus Day/Dia de la Raza Second Monday in October
Veterans Day November 11
Thanksgiving Fourth Thursday in November
Christmas December 25

INSURANCE

Medical care in the United States is prohibitively expensive, and while New Mexico has clinics and programs for uninsured people, you'll be taking a serious risk to both your health and pocketbook if you go without. Health insurance, discussed further in the Health chapter (p196), is imperative.

Travel insurance should cover you for medical expenses, emergency care and evacuations, luggage theft or loss, cancellations or delays in your travel arrangements, and everyone should be covered for the worst possible case, such as an accident that requires hospital treatment and a flight home. Buy insurance as early as possible, and take a copy of your policy, in case the original is lost.

INTERNET ACCESS

Almost every New Mexico library offers Internet access for free or a nominal charge. Youth hostels, visitors centers and senior centers also often offer Internet access. All New Mexico Kinko's offer 24-hour Internet access ($6-12/hour). Internet cafés, which charge similar prices, are a growing business but are still hard to find outside Albuquerque, Santa Fe and Taos.

LEGAL MATTERS

If you are stopped by the police for any reason, remember that there is no system of paying fines on the spot, and offering to do so constitutes bribery. Smile, be friendly and cooperate (this only helps you), and provide photo identification when asked. If you are arrested, you have the right to remain silent until speaking to an attorney, and are presumed innocent until proven guilty. Note that all pueblos and Indian reservations are basically sovereign nations, with their own police and laws.

You must be 16 years old to drive, 21 years old to drink alcohol, and are considered a drunk driver at .08% blood alcohol content – roughly two alcoholic drinks. Ask the bartender to call you a cab.

Marriage licenses are easier to get in New Mexico than a taxi: the bride and groom must each appear in person and present a driver's license, passport or birth certificate, plus $25 in cash, to the **Santa Fe County Clerk's Office** (☎ 505-986-6281; 102 Grant Ave; 🕑 8am-4pm Mon-Fri). That's it – no blood test, no need for residency, and they'll even help find a judge and give you a 'Wedding Gift Pack,' including free samples of dish soap.

MAPS

The maps provided in this book are fine for paths more traveled, and all visitors centers stock free maps of varying (usually poor) quality. Folding street maps, usually $4 at any gas station, are a good investment. *The Horton Family Map*, a locally produced atlas of street maps covering Santa Fe and the surrounding communities, is worthwhile if you'll be in the area for a while.

If you plan to get out into the wilderness, the *New Mexico Road & Recreation Atlas* is indispensable; if you're only going to dip your toes into the great outdoors, the excellent *Highroad Map of North Central New Mexico* is a great, if somewhat outdated, folding map covering Northern New Mexico. Serious hikers should get USGS topos for the region they plan to

explore; these are available at ranger stations and map stores, or for free online through **LANL** (http://sar.lanl.gov/maps_by_name.html).

Travel Bug (Map pp76-7; ☎ 505-992-0418; www .mapsofnewmexico.com; 328 S Guadalupe St), in Santa Fe, and **Holman's** (☎ 505-449-3810; 6201 Jefferson St NE), in Albuquerque, have the best selections of maps in the state.

SENIOR TRAVELERS

Travelers aged 50 years and older can expect to receive cut rates and benefits. Be sure to inquire about such rates at hotels, museums and restaurants. The National Park Service issues Golden Age Passports that cut costs greatly for seniors. Other organizations worth looking into include:

American Association of Retired Persons (AARP; ☎ 800-424-3410; www.aarp.org) This advocacy group for Americans 50 years and older is a good resource for travel bargains.
Elderhostel (☎ 617-426-8056; www.elderhostel.org) This nonprofit organization offers folks 55 years and older one- to three-week tours throughout the USA and Canada, including meals and accommodations.
Grand Circle Travel (☎ 617-350-7500, 800-350-7500; www.gct.com) This group offers escorted tours and travel information, mainly for mature travelers.

TOURIST INFORMATION

All major cities and most rural communities have a visitors center or chamber of commerce with flyers, maps and other information. Some pueblos have visitors centers, while others provide information through their Governor's Office. Ranger stations stock information on public lands as well as the surrounding communities. These websites are excellent sources of information for planning your trip:

New Mexico Department of Tourism
(www.newmexico.org) Information and links to accommodations, attractions and other great websites.
North-Central New Mexico Guide
(www.newmexiconorth.com) Museums, missions, landmarks and pueblos, plus links and recommended driving tours in the Santa Fe-Taos region.
Indian Pueblo Cultural Center
(www.indianpueblo.org) Schedules of feast days and dances, plus cultural information, for all 19 Indian Pueblos.
New Mexico's Cultural Treasures (www.nmculture.org) A fabulous searchable and comprehensive listing of every last museum and cultural attraction.

(Continued on page 190)

INTERNATIONAL VISITORS

ENTERING THE COUNTRY

Welcome to Fortress USA: security protocols at all points of entry into the country are tightening, with new procedures being added almost monthly. These range from increasingly invasive baggage checks and searches to stricter visa requirements. Contact your US embassy or log on to the US Department of Homeland Security's Customs and Border Protection website (www.customs.ustreas.gov) for the latest safety and security measures, and expect long waits at the airport.

Passports

At press time, seven nations were identified by the US government as state sponsors of terrorism: North Korea, Cuba, Syria, Sudan, Iran, Iraq and Libya. Visitors from these countries must fill out giant stacks of paperwork and arrange an interview with a US consulate. If you have passport stamps from these countries, you will not be automatically denied entry into the USA, but it will probably be noted.

New Mexico has three border crossings with Mexico, but the most convenient is at El Paso, Texas, and Ciudad Juarez, Chihuahua. Canadian and US citizens do not need a passport for a 72-hour visit. Mexican nationals and travelers from other countries must have a passport (and nonimmigrant visa) to cross into the USA.

Visas

Canadians must have proper proof of Canadian citizenship or a passport. Visitors from other countries must have valid passports, and many visitors also must have a US visa.

Citizens of these 27 countries can participate in the Visa Waiver Program, which allows visitors with roundtrip, nonrefundable tickets to visit for 90 days without a visa: Andorra, Argentina, Australia, Austria, Belgium, Brunei, Denmark, Finland, France, Germany, Iceland, Ireland, Italy, Japan, Liechtenstein, Luxembourg, Monaco, the Netherlands, New Zealand, Norway, Portugal, San Marino, Singapore, Slovenia, Spain, Sweden, Switzerland and the UK.

As of October 2004 all visitors on this program must have a Machine Readable Passport (MRP) to participate, which includes your biographical information digitally encoded into the passport.

Otherwise you will need a nonimmigrant visa. Check with the State Department Visa Services (http://travel.state.gov/visa_services.html) for the latest information.

If you need a visa, begin the procedure as early as possible. Many foreign nationals who could previously obtain visas by mail are now required to report to a US embassy for a personal interview, which may need to be scheduled weeks in advance. Reports of regular visitors to the USA being suddenly denied visas have become ridiculously common. Plan ahead.

International Driver's License

An International Driving Permit is a useful accessory for foreign visitors in the USA. Local police are more likely to accept it as valid identification than an unfamiliar document from another country. Your national automobile association can provide one for a nominal fee. They're usually valid for one year.

Customs

US Customs allows each person over the age of 21 to bring one liter of liquor and 200 cigarettes duty-free into the USA, and non-US citizens can bring in $100 in gifts and US$10,000 in cash, traveler's checks and money orders; you must declare excess amounts. Visitors must also declare all purchases and gifts received while in the USA when leaving the country; bring your receipts. Each person is allowed to transport $800 worth of goods duty-free. For more information, contact the US Custom Service Albuquerque Field Office (☎ 505-766-2621).

EMBASSIES & CONSULATES

USA Embassies & Consulates

Some US diplomatic offices abroad include:

Australia (☎ 2-6270-5900, 21 Moonah Place, Yarralumla ACT 2600; ☎ 2-9373-9200, Level 59 MLC Centre 19-29 Martin Place, Sydney NSW 2000; ☎ 3-9526-5900, 553 St Kilda Rd, Melbourne, Victoria)

Canada (☎ 613-238-5335, 490 Sussex Dr, Ottawa, Ontario K1N 1G8; ☎ 604-685-4311, 1095 W Pender St, Vancouver, BC V6E 2M6; ☎ 514-398-9695, 1155 rue St-Alexandre, Montréal, Québec)

France (☎ 01 43 12 48 76, 2 rue Saint Florentin, 75001 Paris)

Germany (☎ 30-8305-0, Neustädtische Kirchstr.4-5, 100117 Berlin)

Ireland (☎ 1-668-8777, 42 Elgin Rd, Ballsbridge, Dublin 4)
Israel (☎ 3-519-7575, 71 Hayarkon St, Tel Aviv 63903)
Japan (☎ 3-224-5000, 10-5 Akasaka Chome, Minato-ku, Tokyo 107-8420)
Mexico (☎ 5-209-9100, Paseo de la Reforma 305, Colonia Cuauhtémoc, 06500 Mexico City)
New Zealand (☎ 644-722-2068, 29 Fitzherbert Terrace, Thorndon, Wellington)
Spain (☎ 91587- 2200, Serrano 75, 28006 Madrid; ☎ 93 280 22 27, Paseo Reina Elisenda de Montcada 23, 08034 Barcelona)
United Kingdom (☎ 20-7499-2000, 24 Grosvenor Sq, London W1A 1AE; ☎ 31-556-8315, 3 Regent Terrace, Edinburgh EH7 5BW; ☎ 28-9032-8239, Queens House, 14 Queen St, Belfast BT1 6EQ)

Other US Embassies and Consulates can be found on the government's website at http://usembassy.state.gov.

Embassies & Consulates in New Mexico

Most countries maintain embassies in Washington, DC. The closest consulates for the UK, Canada and Australia are in Los Angeles, California. The **New Mexico Council on International Relations** (☎ 982-4931; www.santafecouncil.org), in Santa Fe, may be able to advise international travelers in the event of an emergency.

French Consulate (☎ 505-989-8929; gmilinaire @aol.com; PO Box 247, Tesuque 87584)
German Consulate (☎ 505-872-0800; mesersmith @aol.com; 4300 San Mateo NE, st B-380, Albuquerque 87110)
Italian Consulate (☎ 505-243-1924, 765-1665; paolaq @umia.com; 1710 Old Town Rd NW, Albuquerque 87104)
Japanese Consulate (☎ 505-293-2322; ikukosnm @aol.com; Albuquerque)
Mexican Consulate (☎ 505-247-2147; 1610 4th St NW, Albuquerque 87102)
Spanish Consulate (☎ 505-898-1082; PO Box 91388, Albuquerque 87199)

MONEY

United States currency is based on the dollar. Bills come in denominations of $1, $5, $10, $20, $50 and $100. The dollar is divided into 100 cents. Coins are the penny or cent (1 cent), nickel (5 cents), dime (10 cents), quarter (25 cents) and half-dollar (50 cents). Dollar coins and two-dollar bills are rarely used.

Traveler's checks can be changed at any bank, and most banks in Santa Fe and Taos will exchange foreign currency. ATMs are common, and you can use debit cards at most businesses, including restaurants.

POST

Postage rates increase every few years, and at press time it cost 37¢ for letters and 23¢ for postcards. International rates were 80¢/48¢ for letters/postcards, slightly less to Canada and Mexico. For rates and zip code information, contact the **United States Postal Service** (☎ 800-275-8777; www.usps.gov).

Mail (poste restante) can be sent General Delivery to any post office that has its own five-digit zip code. Mail is usually held for 10 days before it's returned to sender; request that your correspondents write 'hold for arrival' on their letters. Mail should be addressed like this:

Name
c/o General Delivery
Albuquerque, NM 87106

PRACTICALITIES

- The USA uses the National Television System Committee (NTSC) color TV standard, which is incompatible with other standards (PAL or SECAM) used in Africa, Europe, Asia and Australasia.

- The USA uses 110V and 60 cycles, and the plugs have two (flat) or three (two flat, one round) pins. Most European appliances will require voltage converters and plug adapters.

- Distances are in feet (ft), yards (yds) and miles (m or mi). Three feet equal 1 yard; 1760 yards or 5280 feet equal 1 mile (1.61 kilometers).

- Dry weights are in ounces (oz), pounds (lb) and tons (16 ounces are one pound; 2000 pounds are one ton), but liquid measures differ from dry measures. One pint equals 16 fluid ounces; 2 pints equal 1 quart, a common measure for liquids like milk, which is also sold in gallons (4 quarts).

- Gasoline is dispensed in US gallons, about 20% smaller than Imperial gallons. Pints and quarts are also 20% smaller

(Continued on page 190)

(Continued from page 189)

than Imperial ones. There is a conversion chart on the inside back cover of this book.

TELEPHONE

Currently New Mexico uses only the 505 area code but may introduce the 575 area code for areas outside Albuquerque and Santa Fe before this book is updated. If so, a recorded message will tell you how to redirect your call.

All phone numbers within the USA consist of a three-digit area code followed by a seven-digit local number. If you are calling locally, just dial the seven-digit number. If you are calling long distance, dial 1 + the three-digit area code + the seven-digit number. If you're calling from abroad, the international country code for the USA is ☎ 1.

For nationwide directory assistance, dial ☎ 411.

The 800, 888 or 877 area codes are for toll-free numbers within the USA; some work from Canada. Call ☎ 800-555-1212 to request a company's toll-free number. The 900 area code is for numbers for which the caller pays a premium rate.

Local calls usually cost 50¢ at pay phones, and hotels often add a hefty surcharge for local calls made from their rooms. The best plan is to invest in a phone card, which allows purchasers to pay $5, $10, $20 or $50 in advance, with access through an 800 number. Rates vary widely, so be sure to ask.

To make an international call direct, dial ☎ 011 + the country code + the area code + the phone number.

TIME

The Southwest is on Mountain Time, which is seven hours behind Greenwich Mean Time. When it's noon in Santa Fe, it's 11am in Los Angeles, 2pm in New York City, 7pm in London and 4am in Sydney. Daylight saving time begins on the first Sunday in April, when clocks are put forward one hour, and ends on the last Sunday in October, when the clocks are turned back one hour.

(Continued from page 187)

TOURS

Several operators provide a range of guided tours for groups and individuals; most cost less if you share accommodations.

Rojo Tours and Services (☎ 505-474-8333; www.rojotours.com) Arranges corporate, group and custom trips to Native American sites, artist studios, outdoor attractions and more.

Santa Fe Destinations (☎ 505-995-4525; www.santa fedestinations.com) Specializes in providing groups of 10 to 1200 with upscale packages.

Known World (☎ 800-983-7756; www.knownworld guides.com) Outdoor adventures – including bike treks, fly fishing, rafting and kayaking – with vegetarian meals.

Open Roads, Open Minds (☎ 703-527-6335; www .openroadsopenminds.com) Anasazi ruins and modern Native communities via steam train, raft and horseback.

The World Outdoors (☎ 303-413-0926, 800-488-8483; www.theworldoutdoors.com) Raft the Taos Box, bike the Enchanted Circle and hike, too.

Odyssey Adventures (☎ 800-677-7099; www.hikepaddle.com) Customizable tours of historic sites, plus adventure sports and B&Bs.

Royal Road Tours (☎ 505-982-4512; www.royalroadtours.com) A nonprofit agency with customized group tours emphasizing art, architecture and historical sites.

WOMEN TRAVELERS

The first thing female visitors younger than, say, 70, will notice upon visiting New Mexico are the wide variety of catcalls from passing cars. Generally this is not meant to be threatening; in fact, loosely translated it means, 'Golly, you're attractive.'

There are three ways to deal with this: smile (which may invite further interaction), become frustrated and indignant (which may cause high blood pressure), or ignore it (recommended). Alternately, you could stay in your hotel room.

Women should note that New Mexico ranks third in the country for reported rapes (and second in all crimes), so take all the precautions you would in a major city downtown, no matter how quaint-seeming the village: Park in well-lit areas, stick to populated neighborhoods after dark and trust your gut at the bar.

Transport

WARNING

The information in this chapter is particularly vulnerable to change – prices, routes and schedules change, special deals come and go, and rules and visa requirements are amended. Check directly with the airline or travel agency to make sure you understand how a fare (or a ticket you may buy) works. Get opinions, quotes and advice from as many airlines and travel agencies as possible before you part with your hard-earned cash. The details given in this chapter should be regarded as pointers: they are not a substitute for careful, up-to-date research.

GETTING THERE & AWAY

Historically the region covered by this book has been isolated by geography, which is why it's such a neat place. To reach these settlements along the Rio Grande – basically a long, slender oasis through an otherwise sparsely populated desert – you're either going to spend several hours on the road or rails from other US population centers, traversing some fairly boring stretches of scrub, or take a plane.

AIR
Airports & Airlines
The main hub for all air travel in New Mexico is the Albuquerque International Sunport, with connecting flights to Taos and 27 other cities (Santa Fe's not one of them).

ALBUQUERQUE INTERNATIONAL SUNPORT
This attractive pueblo revival–style airport (Map p64; ABQ; ☎ 244-7700; www.cabq.gov/airport; 2200 Sunport Blvd) is easy to navigate, with two small terminals, lots of art, and a visitors center on the second floor. Though it doesn't offer connecting flights to Santa Fe, bus shuttles make the run several times daily. Rio Grande Air provides service to Taos Municipal Airport three times daily.

Nine major carriers and three regional airlines serve ABQ, with direct flights to 28 US cities. More than half of all flights are operated by **Southwest Airlines** (☎ 800-435-9792 English, 800-826-6667 Spanish; www.iflyswa.com), which serves most of the country from here. Others serving ABQ, along with their most popular direct flights, are:

America West (☎ 800-235-9292; www.americawest.com) Houston and Las Vegas, Nevada.
American (☎ 800-433-7300; www.aa.com) Chicago and Dallas-Fort Worth.
Continental (☎ 800-523-3273; www.continental.com) Newark and Houston, connecting to international flights.
Delta (☎ 800-221-1212; www.delta.com) Salt Lake City, Cincinnati, Dallas-Fort Worth and Atlanta, connecting to international flights.
Frontier (☎ 800-432-1359; www.flyfrontier.com) Denver.
Great Plains (☎ 866-929-8648; www.gpair.com) Oklahoma City, Austin, Nashville and Colorado Springs.
Mesa (☎ 800-637-2247; www.mesa-air.com) Colorado Springs and several New Mexico cities including Roswell, Carlsbad and Farmington.
Northwest (☎ 800-225-2525; www.nwa.com) Minneapolis-St Paul, connecting to international flights.
Rio Grande (☎ 737-9790, 877-435-9742; www.iflyrga.com) Taos.
SkyWest (☎ 800-453-9417; www.skywest.com) Salt Lake City, connecting to Delta and international flights.
United (☎ 800-241-6522; www.ual.com) Denver, connecting to international flights.

There are eight **rental car agencies** at the Sunport. Note that you'll pay an extra 10% concession fee for the privilege of renting directly from the airport. A better bet is to rent from these agencies' city locations, many of which will drop off the car to any Albuquerque address. For more off-site choices, see Rentals under Car in Getting Around, later.

Advantage (☎ 247-1066; www.arac.com) Another location near UNM.
Alamo (☎ 800-327-9633; www.alamo.com)
Avis (☎ 800-331-1212 English, 800-874-3556 Spanish; www.avis.com) Another location near UNM.
Budget (☎ 800-527-0700; www.budget.com)
Dollar (☎ 800-800-4000; www.dollar.com)
Enterprise (☎ 800-736-8222; www.enterprise.com) Several other Albuquerque locations.
Hertz (☎ 800-654-3131; www.hertz.com)
National (☎ 800-227-7368; www.national.com)
Thrifty (☎ 800-847-4389; www.thrifty.com) Another office is right down the street.

SunTran, Albuquerque's public bus system, serves the airport, while **Airport Shuttle** (☎ 505-765-1234) and **Sunport Shuttle** (☎ 505-883-4966, 866-505-4966) both run between the Sunport and Albuquerque addresses 24 hours daily.

Several shuttles make the run from the Sunport to Santa Fe:

Twin Hearts Shuttle (☎ 800-654-9456; www.twin heartsexpress.com; $20; ☉ 7am-9pm daily) Also to downtown Albuquerque and to Taos ($45).
Sandia Shuttle Express (☎ 888-775-5696; www.sandiashuttle.com; $23; ☉ 7am-6pm Mon-Fri, 7am-5pm Sat & Sun)
Herrera Santa Fe Shuttle Coach (☎ 888-833-2300; $21; ☉ 8am-8pm daily)
Faust Transportation (☎ 505-758-3410, 888-830-3410; www.newmexiconet.com/trans/faust/faust.html; $20; ☉ 7am-2pm daily) Also connects to Taos ($40).

SANTA FE MUNICIPAL AIRPORT
This slightly larger airport (Map p116; SAF; ☎ 505-955-2908; 2511 Camino Entrada) is served only by **Great Lakes Air** (☎ 474-5300, 800-554-5111; www.greatlakesav.com), a United Airlines partner, with six flights a day to Denver International Airport for $250 to $350 roundtrip.

Two car rental agencies are located at the airport: **Avis** (☎ 505-471-5892, 800-230-4898; www.avis.com; Airport Rd) and **Hertz** (☎ 244-7211, 800-654-3001; www.hertz.com; Airport Rd).

Roadrunner Shuttle (☎ 505-424-3367; one way/roundtrip $12/20) meets all incoming planes and provides service to any Santa Fe address.

TAOS MUNICIPAL AIRPORT
This tiny airport (Map p147; SKX; ☎ 505-758-4995; Hwy 64) is served by only one commercial carrier, **Rio Grande Air** (p193), with service three times daily from ABQ.

Two rental car agencies are located at the airport: **Enterprise** (☎ 505-737-0514; www .enterprise.com) and **Dollar** (☎ 505-758-3500, 800-800-4000; www.dollar.com). **Faust Transportation** and **Twin Hearts Shuttle** (see above) can arrange transportation from the airport in advance.

LAND
Bus
Greyhound (☎ 800-231-2222; www.greyhound.com), the USA's major bus system, operates throughout New Mexico in conjunction with **TNM&O** (Texas, New Mexico & Oklahoma; ☎ 806-763-5389; www.tnmo.com), a regional carrier that has expanded to cover parts of Colorado, Kansas and Wyoming. Buses connect many larger cities and will drop you off in smaller towns along the way.

Meal stops, usually in inexpensive and unexciting cafés, are made on long trips; you pay for your own food. Buses have on-board toilets, and seats recline for sleeping. Smoking is not permitted. Long-distance bus trips are often available at bargain prices if you purchase or reserve tickets in advance.

Tickets can be bought over the phone or online with a credit card and mailed to you if purchased 10 days in advance, or they can be picked up at the terminal with proper identification. Greyhound terminals also accept traveler's checks and cash. Reservations are made with ticket purchases only.

Fares vary tremendously. Sometimes you can get discount tickets if you buy them three, seven or 21 days in advance. At press time, tickets ran between $10 and $35 for travel within New Mexico, $60 for any journey under 1000 miles and $120 for any journey 1000 to 3000 miles, if purchased two weeks in advance. Generally bus terminals are served by local public buses, but take a cab to your hotel if you arrive after dark.

GREYHOUND DISCOVERY PASSES
Greyhound Discovery Passes offer unlimited travel on Greyhound buses and other regional carriers. US citizens pay between $228 for seven days and $700 for 60 days, with discounts for students and seniors. These tickets can be purchased in advance or from any Greyhound terminal.

Foreign tourists can buy International Discovery Passes, which are about 20% cheaper, usually online or through a travel agency. A variety of passes covering different regions of the USA and Canada are accepted by many regional carriers. TNM&O honors AmeriPass (covering the USA) and CanAmPass (which includes Canada) but does not accept the WestCoast CanAmPass, which can be used on Greyhound buses throughout the western states.

Car

Two major interstates cross in Albuquerque. I-25 (north-south) roughly traces the old Camino Real, connecting Taos with Mexico City. From Albuquerque, I-25 South runs 270 miles (four hours), officially ending at the USA-Mexico border crossing at El Paso, Texas, and Ciudad Juárez, Chihuahua. The road continues to Ciudad Chihuahua and points south as M-45D.

From Santa Fe, I-25 North actually dips southeast for a 65-mile (one-hour) drive to Las Vegas, then turns north for a 300-mile (five-hour) stretch to Denver, Colorado, and points north.

Interstate 40 (east-west) runs basically from sea to shining sea, connecting Albuquerque to Los Angeles, California, via an 800-mile, 12-hour slog past Flagstaff, Arizona, and the Grand Canyon (330 miles, 5½ hours). Heading east, I-40 runs 1800 miles to Durham, North Carolina, just a few hours from the Atlantic Ocean.

Train

Amtrak (☎ 800-872-7245; www.amtrak.com) runs its *Southwest Chief* between Chicago and Los Angeles twice daily, with stops in **Las Vegas** (☎ 800-872-7245); **Lamy** (☎ 505-466-4511), 18 miles south of Santa Fe; and **Albuquerque** (☎ 842-9650; 214 1st St SW). Travel within the state runs from $20 to $30 one way.

Tickets should be booked in advance. Only the Albuquerque station has regular facilities, and trains stop in Lamy and Las Vegas only if you have purchased a ticket in advance. You can arrange a shuttle in advance between Lamy and Santa Fe.

For non-US citizens, Amtrak offers various USA Rail Passes that must be purchased outside the USA (check with a travel agent). Amtrak is not particularly useful for getting around New Mexico; a better bet is to travel here by train, then either use the bus system, such as it is, or rent a car.

GETTING AROUND

New Mexico has a fairly well-developed bus system, augmented by private shuttles that can get you around the corridor between Albuquerque, Santa Fe and Taos, including the (pricey) option of arranging transport into the immediate wilderness areas. That said, renting a car is by far the quickest and easiest way to see the state, and the only way you'll be able to see many smaller towns and pueblos.

AIR

The **Albuquerque International Sunport** (see Getting There & Away, earlier) is the major air hub for New Mexico and offers connecting flights to cities throughout the region. **Rio Grande Air** (☎ 505-737-9790, 877-435-9742; www.iflyrga.com) offers service three times daily to Taos ($70 one way with two weeks advance purchase, $125 the same day). **Mesa Air** (p191) serves several New Mexico cities including Roswell, Carlsbad and Farmington, as well as Colorado Springs, Colorado.

You can catch shuttles to Santa Fe from the Sunport, but to fly into **Santa Fe Municipal Airport** (see Getting There & Away, earlier), you'll have to make the connection in Denver.

BICYCLE

Bicycle activism is huge in New Mexico, where you'll spot stickers reading 'Bikes not Bombs' and 'One Less Car' plastered all over fine rides competing with cars for the roadways. Urban areas, in particular Albuquerque (see p63), have developed elaborate bike paths and multiuse trails, and most public buses have front-loading bicycle racks.

Scenic highways, including the Enchanted Circle and the Turquoise Trail, are popular among road bikers, and locals traverse the entire state without internal combustion year-round.

The state boasts some of the finest mountain biking anywhere, including summertime downhill runs in ski areas, which keep their lifts open for the occasion. Several outfitters offer guided bicycle trips.

TRANSPORT

A couple caveats to this two-wheeled wonderland: aridity, altitude and heat conspire to fell newbies; allow yourself time to acclimate before taking on any serious rides, and drink more water than you ordinarily would. Also keep in mind that New Mexico ranks near the top of traffic deaths – be careful out there!

Bicycle rentals are available in most urban areas and are noted in the text. Some hostels and B&Bs also rent bikes. Bicyclists must follow the same traffic laws as auto drivers, and technically you are required to have a bicycle license and bell, plus a light for night rides.

For more information, contact the **State Highway and Transportation Department** (☎ 505-827-5100; 1120 Cerrillos Rd, Santa Fe), which issues bicycle licenses, good for one year, or the **Bike Coalition of New Mexico** (www.bikenm.org).

BUS

It's possible, though somewhat inconvenient, for travelers with time on their hands to tour most of New Mexico's major population centers by bus. **Greyhound** and **TNM&O buses** (p192) connect many city centers with the rest of the country, including Albuquerque, Santa Fe, Española, Pilar, Taos and Las Vegas. Many stops have convenient connections with public bus systems.

These systems are augmented by several private shuttles, which are listed in the Getting There & Away section, earlier.

CAR & MOTORCYCLE

The very best way to explore New Mexico is by car. Many smaller towns and pueblos, as well as the vast wilderness areas that deserve your full attention, are unreachable by public transportation, and arranging a private shuttle or guided tour can be inconvenient and expensive. Note that New Mexico ranks near the top of traffic deaths, drunk-driving arrests and overall accidents. Drive carefully!

Whether you rent a vehicle or bring your own, begin your trip by stocking it with at least a gallon of water per person, a blanket or jacket, extra medication and any other provisions you might need if stranded for a day or two. Always carry a spare tire, and know how to put it on. And note that cell phones don't always work in the hinterlands.

American Automobile Association (AAA; ☎ 505-471-6620 Santa Fe, 800-222-4357; www.aaa.com) For $20 to $40 annually (plus a one-time initiation fee of $20), AAA provides free maps, roadside assistance, towing and low-cost insurance, and can book car rentals, air tickets and hotel rooms at discount prices.

State Highway and Transportation Department (☎ 800-432-4269) This toll-free line has information about weather, state travel laws and road advisory updates.

Rental

Although there are lots of car rental places in Albuquerque and Santa Fe competing for your dollar, don't just show up unannounced and expect a good deal. Shop around, and make reservations at least two weeks in advance to lower your bill. Many chains also offer far better deals on weekly rentals rather than for two or three days. You can find good deals on **Orbitz** (www.orbitz.com), **Expedia** (www.expedia.com), **Travelocity** (www.travelocity.com), **Discount Cars** (www.discountcars.com) and other online agencies.

Don't limit yourself to the convenient locations at the Albuquerque Sunport, either. You'll often get better rates elsewhere, and most companies can arrange to drop off the car at your hotel.

Rental rates skyrocket from late July through early September, as well as during the Albuquerque Balloon Fiestas and the Christmas holidays. Make reservations at least a month in advance, if possible. Also consider relying on public transportation, which is upgraded across the board to handle extra traffic during those periods.

In general, you'll need to be 25 years old and have a US driver's license or international driver's permit, as well as a major credit card (or ability to make a large cash deposit), to rent a car. Smaller, independent companies are more likely to make exceptions, however, so give it a try. Very few companies will rent cars to drivers under 21, and those that do charge significantly higher rates.

Rates usually include unlimited mileage, but make sure they do. If there is a mileage charge, your costs can go up quickly and disconcertingly. You are expected to return the car to the same place where you picked it up; you can sometimes arrange to drop the car off elsewhere, but there is often a large surcharge. Be aware that the person who rents the car is the only legal driver, and in the event of an accident, only the legal driver is covered by insurance. However, when you rent the car, additional drivers may be signed on as legal drivers for a fee, usually $5 per day per person.

You will be offered a variety of insurance options, most of which insured US drivers don't need. Review your own policies before committing to collision insurance (CWD). If you don't have uninsured driver's insurance, however, go ahead and invest – one-fifth of New Mexicans drive uninsured. Basic liability insurance, which will cover damage you may cause to another vehicle, is required by law and comes with the price of renting.

Many credit cards will cover collision insurance if you rent for 15 days or fewer and charge the full cost of rental to your card. If you have collision insurance on your personal car insurance policy, this will often cover rented vehicles. The credit card will cover the large deductible. Call and make sure.

Note that many rental agencies stipulate that damage a car suffers while being driven on unpaved roads is not covered by the insurance they offer. Check with the agent when you make your reservation.

In addition to the large chains serving the Sunport, Santa Fe and Taos, try these smaller chains and independent rental companies (all but one in Albuquerque), which usually offer better rates, more flexibility for younger drivers and, best of all, no 10% airport concession tax:

ABC Car Rental (☎ 505-256-1169; 2501 Lead Ave SE) Rents to under 21-year-olds and folks without credit cards.
Beaver Toyota (☎ 505-982-1901; www.beavertoyota.com; 1500 St Michaels Dr, Santa Fe)
Capps Van & Car Rental (☎ 505-848-8267; www .cappsvanrental.com; 2200 Renard Pl SE) Rents huge vans, some wheelchair accessible.
Eagle Rider (☎ 505-345-7600; 866-368-5611; www.eaglerider.com; 1220 Renaissance NE) Rents Harley Davidson motorcycles.
Farr Better Car Rental (☎ 505-265-2600; 707 Wyoming NE)
Rent-A-Wreck (☎ 505-232-7552; 504 Yale Blvd SE) Accepts cash deposits, and the cars are nice.
Outwest Auto Rental (☎ 505-255-9400; 6419 Central Ave NE)

Road Rules

Foreign motorists and motorcyclists (traveling with their own foreign vehicles) will need the vehicle's registration papers, liability insurance and an international driver's permit in addition to their domestic license. Canadian and Mexican driver's licenses are accepted.

The speed limit on New Mexico highways tops out at 75 miles per hour. You are expected to yield to pedestrians and bicyclists in cities and towns, and all accidents resulting in damages more than $500 must be reported.

Road Conditions

Also known as the 'Orange Barrel State,' New Mexico generally performs road construction and maintenance in the spring and fall, though summer months see their share of bypasses and impasses.

Generally road conditions in urban centers and along major arteries are excellent, but stray much off the beaten path and many roads remain unpaved. Most of these roads are dirt, not gravel, and after rain may become temporarily impassable to folks without 4WD. Such roads on public land may be heavily rutted throughout the year, which can be hard on a car.

LOCAL TRANSPORT

Several cities offer public buses, most of which run from around 7am to 7pm daily, with limited service on Sunday. They charge a nominal fee for one-way rides, and offer day and week passes. All have convenient connections to **Greyhound** except for the Los Alamos entry, which connects with Española Transit.

Albuquerque SunTran (p63) Daily service to most tourist areas, plus trolleys.
Taos Chile Line (p166) Serves the Ski Valley and Arroyo Seco in winter only.
Santa Fe Trails (p114) On-demand transit for folks with ADA-certified disabilities and anyone older than 60.
Española Transit (p124) Also serves San Juan and Santa Clara Pueblos, plus connections with Los Alamos Public Transit.
Los Alamos Bus System (p136)

Taxis are your other option; they serve Santa Fe, Taos, Las Vegas and Albuquerque. Generally they don't cruise the streets, so you'll have to call for pickup.

TRANSPORT

Health by David Goldberg MD

Northern New Mexico encompasses a wide range of climates and temperatures, from the blistering heat of the desert summer to several 12,000ft-plus peaks where snow lingers almost year-round. Because of the high level of hygiene here, as in the rest of the USA, infectious diseases are rarely a significant concern for most travelers.

BEFORE YOU GO

INSURANCE

The United States offers possibly the finest health care in the world. The problem is that unless you have good insurance, it can be prohibitively expensive. If you're coming from abroad, you're advised to buy supplemental travel health insurance if your regular policy doesn't cover you for overseas trips. (Check the Subway section of the Lonely Planet website at www .lonelyplanet.com/subwwway for further information.) If you are covered, find out in advance if your insurance plan will make payments directly to providers or reimburse you later.

Domestic travelers who have insurance coverage should check with their insurance company for affiliated hospitals and doctors. US citizens who don't have regular health coverage can purchase domestic travel insurance, but be aware that most plans only cover emergencies.

Bring any medications you may need in their original containers, clearly labeled. A signed, dated letter from your physician describing all medical conditions and medications, including generic names is also a good idea.

ONLINE RESOURCES

There is a wealth of travel health advice on the Internet. The World Health Organization publishes a superb book, called *International Travel and Health*, which is revised annually and is available online at no cost at www.who.int/ith. Another website of general interest is MD Travel Health at www.mdtravelhealth.com, which provides complete travel health recommendations for every country, up-dated daily, also at no cost.

It's usually a good idea to consult your government's travel health website before departure, if one is available:

United States www.cdc.gov/travel
Canada www.hc-sc.gc.ca/pphb-dgspsp/tmp-pmv/pub_e.html
United Kingdom www.doh.gov.uk/traveladvice/index.htm
Australia www.dfat.gov.au/travel

IN NEW MEXICO

AVAILABILITY & COST OF HEALTH CARE

In general, if you have a medical emergency, the best bet is to find the nearest public hospital and go to its emergency room; these hospitals are committed to providing emergency care to anyone who walks in the door, regardless of ability to pay.

If the problem isn't urgent, you can call a nearby hospital and ask for a referral to a local physician, which is usually cheaper than a trip to the emergency room if you have insurance. You should avoid stand-alone, for-profit urgent care centers, which tend to perform large numbers of expensive tests, even for minor illnesses.

Pharmacies are abundantly supplied, but international travelers may find that some medications that are available over-the-counter at home require a prescription in the US, and, as always, if you don't have insurance to cover the cost of prescriptions, they can be shockingly expensive.

INFECTIOUS DISEASES
In addition to more common ailments, there are several infectious diseases that are unknown or uncommon outside North America. Most are acquired by mosquito or tick bites.

West Nile Virus
These infections were unknown in the United States until a few years ago, but have now been reported in almost all 50 states. The virus is transmitted by Culex mosquitoes, which are active in late summer and early fall and generally bite after dusk. Most infections are mild or asymptomatic, but the virus may infect the central nervous system, leading to fever, headache, confusion, lethargy, coma and sometimes death. There is no treatment. For the latest update on the areas affected by West Nile, go the US Geological Survey website at http://westnilemaps.usgs.gov.

Rabies
Rabies is a viral infection of the brain and spinal cord that is almost always fatal. The rabies virus is carried in the saliva of infected animals and is typically transmitted through an animal bite, though contamination of any break in the skin with infected saliva may result in rabies. In the US, most cases of human rabies are related to exposure to bats. Rabies may also be contracted from raccoons, skunks, foxes and unvaccinated cats and dogs.

If there is any possibility, however small, that you have been exposed to rabies, you should seek preventative treatment, which consists of rabies immune globulin and rabies vaccine and is quite safe. In particular, any contact with a bat should be discussed with health authorities, because bats have small teeth and may not leave obvious bite marks. If you wake up to find a bat in your room, or discover a bat in a room with small children, rabies prophylaxis may be necessary.

Giardiasis
This parasitic infection of the small intestine occurs throughout North America and the world. Symptoms may include nausea, bloating, cramps and diarrhea and may last for weeks. To protect yourself from Giardia, you should avoid drinking directly from lakes, ponds, streams and rivers, which may be contaminated by animal or human feces. The infection can also be transmitted from person to person if proper hand washing is not performed. Giardiasis is easily diagnosed by a stool test and readily treated with antibiotics.

HIV/AIDS
As with most parts of the world, HIV infection occurs throughout New Mexico. You should never assume, on the basis of someone's background or appearance, that they're free of this or any other sexually transmitted disease. Be sure to use a condom for all sexual encounters with men.

Plague
While rare, plague (aka the Black Death, the little flea-borne bacterium that killed some 25 million Europeans in the 1350s) still infects about a dozen people in Northern New Mexico each year, usually between April and November. Medical technology has improved a bit since the Middle Ages, and prompt diagnosis and treatment almost always mean a full recovery.

Plague has an incubation period of two to seven days and rather nonspecific symptoms: headache, chills, high fever and painful, swollen lymph nodes in the groin, armpit and/or neck. If you display these symptoms shortly after your vacation, tell your doctor that you've been in a plague area and ask her to test for the disease.

Plague is usually contracted by hikers and campers bitten by fleas shared with infected rodents and small animals, in particular rock squirrels and gophers. Stay on trails, avoid stirring up the undergrowth in piñon forests, and give wide berth to sick, slow-moving or disoriented animals. It cannot be transmitted directly from person to person in the bubonic form.

ENVIRONMENTAL HAZARDS
Altitude Sickness
Visitors from lower elevations undergo rather dramatic physiological changes as they adapt to Northern New Mexico's high altitude, and while the side effects

HEALTH

are usually mild, they can be dangerous if ignored. Some people – age and fitness level are not predictors of who these will be – will feel the effects strongly, while others won't even notice.

Symptoms, which tend to manifest after four days and continue for about two weeks, may include headache, fatigue, loss of appetite and/or nausea, sleeplessness, increased urination and sometimes hyperventilation due to overexertion. More severe cases (usually affecting hikers over 10,000ft who didn't take time to acclimate) display extreme disorientation, breathing problems and vomiting. These folks should descend immediately and get to a hospital.

To avoid the discomfort characterizing the milder symptoms, drink plenty of water (dehydration exacerbates the symptoms) and take it easy – at 7,000ft, a pleasant walk around Santa Fe can wear you out faster than a steep hike at sea level. Schedule a nap if you have a sleepless night, and put off serious hiking and biking for a few days, if possible. A mild painkiller like aspirin should take care of the headache.

Dehydration

Visitors to the desert may not realize how much water they're losing, as sweat evaporates almost immediately and increased urination (to help the blood process oxygen more efficiently) can go unnoticed. The prudent tourist will make sure to drink more water than usual – think a gallon a day if you're active. Parents can carry fruits and fruit juices to help keep kids hydrated.

Severe dehydration can easily cause disorientation and confusion, and even day hikers have gotten lost and died because they ignored their thirst. So bring plenty of water even on short hikes, and drink it!

Insect Bites & Stings

Commonsense approaches to these concerns are the most effective: wear boots when hiking to protect from snakes, wear long sleeves and pants to protect from ticks and mosquitoes. If you're bitten, don't overreact. Stay calm and follow the recommended treatment.

Mosquito Bites

When traveling in areas where West Nile or other mosquito-borne illnesses have been reported, keep yourself covered (wear long sleeves, long pants, hats, and shoes rather than sandals) and apply a good insect repellent, preferably one containing DEET, to exposed skin and clothing. Don't overuse the stuff, though, because neurologic toxicity – though uncommon – has been reported from DEET, especially in children. DEET-containing compounds should not be used at all on kids under age two.

Insect repellents containing certain botanical products, including oil of eucalyptus and soybean oil, are effective but last only 1½ to 2 hours. Products based on citronella are not effective.

Visit the **Center for Disease Control's** (CDC's) website (www.cdc.gov/ncidod/dvbid/westnile/prevention_info.htm) for prevention information.

Tick Bites

Ticks are parasitic arachnids that may be present in brush, forest and grasslands, where hikers often get them on their legs or in their boots. Adult ticks suck blood from hosts by burrowing into the skin and can carry infections such as Lyme disease (uncommon in New Mexico).

Always check your body for ticks after walking through high grass or thickly forested area. If ticks are found unattached, they can simply be brushed off. If a tick is found attached, press down around the tick's head with tweezers, grab the head and gently pull upwards – do not twist it. (If no tweezers are available, use your fingers, but protect them from contamination with a piece of tissue or paper.) Do not rub oil, alcohol or petroleum jelly on it. If you get sick in the next couple of weeks, consult a doctor.

Animal Bites

Do not attempt to pet, handle, or feed any wild animal, no matter how cuddly looking; most injuries from animals are directly related to people trying to do just that.

Any bite or scratch by a mammal, including bats, should be promptly and thoroughly cleansed with large amounts of soap and water, followed by application of an antiseptic such as iodine or alcohol. The local health authorities should be contacted immediately for possible post-exposure rabies treatment, whether or not you've been immunized against rabies. It may also be advisable to start an antibiotic, since wounds caused by animal bites and scratches frequently become infected.

Snake Bites

There are several varieties of venomous snakes in the USA, but unlike those in other countries they do not cause instantaneous death, and antivenins are available. First aid is to place a light constricting bandage over the bite, keep the wounded part below the level of the heart and move it as little as possible. Stay calm and get to a medical facility as soon as possible. Bring the dead snake for identification if you can, but don't risk being bitten again. Do not use the mythic 'cut an X and suck out the venom' trick; this causes more damage to snakebite victims than the bites themselves.

Spider & Scorpion Bites

Although there are many species of spiders in New Mexico, the main two that cause significant human illness are the black widow and brown recluse. The black widow is black or brown in color, measuring about 15mm in body length, with a shiny top,

fat body, and a distinctive red or orange hourglass figure on its underside. It's usually found in barns, woodpiles, sheds, harvested crops and bowls of outdoor toilets. The brown recluse spider is brown, usually 10mm in body length, with a dark violin-shaped mark on the top of the upper section of the body. It's active mostly at night and lives in dark sheltered areas such as under porches and in woodpiles, and typically bites when trapped.

If bitten by a black widow, you should apply ice or cold packs and go immediately to the nearest emergency room. Complications of a black widow bite may include muscle spasms, breathing difficulties and high blood pressure. The bite of a brown recluse typically causes a large, inflamed wound, sometimes associated with fever and chills. If bitten, apply ice and see a physician.

If stung by a scorpion, you should immediately apply ice or a cold pack, immobilize the affected body part, and go to the nearest emergency room. To prevent scorpion stings, be sure to inspect and shake out clothing, shoes and sleeping bags before use, and wear gloves and protective clothing when working around piles of wood or leaves.

HEALTH

Glossary

NORTHERN NEW MEXICAN DIALECT

Although American English is most widely spoken, the state's constitution designates New Mexico as officially bilingual, and about 30% of New Mexicans speak Spanish at home. Visitors are likely to hear 'Spanglish,' in which speakers switch smoothly between Spanish and English, even within the same sentence. You'll also see Spanish and Native American terms on menus, in galleries and at historical sights. The following list should help you translate, as well as make sense of some of the government acronyms and New Age terminology you'll hear in these parts.

A

abierto – Spanish for 'open,' so come on in.

acequia – The ancient irrigation ditches, still used in Santa Fe and throughout the Rio Grande Valley, that were communally owned and maintained by local landowners for centuries before plumbing was introduced; today they are maintained by associations that operate in much the same fashion.

adobe – A building material originally made with bricks cut directly from root-filled sod by Pueblo Indians, and later improved by mixing straw and mud by the Spanish; today it refers to almost any building material designed to resemble adobe.

AIPC – All Indian Pueblo Council, an intertribal governmental organization comprising the 19 New Mexico pueblos: Acoma, Cochiti, Isleta, Jemez, Laguna, Nambé, Picuris, Pojoaque, Sandia, San Felipe, San Ildefonso, San Juan, Santa Ana, Santa Clara, Santo Domingo, Taos, Tesuque, Zia and Zuni.

arroyo – A usually dry ditch or waterway, which can fill quickly and violently even if there's no rain in your area; as schoolteachers say, 'ditches are deadly, stay away.'

avanyu: The water serpent motif popular on pueblo pottery, symbolizing the prayer for rain and flowing water.

ayurveda – An Indian (as in India) holistic healing philosophy based on balancing three body types, or doshas, which can be accomplished in a variety of ways at spas, restaurants and holistic healing centers throughout the state.

Aztlán – Nahuatl for 'Place of the Blue Herons,' and ancestral home of the Aztec peoples, probably Northern New Mexico; also refers to those parts of the American Southwest annexed during the Mexican-American war, including New Mexico, Arizona, Texas, California and parts of Wyoming and Colorado.

B

barrio – Spanish for 'neighborhood,' used to describe primarily Hispanic parts of town.

bienvenidos – Spanish for 'Welcome.'

biscochito – The New Mexico state cookie! Simple and sweet with a hint of anise, traditionally made around Christmas.

bolo – A replacement for a man's tie (often worn by women) that cinches a thick cord with a silver disc or semiprecious stone; around here, it counts as formalwear.

bosque – Spanish for 'forest,' and refers to the wooded area along rivers that flow year-round.

breakfast burrito – A burrito usually filled with scrambled eggs, sausage or bacon, cheese and chile.

bultos – Carved Catholic saints, often roughly hewn from wood.

burnish – The Native method of bringing unglazed pottery to a high sheen, using special smoothed rock tools often handed down for generations.

C

Camino Real – Spanish for the 'Royal Highway,' here it refers to the old route that has connected Santa Fe and Mexico City since before the time of the Aztec empire, and which has since been used by Indians, Spanish and NAFTA truck drivers for trade.

carne adovada – Pork cooked until it's so tender you barely have to chew it, then marinated and baked in a rich mixture of red chile and spices.

casita – Spanish for 'little house'; B&Bs and hotels use it to designate small, usually freestanding accommodations, often suite-style with a full kitchen.

cerrado – Spanish for 'closed,' sorry, folks.

ceviche – Sort of Mexican sushi, it's fish that's not cooked per se, but soaked in citrus juices and other ingredients that catalyze a similar chemical reaction.

chakra – Seven power points in the human body that often need to be realigned by experienced metaphysicians.

Chicano – Sometimes traced to a Spanish corruption of the Nahuatl word for 'poorest of the poor,' this was almost a racial slur for Hispanic Americans until adopted in the late 1950s by young Latinos as a badge of pride, and later popularized by the Chicano Civil Rights Movement of the 1960s.

chicharones – Spanish for 'pork rinds.'

chile – The correct spelling for the fruit of the chile plant, despite what editors elsewhere in the USA would have you think.

chile relleno – Poblano or green chiles stuffed with cheese and sometimes meat or other fillings, then breaded and deep fried.

chili – A meat and bean stew eaten primarily in Texas, or the incorrect spelling of the word 'chile' (see above).

chorizo – A spicy Mexican sausage often served at breakfast.

churro sheep – The sheep originally brought here by Spanish settlers and used for wool, milk and, in times of desperation, meat. They were almost entirely replaced by generic meat sheep in the last century, until the recent weaving renaissance inspired more interest in preserving this unique and historic breed.

concha – Spanish for 'shell'; generally refers to the thin silver discs, usually with scalloped edges and decoratively engraved, used to make those Navajo-style belts and hat bands you see everywhere.

D

descansos – Small shrines, usually by the side of the road, marking where travelers have died; drive extra carefully when you see one.

Diné – The more proper name for the Indian tribe more often referred to as Navajo, or the language thereof.

DOE – The Department of Energy, which administrates LANL (Los Alamos National Laboratory) and which was headed by Governor Bill Richardson during the Clinton administration.

E

enchiladas – Corn tortillas either rolled (Mexican style) or stacked (New Mexican style) with cheese, chile sauce and often meat.

ENIPC – Eight Northern Indian Pueblos Council, an organizing body for the pueblos of Nambé, Picuris, Pojoaque, San Ildefonso, San Juan, Santa Clara, Taos and Tesuque.

F

farolito – Paper bags weighted with sand and illuminated with candles, usually around Christmastime; they're also often referred to as luminarias.

fetish – No, not that, silly. These are the carved stone animals that some Zuni Indians believe impart their carrier with the traits of the critter portrayed: a bear for strength, frog for fertility, etc. Different rituals may be required to activate their powers, usually described in the attractive brochures provided by the shops and galleries that sell them.

fiesta – Spanish for 'celebration,' and usually refers to weeklong parties throughout New Mexico that nominally honor Catholic saints.

fonda – Spanish for inn; 'La Fonda' is often the oldest hotel in town.

G

gray water – Recycled water from sinks and showers that's been purified by natural and/or artificial means, then typically used to water lawns and gardens.

green chile stew – The barometer of competitive home cooks, this is stew made of green chile and usually ground beef, potatoes and other vegetables.

H

hacienda – Spanish-style house built around a courtyard; refers to anything adobe of mansion-sized proportions.

horno – A beehive-shaped outdoor adobe oven, originally used by Spanish settlers and still popular among many Pueblo Indians; also refers to the chewy bread baked after heating the oven with coals, then removing them.

huevos rancheros – Eggs cooked to order atop lightly fried corn tortillas and swimming in chile, served with beans and potatoes.

I

Indian taco – Also 'Navajo taco,' it consists of soft fry bread often topped with beans, meat, cheese, lettuce, tomato and chile.

J

jerga – A type of weaving popular among Spanish colonists and usually used as a wall hanging, characterized by streaks of colorful yarn without the geometric patterns favored by Native weavers.

K

kachina (or katsina) – Religious dolls carved primarily by the Hopi from the root of a cottonwood tree, representing the spirits and spirit dancers sacred to the tribe; cheap knockoffs abound but are still pretty neat.

Kokopelli – The flute-playing rain deity you'll see on advertisements, corporate logos and sometimes Native crafts.

kiva – A circular, partially underground Native American house of worship, or a bulbous fireplace built into a corner and boasted about by B&Bs.

L

LANL – Los Alamos National Laboratory, the USA's top weapons lab.

lowrider – A car with lowered suspension, clean paint, nice rims and often a plush interior and hydraulics that lift the car up and down; also refers to the driver thereof, as well as the art, fashion and style associated with folks who build such fine cars.

M

mañana – Not just Spanish for 'tomorrow,' it's the word that sums up the New Mexico lifestyle.

Manhattan Project – The top secret WWII project that built the first atomic bomb

milagrosa – A small tin charm usually representing a body part you hope to heal.

GLOSSARY

menudo – A spicy tomato-based breakfast stew of tripe (yes, animal intestines, and if that grosses you out, consider what sausage casings are made with) and other ingredients, long venerated as a hangover cure.

micaceous clay – Clay flecked with sparkling mica and made into cooking vessels by potters at Picuris, Taos and other pueblos; many New Mexicans consider micaceous kitchenware to be the ultimate pots for cooking beans.

morada – A chapel or meeting place for penitentes.

O

ojo – Literally, Spanish for 'eye,' but in New Mexico usually refers to an artesian spring; an ojo caliente is a hot spring, while an ojo sarco is a clear spring.

P

paraje – Spanish for 'campground' or stopping place.

passive solar energy – A term coined in New Mexico that refers to architectural elements that maximize use of the sun for heating, cooling and other purposes.

pawn – Items traded for cash on a short-term loan that couldn't be paid back; and used to refer to Native American jewelry traded as such. Dead pawn was used as collateral before WWII and therefore has less weird karma associated with it.

penitentes – A secretive Catholic sect that became popular in Northern New Mexico after the Franciscans more or less closed up shop. Though known for self-flagellation, the actual rituals involved are not advertised to the general public (thus most of what you hear is probably not true).

petroglyph – Line drawings etched into rock; usually refers to those that are centuries old.

photovoltaic cells – Plates of silicon alloy specially treated to absorb sunlight and then allow free electrons to migrate to the surface, creating a negative charge on top while leaving behind a positive charge on the bottom; the resulting imbalance creates a voltage potential that can be used to generate solar electricity.

piñon – A high desert tree indigenous to Northern New Mexican deserts, or its rich nut.

piñon bark beetle – *Ips pini*, the rice-grain-size beetle currently devouring piñon trees throughout the Southwest.

placita – Spanish for 'small square,' these are plazas usually fortified by being entirely surrounded with strong adobe structures to protect them from attack; the plaza in Chimayó is a good original example.

posole – A usually tomato-based stew made from hominy (corn soaked in lye until it gets puffy) and other ingredients.

pueblo – Literally, Spanish for 'people' or 'town'; used to designate the villages or reservations of the 19 tribes along the Rio Grande, or the multistoried adobe buildings built by these tribes.

pueblo revival – Modern architecture based on the look of pueblo buildings.

R

rajas – The rough cedar sticks closely packed at 45-degree angles to vigas, making a popular ceiling for pueblo-revival (or actual pueblo) interiors.

raza – Spanish for 'race' and used to describe the Spanish-speaking peoples of the Americas; it is a reference to Jose Vasconcelos' poem, *La Raza Cosmica*.

recuerdo – A memory or souvenir.

reredo – A series of religious paintings, as on an altar.

retablo – A religious painting, usually of a saint or the Virgin Mary, done in Spanish colonial style.

ristra – A string of vegetables, usually red chiles, designed for drying; both decorative and delicious.

S

santero/a – A person who makes reredos, retablos or bultos.

sopapilla – Flaky pillows of delicately puffed fried dough, perfect with honey.

squashblossom necklace – The heavy silver necklaces, once considered an integral part of Santa Fe style, with several flower-shaped beads and a central crescent-shaped pendant, called a naja, which represents both the moon and female spirit.

storyteller doll – A popular style of ceramic figure depicting an adult swarming with small children, originally created by Cochiti artist Helen Cordero.

T

tilde – The accent above the 'n' in Española; the letter 'ñ' is called an eñe.

V

viga – A substantial roof beam used in Spanish adobe architecture, often carved into decorative patterns.

virga – Rain, visible to the naked eye, that evaporates before it hits the ground.

W

WPA (Works Progress Administration) – Created in 1935 as part of President Franklin D Roosevelt's 'New Deal' to lift the country from the Great Depression, the WPA provided public funds for a variety of projects and professions nationwide, playing patron to some 5000 artists who produced more than 200,000 works of art, including many of the Taos Society of Artists, Patrociño Barela and many other New Mexico masters.

X

xeriscaping – Landscaping using only drought-resistant plants, and usually lots of rocks (very drought-resistant).

Z

zia – New Mexico's state symbol (for now; see p87), the sun sign that's all over everything.

Behind the Scenes

THE LONELY PLANET STORY

The story begins with a classic travel adventure: Tony and Maureen Wheeler's 1972 journey across Europe and Asia to Australia. There was no useful information about the overland trail then, so Tony and Maureen published the first Lonely Planet guidebook to meet a growing need.

From a kitchen table, Lonely Planet has grown to become the largest independent travel publisher in the world, with offices in Melbourne (Australia), Oakland (USA), London (UK) and Paris (France).

Today Lonely Planet guidebooks cover the globe. There is an ever-growing list of books and information in a variety of media. Some things haven't changed. The main aim is still to make it possible for adventurous travelers to get out there - to explore and better understand the world.

At Lonely Planet we believe travelers can make a positive contribution to the countries they visit – if they respect their host communities and spend their money wisely. Since 1986 a percentage of the income from each book has been donated to aid projects and human rights campaigns, and, more recently, to wildlife conservation.

THIS BOOK

This is the first edition of *Santa Fe & Taos*. It was researched and written by Paige R Penland. The Health chapter was written by David Goldberg MD.

THANKS from the Author

Paige R Penland Thanks, first, to the benevolent strangers and beloved old friends who unselfishly (and often unknowingly) offered their insights, information, encouragement and storage space – in particular Charles Tuttle, Erin Corrigan, Patrick Huerta, cultureshock and Lu Yoder. Thanks especially to my mom, Wanda Olson, for holding down the fort while I tackled this project.

Special thanks also go out to Mike and Anita Stevenson for lending me their home, their knowledge and their wisdom; artist and ski-bunny Julia Coyne, for her hospitality and helpful hints; and Gordon Jones, for letting me take over the laundry room.

Sidebar writers Annette Rodriguez, Beth Penland and Bridgette Wagner, who also helped compile information for the literature section, provided special knowledge I simply did not have. You all rock. And, of course, thanks to all the editors, cartographers, proofreaders and designers who made this book work, in particular Kathleen Munnelly – thanks for everything.

CREDITS

Santa Fe & Taos 1 was commissioned and developed in the US office by Kathleen Munnelly. Series Publishing Manager Susan Rimerman oversaw the redevelopment of the regional guides series and Regional Publishing Manager

---

SEND US YOUR FEEDBACK

We love to hear from travelers – your comments keep us on our toes and help make our books better. Our well-traveled team reads every word on what you loved or loathed about this book. Although we cannot reply individually to postal submissions, we always guarantee that your feedback goes straight to the appropriate authors, in time for the next edition. Each person who sends us information is thanked in the next edition – and the most useful submissions are rewarded with a free book.

To send us your updates – and find out about LP events, newsletters and travel news – visit our award-winning website: www.lonelyplanet.com.

Note: we may edit, reproduce and incorporate your comments in Lonely Planet products such as guidebooks, websites and digital products, so let us know if you don't want your comments reproduced or your name acknowledged. For a copy of our privacy policy, email privacy@lonely planet.com.au.

Maria Donohoe steered the development of this title. The guide was edited by Emily K Wolman and proofed by Valerie Sinzdak. Cartographer Bart Wright drew all the maps. The book was laid out and the color pages designed by Candice Jacobus, with assistance from Andreas Schueller. Pepi Bluck designed and prepared the cover artwork. Ken DellaPenta compiled the index. Darren Burne helped decode the mysteries of Sylvester, and Alex Hershey provided invaluable support.

Index

000 Map pages
000 Location of color photographs

000 Map pages
000 Location of color photographs

INDEX

216

LEGEND

ROUTES

Tollway	Walking Path
Freeway	Unsealed Road
Primary Road	Pedestrian Street
Secondary Road	Stepped Street
Tertiary Road	Tunnel
Lane	One Way Street
Walking Tour	Walking Tour Detour

TRANSPORT

Ferry	Rail
Metro	Rail (Underground)
Monorail	Tram

HYDROGRAPHY

River, Creek	Lake (Salt)
Intermittent River	Mudflats
Canal	Reef
Glacier	Swamp
Lake (Dry)	Water

BOUNDARIES

International	Ancient Wall
State, Provincial	Cliff
Regional, Suburb	Marine Park

POPULATION

○ CAPITAL (NATIONAL)	◉ CAPITAL (STATE)
● Large City	○ Medium City
○ Small City	○ Town, Village

AREA FEATURES

Area of Interest	Land
Beach, Desert	Mall
Building	Market
Cemetery, Christian	Park
Cemetery, Other	Sports
Forest	Urban

SYMBOLS

SIGHTS/ACTIVITIES	INFORMATION	SHOPPING
Beach	Bank, ATM	Shopping
Buddhist	Embassy/Consulate	**TRANSPORT**
Castle, Fortress	Hospital, Medical	Airport, Airfield
Christian	Information	Border Crossing
Confucian	Internet Facilities	Bus Station
Diving, Snorkeling	Parking Area	Cycling, Bicycle Path
Hindu	Petrol Station	General Transport
Islamic	Police Station	Taxi Rank
Jain	Post Office, GPO	Trail Head
Jewish	Telephone	**GEOGRAPHIC**
Monument	Toilets	Hazard
Museum, Gallery	**SLEEPING**	Lighthouse
Picnic Area	Sleeping	Lookout
Point of Interest	Camping	Mountain, Volcano
Ruin	**EATING**	National Park
Shinto	Eating	Oasis
Sikh	**DRINKING**	Pass, Canyon
Skiing	Drinking	River Flow
Taoist	Café	Shelter, Hut
Winery, Vineyard	**ENTERTAINMENT**	Spot Height
Zoo, Bird Sanctuary	Entertainment	Waterfall

NOTE: Not all symbols displayed above appear in this guide.

LONELY PLANET OFFICES

Australia
Head Office
Locked Bag 1, Footscray, Victoria 3011
☎ 03 8379 8000, fax 03 8379 8111
talk2us@lonelyplanet.com.au

USA
150 Linden St, Oakland, CA 94607
☎ 510 893 8555, toll free 800 275 8555
fax 510 893 8572, info@lonelyplanet.com

UK
72–82 Rosebery Ave,
Clerkenwell, London EC1R 4RW
☎ 020 7841 9000, fax 020 7841 9001
go@lonelyplanet.co.uk

France
1 rue du Dahomey, 75011 Paris
☎ 01 55 25 33 00, fax 01 55 25 33 01
bip@lonelyplanet.fr, www.lonelyplanet.fr

Published by Lonely Planet Publications Pty Ltd
ABN 36 005 607 983

© Lonely Planet 2004

© photographers as indicated 2004

Cover photographs by Lonely Planet Images: First Presbyterian church built circa 1867, Richard Cummins (front); Chilli ristras hanging on a wall, John Elk III (back). Many of the images in this guide are available for licensing from Lonely Planet Images: www.lonelyplanetimages.com.

All rights reserved. No part of this publication may be copied, stored in a retrieval system, or transmitted in any form by any means, electronic, mechanical, recording or otherwise, except brief extracts for the purpose of review, and no part of this publication may be sold or hired, without the written permission of the publisher.

Printed through Colorcraft Ltd, Hong Kong.
Printed in China

Lonely Planet and the Lonely Planet logo are trademarks of Lonely Planet and are registered in the US Patent and Trademark Office and in other countries.

Lonely Planet does not allow its name or logo to be appropriated by commercial establishments, such as retailers, restaurants or hotels. Please let us know of any misuses: www.lonelyplanet.com/ip.

Although the authors and Lonely Planet have taken all reasonable care in preparing this book, we make no warranty about the accuracy or completeness of its content and, to the maximum extent permitted, disclaim all liability arising from its use.